Defining and Designing Multiculturalism

SUNY series, The Social Context of Education

–Christine E. Sleeter, editor

Defining & Designing Multiculturalism

ONE SCHOOL SYSTEM'S EFFORTS

Pepi Leistyna

STATE UNIVERSITY OF NEW YORK PRESS

Published by
State University of New York Press, Albany

© 2002 State University of New York

All rights reserved

Printed in the United States of America

For information, address State University of New York Press,
90 State Street, Suite 700, Albany, NY 12207

Production by Kelli Williams
Marketing by Anne M. Valentine

Library of Congress Cataloging-in-Publication Data

Leistyna, Pepi.
    Defining and designing multiculturalism: one school system's efforts / by Pepi Leistyna.
        p.cm.—(SUNY series, the social context of education)
    Includes bibliographical references (p. 303) and index.
    ISBN 0–7914–5507–6 (alk. paper)—ISBN 0–7914–5508–4 (pbk.: alk. paper)
    1. Multicultural education. 2. Critical pedagogy. I. Title. II. SUNY series, social context
of education
    LC1099.L45 2002
    370.117—dc21

                                                                            2002017612

This book is dedicated to all the kids in this world who are disgracefully offered so little, blamed for so much, and yet still manage to dream so high.

Contents

⌒

Foreword

Multiculturalism Revisited

Pepi Leistyna's Politics of the Concrete

Once held to be the divining rod that would lead humanity to a new democratic imaginary of diversity and inclusion, multiculturalism today resembles more a forked stick in the hands of a boy scout than a magic wand capable of bringing about a social revolution. While it arrived on a flood tide of vibrant ideas about rekindling the relationship between racial equality and democracy, multiculturalism largely remains a domesticated agenda, riding to national prominence on the current wave of buttoned-down progressive reformism and neoliberal educational policy making. Multiculturalism seemingly has lost its relationship to wider class and social struggles, and has been debarred from serious consideration as a tool of the left. And it doesn't take much in the way of analysis to realize that the current state of ambivalence toward multiculturalism serves the interests of the dominant class. The question, therefore, has to be raised: To what extent does mainstream multiculturalism reflect the cultural logic of late capitalism?

Mainstream multiculturalism has become the bellwether of ever shifting currents of bourgeois liberal opinion and a marker for the diminishing tide of revolutionary class struggle. Largely an unprincipled fusion of corporatism, incremental reformism, and bourgeois humanism, mainstream multiculturalism has become a perennial cauldron of competing factions pursuing counterposed lives dictated by conflicting notions of identity. The juggernaut of global capitalism (and its social equivalent, imperialism) and the demise of the Soviet Union and the Eastern Bloc socialist regimes have sent the educational left into a tailspin. It appears that no local or global proletarian inclination to organize currently exists that has the potential to bring about a massive world-historical challenge to capital. Consequently, the question is frequently put forward: Is there any viable alternative to capitalism and what are the major points of criticism that should animate the educational left?

Believing perhaps that capitalism is here to stay, and that other struggles are more urgent, the educational left for the most part has been concentrating on local and regional reform efforts dealing with issues involving race and ethnicity. For instance, the struggle to preserve affirmative action currently occupies many progressive educators and cultural workers. Also, there have been concerted attempts at mobilizing around antiracist and multicultural initiatives, including the development of multicultural curricula in elementary and secondary school settings. While such efforts continue to be exceedingly important—even urgent— they have been conceptually handicapped and politically compromised by a retreat from larger struggles affecting the working class on a global basis. Pepi Leistyna has surveyed the state of multiculturalism and has arrived at a similar conclusion. Attempting both to understand multiculturalism better, and to unleash its most progressive potential, Leistyna embarked on a three-year study to document systemwide efforts at multicultural reform in a school district in a major urban center on the U.S. East Coast. At the outset, he recognized many of the shortcomings of multicultural education, including its retreat from class struggle. Early on he remarks that "capitalism and social class are often not considered significant issues when dealing with raising consciousness about multiculturalism. . . . Consequently, economic exploitation and the concomitant social antagonisms and cultural values, beliefs, languages and world views that are shaped by class relations . . . are rendered invisible, as are the ways in which schools act as socializing agencies for capitalist logic, and as sorting machines for a hierarchically divided labor force" (p. 29). Leistyna is concerned with how racism interlocks with other social relations of oppression and exploitation, and seeks to undress the debate over inclusion and diversity in order to redress its structured absences. Multiculturalists who teach tolerance of—or better, who celebrate—the multiple cultures interlocked within our postmillennium historical conjuncture, have too often formalized out of existence the hegemonic center where the contested and embattled concepts of multicultural citizenship are played out. Leistyna notes, for instance, that efforts by mainstream multiculturalists remain trapped in an individualistic Human Relations approach, abstracted from any critical discussion of the systematic inequalities that reproduce the status quo. In other words, in their attempt to bring marginalized groups into the center of society as equal participants in civil society, there remains among mainstream multiculturalists a structured ambivalence surrounding just what constitutes the center (for criticalists, the center means the power to name, the power to exercise power, to extract labor power from the workers, the power to narrate and adjudicate, to define the limits of what is normal). In fact, the center—what some critical multiculturalists have connected to the social terrain of white supremacist capitalist patriarchy—often remains unaddressed. There is good reason to believe that this is because it has been naturalized as normal, as commonsensical, as inevitable. Leistyna extends this point by arguing that "the insistence upon solely affirming diversity creates a pedagogical process that is reduced to an empty form of pluralism which largely ignores the workings of power and privilege" (p. 25).

In the annals of the mainstream multiculturalists, there appears to be a studied avoidance of and at times a caution against linking the struggle over and for diversity to the practices of capitalist exploitation and specific instances of the construction of white supremacist ideology, or to manifestations of racism, sexism, homophobia and imperialism to which such practices are inescapably and unalterably interwined. Here, Euro-Americans not only fail to recognize that the radical Otherness to which they aspire is built upon systematic oppression through a criminal justice system, an educational system, and a political system that targets some groups as little more than human refuse, but they also succumb to a structural refusal to recognize how their own identity is mediated by the Other. This process constitutes a special form of disavowal implicated in a double-amnesia. Euro-Americans too often forget that what constitutes their social subjectivity is an active refusal of historical memory. Their inability to activate such memory has less to do with an unwillingness to confront past history than an inability to confront the history of the present.

Unless this center of social power in the United States is systematically interrogated, mainstream multiculturalism always will remain trapped within the confines or coordinates of its own symbolic horizon: that of whiteness and the politics of selectively rewarded cultural capital. Leistyna recognizes this dilemma and calls for a mode of analysis that draws from the tradition of critical multiculturalism and critical pedagogy. Although he doesn't explicitly state it in these terms, Leistyna recognizes that contemporary mainstream calls for diversity represent a synecdoche for larger, deeper structural contradictions within United States society. We could raise yet another question in relation to this dilemma: Is the current call for diversity instigated by both the Republican and Democratic Parties perhaps a way of directing attention away from the harsh reality of deep-seated institutionalized racism? And could it also be a way of distracting the public from the casualties of now well-entrenched neoliberal policies promoting the globalization of capitalism? Could it be a way of deflecting the public's attention from the way in which racism and capitalism are co-implicated in the reproduction of dominant social relations? It is within the context of these questions that Pepi Leistyna undertakes his important study of a community struggling over how to define, bring about, and evaluate multicultural education. By arguing that "multicultural education will be fruitless if frozen in the fictitious realm of the apolitical and ahistorical," (p. 5) Leistyna in effect raises an even more fundamental question: Multiculturalism on what basis, on what terms, in the interest of whom?

That exploitation targets certain racial groups disproportionately—both within the United States and elsewhere—should be reason enough to bring the development of critical multiculturalism in line with the struggle against global capitalism and various forms of racism, sexism, and homophobia that follow in its wake. But reason is not always the coin of the realm in the field of education, especially in light of the recent politics of educational policy making and practice. Few people recognize this truism as well as Pepi Leistyna.

For years Leistyna has been engaged in the struggle for bringing about educational transformation. Before entering the academy, Leistyna taught for a number of years in the area of community-based adult education/literacy and English as a second language. His classrooms have ranged from a bathroom floor and the assembly line to the walls of the Harvard Graduate School of Education. As a graduate student in Harvard's doctoral program in education, Leistyna took a stand against the anti–intellectualism of the program, and against the practices deskilling teachers from understanding and theorizing the complex realities that they face in contemporary society. While his tactics have been bold, they have also been carefully reasoned and politically seasoned. In discussing Leistyna's approach, I emphasize the term "transformation" in contrast with the more common term "reform" because I want to underscore what is at stake in Leistyna's call for a critical multicultural praxis. Leistyna is acutely aware that calls for diversity (such as those undertaken by General Colin Powell of the Republican Party) are not, in themselves, necessarily progressive. The larger social order can certainly accommodate such calls for diversity, as long as its structural arrangements (that is, exploitation of surplus value of the workers, the international division of labor) are not touched. In a setting where, as Ricardo Rosa notes, currently 1 percent (mainly white) of the population of the United States controls 45 percent of the wealth in the United States, and where one out of four children is born into poverty (p. 266), calls for diversity do not necessarily add up to a serious challenge to the status quo.

What makes Leistyna's work in multiculturalism of singular importance is that it attempts to unburden multiculturalism of its superficial and bumptious calls for equality and to analyze the absent center of multicultural education— that intersection of history, culture, capital, language, and power that constitutes the dominant social order. *Defining and Designing Multiculturalism* is not only a finely tuned empirical investigation of the systemwide efforts of Changeton's Multicultural Central Steering Committee to bring about substantive change within its Northeastern community, but also demonstrates Leistyna's sophisticated understanding of the relationship of culture to wider social arrangements. In order to highlight what this entails, I would like to shift gears somewhat and ask the reader to indulge me for a moment as we make a brief excursion into the concept of *culture*.

The anthropologist Gavin Smith, in *Confronting the Present: Towards a Politically Engaged Anthropology* (1999), has recently revisited the concept of culture and asks the following: Is culture primarily a heuristic device to help fathom the warp and woof of people's lives? Is it a generic blueprint that captures the concrete means that people employ to articulate their participation in day-to-day social life? Or is culture an identifiable place, something that occupies time and space that can be named as such—and possibly transformed? There are numerous positions that scholars have taken over the years in staking out their conceptual and political relation to the concept of culture. These have been extensively summarized and discussed by Smith. One relatively common position on culture could be called the preemptive view. Here, culture is viewed as a fairly integrated and coherent arena consisting of local phenomena detached from systematic mediations of larger social and civic apparatuses of the state. Within this perspective, culture is perceived as a set of shared ideas, taken-for-granted regulations that give shape and meaning to everyday life, or similarly as systems and concepts that inform or give coherence to the ways that human beings live. Culture, in other words, is viewed as both working through and being mediated by a local *habitus* that is distinct from more formalized practices of other settings such as those associated with state institutions. By and large, Smith notes, cultural practices provide identities that legitimize specific claims to rights.

A broader view of culture evokes standards, norms and idiosyncrasies of a broader range of people than those involved in daily interaction. This broader—what some have called "nationalist"—view stresses the idea of a code to which people refer or to which they conform—that is, in the notion of French culture or Mexican culture—as against the way in which their practices generate cultural patterns. Unlike the preemptive or "closed" view of culture, this position is more attentive to historical processes but still is limited in its grasp of the complexities of culture. Like the preemptive view of culture, the idea of national origin stresses a life of its own, an independence from institutionalized state apparatuses. It also refers to a prior set of patterns and ideas through which a distinctive politics is practiced. But such a view cannot grasp the complex layering of culture and its tangential lines of hegemonic forces. Leistyna recognizes this when he writes that

> Unfortunately, many educators who are actively engaged in current multicultural practices, reduce the idea of culture to national origin. This assumption not only boils down the myriad of identities within a nation to one homogenized image, but it fragments groups of people via real borders, pulling culture out of its antagonistic intergroup and transnational relations, and institutional formations. (p. 28)

A third view, which is often reflected in the work of Marxist scholars, suggests that people work in cultural settings that are integrated into nation states, in the case, for example, of schools, courts, police departments. This view approaches the notion of culture as forms of identity that emerge from participation in collective struggles across a wide horizon of the social. Here, culture is viewed as emergent from collective forms of resistance to hegemonic forces in the larger society or social totality. Marxists raise the issue of how culture as a system of meanings and shared ideas came into being as an historical process—as, in other words, habits, customs, and traditions. Culture is constitutive of struggles often over collective and individual social membership. In other words, culture is intertwined with collective claims to identity and such claims are always made within a larger politicized setting where other particularities are struggling to make themselves heard. Whereas the integrated view of culture sees politics as something that is expressed through culture, the Marxist or "conflict" perspective on culture interrogates how cultural collectivities arise out of political engagement. As Smith (1999) notes:

> Rather than seeing any one of these three perceptions of culture as sharply distinct, we need to see the way they inform one another. If the contours of local distinctiveness and identity, as well as the broader field of "national culture," arise out of historically quite specific struggles within and between existing and emergent sets of collectivities, then any sense of culture—what "culture" may actually mean at any given moment—must arise as a result of the nature of these struggles. (p. 204)

Smith claims that it is impossible to rest with a neat distinction between anthropological notions of culture and Marxist versions. The issue is to see both how politics is expressed through cultural formations but also how cultural collectivities arise out of political engagement. First, we need to ask those questions Leistyna raises in his book: How does common, everyday experience play out in the context of local struggles? How does such experience play out in the context of wider conflicts that inflect upon local expression, providing opportunities for the development of particular idioms and discourses?

Of course, we would be remiss if we remained hitched to this view. This is because the concept of culture overlaps with the concept of "civil society." In fact, a number of social theorists view culture as an arena of expression beside, above, and beyond the state—in the domain of civil society and farther, to that of the state. In fact, it could be argued that civil society and the state represent culture stretched to its broadest degree. Many Gramscian scholars, for instance, consider culture to be the process by which power is exercised through civil society. But if we believe this to be the case, we are faced with defining civil society in relation to its embeddedness in the state. This provokes the questions: Does civil society arise out of struggles against the state or is it the internal character of the state? Does civil society constitute all that is not commodified or subject to the market? How are social practices within civil society different from those associated with the state? Are they intermediate institutions controlled by the state? Civil society, according to Smith, arises out of struggle against external regulation but within such a struggle reproduces within itself institutionalized regulatory practices. At the local level, claims and patterns of conduct take on distinct cultural formations within the framework of different types of states. There is, Smith notes, always confusion in trying to sort out the local, the cultural, the civic, and the state in terms of understanding the forces that mediate between an individual and society. So if we stretch the concept of culture to embrace not only local events but also national culture, civil society, and state formations, how do we grasp its essential function? How do we make sense of the way in which culture works? How can we understand its processual character?

Antonio Gramsci comes the closest to answering this challenge through his development of the concept of hegemony (a term first used by Lenin). Gramsci focuses on what is inherited from the past and uncritically absorbed by individuals and groups, and the practical transformation of the real world. As Smith notes, there exists a dialectical tension between the historical conditions that give us our specific subjectivity and the central role of human will or agency. In this regard, if we want to understand the way in which culture intersects with history and power, we not only need to look back and analyze how specific historical conditions have produced the social and cultural relations that make up our subjectivities, but we also need to look forward to the practical transformation of the social world. In other words, how are we going to transform the conditions under which we love and labor? This Gramscian position of looking backward and forward simultaneously is the one taken by Leistyna in *Defining and Designing Multiculturalism*. When he describes culture as "being shaped by the lived experiences and institutionalized forms organized around diverse elements of struggle and domination" (p. 28), Leistyna is attempting to urge educators to view culture dynamically, as both the medium and the outcome of contested knowledges, social relations, and historically mediated styles of interaction.

Within mainstream multiculturalism, an emphasis on racism as essentially an attitude or stereotyped representation has, at times, reinforced our understanding of difference as a form of representation or signification detached from its relationship to the labor process, or decapitated and cauterized from its messy insinuation in the production of social value linked to the social relations of production. Leistyna recognizes that such a studied avoidance of the relationship between racism and capitalism effectively appends the struggle of people of color to a narrative of diversity orchestrated and coordinated by a white paternalism and Eurocentered humanism. By employing a concept of culture as a dynamic, multilayered, and contradictory site of struggle, Leistyna admonishes those multiculturalists who trawl through the vast ocean of cultural difference only to arrive at a destination where the Other is characterized as unassailably Other, that is, as static in nature and parochial in worldview.

Leistyna is careful not to reduce identity to the level of representation alone, but always locates representations (of race, of class, of sexual orientation, etcetera) within larger terrain of historically specific social struggles. Whether identity is located in the concept of color-blind liberal citizenship or in forms of race and ethnic essentialism and separatism, Leistyna urges that we approach identity-formation historically and critically. Leistyna is not content to allow representation to be misunderstood as a mere attitude or opinion that is either misguided or uninformed but chooses to link such forms of representation to the messy world of value created by class contradictions, institutionalized racism, and white supremacy. Difference can never stand alone, but must be seen interrogated in terms of the historical and contextual specificity of its formation.

Leistyna underscores the importance of struggling against relations of power and privilege that have been sedimented into racist and patriarchal systems of classification and that support existing capitalist social relations. But he also emphasizes the importance of human agency in struggling against the commodification and dispossession of the will. He pays tribute to the twin dimensions of social critique and transformative praxis when he rebukes mainstream multiculturalists for "not paying enough attention to structural inequalities and student agency" (p. 25). Of course, what we inherit from the past uncritically and what we use to shape the real world are not "mere" cultural processes but cultural processes both rooted and routed in social relations of capitalist production that shape the historically formed power differences that exist between social agents (that is, between the ruling class and the workers, between Euro-Americans and Afro-Americans and Latino/as). These "differences" that make a difference (that serve to locate individuals and groups differentially in terms of power and social position within the existing capitalist hierarchy) take on different, and often contradictory, meanings at different historical moments and depending upon both the broader geopolitical contexts in which they occur and the local cultural formations that give immediate shape to daily life.

The social relations of production linked to global capitalism both form and deform individual and collective subjectivities through the active production of hegemonic relations of power and privilege. Such a recognition stipulates that when we undertake the task of creating a multiculturalist praxis, it is imperative to see how "culture" is embedded in a wide range of social forces, relations, and practices. I rehearse these ideas here not because I feel nostalgia for the anthropology seminar room, but because I believe that they are of fundamental importance in how we approach the concept of multiculturalism. Furthermore, they may prove helpful in our approach to *Defining and Designing Multiculturalism*.

An active engagement with Leistyna's work will help educators, administrators, and community activists to break ranks with the misleading conceptions of mainstream multiculturalism and to lay the groundwork for the development of a critical multiculturalism. True to Freirean praxis, *Defining and Designing Multiculturalism* is not a cookbook or toolbox of strategies, but a problem-posing narrative written with a commitment to critique and transformation. Readers are not provided with a prefabricated model to be implemented, but with an invitation to engage, to question, and to challenge received orthodoxies, as uncomfortable as this challenge might be for some teachers and for those in the universities who claim to be educating them.

Peter L. McLaren
Los Angeles, California

Acknowledgments

⤙

First and foremost, I want to express my heartfelt appreciation and respect for all of the members of the Changeton Multicultural Central Steering Committee for their courage in taking the risk of allowing me to record and critique their every move. I was so fortunate to have started this empirical sojourn with the guidance of Lilia Bartolomé, Donaldo Macedo, and Eileen De Los Reyes. Without the wisdom of these three scholars, the study would have never gotten off the ground. Along the rocky road of longitudinal research, I also had the comfort of knowing that I could count on the brilliance and integrity of Peter McLaren, Henry Giroux, Antonia Darder, Christine Sleeter, Sonia Nieto, Ken Saltman and Roberto Bahruth. I've not only grown from their profound contributions to public education, but I've learned a great deal from them about intellectual generosity and solidarity. In addition, I would like to thank my colleagues at UMass Boston for helping to keep vibrant the ethical art of teaching—with special thanks to Michelle Fazio and my research assistant Kerri Lamprey. I'm also indebted to Liz Freedman and Ricardo and Joao Rosa for their courage to speak out against oppression. Many thanks to the entire SUNY Press staff, especially Kelli Williams, who have helped to bring this book to fruition, including Carol Inskip for indexing. Last but not least, I want to express my love and appreciation to the Kubik family for their continued support over the years, to Buddy and Charlie for making sure that I don't get any sleep, and most importantly, to Susan for keeping me on track in the insane roller coaster ride of writing a book.

Introduction

⌒

During the civil rights movement of the 1960s, various groups, motivated by the contention that educational institutions were systematically denying certain people fair and equal treatment, demanded the revision of curricula and pedagogical practices in primary and secondary schools. Ostensibly, the goal was to provide all students, regardless of their background, with an equal opportunity to learn.

While a majority of educators across the ideological spectrum would subscribe to the idea of equality for all students, they by no means agree upon the content, pedagogy, or purposes of public education. The struggle over which bodies of knowledge, values, and interests are to be legitimated through the educational process has represented a terrain of fierce debate in the United States.

Caught in the middle of these culture wars, and often ill-prepared to accommodate the demographic shifts and antagonistic social relations in their ever changing communities, increasingly educators and school systems are turning to the plethora of literature and research in multiculturalism to help ensure cross-cultural understanding (among students, faculty, and staff), academic success, and overall school/community harmony. Those involved with such efforts immediately confront the confusing reality that, over the years, multicultural education has come to mean many different and even contradicting things.

In an attempt to categorize the myriad of theoretical and practical approaches for addressing diversity within schools, researchers have developed a number of typologies (Gibson, 1976; McCarthy, 1993; McLaren, 1994; Parekh, 2000; Pratte, 1983; Sleeter & Grant, 1988). However, while all of these theoretical models suggest ideas about what should be done—a very important contribution to say the least—few of them adequately deal with how (or attempt) to develop comprehensive and detailed programs that can actually meet such ends. In other words, we still ask what are some of the ways in which educators and communities can work together to conceptualize and create system-wide multicultural programs.

Changeton: A Need to Document Their Efforts

Unfortunately, there are virtually no theoretical or tangible comprehensive models that have been documented that actually depict the development of a system-wide multicultural education program. There is a limited body of literature that discusses what is presently being done in several school systems; however, these research examples are constrained by their focus on classroom content and professional development.[1] More importantly, detailed depictions of how the multicultural practices were conceptualized and developed over time have been virtually omitted from the literature. Consequently, educators have no elaborate theoretical or practical blueprints with which to begin their own systemic multicultural transformations.[2]

Just outside of a major urban center on the East Coast of the United States, the Changeton school district is witnessing the harsh realities of cultural misunderstanding, poverty, interracial tensions, and violence.[3] To combat the sociocultural trauma that the city is facing, an effort is being made by the school district to create a system-wide multicultural education program. A volunteer group, referring to itself as the Changeton Multicultural Central Steering Committee (the CSC for short), has been established in order to shape and direct what the members hope will provide a foundation for working toward mitigating the racism and cultural strife that plague their schools and community—an effort that the organization itself described at its first all-faculty in-service workshop as "the affirmation of diversity through educational equity and social justice."

The CSC, which is made up of teachers, guidance counselors, specialists, principals, and other administrators, has been officially sanctioned by the superintendent of schools to direct this system-wide effort. The committee has been given the responsibility to extract from participants' own individual experiences, as well as from the bounty of research on cultural diversity, ideas that they think will help their city's schools.

Through a qualitative three-year study (which began in 1993, on the day that the CSC was formed), data was collected and analyzed in order to focus on the following research question: What are the developments in the work of a Multicultural Central Steering Committee to conceptualize and infuse a system-wide multicultural education program? In other words, this has been an investigation into how the CSC got created, how this group came to define multicultural education, and how these educators subsequently went about infusing this definition into daily operations. In order to provide a more longitudinal analysis to see if such efforts were having a significant impact on school/community life, three years of follow-up research was conducted.

An Overview of the Chapters

Defining and Designing Multiculturalism comprises twelve chapters that are broken up into three sections. Part One, "Theoretically and Historically Contextualizing the Study," contains four chapters that introduce the reader to the overall project and the research site. Chapter One—"Critical Multicultural Education: What Is It?"—sets the stage for the entire study by covering what critical multiculturalists theoretically and practically embrace and reject from mainstream models of multicultural education. The intention here is twofold: first, to scaffold the unfamiliar reader into the debates over diversity and schooling and to present a clear idea of what critical multiculturalism, in general, theoretically sets out to accomplish; second, to provide a lens through which Chapters Five through Nine, which encompass the research participants' efforts, are analyzed.

Chapter Two—"A History of Changeton and Its Public Schools: Taking a Sociohistorical Perspective"—historically contextualizes the present predicaments that the city and its educational institutions are facing. This chapter explores the demographic shifts and the struggles for power and voice that have emerged in the immediate locale over time. Chapter Three—"Facing Oppression: Youth Voices from the Front"—through a dialogue with a diverse group of students who all dropped out of school (or more accurately, were forced out), puts human faces to the present history of cultural strife and hardship in the city. Chapter Four—"The Formation of the Multicultural Central Steering Committee: Its Basic Processes, Functions, and Structures"—depicts the CSC getting together and shaping the organization's procedural routines and practices.

Part Two of the book, "The Work of the Multicultural Central Steering Committee," consists of five chapters that explore the group's actual efforts. Chapter Five—"The Development of the Multicultural Central Steering Committee's Mission Statement"—covers the evolution of the CSC's work in drafting its basic philosophical foundation. Chapter Six—"Professional Development: Raising Consciousness among the Faculty and Staff"—deals with the group's trials and tribulations in conceptualizing multicultural professional development activities. Chapter Seven—"Curriculum Development and Instruction"—covers the committee's concerns with practical classroom content and pedagogy. Chapter Eight—"Diversifying the Faculty and Staff"—discusses how the multicultural organization attempted to diversify school personnel in order to match the basic student/community makeup. Chapter Nine—"Creating a Partnership between the School and the Public"—explores the committee's efforts to work with local organizations, businesses, and houses of faith, as well as parents and caregivers.

The descriptions/stories that make up Chapters Five through Nine are followed by a critical interpretation and discussion section. It is the critical multicultural theoretical framework developed in Chapter One that informs these analyses.

It is important to note that while the level of criticism throughout this book is extensive, the goal of such research analysis is by no means intended to dismiss the crucial work being done by the CSC, or to ridicule the individual contributions of its members. On the contrary, in deconstructing their work, the task at hand is to theoretically approach the complex social conditions that gave rise to the committee in the first place. Such analysis is thus undertaken with the utmost optimism; however, hope for the future requires awareness of the grim realities of so many students in this country and the reconcilable limitations of mainstream efforts to bring about equity and social justice in schools in the United States. It is also important to recognize this study is a micro-analysis in the sense that there are obviously much larger social and institutional forces that keep an organization like the CSC contained in terms of its possibilities for social activism. The suggestions for the future of multicultural education made throughout these analysis sections are intended to extend the possibilities of the efforts in Changeton so as to radically democratize public schooling.

An effective use of this book, to encourage readers/students to actively theorize (that is, an exercise in critical pedagogy), would be to first read the narrative section of a chapter and then use the insights in Chapter One's elaboration of Critical Multiculturalism, as well as one's own personal insights, to critique the work of the Central Steering Committee. Then readers/students can explore the critical interpretation and discussion section of that chapter and compare analyses.

Part Three of the book, "The Impact of Multicultural Education in Changeton over the Years," consists of three chapters. This final section takes a look at the progress that has been made in the Changeton school system in terms of the palpable effects of this extensive multicultural education project. Chapter Ten—"In the Aftermath: A Dialogue with Changeton Teachers in the Trenches"—is a poststudy overview that includes a review of outside audits of the Changeton school system, as well as a dialogue with three teachers in the Bilingual/English as a Second Language Program who, five years after its inception, discuss the impact that such efforts to infuse multicultural education have had on their daily lives as educators. Chapter Eleven—"Two Letters to Changeton Educators"—also provides a teacher analysis of the situation in the city and its schools. Chapter Twelve—"Challenges for the Future"—concludes the study and makes suggestions as to what can be done nationwide to extend the possibilities of multicultural education. The book's appendix is an elaboration of the research methodologies used throughout this project.

It is my hope that, after reading *Defining and Designing Multiculturalism*, educators who truly believe in democracy and the important role of public schooling in promoting political awareness and civic responsibility will realize that any effort limiting the dynamics of culture and the politics of identity and difference to the neutralized and romanticized exotics of food, dance, and cut-and-paste add-ons to existing curricula can never lead to more participatory and transformative structures. In other words, multicultural education will be fruitless if frozen in the fictitious realm of the apolitical and ahistorical. Instead, critical educators should seriously question existing unequal relations of power and privilege throughout society. With a developing understanding that the struggle over culture and identity is not just one of recognition but of economic and political redistribution (Fraser, 2000), people can better work in solidarity to develop coalitions with other public forces in order to understand and eradicate what it means to live in poverty, exclusion, and despair.

Democratic educators also need to recognize that while solidarity presupposes a profound grasp of what it means to live in opposition to forms of domination, it does not imply conformity and homogenization. As Paulo Freire (1999) has argued:

> There are a lot of people who think that we will have unity in diversity by a reduction of the differences, creating a whole by this reduction. Unity in diversity does not mean homogenization. . . .Unity in diversity would call for [all of our] association with other oppressed groups in order to be truly engaged in a fight for freedom. (As cited in Leistyna, 1999, pp. 53–54.)

In the spirit of Freire's work, a democratic society should be struggling toward the kinds of education that liberate rather than domesticate. *Defining and Designing Multiculturalism* is offered as the inspiration necessary for a step in that very direction.

Part One

*Theoretically and Historically
Contextualizing the Study*

CHAPTER ONE

Critical Multicultural Education

What Is It?

> Multicultural education: Schooling that helps students understand and relate to cultural,
> ethnic, and other diversity. . . . Multicultural education should be a process to work
> together and to celebrate differences, not to be separated by them.
> —J. Lynn McBrien and Ronald S. Brandt,
> *The Language of Learning: A Guide to Education Terms*

Although multicultural education is often talked about as if it were a monolithic entity, as illustrated in the above definition, in fact, the rubric contains a multiplicity of theoretical and practical insights that may even be contradictory. After an extensive review of the literature, Christine Sleeter and Carl Grant (1988) divided the available approaches into five groups: (1) Teaching the Exceptional and the Culturally Different; (2) Human Relations; (3) Single-Group Studies; (4) Multicultural Education; (5) Education that is Multicultural and Social Reconstructionist. This chapter presents a brief overview of the first four of these existing models in a way that allows for their juxtapositioning to what will be referred to as Critical Multiculturalism (a concept that will be used interchangeably throughout this book with critical pedagogy and critical multicultural education).[1] Once Sleeter and Grant's (1988) first four models have been interpreted, an elaboration will be provided to establish which tenets Critical Multicultural Education appropriates and which it rejects. Additional concerns and insights will complement this analysis.

Teaching the Exceptional and the Culturally Different

Proponents of Teaching the Exceptional and the Culturally Different are concerned with helping students from different cultural backgrounds, including those with disabilities, adapt to the mainstream demands of public schooling and society. The ultimate goal of this approach is to "remediate deficiencies or build bridges between the student and the school" (Sleeter & Grant, 1988, p. 35).

Viewing public education as systemically sound, just, and democratic, educators who embrace this type of multicultural model believe in meritocracy—where the so-called talented are advanced by virtue of their achievements. Proponents of this approach feel that the only reason culturally different people are not succeeding academically, and consequently in the workforce, is because they do not possess the necessary, standard human capital (such as language and bodies of knowledge) necessary to navigate the everyday demands of society. Consequently, advocates of this type of education attempt to prepare students—only those who are considered "in need"—with the crucial skills, values, and information to compete in the classroom and eventually in the job market.

Using educational approaches that are culturally compatible with learners' backgrounds, Teaching the Exceptional and the Culturally Different is intended to "teach traditional school knowledge more effectively by building on knowledge and skills students bring with them" (Sleeter & Grant, 1988, p. 43). As a process of remediation, educators who work within this paradigm use what information, skills, learning styles, languages (which may include the implementation of Transitional Bilingual Education) students possess, as well as creative teaching strategies, only to the extent that they act as vehicles for more efficiently transferring the learner into the so-called regular classroom. Such background information is not intended to displace or transform more conventional school content. Although this multicultural philosophy does not overtly discourage people from maintaining their native cultures and languages outside of public institutions, parents/caregivers are encouraged to show support for the school's agenda.

Human Relations

The main goal of this approach to multiculturalism is to promote positive relations among groups in schools by eradicating stereotypes and encouraging tolerance and unity. The basic idea is to bring about the realization that all people share the universal human experience. It is this common bond, combined with a newly acquired appreciation for difference, that is thought to lead to social harmony within existing societal structures. Intended to be implemented schoolwide, according to Sleeter and Grant (1988):

> the Human Relations approach is directed toward helping students communicate with, accept, and get along with people who are different from themselves; reducing or eliminating stereotypes that students have about people; and helping students feel good about themselves and about groups of which they are members without putting others down in the process. This approach is aimed mainly at the affective level: at attitudes and feelings people have about self and others. (p. 77)

Heterogeneous grouping, cooperative learning, and role playing are considered important elements of this philosophy of education, as is the open invitation to community members to come into the schools and share information about their cultural backgrounds.

Single-Group Studies

Single-Group Studies is based on a philosophy of identity politics. That is, this model promotes an in-depth exploration of the lived experiences of an individual group, for example, women, gays, blacks, or the working class. Unlike the two previous models, advocates of Single-Group Studies argue that schools are socializing institutions, and thus inherently political sites. To engage the ideological nature of schooling—the basic values, beliefs, interests, and intents that inform the learning process—this kind of multiculturalism embraces critical thinking, cultural analysis, and social action and transformation.

Essentially, the Single-Group Studies approach attempts to change attitudes and provide a basis for social action by exposing information (in this case through schooling) about a particular group and about the effects of discrimination on that group. As such, students and teachers are encouraged to question bodies of knowledge in a way that links power, ideology, and marginalization, offering an alternative view of the dominant culture and history of the country from the perspective of the group under study.

Differing from Teaching the Exceptional and the Culturally Different, Single-Group Studies is not solely intended for marginalized students. However, unlike Human Relations, which is also meant for all students, this more critical model serves the purpose of "empowering group members, developing in them a sense of pride and group consciousness, and helping members of the dominant groups appreciate the experiences of others and recognize how their groups have oppressed others" (Sleeter & Grant, 1988, p. 116). This approach also demands that teachers develop a more profound understanding of students' existential realities and needs, helping them to actualize a better sense of their own histories and the sociopolitical influences that shape their lives in the United States—the logic being that when people possess a deeper understanding of themselves and their communities, they are more adequately equipped to bring about positive social change.

Multicultural Education

Multicultural Education encompasses educational policies and practices that attempt to affirm cultural pluralism across differences in gender, ability, class, race, sexuality, and so forth. Educators who embrace such an approach stress the importance of cultural diversity, alternative life styles, native cultures, universal human rights, social justice, equal opportunity (in terms of actual outcomes from social institutions), and equal distribution of power among groups. Teaching diverse traditions and perspectives, questioning stereotypes, learning the appropriate cultural codes in order to function within a variety of settings, recognizing the contributions of all groups to society (especially those that have been traditionally excluded), encouraging teachers to learn more about their students' experiences and realities, and eliminating negative biases from materials are all deemed important everyday practices. This model also embraces cooperative learning, having high expectations on all participants involved in the learning process, nurturing a positive self-concept among students, and developing forms of evaluation that are free of stereotypical language and that reflect multicultural curricula.

Proponents of Multicultural Education recognize the sociocultural nature of behavioral patterns, literacy practices, bodies of knowledge, language use, and cognitive skills. These educators demand culturally compatible forms of teaching that build on students' learning styles, needs, and realities. In order to accomplish this goal, there is a call within this model to diversify the faculty and staff so that they better reflect the students and their communities.

Similar to Human Relations, though far more involved, Multicultural Education also aspires to bring the community into the schools, and vice versa. Unlike Teaching the Exceptional and the Culturally Different, which simply solicits the passive acquiescence of parents, proponents of this model

> believe that when it comes to the education of their children, parents and community members must be more than mere spectators, simply attending graduation ceremonies, open house, or sporting events. They argue that just as citizen participation is fundamental to American democracy, so is it fundamental to school success. . . . Advocates of the Multicultural Education approach want to

see the community involved in budgetary procedures, the selection of school personnel, and curriculum development. (Sleeter & Grant, 1988, p. 160)

The ultimate goal of Multicultural Education is to transform the entire academic environment and not just the curriculum or the attitudes of individuals.

Critical Multicultural Education

Contrary to common misperceptions of Critical Multicultural Education as a monolithic entity, the vast literature and positions that generally fall under this category not only demonstrate that there are multiple theoretical camps and differences, but also that there is no generic definition that can be applied to the term (Leistyna & Woodrum, 1996). Even the conceptual descriptors used to name such educational endeavors vary a great deal: Paulo Freire (1970) refers to this type of education as "critical pedagogy"; Henry Giroux (1994a) often uses the title "insurgent multiculturalism"; Peter McLaren (1994) prefers the use of "critical and resistance multiculturalism" or "revolutionary multiculturalism"; Donaldo Macedo (1994) speaks of "liberatory pedagogy"; and bell hooks (1994) embraces the idea of "engaged" or "transgressive pedagogy."

Regardless of the abundance of names that are summoned to describe Critical Multiculturalism, there are important theoretical insights and practices that are woven throughout these various concepts, which often grow out of a common set of issues and conditions, that provide the focus for critical education within shifting spheres of political conflict. It is with these basic tenets, and through the voices of a number of critical social theorists, that the approaches in Sleeter and Grant's (1988) typology will be analyzed. However, it is important to first present Critical Multiculturalism's rejection of conventional schooling.

A Critique of the Traditional Classroom

Critical educators (Apple, 1996; Cherryholmes, 1988; Freire, 1985; Giroux, 1983) have argued that traditional conservative technocratic models that dominate mainstream educational programs, which narrowly conceptualize teaching and learning as a discrete and scientific undertaking, embrace depersonalized methods for educating students that often translate into the regulation and standardization of teacher practices and curricula. As such, the role of the teacher, who is "trained" instead of actively educated, is reduced to that of a passive and efficient distributor of information.

Endorsing a mechanical approach to reading, writing, and math, this movement, referred to as "back to basics," has focused primarily on the transfer of basic skills and knowledge from the instructor to the student through mindless drills and rote memorization of selected facts that can easily be measured through standardized testing. Critical multicultural educators often depict how this pedagogical model, which focuses exclusively on preparing students for the workforce, abstracts education from the challenges of developing a conscious, socially responsible, and politically active student body and citizenry.

Many conservatives (Bennett, 1992; Cheney, 1988; D'Souza, 1995; Hirsch, 1996; Kimbal, 1990; Ravitch, 1995) have argued that attempts to reveal the underlying values, interests, and power relationships that structure educational policies and practices have corrupted the academic environment. As a rebuttal, critical educators assert that such efforts to depoliticize the public's understanding of social institutions, especially schools, in the name of neutrality and democracy is merely a reactionary ploy to maintain the status quo.

It is important to note that conservatives are not the only ones guilty of this unwillingness, or failure, to name the inherently political nature of formal education. Take, for example, former President Bill Clinton's two separate and contradicting statements made while he was still in office: "Politics must stop at the schoolhouse door!" and

> I support efforts to empower local school districts to experiment with chartering their schools . . . or having more public school choice, or to do whatever they wish to do as long as we measure every school by one high standard: Are our children learning what they need to know to compete and win in the global economy?

Clinton is complicit in perpetuating the idea that politics can be left at the schoolhouse door, though he himself is placing the central value of public education on careerism and global capitalism: "Are our children learning what they need to know to compete and win in the global economy?" Even if he chooses the language of democracy and civic responsibility over neoliberalism when speaking openly about educating the public, Clinton would nonetheless be taking a political stance. As Sleeter and Grant (1988) point out:

> Schooling that teaches about democracy is not neutral, but offers a particular point of view. Although this view may be related to freedom, justice, and equality, it is nevertheless a point of view. (p. 110)

Critical pedagogues insist that, as a consequence of mainstream technocratic models of public education, the larger historical, ideological, economic, and cultural conditions out of which today's social and institutional crises have grown, generally go unquestioned. It is precisely this lack of inquiry, analysis, and agency that a critical philosophy of learning and teaching hopes to reverse.

Critiquing and Appropriating from Teaching the Exceptional and Culturally Different

Teaching the Exceptional and the Culturally Different, like traditional pedagogy and curriculum in the United States, is based on an assimilationist agenda. This is clearly the case when any and all materials that are relevant to learners from different backgrounds are only used temporarily and are ultimately discarded. From a critical point of view, this culturally homogenizing process, which in the end contributes to students losing a sense of themselves in order to become "Americans," is fundamentally antimulticultural and antidemocratic.[2] In rhetoric, advocates of this model claim that people can do whatever they want in their homes, but in public they must abide by certain codes. However, it is naïve at best, and malicious at worst, to assume that the two spheres can exist in isolation from each other.

Similar in many ways to conventional schooling, this depoliticized model of multicultural education also embraces the existence of an objective/neutral and universal body of knowledge that is referred to as "human capital." Rejecting the idea of a universal foundation for truth and culture, as well as any claim to objectivity, critical pedagogy reveals that educational practices and knowledge are always produced within particular social, economic, and historical conditions, and therefore any understanding of their production and dissemination must be accompanied by an investigation of their relation to ideology and power (Foucault, 1972). Education, for example, as an integral part of the socialization process, is directed by particular beliefs, values, and interests. Knowledge, which in broad terms is understood as the way a person explains or interprets reality, is similarly constructed. Examining schooling, not as a neutral process, but rather as a form of cultural politics, critical multiculturalists argue that, as microcosms of the larger society, educational institutions reflect and produce social turmoil by maintaining dominant beliefs, values, and interests through particular teaching practices and bodies of knowledge that are legitimized, circulated, and consumed (or resisted) in the classroom. This surreptitious mirroring of dominant values, at the exclusion of "others," is often referred to in the literature as the hidden curriculum (Anyon, 1980; Apple, 1990; Giroux & Penna, 1979; Vallance, 1973). Giroux (1983) broadly defines the "hidden curriculum" as

those unstated norms, values, and beliefs embedded in and transmitted to students through the underlying rules that structure the routines and social relationships in

school and classroom life. The hidden curriculum functions not simply as a vehicle of socialization but also as an agency of social control, one that functions to
provide differential forms of schooling to different classes of students. (p. 47)[3]

This covert agenda also works to erase or distort the experiences and perceptions
of individuals and groups from other social realities that are shaped by the ideologically constructed categories of race, gender, sexual orientation, and so forth.[4]

Critical pedagogy reveals how only those characteristics and practices reflecting that dominant ideology will potentially facilitate academic achievement in
mainstream schools (Anyon, 1980; Apple, 1990; Bourdieu & Passeron, 1977;
Bowles & Gintis, 1976). With this in mind, the idea of universal human capital
that is enthusiastically embraced by proponents of Teaching the Exceptional and
the Culturally Different needs to be problematized and replaced. A more appropriate term, "cultural capital," is extremely helpful in openly naming how different practices, behaviors, forms of language, and meaning are ideologically produced and hierarchically valued in society (Bourdieu & Passeron, 1977). From this
perspective, knowledge is accurately portrayed as being generated within historical relations of power and not as some form of universal human understanding.

Contesting modernist traditions that are based on the notion that emancipa-
tion is only realizable through objective inquiry, universal reason, and absolute
truth, students and teachers involved in critical multicultural learning and teaching are encouraged to examine the values, assumptions, and interests reflected in
bodies of knowledge and representations, link such information to their own experiences if possible, and subsequently pose questions about the construction of
knowledge—questions that address whose interests are served and whose voices
and narratives have been systematically excluded. For example, educators should
immediately question descriptors such as "normal" or "regular," which are often
used to compare the Bilingual and Special Education Programs to the so-called
mainstream—terms that dialectically imply that everyone outside of this dominant category is "abnormal" or "irregular."

Proponents of Critical Multicultural Education would agree with the idea
embraced by Teaching the Exceptional and the Culturally Different that all students should possess the tools necessary for navigating the current social order.
However, unlike the conservative model that never questions the status quo, there
is a call within critical pedagogy for the selective appropriation of dominant discourses—language, interaction styles, and knowledge—so that people of all backgrounds are not only able to survive within the mainstream, but more importantly they are armed to transform it. In this way, teachers and students do not fall
into what Freire (1970) refers to as the "banking model of education," which occurs when educators perceive students as empty containers that need to be filled
with preestablished bodies of knowledge. Within the confines of a pedagogy of

transmission, learners are treated as objects that are acted upon, rather than knowledgeable participants in the construction of deep, meaningful, and transformative learning experiences.

By accepting the status quo, Teaching the Exceptional and the Culturally Different neglects, or simply ignores, the institutional and socially sanctioned practices of discrimination and oppression. Instead, this model perpetuates the myths of meritocracy and life in a melting pot where the patterns of a so-called common culture miraculously emerge. Through a critical lens, any conservative effort to enforce a common culture, which in actuality is an unnegotiated foundation of values, ethics, meaning, histories, and representations, is viewed as the imposition of a homogenizing social paradigm that severely limits the possibility for a participatory democracy within a pluralistic society.

The reactionary idea of commonality disregards the real inter- and intragroup cultural differences and histories that exist in the United States. For example, as race and culture, class and culture, and gender and culture are inextricably related through discrimination, racially subordinated realities are substantially different from those of whites, as the ruling class is different from the working class, and as men are from women. The key question is, whose perspectives and interests are defining societal norms—the common culture—as well as what it means to be an official member of the nation?

Focusing on the imposition of particular values in society, as well as on the antagonistic relations and the opposition that surfaces as a response to such domination, critical multicultural educators view the contemporary cultural landscape not as a vista of common traditions and memories, but rather as a terrain of conflict. From this perspective, it is democracy alone that is the common element intended to unite the nation and eradicate the abuses of power and inequities that produce and maintain social injustice. However, it is crucial to acknowledge that a participatory democracy thrives on diversity and dissent, and not on coercive acts that rely on symbolic and physical violence to enforce conformity.

Ignoring the fact that U.S. society is not built on a level playing field for all groups, and that the elements of race, gender, class, health, religion, age, and sexuality have been used systematically to marginalize or exclude many people, conservative approaches to multicultural education never engage the politics of difference. Although Teaching the Exceptional and the Culturally Different uses the word "different," the model disallows any exploration of how difference is constructed within unequal relations of power. Working from such a limited and limiting framework, one that focuses exclusively on the so-called other, the concept of difference is often not taken up in terms of recognizing and critically engaging the dominant referent group—the invisible norm of the white, affluent, heterosexual, healthy, Christian male by which all people are measured. Without ever questioning the inhibiting aspects of this dominant referent, Teaching the Exceptional and the Culturally Different implicitly works from a deficit-model orientation that equates different cognitive and learning styles, literacies, language use, and low academic achievement of students from certain groups, with individual or group pathology, cultural deprivation, or genetic limitations.

Instead of recognizing schools as a product of the larger society of inequities and struggles, they are viewed within this reactionary multicultural model as the great equalizers, the all-encompassing panaceas to "cultural and physical deficiencies," as well as to societal problems. Educational institutions are thus understood as the solution to, rather than perpetuators of, social injustice and demise.

Critiquing and Appropriating from Human Relations

There are a number of qualities that Critical Multicultural Education appropriates from the Human Relations approach to diversity: the idea that education of this kind is for all students and not just those on the margins, the stress on infusing such principles systemwide, and the use of heterogeneous grouping, cooperative learning, and role playing in the classroom. The two models also mutually embrace teaching social skills and providing an open invitation to community members to come into the schools and share information about their cultural backgrounds. However, Human Relations, like Teaching the Exceptional and the Culturally Different, neglects to analyze the larger social and institutional structures that create intergroup tensions, poverty, disenfranchisement, and oppression. Instead, this multicultural model is built around the idea of cultural relativism, a philosophy in which all cultures are valued equally.

By not addressing structural inequalities and the reality that all groups and experiences are not treated with the same respect in society, Human Relations implicitly accepts the present social order. In fact, by using the word "human" in place of the term "cultural," this educational model avoids any kind of engagement with antagonistic intergroup relations, collapsing into a kind of benign universal humanism (McCarthy, 1993). As a result, proponents openly reject talking about oppressive practices, claiming that exploration of this sort will exacerbate differences, tensions, and hostility among groups. In reference to such approaches, Paul Gilroy (1987) argues, "They have been concerned not directly with the enhancement of the power of the oppressed or disadvantaged groups but with the development of racially harmonious social and political relations" (p. 117).

In actual practice, Human Relations rarely moves beyond the surface features of traditional foods, clothing, and music. Schooling is consequently dealt with as a public ground where people, given the opportunity, can remove themselves from the turmoil of the rest of the world. Sleeter and Grant (1988) contend that within multicultural practices of this type, "students may learn to interact pleasantly with Victor and to enjoy Chinese food, but this is no guarantee that they will learn about issues such as the poverty of Chinatown or the psychological devastation many Asian immigrants face when they realize they must surrender much of their identity to assimilate into American society" (p. 98).

Grounded in a relativistic stance on culture and identity, a major problem with Human Relations in the classroom is that the attitudes and beliefs of educators are often taken for granted. When advocates of this approach identify the need to question the affective domain of teachers, this often translates into an innocuous call for individuals to be more sensitive to differences and more inclusive. In fact, many well-intentioned educators working from within this conceptual framework believe that they can be more welcoming and just by miraculously leaving their own cultural baggage and biases at the schoolhouse door. Rather than confronting any potentially negative, inhibiting, and exclusionary ideologies that inevitably enter the classroom, they are in many cases rendered invisible. The idea that personal politics can be left at the door gives the erroneous impression that teachers can in fact be neutral distributors of information, and that objective truth is attainable.

From a more critical perspective, teachers are viewed as working and speaking from within historically and socially determined relations of power and privilege that are based on such markers as their race, class, ability, sexuality, and gender. Diametrically opposed to ignoring educators' attitudes and beliefs, critical multiculturalists call for the ongoing process of self-reflection and self-actualization. This evolving awareness, or presence of mind, is intended to help people not only understand the sociohistorical and economic nature of their own cultural assumptions, and how they may affect the educational process, students, and the school's overall social relations, but also the asymmetries of power that exist within the institutions where they work and live. This ability to interrogate the values and beliefs that inform knowledge also allows educators and concerned citizens to recognize the ideology of groups, such as teachers unions and school committees, that control school life, as well as "the hierarchical and often authoritarian relationships of school management, the conservative nature of school ideology, the material conditions of the classroom, the structural isolation teachers often face, and the fiscal and ideological constraints imposed by school boards on faculty" (Giroux, 1983, p. 56).

Educators need to reflect deeply on the assumptions that they carry about learning, evaluation, and different cultural identities. Self-actualization and prejudice reduction are essential to social transformation. However, self-actualization and prejudice reduction do not in and of themselves address where the "self" or the prejudice comes from. By solely looking within oneself, an individual is unable to make the links to the larger sociopolitical reality that shapes the psychological so as to be able to change it.

It is also crucial to recognize the fact that consciousness raising should not simply be about the process of unlearning. Of equal importance is developing an understanding of where and how such values and beliefs were produced so that any such sources can be confronted and eradicated if need be. For example, when it comes to actual classroom practices, Antonia Darder (1991) argues, "Another significant factor in the production of self-awareness in teachers is the ability to decode and critique the ideologies inscribed in the forms of structuring principles behind the presentation of images in curriculum materials" (p. 87).

When Human Relations manages to move beyond the mere sensitizing of teachers and students, and focuses on changing their attitudes, such a philosophy in action often implicitly individualizes and psychologizes oppression, decoupling one's personality from the sociohistorical factors that in fact shape human subjectivities. Instead of examining the inherently ideological and thus political nature of identities and educational practices, and the systemic nature of multicultural tensions, this approach abstracts the historical from the present, the institutional from the personal, and thus, the social from the psychological. It deals with discrimination as if it were the product of ignorance or personal acts of mean-spiritedness, rather than the result of socially sanctioned practices and institutions. Cameron McCarthy (1993) observes: "Within these frameworks, school reform and reform in race relations depend almost exclusively on the reversal of values, attitudes, and the human nature of social actors understood as 'individuals'" (p. 293).

Trapped by the inherent myopia of this paradigm, it is no wonder that there is little to no call for an in-depth transformation of the ways in which society and public education have been organized. If discrimination can be reduced to the level of personal attitudes, disconnected from the cultural institutions and everyday practices that have in fact shaped those personality traits, then there is no need to question reality beyond an individual's consciousness and actions.

Within the Human Relations model of multicultural education, those who discriminate or abuse particular students are said to be "ignorant." The use of the term "ignorance," by apologists who are looking for excuses for particular forms of individual behavior, actually conjures up images of a lack of experience, as if a person simply doesn't know any better. However, the experience of ignorance is not empty of content. On the contrary, it is full of information that is worked deeply into the fabric and texture of identity. Such experience not only distorts social reality, but it also deskills people from understanding what guides their thoughts and feelings.[5]

Psychologizing the world also manages to create an individualized and relativistic understanding of difference, which has the tendency to lead to a color-blindness mentality that disarticulates students' identities in the classroom from the diverse social realities of the everyday. When educators attempt to look at students all in the same way, as well-intentioned as this may be, the lack of acknowledging and engaging the ideological markers of difference, especially within a project of social change, has negative consequences (Nieto, 1992). That is, teachers can't value all students if they deny any engagement with their different life experiences, especially those related to and shaped by homophobia, ableism, sexism, classism, and racism. Unfortunately, the Human Relations philosophy of empty humanism and benign pluralism obfuscates the reality that difference exists within historically determined asymmetries of power in which some identities are valued and encouraged, while others are disparaged and discouraged. Responsible educators working toward more democratic structures and social justice can't simply hide behind what appears to be an objective and just way of interacting with all students in the very same ways.

One of the major obstacles of critical transformative education in the United States is that theory of any kind is often devalued among educators. Such ambivalence is not surprising when it comes to schooling considering the fact that most educational theory has been removed from everyday practice and left in the hands of academic "experts" who have little contact with the actual classroom dynamic. Furthermore, theories of learning and teaching are often uncritically passed down to future teachers to inform more efficient ways that students can assimilate basic skills.

This divorce of theory and practice is reflected in a system of public primary and secondary schooling that continues to be inundated with the practical: prepackaged methods, teacher-proof materials, and standardized evaluation. Within these rigid and disempowering pedagogical conditions, educators generally have no opportunity to develop an understanding of the historical specificities and presuppositions that inform such practices (Bartolomé, 1994), let alone those that inform the larger social order.

Advocates of the Human Relations approach to multicultural education actually work against the possibility of understanding and creating social theory. Psychologizing people's behavior—collapsing the world into the realm of the individual, at the expense of recognizing the sociohistorical construction of the psyche—makes it is virtually impossible to interpret, critique, and draw generalizations about what socially takes place around and within people. Educators who exclusively embrace the individualization of life thus run the risk of crippling the possibilities for theorizing what it means to be associated with a particular group or shared experience.

The basic theoretical underpinning of Human Relations is that educators need to be more sensitive and affirming. The inherent problem with this conceptual approach, in practice, is that striving solely for sensitivity and a safe environment creates a paradigm of interaction that is based on the idea of good relations and not necessarily on consciousness, social critique, and action. In most cases, the formation of a comfort zone does not allow for critical interrogation of ideas and assumptions. This not only puts some serious constraints on the role of critical dialogue, but such a model allows discriminatory values, beliefs, and actions to go uncontested. Multicultural education is thus reduced to the nice, neat, and sweet of food and fun. As Ana Maria Villegas (1988) states, "Culturally sensitive remedies to the educational problems of oppressed minority students that ignore the political aspect of schooling are doomed to failure. Worse still, they give the illusion of progress while perpetuating the academic problem, and by extension, the social inequalities they mask" (p. 263).

Perhaps creating comfort zones is a strategy to keep peoples' eyes and ears open to the issues being discussed; however, if education never moves into the unknown and the uncomfortable, and silenced voices are never heard from, then oppressive institutions and identities remain virtually unchallenged. It is crucial that multiculturalism gets beyond the politeness muzzle of solely affirming diversity, which discourages individuals from intellectually rigorous discussions. This is not intended to be an argument against acknowledging where people come from, being sensitive to the plight of others, or creating a safe environment to dialogue. Rather, it's simply a contention that without critical engagement, sensitivity alone can not adequately address what needs to be changed in schools and society.

Educators need to create a space that allows for a more critical and democratic exchange of ideas in which everyone's location, experiences, and perceptions in their private and public lives become the point of departure for dialogue and a text for debate. In examining the social construction of knowledge, values, and interaction across difference, the idea is not for the process to be abusive by silencing participants or placing their identities on trial. Rather, the process is to be unsettling only to the degree that it forces all of those involved to recognize and challenge their role in accepting and perpetuating oppression of any kind. By not confronting the sources of stereotypes, and by hiding behind superficial, positive portrayals of all groups, Human Relations works to create and perpetuate what Macedo (1994) refers to as "the social construction of not seeing" and "complicity through denial"—both of which contribute to cultural reproduction of the status quo.

Critiquing and Appropriating from Single-Group Studies

In theory, Single-Group Studies has a good deal in common with Critical Multicultural Education. These two approaches embrace a schoolwide discussion of the group's contributions and struggles in society. Perhaps the strongest connection between the two camps is the mutual recognition of, and engagement with, the ideological and thus inherently political nature of schooling. This entails questioning bodies of knowledge and providing alternative perspectives and counterdiscourses—languages of critique and demystification capable of contesting oppressive beliefs and practices. Such interaction is intended to rupture stereotypes, myths, and social inequities.

Single-Group Studies and Critical Multicultural Education also call for the development of political awareness among classroom participants, which necessitates constant engagement with history, as well as with teachers' and students' existential realities, in ways that develop the kinds of cultural analyses and personal connections that are fundamental to transformative education. Unfortunately, instead of having students explicitly link their actual lives to the legacy of discrimination being explored in the classroom, Single-Group Studies, in practice, has a tendency to deal with oppression as disconnected from the here and now. Even worse, as noted by Sleeter and Grant (1988), a softer form of this model often turns into "the four Fs: fairs, festivals, food, and folk tales" (p. 121). Generally collapsed into one course, such an approach to diversity and discrimination frequently consists of simply adding on to the existing curriculum, instead of achieving the ostensible goal of challenging and changing the entire educational process.

One of the major flaws of Single-Group Studies—a common problem among all mainstream models of multicultural education—is that it has a tendency to essentialize and thus objectify and stereotype identities. Essentialism ascribes a fundamental nature or a biological determinism to humans through attitudes about experience, knowledge, and cognitive development. From a monolithic and homogenizing point of view, the category of gender, for example, appears as a gross generalization and single-cause explanation for individual character and behavior. As such, this model is inclined to ignore intragroup differences across social class, health, race, religion, sexuality, and so forth. Pointing out the limitations of such a reductionistic propensity, Sleeter and Grant (1988) observe, "Specifically, ethnic studies often focus on the males of a given ethnic group; labor studies often focus on the working-class males; and women's studies often focus on white, middle-class women" (p. 129). It is as if the multiple forms of diversity—the complex and interconnecting relationships that speak to a more dialectical understanding of the politics of difference—exist in isolation from each other.

An additional recurring problem with a pedagogy based on identity politics is that experience is often left at the level of description, that is, storytelling is welcomed at the expense of theoretical analysis. Such an atheoretical posture gives the erroneous perception that subject position (the place that a person occupies within a set of social relationships, often determined by gender, class, race, language, sexual orientation, religion, age, and ability) leads to presence of mind. In other words, when a subordinated person shares experiences of discrimination, this narration, in and of itself, would necessarily bring about the intra- and interpersonal political awareness to understand such oppressive acts. McLaren (1995) warns of this very pitfall:

> Either a person's physical proximity to the oppressed or their own location as an oppressed person is supposed to offer a special authority from which to speak. . . . Here the political is often reduced only to the personal where theory is dismissed in favor of one's own personal and cultural identity—abstracted from the ideological and discursive complexity of their formation. (p. 125)

The pretense that location predisposes presence of mind is like saying that a patient who is sick, who feels the pain, necessarily understands why the disease exists, how it works, and how to combat it. If subject position ensured consciousness, then the white working class and white women would not be so easily diverted, as they historically have been, by issues of race and sexuality, and would rise up in solidarity with others against their own oppression (Allen, 1994; Baldwin, 1985; DuBois, 1935; Frankenburg, 1993; Hill, 1997; hooks, 1981; McIntyre, 1997; Mohanty, Russo, & Torres, 1991; Roediger, 1991; Wallace, 1990). It is only with exposure to a multitude of competing information, and in dialogue with the disempowered, that all of those opposed to the present social order can work from a position of awareness to one of informed solidarity.[6]

Countering the reductionistic tendency to conflate location and consciousness, Critical Multicultural Education requires the kinds of theoretical analyses and dialogue necessary for explaining why it is that something (a particular experience) occurred in the first place. For educators influenced by Freire's wisdom, it is important to keep in mind that the concept of dialogue is not simply about having a conversation with students and their respective communities. Rather, this type of discursive relationship is meant to facilitate critical interaction that focuses on the kinds of ideological analyses of knowledge and experience that lead to political awareness and action capable of eradicating oppressive practices, institutions, and identities, both in schools and society.

Critiquing and Appropriating from Multicultural Education

Critical pedagogy, like Multicultural Education, recognizes the importance of cultural diversity, alternative life styles, maintaining native cultures, universal human rights, social justice, equal opportunity (in terms of actual outcomes from social institutions), and equal distribution of power among groups. Both models call for teaching diverse traditions and perspectives, questioning stereotypes, learning the cultural codes to function within a variety of settings, recognizing the contributions that all groups have made to society (especially those that have been traditionally excluded), and encouraging teachers to learn more about their students' experiences and realities. They also embrace learning cooperatively, having high expectations on all classroom participants, nurturing a positive self-concept among students, and developing forms of evaluation that are free of stereotypical language and that reflect a diverse curriculum.

Although Multicultural Education and critical pedagogy, in theory, have a great deal in common, critical educators argue that in practice this is not the case. Similar to Human Relations, Multicultural Education often endeavors to simply affirm diversity and identities through positive images of subordinated groups and does so in a limited fashion by focusing on color coordination (disconnected from issues of ideological differences among people from the same racial/ethnic group), food festivals (in which multicultural education is reduced to having fun), cut-and-paste add-ons to the existing canon, and group-based methodologies (which often essentialize and objectify students by making them fit to the method, rather than the other way around).

Not paying enough attention to structural inequalities and student agency, Multicultural Education, through a superficial pedagogy of inclusion, often becomes a romanticization and celebration of differences, without any interrogation of the power differentials that give rise to exclusive practices, distorted representations of otherness, and social strife. As previously discussed in the critique of Human Relations, the insistence upon solely affirming diversity creates a pedagogical process that is reduced to an empty form of pluralism which largely ignores the workings of power and privilege. Consequently, diversity is not experienced as a politics of cultural criticism and change—a process of engaging all lived experiences for their strengths and weaknesses, nor is it embraced as an ongoing democratic struggle to achieve social justice. When activities in schools are based on fun and superficial exposure to other cultures than that of the dominant group, and artificially cleansed of any analysis of harmful institutional structures, social practices, and identities, there can never be the kinds of edifying conditions that generate presence of mind and social activism among educators and students. Giroux (1994) warns of this radical omission:

> In opposition to quaint liberalism, a critical multiculturalism means more than simply acknowledging differences and analyzing stereotypes; more fundamentally, it means understanding, engaging, and transforming the diverse histories, cultural narratives, representations, and institutions that produce racism and other forms of discrimination. (p. 328)

As argued earlier, curricula and pedagogy can either affirm or exclude certain voices and lifestyles. What is worse, in the hands of unreflective teachers, they can demean, deny, or disfigure the lived experience of many people who are not part of dominant groups. Instead of simply adding elements of diversity to existing classroom content, educators need to recognize that the ways in which conventional subject matter often blatantly ignore or distort the realities of the oppressed is not a mere matter of circumstance or oversight, but rather, they are more often systematic ideological impositions intended to shape public memory along the lines of race, religion, gender, class, sexual orientation, and disability. Otherwise, educators risk embracing a pedagogy of content addition, which does not question the basic structures of public schooling, nor does it contest the ways in which such institutions are implicated in the politics of difference and domination.

Multicultural educators often mention the importance of not treating lightly such events as black History Month, and that any philosophy of diversity should be interdisciplinary and ever present throughout the curriculum. However, far too often, there is little attempt to point out the oppressive cultural conditions within which the need for such an emphasis evolved. As Darder (1991) states:

> Often the dominant culture is able to manipulate alternative and oppositional ideologies in a manner that more readily secures its hegemony. The celebrations of Cinco de Mayo and Martin Luther King's birthday are prime examples of how these initially radical concepts—intended to resist cultural invasion—have been appropriated in such a fashion that they now do little to challenge the real basis of power of the dominant culture. (p. 43)

It is extremely important that teachers and students develop a more critical sense of knowledge, its inextricable link to ideology and power, and the risks of the co-optation of meaning.

When mainstream models of multicultural education do address the politics of the curriculum, it is usually in a limited fashion that superficially points out the problems with Eurocentrism. However, instead of using Eurocentrism to name white supremacy, the term more often than not functions in a relativistic manner to simply quantify and balance out classroom content by focusing on how often a certain world view is or isn't mentioned. This level of critique does not confront and challenge knowledge bases and the construction of identities, but rather, it collapses into the benign idea that educators need to teach all cultures. One seriously debilitating result of this relativistic approach to difference is that white students are effectively taught to disregard the fact that they are also historical and ideological beings that are racialized, gendered, and sexualized. Louis Castenell and William Pinar (1993) maintain that, "The 'Eurocentric' character of the school curriculum functions not only to deny 'role models' to non-European American students, but to deny self-understanding to 'white' students as well" (p. 5). With this in mind, any model of multicultural education based on a pedagogy of inclusion that simply functions to raise self-esteem is not only working to boost the confidence of stigmatized students, but also to celebrate the development of oppressive identities.

Rather than merely filling in the blanks of the existing Eurocentric curriculum with superficial elements of diversity, educators need to encourage, among all students, a great deal of self-reflection and self-actualization. This, in part, entails a discussion about content omissions and structured silences, as well as why history has been written in certain ways. It is important to recognize that the call to critically examine existing curricula is not a demand to throw the baby out with the bath water, so to speak. That is, "We need not necessarily indiscriminately abandon the traditions of Western civilization; instead, we need to engage the strengths and weaknesses of such a complex and contradictory tradition as part of a wider effort to deepen the discourse of critical democracy and responsible citizenship" (Giroux, 1992, p. 105).

It is not only what teachers teach that is important but how they teach. Educators can have very progressive content but an authoritarian style of interaction that excludes the perspectives of students. Regardless of intention, this style represents a pedagogy of imposition rather than exposition. By including all voices in the classroom, and having theory work through students, rather than on them, teachers move away from the traditional relational restraints—that is, the limits of the relation of knowledge imparter to passive recipients. Real dialogue, which demands critical reflection, debate, and negotiation, affords the necessary conditions for everyone, especially students, to act as knowers, learners, and teachers, and to reach beyond their own cultural boundaries. It is extremely important for teachers to also participate as learners if they hope to truly discover who their students are, what they need, and how best to accommodate or demystify those needs.

Unfortunately, instead of tapping learners as rich sources of information and guidance, the majority of curricula activities within uncritical approaches to multicultural education attempt to affirm diversity by randomly providing such superficial aspects as flag displays, units on particular countries, and food. Educators seem to prefer to use abstract objects and practices from the outside world, rather than the living breathing cultural entities—the students themselves—as text for exploration and debate. Although affirming aspects of distant cultures is a step in the right direction (as long as it's not stripped of its actual meaning), without serious consideration of the existential realties of people here in the United States, multicultural education can accomplish very little. A great majority of the people who are perceived as culturally different in schools in the United States have roots elsewhere, but the reality is that many of their cultural characteristics are more the result of local developments than more privileged citizens care to recognize or believe. This points to a central problem with Multicultural Education—and with all mainstream approaches for that matter: its proponents usually work from an a limited theoretical, ahistorical, and depoliticized understanding of culture.

While the first four models in Sleeter and Grant's (1988) typology readily make use of the word "culture," none of them, even the more progressive approach of Single-Group Studies, offers a comprehensive explanation of the term. Beyond the typical depoliticized, ahistorical, and thus vacuous conception of culture as artifacts, social practices, and traditions, in the critical sense it also embodies the lived experiences and behaviors that are the result of the unequal distribution of power along such lines as race, class, gender, sexuality, religion, and ability (Fanon, 1952; Foucault, 1972; Marx, 1859; Spivak, 1987; Williams, 1958). Therefore, culture is perceived as being shaped by the lived experiences and institutional forms organized around diverse elements of struggle and domination. Critical multiculturalists argue that as people interact with existing institutions and social practices in which the values, beliefs, bodies of knowledge, styles of communication, and biases of the dominant culture are imposed, they are often stripped of their power to articulate and realize, or are forced to rearticulate, their own goals. From this perspective, cultures in the United States develop in relation to (whether it's actual human contact or through institutionalized norms) and not in abstraction from each other.[7]

Unfortunately, many educators who are actively engaged in current multicultural practices reduce the idea of culture to national origin. This assumption not only boils down the myriad of identities within a nation to one homogenized image, but it also fragments groups of people with borders, pulling culture out of its antagonistic intergroup and transnational relations and institutional formations. It also creates deterministic connections that are fundamentally racist. For example, talking about Nigeria to a young black man, born and raised in the Bronx, often removes the classroom from the immediacy of the lived experiences of the learner. Such an exercise risks implying that there is some genetic link between the student and a faraway land.

Hopefully, Critical Multicultural Education will lead to a recognition of the community learning patterns and world views that youth(s) bring to school with them. As Joyce King (1994) states, "Teachers need sufficient in-depth understanding of their students' background to select and incorporate into the education process those forms of cultural knowledge and competence that facilitate meaningful, transformative learning" (p. 42).

The reduction of culture to the idea of nation has also led to a trend in mainstream discussions of multiculturalism to talk about immigrant experiences. Although an understanding needs to develop about students who have recently endured cultural and geographical transitions, such an effort should not conceal the reality that many of the students that are not academically succeeding in public schools have been in the United States for generations—African

Americans, Native Americans, Native Hawaiians, Chicano/as, Puerto Ricans, Filipinos, and so on. Rather than being the byproduct of immigration, such groups are the victims of enslavement, genocide, colonization, and conquest.

Understanding immigration is important; however, it is imperative that educators problematize their understanding of this phenomenon. Contrary to researcher John Ogbu's (1987) idea of "voluntary immigrants," most groups do not come to the United States by choice. In fact U.S. foreign policy in places like Latin America, the Middle East, Southeast Asia, Africa, and the Caribbean has led to mass destruction and chaos, forcing people away from their homes (Bhabha, 1994; Chomsky, 1993; Gilroy, 1993; Said, 1993). Teachers need to develop a more profound awareness as to why people make their way to the United States. Educators need to move beyond the anti-multicultural, conservative ideology that claims that "you immigrants came to our house for dinner and now you want to decide what's on the menu."

Although Multicultural Education, in theory, is intended to encompass issues of race, gender, class, ability, and sexuality, often this approach reduces culture to unelaborated inclusions of race and ethnicity, at the exclusion of all other markers of identity. As such, it neglects to engage how these multiple and interconnecting relationships that define a politics of identity and difference shape the cultural realities of everyday life. For example, capitalism and social class are often not considered significant issues when dealing with raising consciousness about multiculturalism. In fact, they are generally not understood as culturally formative entities. Consequently, economic exploitation and the concomitant social antagonisms and cultural values, beliefs, languages, and world views that are shaped by class relations are rendered invisible, as are the ways in which schools act as socializing agencies for capitalist logic and as sorting machines for a hierarchically divided labor force (Anyon, 1980; Aronowitz, 2000; Bourdieu & Passeron, 1977; Bowles & Gintis, 1976; Saltman, 2000; Willis, 1977).

The ways in which culture is produced through the media are also overlooked by most models of multicultural education. From a critical perspective, pedagogy—that is, how, and in what context, people learn what they learn—does not simply take place in schools. The electronic media (for example, television news, movies, and music) not only serve up information, but they also shape human perceptions. These media are not simply expressive or reflective, they are also formative in that they can influence how people see themselves and others. What inevitably becomes a struggle over identity and representation (that is, over who has the power to articulate experience, fashion identities, define the nature of problems, and legitimate solutions) contributes to shaping the sociocultural relations of everyday life—how people look at, feel about, fear, and interact with one another and how they perceive themselves.

As popular culture has a tendency to produce and maintain stereotypes and destructive identities, Critical multiculturalists argue that there is a serious need in public education to have students develop critical media literacy, so as to be able to deconstruct the ideologies embedded in the images that they are constantly subjected to and protect themselves against, and rewrite, any harmful messages (Durham & Kellner, 2001; Dyer, 1993; Freire & Macedo, 1987; Giroux, 1996; Hall, 1997; Herman & Chomsky, 1988; Jhally, 1991; Lankshear & McLaren, 1993; Said, 1993; Strinati, 1995). By investigating the historical situatedness of particular forms of representation, and how such images are constructed and for whom, the class participants can examine and extend their understanding of the ways in which multimedia can work toward both a liberatory self and collective definition, and toward distorting perceptions of social reality that can act maliciously as agents of containment and cultural reproduction. Thus, students develop the ability to recognize and confront their own cultural assumptions, especially those that are the result of the vicarious teachings of popular culture. Embracing critical media literacy, David Sholle and Stan Denski (1994) argue that active classroom participants should be posing such questions as:

> What names do the media give as they define the world? What language do they speak as they shape the central concepts of our culture? How does the symbolic system work? And who does it work for? What are the institutional determinants of media messages? Under what constraints do media producers work? How do the prevalent symbolic and institutional systems mesh with other systems? How do they mesh with other such social values as democracy, freedom, equality, culture, progress? (p. 141)

These are the kinds of inquiry that lead to a deeper understanding of the sociopolitical realities that shape peoples' lives—demanding a great deal of self-reflection about the ways in which subjectivities, dreams, and behaviors are ideologically and discursively mobilized.

As previously mentioned, proponents of Multicultural Education and critical pedagogy recognize the social construction of behavioral patterns, literacy practices, bodies of knowledge, language use, and cognitive skills. Advocates of such models demand culturally compatible forms of teaching that build on students' learning styles, and that adjust to their needs and cultural realities. In order to accomplish such goals, there is a concerted effort to diversify the faculty and staff of schools so that they reflect the student body and the public at large. The basic idea is that teachers from marginalized groups could potentially bring a great deal to the school community in terms of providing role models, alternative worldviews, critiques of oppressive practices, and ideas and energy for reworking the system in order to meet the needs and interests of all students.

While the struggle to gain representation of different groups on school faculties and staff is crucial, educators should be weary of the misconception that the mere presence of different people implies presence of mind, or that color coordination ensures ideological diversity. In other words, having Colin Powell, Linda Chavez, and Richard Rodriguez at the table—three extremely conservative public figures—would not represent the interests of a great many racially subordinated people, women, the poor, or gays and lesbians. On the contrary, multicultural education of any kind should not only be interdisciplinary in content, but it should also draw upon the lived experience of people from a diversity of backgrounds and ideologies who cross and engage the multiple and shifting interconnecting relationships that constitute a pedagogy and politics of identity and difference. Multicultural education needs to develop from, and thus reflect, the plethora of communities that make up this country.

As with all other models of education that attempt to work with diversity, Critical Multicultural Education embraces the active participation of parents/caregivers and the public at large in the process of schooling, because, as Sonia Nieto (1992) states:

> The research is quite clear on the effectiveness of parent and community involvement: In programs with a strong component of parent involvement, students are consistently better achievers than in otherwise identical programs with less parent involvement. In addition, students in schools that maintain frequent contact with their communities outperform those in other schools. (p. 81)

The problem is that most mainstream multicultural research, literature, and practices fail to define what exactly involvement and community mean. There are multiple, even contradicting, definitions of parent involvement in public education.

While critical multiculturalists support the idea of being sensitive to diverse needs and perceptions of parents and caregivers, they also call for a more profound relationship between families and schools, one that moves beyond parent/teacher conferences, bake sales, and extra curricular activities such as sports. They believe that there should be shared responsibility and decision-making power in the conceptualization, implementation, and evaluation of school change. This collaboration (not competition) is intended to be based on respect for parents'/caregivers' insights about their children and the educational process. Critical models of school/community collaboration work to move away from the reality that parent involvement policies and opportunities are usually controlled by very particular contingencies in the schools that neglect to solicit decision-making input from the individuals and groups that they claim to serve.

Unfortunately, far too often the rhetoric of parent/community involvement in mainstream practices of power sharing reduces concrete engagements of deliberation and action to mere lip service. In their research, Marianne Bloch and Robert Tabachnick (1994) argue:

> The rhetoric and the reality of parent involvement, despite the good intentions of actors and participants in such programs, appear to us to be symbolic reform. The concept of parent involvement, as currently used in the schools we've examined, is an "educational quick fix" that is constrained by economic, ideological, and social relationships of power as well as perceptions of unequal expertise. (p. 289)

Consequently, many efforts to democratize schools do not go beyond the inclusion of a few token parents. Dale Snauwaert (1993) warns "that the so-called community empowerment approaches to school restructuring and school-based management are also designed primarily to increase efficiency rather than to empower the community" (p. 95).

The critical problem with most mainstream efforts to create a school/public partnership is that parental involvement is often not recognized as being determined within specific and unequal relations of power and cultural capital. However, the reality is that attempts at such coalitions are "often based on a mainstream, middle-class model that assumes that parents have particular outlooks, resources, and time frames available for schoolwork" (Miramontes, Nadeau, & Commins, 1997, p. 202). The constraints of discrimination along the lines of social class (which includes employment prestige), language, gender, race, and so forth, that act as boundaries between school personnel and parents, dramatically affect the ways in which people are actually able to participate in the educational process. Referring to broader political struggles in society, Nancy Fraser (1994) adds, "Discursive interaction within the bourgeois public sphere was governed by protocols of style and decorum that were themselves correlates and markers of status inequality. These functioned informally to marginalize women and members of the plebeian classes and to prevent them from participating as peers" (p. 81). Taking into consideration these subtle forms of exclusion, let alone more overt manifestations of cultural devaluation, indigence, and disrespect, it should come as no surprise that low income people, persons with disabilities, religions other that Christianity, gays and lesbians, and racially subordinated families are rarely found on school boards or at PTA/PTO meetings.

Refusing to acknowledge that society unjustly values certain cultures and languages over others only serves to reproduce the very same hierarchy of power and exclusion in the guise of participation. In the best interest of democratic deliberations, Fraser (1994) argues that we can't simply set aside inequalities of status, as if we are all on the same playing field—what she refers to as "a space of zero-degree culture" (p. 82). Such discrepancies need to be acknowledged, and the exclusionary practices dismantled.

Concluding Comments

It would be impossible to capture the diversity of perspectives and issues that are part and parcel of a critical multicultural philosophy of education, especially since there is no universal theory of critical pedagogy. However, this chapter is intended to help people jump on board the debates over diversity and democracy. Educators are encouraged to realize that any uncritical approaches to multicultural education can invite surface reforms, but merely recognizing differences among people, and ignoring such related problems as racism, social justice, and power as a broader set of political and pedagogical concerns, will not lead to a transformation of the exclusionary structural and ideological patterns of any unjust society.

Critical Multicultural Education is enormously important for developing theoretical frameworks that historically and socially situate the deeply embedded roots of racism, discrimination, violence, and disempowerment. Rather than perpetuating the assumption that such realities are inevitable, avoidable, or easily dissolvable, this philosophy of education invites everyone, especially teachers and students, across all disciplines and spaces, to further explore and act upon the relationship between these larger historic, economic, and social constructs and their inextricable connection to ideology, power, and identity. In this way, people can engage in real praxis, and develop, as they interact with one another, their own possibilities for the future.

Taking a Look at the Research Findings

In order to examine the developmental efforts of the Changeton Central Steering Committee, the basic theoretical foundation of what has been described in this chapter as Critical Multiculturalism will be used. The interpretation and discussion sections will first summarize what the CSC accomplished and then compare and contrast these efforts to mainstream and critical models of multicultural education. The investigations of Chapters Five through Nine will consider whether or not the CSC's conceptualization of multicultural education (in its Mission Statement; its efforts at professional, pedagogical, and curriculum development; and its attempts to diversify the staff and to create a partnership with the community) takes into consideration issues of power and ideology.[8]

CHAPTER TWO

A History of Changeton
and Its Public Schools

Taking a Sociohistorical Perspective

Contrary to the prevailing legacy of positivism, which embraces the neutrality and universality of culture, truth, and the empirical eye, researchers cannot assume that what is being observed and examined exists in a vacuum, abstracted from the ideological conditions that in fact shape the object/subject of analysis, the very question that is being entertained, as well as the lens of the researcher. This is especially true in approaches to history.

As history is inevitably the product of interpretation, it is always a form of representation. Problematizing the inevitability and risks of historical engineering in the development of textbooks, Howard Zinn, at a public talk in 1998 at the University of Massachusetts, Boston, stated, "Even choosing which facts to include, and which to exclude, is a subjective process. . . . Why these and not those?"

To become subjects of history, that is, to be active participants in shaping the present and future, rather than passive objects that are acted upon, manipulated, and controlled, people need to be attentive to the structural and ideological limits and possibilities of the past (Friere, 1970). That is, people need to engage the multiple representations of days and events gone by for their strengths and weaknesses—a sort of history of history. In this way, the past can be better understood and more justly rewritten as it is in the process of formulating the present.

Excavating the past is imperative in that, as critical social theorists argue (far too many to list here), without digging into history the dominant ideologies and knowledge that have been built into social institutions—such as schools, that privilege and exclude particular perspectives, voices, authorities, and representations—work to reproduce themselves. Since those in power have controlled the means of production and publishing, they have maintained the ability to draft, legitimate, justify, and disseminate their versions of history, or what Michel Foucault (1972) in his illumination of the power/knowledge relationship has called "a regime of truth." Emanating from these regimes are discursive practices that are deeply implicated in the production and perpetuation of poverty, racism, sexism, illiteracy, and other such oppressive formations and structures.

All of the events described in this chapter, which explores Changeton's past, take place within a specific time frame and set of material conditions. This particular history, drawn in order to contextualize this multicultural research project, is intended to be inclusive of the voices and countermemories that have been traditionally excluded from dominant versions of the city's past. In this way, readers of this book will have an idea of the relations of power that have and continue to shape the lived experiences and cultural terrain on which this study takes place.

This chapter presents a detailed view of the history of Changeton and its public schools, exposing a long legacy of demographic shifts, cultural divisions and segregation, social-class hierarchies, misrepresentations, discrimination, and unequal power relations among groups. These historical conditions continued to be prevalent in the 1990s and thus during the work of the Multicultural Central Steering Committee.

The roots of historical materialism and cultural strife in Changeton must be excavated and understood if critical transformative researchers and educators hope to develop a profound sense of the current social and institutional predicaments and cultural challenges that they face on the road to philosophically and practically infusing multicultural education. It is only then that they will be able to recognize the fact that cultural diversity and conflicts in this city are not novelties brought on by recent demographic shifts, as conservatives would have them believe. Instead, cultural politics, antagonistic social relations, and the struggle over capital (both material and symbolic) have been central forces in the forging of the city's historical present.

It is also important to bear in mind that Changeton is not some historical anomaly. While the area has its own idiosyncrasies, in large part its story speaks to the realities of most of the towns and cities across the United States.

Pre-Changeton: The Early Days

For over 10,000 years Native Americans inhabited the land now known as Changeton. In the 1600s their total population ranged from 60,000 to 144,000. The Wampanoags, the largest of the Native communities, consisted of 21,000 to 24,000 people.

Led by Miles Standish, English settlers happened upon the territory occupied by the Wampanoags. From the ontological and epistemological view of the Native Americans of this region, all people, including those who were not members of their immediate community, had a right to share the land. In 1649, the leader Massasoit, Grand Sachem of the Wampanoags, was talked into "deeding" the area to the newcomers. The chief allowed the use of forty-nine square miles of untouched earth by the whites. In return, Standish reciprocated with thirty dollars worth of goods.

The cross-cultural confusion over the implications of sharing and deeding the land proved to be devastating for the Wampanoags. They had understood that the allotted terrain would be used for basic needs and they by no means interpreted the agreement as permanent. On the other hand, as Walter Carroll (1989) describes:

> The colonists did not understand the Native use of resources or landowning and tended to see them as lazy or misusing the resources available to them. This was no doubt partially based on lack of knowledge or understanding of Native ways of life, but it may also have been a justification for taking the Native's land and pushing them to the periphery of the Portman Colony. (p. 10)

The colonizers immediately began to farm what they considered to be their property, which they referred to as the Bluewater Plantation, and restricted access to the Native populations in the name of private ownership. The inevitable tensions created over land encroachment and exploitation, as well as the ideological imposition of Christianity, played a significant role in sparking King Philip's War (1675–76). Upon defeat by the colonists/colonizers, the Wampanoags were subjected to even greater forms of disempowerment, exclusion, and oppression. This would include the execution of many of their leaders, and for others, being sold into slavery in the West Indies (Current, Williams, Freidel, & Brinkley, 1983). Combined with epidemics brought on by exposure to the Europeans, the population of Native Americans in the area was rapidly reduced by at least 90 percent (Carroll, 1989).

Becoming a Rural Parish

Having pushed out the surviving Natives, the usurped lands were destined to be developed by the whites. While the first new home was constructed in the area in 1697, the status of a permanent Euro-settlement was not realized until 1700. In 1737 the first meeting house was built, giving birth to the "White Parish."

By 1738, the Irish began to settle alongside the English in the parish; African Americans followed suit as early as 1744. "Records for that year indicate that a black man named Zepio, or Scipio, had paid a substantial poll tax. In 1746 Zepio apparently owned two parcels of land and was clearly not a slave" (Carroll, 1989, p. 17).

Given that two of the community's most prominent citizens were slave owners, this interracial dynamic in the White Parish would prove to be highly problematic. Regardless of their status, economic or otherwise, blacks were not treated as equals. Epitomizing the area's early roots of racism, segregation, and intergroup tensions, it was not until 1789 that black residents were allowed to attend local church services. Even then, whites insisted upon separate seating.

Beyond the institutionally sanctioned practices of slavery that were in place in parts of the country, laws were being passed throughout the nation that would help to maintain a racial hierarchy in which "white" would come to define "American." In 1790 the first Congress demanded that any naturalized citizen of the United States had to be "white." Adhering to such an ambiguous discriminatory category, this racial marker proved to be extremely difficult to interpret. As David Roediger (1994) states, "the legal and social history of immigration often turned on the question 'Who was white?'" (p. 181).

This ideological stronghold based on whiteness would function to shape perceptions of racial difference and significantly influence the formation of ethnic/ cultural identities throughout the United States. Cornel West (1993) clearly articulates this dynamic:

> European immigrants arrived on American shores perceiving themselves as "Irish," "Sicilian," "Lithuanian," and so forth. They had to learn that they were "white" principally by adopting American discourse of positively valued whiteness and negatively charged blackness. This process by which people define themselves physically, socially, sexually, and even politically in terms of whiteness or blackness has much bearing not only on constructed notions of race and ethnicity but also on how we understand the changing character of U.S. nationalities. (p. 31)

The White Parish would be no exception to the rule.

By 1820, there were a total of twenty-three blacks living in the parish. According to Bradford Kingman (1895), the abolitionist movement did not have a large contingency in the region, but the Freedman's Society did have a local voice. In fact, two Underground Railroad stations were established in the parish in order to assist enslaved blacks in their flight from the shackles of the South.

By that same year, the White Parish population had grown to a size of about 1,500. Acknowledging the substantial increase, the residents petitioned the General Court to recognize the community as an independent town. On June 15, 1821, the township of North Bronson was established. On July 4, 1821, the residents held their first public meeting in which town officials were elected. As Carroll (1989) points out, to this very day certain families have controlled the parish/town/city since its inception: "The citizens of North Bronson wasted little time in organizing the town politically. The officers selected had familiar names. In fact all through the rest of the history of the town, many of the same names recur" (p. 23).

Becoming an Industrial Giant and More Ethnically Diverse

Covering an area of 21.37 square miles, or about thirteen thousand acres, the old agricultural community (which included some forges and saw and gristmills) began to give way to the industrial revolution. Larger mills and factories were built, quickly replacing in-home workshops. In 1813, the Bronson Manufacturing Company purchased most of the local mills in order to increase its production of yarn and cloth. A number of businesses also began producing agricultural and industrial tools. However, splack production became the most significant industry in North Bronson, and splackmakers were successful in marketing their products in the nearby metropolitan city of Nobel.[1] By 1836, this ambitious community had become the world's leading producer of splack, and the top manufacturer in the area had annual sales of up to $50,000. Consequently, there was a huge local demand for fresh cheap labor.

The potato famine in Ireland in the 1840s forced thousands of Irish to flee their homeland and come to the United States. They came for work, to practice their religious beliefs as they pleased, and to escape the oppressive hold of their government. Many Irish immigrants came to North Bronson providing a sizable workforce for the splack industry, as well as hearty construction crews necessary for digging roads and laying down the railway. Many of the Irish women worked as domestic servants.

By 1856, there were four distinct areas in North Bronson that were designated Irish. St. Patrick's parish was built to accommodate this growing Catholic population. Roediger (1994) captures the Irish-American racialized struggle:

> In the mid nineteenth century, the racial status of Catholic Irish incomers became the object of fierce debate, extended debate. The "simian" and "savage" Irish only gradually fought, worked and voted their ways into the white race in the U.S. Well into the twentieth century, blacks were counted as "smoked Irishmen" in racist and anti-Irish U.S. slang. (p. 184)[2]

In 1846, running directly through North Bronson, the Old Colony Railroad, built in large part on the sweat and blood of the Irish, contributed greatly to the town's expansion: "In 1820, 1,480 people resided in the White Parish. By 1830, 1,953 lived in North Bronson, and in 1870, the population had risen to a little more than

8,000" (Carroll, 1989, p. 29). With business booming, the demand for labor continued to draw newly arrived immigrants in the United States to the local area. Many Swedes moved to North Bronson in the 1840s and 1850s. Finding a bounty of jobs in the growing splack industry, they settled, built their own houses of faith (notably the Swedish Lutheran Church in 1869—the first to be established in New England), and organized cultural events that celebrated their ethnic background. Like the Irish, the Swedes also struggled to position themselves in the local political arena.

In 1868, French Canadians began to arrive and establish their own neighborhoods. Predominantly Catholic, they initially attended St. Patrick's along side the Irish, but by 1891 they built their own church and school. The French Canadians also developed their own bank/credit union and a cultural and fraternal organization called the Club National. However, it wouldn't be until November of 1927 that "the Franco-American Civic League was organized in Club National Hall for the advancement and naturalization of the French people throughout the state" (Kane, 1982, pp. 34–35).

While ethnic neighborhoods inevitably emerged in North Bronson, it is important to recognize that a combination of cultural commonalty and discrimination through racialization and social-class segregation played a significant role in the development of these enclaves. The elements of discrimination are extremely important to acknowledge in the establishment of local neighborhoods because ethnic groups, even today, have been accused of balkanization, or self-imposed separatism. Such accusations are disconnected from the realities of oppressive and divisive social practices of the dominant culture that not only lead to creation of imposed geoethnic communities, but also communities of resistance and solidarity. It was only eventually, through the domesticating forces of assimilation, and not mere choice, that such groups as the Irish, Italians, and Eastern Europeans would become "white" and cross the socially constructed racialized borders (Allen, 1994; Roediger, 1994).

In the 1860s, with the outbreak of the Civil War and the invention of the McKay sewing machine and steam-driven technology, North Bronson underwent significant economic change. The U.S. government commissioned large orders of splack to support the war effort for the North, and these new innovations in industrial machinery made mass production possible.

By 1870, North Bronson had achieved a high level of economic success. Feeling a sense of independence, many residents demanded that the town be renamed. The general consensus was that a shorter and more distinctive title would be fitting. After a great deal of public debate, on May 6, 1874, the name Changeton— taken from a Canadian city—was christened.

From 1876 to 1890, there was a 236 percent increase in splack production in Changeton, and splack quickly became one of two of the leading industries in the state. Along with economic growth, a local population burgeoned to about fourteen thousand. On January 10, 1881, the town selectmen held a meeting to discuss petitioning the state capital for a city charter. On May 23, 1881, Changeton officially became a city, and in January of 1882, its first municipal government was inaugurated.

Changeton's economic success, coupled with a progressive industrial attitude, brought national public attention. Thomas Edison came to the ever developing metropolitan area to experiment with the possibility of electric street lights. The city possessed the third electric power station in the country. "On October 1st, 1883, he [Edison] threw a switch giving the city a three-wire underground system—the first in the world" (Carroll, 1989, p. 53). Changeton became the second urban center ever, behind New York City, to use incandescent and arc lamps for street lighting. On December 30, 1884, the ever expanding metropolis boasted the first electrically operated fire station in the nation. And in 1887, its citizens enjoyed the use of one of the country's two electrically operated trolleys. By the end of the nineteenth century, Changeton was described by historian William Cole (1968) as "A booming industry, a skyrocketing population, railroad connections with major markets, an internal transportation system, electric street lighting, local newspapers, a first rate agricultural fair, theaters, schools, concerts, libraries, and all the paraphernalia of social and cultural vitality" (p. 35). A town of only 8,007 inhabitants in 1870, by 1900 the population was up over 40,000 people (Carroll, 1989). This era of prosperity and expansion became known as the "Golden Age."

Immigrants continued to pour into the city for work. By 1880 they made up 15 percent of the community's residents. The Irish were the largest of the immigrant groups, claiming a population of 1,200 people. Through enormous social struggle, and with the help of the city charter, the Irish gained the necessary power to participate in local politics. Kane (1982) notes, "Perhaps more than any other ethnic group, they have dominated over the past one hundred years. To the present time the Irish have run up a total of one congressman, eleven mayors, over twenty representatives, and a remarkable number of school board members, councilmen, aldermen, and councilors" (p.34). Swedes were the second largest immigrant group, totaling 316 in number.

During this same period the African-American population of Changeton also grew. In 1870 there were 55 black residents; by 1890, there were 75. In 1888, Lemuel Ashport, who fought in the Civil War as a member of the state's 54th Regiment—the first black regiment to be formed, was hired as Changeton's first black police officer. In 1894, James E. Atus started the first local black-owned business. Over the next ten years the black population would continue to increase, and by 1900, it would reach 600. However, in large part the racial hierarchy remained in place and as a result very few blacks were hired in the splack factories—the majority were employed as gardeners, coachmen, janitors, housekeepers, or laborers. In addition, blacks were compelled to establish their own local Congregational and Baptist churches.

Labor Unrest: Scapegoating the Poor

The economic prosperity and social successes of the area were not enjoyed by the majority of the population. In fact, the Golden Age was relished by very few. As the splack industry was seasonal and affected by national competition and economic depressions, layoffs were common and poverty was a reality for many. By 1870, being out of work had become a regular feature in many people's lives in Changeton (Keysar, 1986). Although daily life for most people of the city was extremely difficult, as Carroll (1989) points out, "The costs of industrialization often fell disproportionately on immigrants, members of racial minorities, and women" (p. 54).

On November 12, 1885, splack manufacturers released a manifesto that declared their power to mistreat their employees as they pleased. It was the straw that broke the camel's back, after which collective bargaining, strikes, and industrial conflict grew. The Knights of Labor (which also granted membership to women) and the Laster's Protective Union countered capitalist exploitation as best they could.

New immigrants, unlike their native-born counterparts, wished to play a significant role in the major strikes. In fact, various ethnic groups were often cited/scapegoated as the provoking force of labor unrest (Carroll, 1989). However, in the United States, progressive social movements such as the early struggles to form labor unions also gave way to the ideology of racialization in which whiteness split class consciousness, rendering blacks and other non-white groups unprotected outcasts (Goldfield, 1992; Roediger, 1991). The native-born "ethnics" who preferred not to participate in the manifestations perhaps understood how the racialization of working-class identity had become white and that they would not be safeguarded by organized labor as it existed.

Despite the struggles of women, the racially subordinated, the poor, and the working classes to organize, it soon became obvious that union leaders and splack manufacturers were in cahoots. As a result, most workers grew disenchanted and uncooperative with labor organizations and factory owners.

From a combination of labor unrest, intense industrial competition elsewhere in the country, shifts in the styles and prices of splack, and local business's inability or unwillingness to adapt to ever changing industrial and commercial needs, the splack industry in Changeton took a severe dive, bringing the majority of the community with it. Job opportunities and wage levels drastically declined. As Kane (1982) observes, "The 1890s were years of social unrest, the rise of APAism, the populist movement and, finally, at the end of the decade, the emergence of socialism, all of which left marks on the history of Changeton" (p. 9).

In 1895, unemployment in the state reached highs of 8 to 10 percent (Carroll, 1989). The increased demands on public and private welfare agencies, especially in the hardest hit areas such as Changeton, were far too large to meet. As the general population bore the brunt of the financial decline, the popular political vote at the turn of the century was in favor of the Social Democratic Party, which stood by the slogan, "Equal opportunities for all, special privileges for none."[3] In 1897, Eugene Debs, the organizer of this nationally-based organization, came to town to help eight residents establish a local branch. As other populist movements joined forces with the new labor party, Branch 9, as it was referred to, was thought to have had at that time the largest number of dues-paying Socialists in the United States.[4]

By 1902, fifteen members of the Socialist Party were elected to city government: three out of seven alderman, eight out of twenty-one councilmen, two out of three School Committee members, the city marshal, and the mayor. This was the second Socialist mayor ever to be elected in the country. However, by 1903, opposition parties with the help of the Catholic Church put an end to the Socialist influence in the area. As Carroll (1989) describes, they "brought in rabble-rousing speakers to protest against the Socialists. They succeeded. Thus, within a few years, the Socialist successes had evaporated, leaving little permanent change in Changeton or in the state as a whole" (p. 66).

With the Socialists out, the Republicans made their way back into power and stayed there until 1912. However, by that year there was a rift in the GOP led by Theodore Roosevelt, who eventually brought to Changeton his "Bull Moose Party." Weary of Roosevelt's impact on the local vote, two days later, incumbent President William Howard Taft also visited the area in order to campaign—he would return that October to attend the city fair. He was the first U.S. president to come to the city, but not the last. He commented:

> Changeton is not so fortunately situated as most of the great manufacturing centers of the country in the matter of varied transportation facilities for reaching great distributing markets. But the men who built up Changeton's industry showed indomitable pluck and energy in overcoming natural obstacles and to them much credit belongs. (As cited in Kane, 1982, p. 15.)

New Waves of Immigration

From 1890 to 1920, the nation as a whole experienced a great deal of immigration from Southern and Eastern Europe. According to the 1895 state census, with a population of 33,165, almost 26 percent of Changeton's residents (8,027 people) were now of international descent: 16,559 were men and 16,606 were women. Kane (1982) counted the international population as: "Canada 718, China 25, Denmark 31, England 818, France 14, Germany 48, Ireland 2,719, Italy 197, New Brunswick 21, Nova Scotia 739, Poland 53, Portugal 18, Prince Edward Island 157, Russia 146, Scotland 161, Sweden 1,704, and Wales 14" (p. 35).

The seeds of a soon to be local Jewish community were also planted at this time; however, both locally and nationwide, there was a great deal of anti-Semitism. Roediger (1994) captures this unwarranted hatred: "The nativist folk wisdom that held that an Irishman was a black inside out, became transposed to the reckoning that the turning inside out of Jews produced 'niggers.' Factory managers spoke of employees distinctly as Jews and as white men" (p. 184). In 1900, the first local synagogue was built in Changeton; however, it wouldn't be until 1914 that a Jewish politician would be elected to city government. By 1926, the local Jewish population rose to about 3,200, most of whom were living on the east side.

By 1901, from fifty to seventy-five Greeks had arrived in the city. With time, Greek enclaves grew, as did their small restaurants, candy shops, grocery stores, and leather shops.

[In 1909,] 60 members of this community organized a society for the study of American politics. The name of the organization, the first of its kind in the county, was the Pericles Political Society of Changeton. Their aim was to enroll the Greek-speaking men of the city and to act as a naturalization society. (Kane, 1982, p. 37)

The Greek population expanded and by 1917 it reached about nine hundred. There were now over sixty-five Greek stores and a newly established Greek church.

Changeton's 1915 slogan of "City of Workers and Winners" nationally drew the attention of people desperately looking for employment. Italian immigrants began to arrive in the region around this time. Settling initially in the poor areas on the east side, most were involved with the splack industry.

Lithuanian and Polish immigrants settled in the north end of the city, which became known as "the Village," or "Lithuanian Village." These groups also struggled diligently to maintain their ethnic heritage over the years by building cultural centers and churches. During this same period of time, more French-Canadian immigrants, along with the Lebanese, began to arrive.

Labor Unrest Continues

On March 20, 1905, Changeton witnessed the harsh realities of unsafe labor conditions. At one of the major splack factories a boiler exploded, killing 58 workers and injuring 150. Thirty-six of the victims could not be identified and consequently had to be buried in a local common grave.

Poor working conditions, low wages, and frequent unemployment, regardless of the promises of the Republicans who were now in power, continued to instigate labor unrest. On May 14, 1923, there was a major workers strike within the splack industry in Changeton that would last for ten weeks. The manifestation was started by members of the Dressers and Packers Local of the Changeton Splack Workers' Union (CSWU) who walked off their jobs and parted ways with the existing labor organization. Ending in July, the strike brought about the death of the CSWU and the birth of the CSAC—Changeton Splack and Allied Craftsmen. The strike also led to the downfall of the mayor, who had claimed that "the unions were being infiltrated by the Communists with the aim of disrupting the local industry" (Kane, 1982, p. 18).

Fear of communists, anarchists, and ethnic outsiders was rampant. On May 5, 1920, Changeton police arrested on a local streetcar Bartolomeo Vanzetti and Nicola Sacco, two Italian immigrants and Anarchists, accused of robbery and murder. As Carroll (1989) states: "This was the time of the 'Red Scare,' characterized by widespread harassment and jailing of anyone suspected of any radical leanings. In this climate it was unlikely that Sacco and Vanzetti would get a fair trial. The men were found guilty and executed on August 23, 1927." (p. 66)

In the early 1920s, Changeton again made national headlines for its involvement in a controversial court case in which a Lithuanian communist lecturer, organizer, and writer from Brooklyn was charged with two counts of sedition and blasphemy for speaking in the city's Lithuanian National Hall. After a great deal of controversy, and two death threats against the mayor, the man was found guilty of sedition and fined $100.

Although World War I brought with it the call for increased splack production, by 1929 there were one-third fewer splack workers in Changeton than there had been in the previous decade. Once again, unemployment was high and wages were low, but the worst was yet to come. On October 29, 1929, the stock market crashed. Dramatically affected by the national economic plunge, the number of local factories dropped from 431 to 244.

In December of 1929, the city's Common Council agreed to contribute $50,000 to help mitigate the pressures of poverty and unemployment on the community at large. However, the Changeton Board of Alderman, the media, and other members of the local political community blocked the distribution of the funds, holding the workers responsible for the economic decline. As Cole (1968) points out, Changeton's welfare commissioners felt that economic assistance in hard times "tended to make the receiving of something for nothing so eminently respectable that one wonders if wishbones will take the place of backbones in the future" (p. 72). The local paper, the *Nosurprise,* "consistently minimized the seriousness of the Depression and evinced little understanding of what was happening, and less sympathy for the bleak circumstances facing many Changetonians" (Carroll, 1989, p. 78).

The 1930s brought to the industrial world new and more efficient and profitable machinery. However, the technological progress that awed capitalists contributed to the unemployment problem in the city by dramatically reducing the number of workers required. With fewer jobs, and plenty of people desperate for work, wages could be driven down by the factory owners.

In 1938, Franklin Delano Roosevelt came to Changeton, greeted by a cheering crowd, with a promise of helping the city in its time of need.[5] Roosevelt's assurances of government help eventually came true in World War II, as the military buildup inevitably increased the demand for splack. One company in particular led the country in manufacturing the product for the war effort. However, a report to the city's Committee for Economic Development, which was established in order to solve the severe local problems, made it clear that the reduced production of splack from 1919 to 1947 and the concomitant high rates of unemployment were the culprits for the severe local economic and social decline.

Campaigning by train in 1948, President Harry S. Truman came to Changeton to encourage new growth and development. The city struggled in vain to devise ways of revitalizing the local infrastructure. In the 1950s, the state built Route 65, a major expressway that passed through Changeton, giving easy access to the state capital. With more and more people moving out of the nearby big city and into the outer communities, Changeton's population shot upward, but the once bustling industrial urban center was in the midst of an identity crisis.[6] As Kane (1982) observes, "No longer was the city an industrial giant—it had become a 'bedroom community for Nobel'" (p. 27). Population wise, it was now the fastest growing area in the state: from 1920 to 1970 it jumped from 66,254 to 90,000 (Carroll, 1989, p. 85).[7] Unfortunately, local industry was still on its way down: "In 1919 the 39 splack manufacturers in the city employed about 13,000 workers and produced more than $81 million worth of splack. By 1964 there were only 10 Changeton splack factories, and they employed only 2,000 workers" (Carroll, 1989, p. 59).

Shifting Demographics

As had been the pattern since the destruction of the local Native-American populations, Changeton continued to witness demographic changes. Kane (1982) notes that the racial makeup of the city in 1970 was as follows: 86,515 whites (97.2 percent), 2,162 blacks (2.4 percent), 363 other (0.4 percent). He also noted that 25,960 citizens had international parentage, and 6,436 of the local population was of internationally born origins (p. 30). Of the parents of people of European origin in Changeton, 15.9 percent of the Italians, 24 percent of the Canadians, 11.3 percent of the Irish, 7.4 percent of the British, and 5.8 percent of the Russians were internationally born (Kane, 1982, p. 30). By 1982 the city ranked as the sixth largest in the state, with a population of 94,990: 92.2 percent were white, 4.2 percent black, 1.6 percent Cape Verdean/Portugese, and 1.3 percent Latino/a.

At that time, the largest manufacturing firms in the area produced clothing and other textile products. Smaller businesses made leather goods and were involved in printing and publishing. However, with a steady loss of its industrial base, business in general in Changeton continued to decline. In the early 1980s, 44.1 percent of the labor force in the city worked in the service or clerical sectors and 14.6 percent were professional and technical workers. When unemployment statistics were broken down racially/ethnically, 8.6 percent of white men and 9.6 percent of white women were unemployed, 13.8 percent of black men and 20.4 percent of black women were without work, and 20 percent of Latinos and 30 percent of Latinas were searching in vain for jobs (Sennett, 1982). At the same time, the average income for whites in the early 1980s was $11,570; for blacks, $8,731; for Cape Verdeans, $8,500; and for Latino/as, $5,850 (Sennett, 1982).

At the same time, a third of the population had attended fewer than four years of high school, a third had a high school diploma, and a third had an education beyond high school. Only 13 percent of the occupational population had four or more years of college education (Sennett, 1982).

Facing Urban Renewal

Attempting to accommodate these major demographic shifts of the 1950s and 1960s, the city planners initiated a flurry of construction in which schools, libraries, and recreational facilities were built.[8] Unfortunately, while Changeton was witnessing some physical and financial restructuring over the next two decades, overall it was not undergoing the type of massive urban renewal being carried out in many other urban centers across the state and nation. Consequently, the downtown was in ruins.

From 1975 to 1980, there was serious concern about the general state of the downtown. Local business and city government worked together to figure out how to revitalize the community. They attempted to develop better public transportation, along with parking and cultural facilities. The City Planner's Office, the Mayor's Office, the City Council, and the Changeton Redevelopment Authority were involved in these projects.

As one of their first major undertakings, private development firms were hired to build federally subsidized housing for the elderly in the central business district. Equating local demise with crime (surely coded language for racially subordinated groups and the poor), rather than with capital flight and a failing social infrastructure, one city official at the time stated, "If we could get a few hundred elderly downtown, we could justify more police presence, people would come down to visit their folks, it will help turn things around" (as cited in Carroll, 1989, p. 96).

Meanwhile, new immigrants from Southeast Asia, West Africa, Latin America, and Haiti were settling in the city. There was a great deal of displacement in Changeton fueled by escalating housing costs, a widening gap between the rich and the poor, and a declining standard of living. In 1990, 12.9 percent of the local population of 92,788 had bachelor's degrees; the local per capita income was $13,455; and 11.7 percent of the families were living below the poverty level (Parent Information Center, 1995). As always, social class, ethnic, and racial neighborhoods emerged, as did local ethnic community organizations.

By 1993 (the year that this multicultural research project began), the city's estimated population was racially broken down as follows: 74,449 whites, 12,028 blacks, 1,589 Asian/Pacific Islanders, 5,860 Latino/as, 269 Native Americans, and 4,453 "others." In addition, there were more women than men, over thirteen thousand people living in poverty, and the annual crimes committed in the city totaled 6,895, with 1,156 violent acts (Information Publications, 1994).

Changeton's long multicultural history and legacy of oppressive practices—especially the early and advanced forms of capitalist domination, blaming the victim for their bleak circumstances, the racialization of identities, and the results of forced assimilation—are extremely important to recognize if educators and activists are to understand the present sociocultural conditions in the city. Part of understanding this history entails examining the role that schools, which reflect the larger social order, have played in the reproduction of culture in Changeton.

Rather than viewing schools as neutral entities, they need to be examined as "institutions involved in history" (Freire, 1985, p. 121). In other words, as argued in Chapter One, institutions of education along with pedagogy and curricula have historically worked to reproduce and maintain dominant beliefs, values, norms, and discriminatory practices both nationally and locally. Thus it is crucial to explore the history of public education in Changeton, which in many respects reflects the story of the city itself—a twist of multicultural engagements and shifting intergroup antagonisms.

The History of Public Education in Changeton: The Early Years

The first four schoolhouses, traditional one-room structures, were built in the White Parish in the eighteenth century. Because agriculture was the community's livelihood and required long, hard hours of human labor, the academic day and year were short. It was generally understood by the populous that extensive formal schooling was a privilege intended only for the wealthy.

As the importance of public education was increasingly acknowledged, schooling became more important. By 1821, North Bronson had eleven schools and the community decided to increase the school year to six months. Reading, writing, arithmetic, history, geography, and science were part of the curriculum; nonetheless, the locals wouldn't see their first high school established until 1864. By 1867, the first public library was opened. Many of the community's elite were against funding such a project with tax money because they thought that the facilities would not be adequately used.

As the population grew over the years of industrial growth, it was apparent that the local public schools were greatly overburdened. In 1865, "the entering class had numbered 27 students as compared to 305 students in 1905, an increase of more than ten times" (Kane, 1982, p. 14). Amid waves of opposition, on February 15, 1906, the city completed the construction of a new high school, estimated to have cost $273,000. The *Nosurprise* (1906) described the effort as "a home equipped as are few in this great country where education is conceded to be the great bulwark of its liberty" (p. 1). The mayor christened the new building with a speech to the public, in which he stated, "What a splendid illustration of the faith and belief of our citizens in the value and importance of free education . . . that our citizens individually and as a whole may stand in the front rank in the onward march of the world toward a higher and more perfect state of civilization and development."

On June 10, 1913, after receiving a $110,000 gift from Andrew Carnegie, the city celebrated the completion of a new public library.

Educational Modernization

With continued population growth, by the 1950s, there was another concerted effort to accommodate the public by modernizing the city's schools. Consequently, the community witnessed the construction of four new junior high schools and eight elementary schools. In addition, a new high school was completed in 1958. This period of educational renewal continued into the 1960s, costing over $35 million.

Two branches of the public library were also built during this time.[9] In June of 1963, as social and racial tensions were heating up nationwide, there was a major controversy around the Changeton Public Library's refusal to allow the John Birch Society—a well-known conservative and racist organization—to run the film *Operation Abolition*. As Kane (1982) describes:

> The trustees had voted 6 to 3 to grant the request when a group of people demanded the cancellation of the program. The librarian refused. But the day before the meeting the mayor asked the trustees to reverse their position, and they obliged by a vote of 7 to 2. The Birchers then took the film to the YMCA where it was shown to an audience of about 40 people. (p. 30)

The educational renewal in Changeton in 1970 would lead to the construction of two new twenty-four-room elementary schools, estimated to have cost $1.4 million. In September of that year, at a cost of $17 million, the city finished building a new high school on eighty-eight acres of land across from the local fair grounds.

With its nine interconnected, three-story buildings, the high school was considered one of the most impressive in the country. It had an Olympic-sized indoor swimming pool, an outdoor track, nine tennis courts, a football stadium and baseball diamond with a seating capacity of 10,000, ten gyms that could be broken down into fourteen individual spaces (the main gym with a seating capacity of 2,600), a corrective physical education room—including a facility for persons with disabilities, indoor/outdoor basketball courts, four parking lots, a planetarium, a student-run restaurant, a theater, a fine arts center with art studios and drama centers, eighteen industrial arts rooms, a fully equipped radio and television station, a photography lab, three extensive science areas, a family living section, a child study area, four guidance centers, and a job placement office. The new high school also had a civic, social, cultural, and educational center, as well as a school newspaper designed to inform the public about current school activities, programs, and staff.

The large building is divided into smaller units called houses (the only system like it in the country at the time), to give students the intimacy found in smaller schools while offering the perks of an expansive curriculum. Through federal grants, the school system had access to more than $20 million to fund educational programs. Spending the money wisely, each of the academic units had a self-contained instructional materials center, a library of 12,000 volumes, and extensive audio-visual equipment.

Showing signs of a more open and progressive attitude toward classroom content, schoolwide curriculum offerings included: Afro-American history, the Bible as literature, geography in the urban city, Russian, German, Latin, Spanish, Hebrew, French, Lithuanian, cinematography, jazz, design, ceramics, nursing, restaurant training, electronic drawing, service station management, automotive services, anthropology, ecology, aquariology, and computer programming. Among the library's educational videos were: *Edward R. Murrow vs. Sen. Joe McCarthy, Birth of the Bomb, Martin Luther King, Struggle for China,* and *Black Poetry.*

In order to help new students adapt to the school system, the faculty and staff designed and implemented "Operation Smooth-Out." They also developed summer programs for children with speech, hearing, and perceptual problems; as well as a program called "Awakened Awareness and Development of Self," which was created to curb the student dropout rate.[10] The principal of the high school described the overall facilities and offerings: "What all this means is, if a student wants to learn he can go places in this school. . . . He has opportunity after opportunity available to him."[11] With 371 teachers, the new building was ready for its 5,700 students in the fall. It was the biggest school in the East, with the second largest enrollment in the county.

The mayor informed the public that approximately half of the tax dollar of the city of Changeton was devoted to education. It is thus not surprising that not everyone was keen on the idea, size, and expense of the new school. Before the first shovel was sunk for the building's foundation, major battles were fought in the City Council chambers. As one newspaper reported, "The townspeople viewed the new school as a multimillion dollar monstrosity that would eventually choke on itself" (Bullard, 1973, p. 2). With a student capacity of 6,000, dissenters negatively referred to the building as the "Taj Mahal."

After it was officially opened, the first few years were rocky for Changeton High School. With the civil rights movement of the 1960s, which spotlighted issues of social injustice and the need for dramatic social change, schools around the country were experiencing growing pains as democracy stretched to include more people. In Changeton, as a response to the national and local spirit of civil disobedience, there was a serious effort by school officials to limit student freedoms. Lunch was only eaten in assigned buildings, hall passes were required, and student identification cards were regularly checked.

Disgusted with such constraints, the political platforms of candidates for student government were regularly built around the issue of student rights. Proclaiming themselves "prisoners," students protested "being locked in a concrete cave never being able to see natural light." A newspaper was created in order for students to voice their concerns, and young people got involved in such public protests as book banning.

As the tenth largest city in the state, "between 1961 and 1973 the school population rose from 12,500 to over 20,000 students" (Kane, 1982, p. 29). With a $20 million school budget, the per pupil expenditure at this time was slightly above the state average: from $749.13 at the elementary level, to $1,089 at the high school level (Bullard, 1973).

However, regardless of the expenditures and the sheer size of the renewal projects, material conditions alone could not resolve what the civil rights movement had yet to bring to fruition—social harmony through the dismantling of white supremacy and a redistribution of economic and cultural wealth. Antagonistic race relations and discrimination had been woven into the fabric of Changeton, the entire nation for that matter, and incidents of symbolic and physical violence manifested.

Though readily denied, violence and drug abuse throughout the school system and community were common. According to the public school's own newsletter, 343 Changeton school children under the age of seventeen made court appearances the year that the new schools were opened. Twenty-two percent of these children were sent to treatment or detention centers for juveniles.

The most prominent recorded racial incident involving schools in Changeton occurred in November of 1975, when the high school was ordered closed after a number of fights broke out, with rumors circulating of more to come. Students spoke openly about witnessing interracial violence and the potential of a race war on campus. On the day of the closure, the vice-president of the teachers union said that there were many weapons on school grounds during the confrontation.

Concerned for their children's safety, two black mothers came to school and protested the antagonistic, racist climate of the institution. There was a skirmish of sorts, and as a result, two black teens (the sons of one of the mothers who came to school to protest) were charged with assault and battery. The mothers were also arrested and charged with disorderly conduct. Trying to calm a community in turmoil, the acting superintendent of schools told the local press that there were no problems until the parents got involved, and that he wasn't aware of the racial fights that had broken out all that week.

When the school was reopened, hundreds of parents kept their children at home, and blacks boycotted classes. Of the three hundred African-American students, only a few of them came back to school.

The head of the teachers union argued that security needed to be updated at the high school because the existing guards were "not the best trained force." Security measures throughout the building were increased, entrances were guarded, and the halls were filled with detectives. Student activities and movements were limited and all vehicles entering school grounds were checked by the police. By order of the superintendent, the press was not allowed into the high school.

Instead of naming racism, poverty, and other forms of discrimination, and calling for community dialogue around these issues, the principal of the high school ordered that pay phones be locked during school hours. He said that the phones were a contributing factor to trouble because students would often call home with exaggerated reports of impending trouble.

Violence

Into the 1990s, violence would continue to plague the city of Changeton and its schools. Drawing a general picture of the local academic climate, one newspaper article stated, "For some students, a big part of the day is spent dodging gangs of violent youth" (Hoey, 1990b, p. 1). Bomb threats had been made against the high school, and on one occasion the building was closed the next day while a complete search took place.

There were radically different perceptions of the problem of violence in the city. Representational politics would play a huge role in how the issues were presented and addressed. Echoing the past, some politicians, parents, and school officials at the Changeton School Committee meetings chose to play down the violence. As one newspaper reporter wrote, "Parents and school officials at Tuesday's School Committee meeting said incidents of violence at Changeton High School have been blown out of proportion" (Blotcher Guerrero, 1990, p. 1). These school administrators denied any escalation in violence that year, and the Changeton Education Association president stated that few teachers had noted aggressive behavior among students. The superintendent of schools (the position had changed hands since the turmoil of the 1970s), who insisted that student safety was a priority throughout Changeton schools, argued, "I don't think every time you hear a rumor, education stops."[12] Rallying for the support and confidence of parents, and inviting them to contact school officials anytime they had a concern, he assured the group that "the small number of students who disobey rules and regulations are dealt with severely."

Other parents and educators at School Committee meetings said that there is a dangerous atmosphere fostered by gangs in local schools. Violence in this case was being interpreted as reverse discrimination. Some local news reporters, School Committee members, and parents were pointing the finger at black teens who they claimed were forging street gangs, emulating those from Nobel. Reference was made to an incident known as "Black Tuesday," in which it was rumored that Nobel gangs were going to descend on one of the local junior high schools and the high school to cause trouble. Many parents kept their children at home on that suspected day, and over fifty phone calls voicing concerns were recorded at the police station.

Many whites were up in arms with the image of little armies of mean-spirited black youths walking the streets and their school corridors. One mother complained to the School Committee that her son had been regularly hassled by a group of black students, and that he had told her that he can get guns and drugs from other students at school. The mother added that her son also told her that "there is an unwritten code that white students risk a beating and/or having their belongings 'ripped off of them' if they wear articles of clothing emblazoned with the words 'Dukes,' 'Kings,' or 'New York Giants,' names affiliated with gangs" (Blotcher Guerrero, 1990, p. 1).

There were additional testimonies that described groups of youths sometimes armed with knives, readily instigating fights, robbing students of their valuables and clothing, and preventing them from going to the bathroom. One parent publicly revealed that her son had wanted to bring a crowbar to school to defend himself and was instead taking self-defense classes.

A member of the School Committee, a city police sergeant who was also chairing a subcommittee on school security (and who would by 1992 be mayor of the city), was worried about the nature of the escalating violence. After mentioning the twenty-plus phone calls that he had received from parents concerned for their children's safety, he responded to the press, with racist overtones:

> I can flatly tell you there is a problem. I've gotten more calls about these organizations. They're flexing their muscles. . . . My information indicates it is the minority versus the majority. I'm a bit angry about this. If a group of minority students were ever being threatened we'd have the Justice Department down here by now.

This particular School Committee member complained that school administrators were going about "business as usual," and that they had completely disregarded the lethal potential of Black Tuesday. In actuality, the administration had suggested that police monitor the streets around the schools and dispatched school officials throughout the hallways on that day.

The future mayor also stated that the School Department in Changeton kept issues of school security concealed, rarely sending incident reports to the local police department. He stated that such actions made evaluating the extent of the violence in schools difficult to judge. As an example, he shared the story of the school security finding a gun in a student's car. He claimed that the weapon wasn't handed over to the police for an entire week—until he had brought the issue public—"It's all kept very quiet." Wanting some serious police presence on campus, he added, "Educators think they have the right to determine what should be prosecuted. If a larceny of a coat occurs at Changeton High School, the police should be told about it."

A city councilor, also the chairman of the Public Safety Committee, was considering holding public hearings about the violence. He said, "Somebody is going to get seriously injured or even killed up there if nothing is done. . . . Let them try to explain that." He added, "The parents are afraid to send their children to school." Confirming such fear, one mother demanded that her son, a sophomore in high school, call her at work as soon as he arrived home after school. She exclaimed, "That way I know he made it home all right. It's getting so that the kids can't go to school to learn. Now it's how can they make it without getting stabbed or getting drugs forced on them." Needless to say, communications between the police and the schools increased.

Denying the issue of race altogether, and rebutting the racist implications in the idea that gangs of blacks were the root of the problem, some parents at these School Committee meetings argued that "incidents of violence occur at all high schools" and that "the matter should not be treated as racially motivated" (Blotcher Guerrero, 1990, p. 1). Echoing this sentiment, one black father said, "I have never experienced or heard of any racism at the high school." Disappointed by a recent article in the *Nosurprise* that focused on the violence against white students by blacks, he commented:

> Fights go on in any school. If it happens between a white and a black student does that make it racial? The overall picture is of hooligans running through the school and no one doing anything about it. To defame a wonderful educational system like we have in Changeton is criminal.

He added, if the *Nosurprise* "spent more time giving kudos, Changeton wouldn't have half the problems it does now." The father also demanded that any School Committee members who claimed that reverse discrimination is running rampant should be able to prove it with substantial facts.

Motivated by such public scrutiny and complaint, the School Committee member/police sergeant, attempting to publicly respin his revealed racial prejudice (perhaps knowing that he would soon be running for the position of city mayor), rebutted:

> I have not stated in any way, that a serious racial problem exists at Changeton High School. I have, however, stated flatly that a problem exists and that an identifiable group of persons enjoys harassing, intimidating, and assaulting other persons. This group has adopted a nickname for those who are harassed: they are "crackers." I resent that and I do not believe that has any place in our school or community. These are merely facts. They are neither racial nor prejudicial. (As cited in Blotcher Guerrero, 1990, p. 5.)

As a response to the violence in the community, a metal detector was installed in the city's alternative high school, and only there. In response, one student stated, after being frisked by police officers before being allowed to enter the building, "Everybody's going to look down on us. . . . They already think that we're losers" (as cited in Hoey, 1990b, p. 1). According to youths at the alternative school, the weapons were for personal protection in Changeton streets. One young man was quoted as saying, "The reason a guy is carrying is because he needs it outside . . . the world is so bad that you can't change it" (as cited in Hoey, 1990b, p. 6).[13] The total number of crimes in 1989 of 7,352, which included 1,009 violent acts, supported his point (Information Publications, 1993).

Unfortunately, community dialogue about the history of poverty and white supremacy in the city, and the legacy of social antagonisms among racial and ethnic groups, never made it to center stage. Playing down the role of discrimination in the schools, the superintendent publicly stated, "We represent the interest of all the students of Changeton, rich, middle-class and poor. . . . We see that every student is given an equal opportunity."

Drugs

The 1990s also witnessed a wave of drug abuse and media attention in Changeton, regardless of the efforts of the drug and alcohol prevention programs provided by D.A.R.E. (Drug Abuse Resistance Education) and the Comprehensive Health Education Program. Local newspaper headlines such as "Under the Influence" and "More Drug Use in Growth Areas" were common. Drawing statewide attention, one of Nobel's most influential newspapers put out an article entitled, "A Bad Trip for a Blue-Collar Town: Changeton Teen-agers Escape to Drugs and Alcohol" (as cited in Scaglione, 1990, p. 1).

One local article in particular discussed the problems of prostitution and its connection to drug abuse in the city. In it, one of the police detectives commented, pointing to a young prostitute, "She's scared to get in the car, but she has to get her fix. . . . That girl is going to die on the street" (Hoey, 1990a, p. 1). Reporter John Hoey described this particular scene as "just one of the hundreds of horror stories one can find on Changeton streets where three of the city's record-breaking six murders last year were drug-related" (p. 1).

But drug abuse was not exclusive to the urban poor. In 1989, the chief of police was arrested on cocaine theft charges, a crime committed in order to feed his own habit. Two months earlier, he had told the state's chairman of the Subcommittee on Narcotics, that Changeton is "fighting a losing battle" against drugs.

It was unclear just how affected the schools were by drug abuse. According to reporter Donna Scaglione (1990), when the local newspaper "attempted to gauge drug use by Changeton High School students with a survey," the superintendent and the principal "declined" (p. 1). Instead, they wanted the press to refer to research that had been conducted in the late 1980s by the state Department of Public Health. However, while these surveys from 1984 and 1987 identified various regions in the state, they did not deal specifically with Changeton. Exclaiming that "drug and alcohol abuse is alive and well among some Changeton High School students" (p. 1), Scaglione added:

What students and officials disagree on is the extent to which the abuse creeps into students' lives. And if someone tries to generalize and say that substance abuse is a big problem affecting the majority of the students, students and school officials will cry out loud that they have been unfairly judged. (p. 1)

In 1993, the local Teen Council (an organization set up to advise the City Council about issues of youth violence and racism) publicly reported that a large number of students at Changeton High School, between 50 and 80 percent, used marijuana. The superintendent denied the allegations, calling them "totally irresponsible, a blanket indictment of the entire student body" (as cited in Hancock, 1993c, p. 17).

Dropouts

As cultural misunderstanding, poverty, racial tensions, and violence were omnipresent, students—overwhelmingly the racially subordinated, linguistic minorities, and the poor, were dropping out, or being kicked out, of school in Changeton. According to the Fanton State Department of Education (1997b), the dropout rates in grades 9 to 12 went from 9.2 percent (336 students) in 1989 (as compared with a state average of 4.9 percent), to 9.5 percent (331 students) in 1990, and 8.4 percent (276 students) in 1991. The year 1992 would have a rate of 8.5 percent (Steinway, 1994). From 1992 to 1993, dropout rates were 9.6 percent of a student body of 3,100—totaling 295 students (as compared with the state average of 4.3 percent). This number would rise to 9.9 percent (or 296 students) by 1994 (Hancock, 1994; Parent Information Center, 1995). While the school lost nearly a tenth of its population that year, the dropout rate for ninth graders was estimated at 12 to 14 percent.

Taking action, alternative forms of education and additional career services were being developed to combat this high attrition rate. Such efforts would include a program for troubled students, a day care and teen parenting project at the high school, and a specialized school for expelled junior high youth(s) who were "considered good candidates for rehabilitation." However, the superintendent believed, "What really has to happen is a commitment on the part of the student to come to school, attend class and do the required work" (Hancock, 1994, p. 4).

School Demographics Leading into 1993

Throughout the late 1970s and early 1980s the racial and ethnic diversity within the Changeton Public Schools increased.[14] By 1982, there were over 18,500 students in local schools: 89 percent were white, 5.6 percent black, 2.2 percent Cape Verdean, and 2.2 percent Latino/a (Sennett, 1982, p. 2). There were also 949 bilingual students who made up 5.1 percent of the total school population. About half of this linguistic-minority group was placed in mainstream classrooms, and the remaining half participated in the Transitional Bilingual Education Program. About 1,900 students, mostly non-white, linguistic-minority, and poor, were identified as special needs (Pongonis & Malonson, 1983).

By 1984, Changeton was the state's fourth largest public school system, with "the fastest growing minority student population" (Wilson, 1985, p. 76).

By the time of this three-year ethnography in 1993, there were fifteen elementary schools, four middle schools, and one high school. There was a total school enrollment of 14,015 students. That year, the superintendent publicly acknowledged the racial and linguistic demographic shifts of the 1980s and 1990s, when he stated at the "Working with Diversity" all-faculty in-service: "In 1982, the city had a total of 15.7 percent students of color. By October of 1993, this percentage rose to 43.7 percent. In 1972, there were a total of one hundred limited-English proficient students. Today, there are 1025—one in every fourteen students in Changeton is limited-English proficient."

Throughout the years of growth and turmoil in the city's public educational system, it was only a matter of time before democratic changes would have to be attempted if the schools were to adhere to the laws of the state and the federal government, as well as to the emerging voices of racially, economically, gendered, disabled, and sexually subordinated and underserved peoples. However, the efforts of the 1990s were not the first attempts to democratize the educational system through desegregation and some form of multicultural education.

Efforts at Desegregation

Since the reestablishment of the Harrington-Willis Act in 1965, the Board of Education of the state of Fanton set itself the task of dealing with the racial imbalance of schools (Glenn, 1987). It would officially refer to these efforts as "Chapter 636." School desegregation found its way into the federal district courts, and cultural/racial inequalities in education came to the forefront of public debate.

Integration in the 1980s was big business for schools in Fanton, and many systems were more than eager to get access to the tens of millions of dollars that were made available by the state for those who complied (Fanton State Department of Education, Bureau of Equal Educational Opportunities, 1984a).[15] There were significant changes in the racial/ethnic composition of school enrollment in Changeton from 1978 to 1983 (Table 1).

Table 1. School Enrollment in Changeton

	Racial/Ethnic	Black	Latino/a	Asian
1978	11.1%	7%	3%	0%
1983	16.5%	10%	4%	1%

(Fanton State Department of Education: Bureau of Equal Educational Opportunities, 1984a, p. 92.)

Black student enrollment increased by 258 students—from 1,439 to 1,697 (Fanton State Department of Education, Bureau of Equal Educational Opportunities, 1984b, p. 31). The high concentration and increase of racially subordinated students in some of the district's schools were as shown in Table 2. At the same time, the Raddleson School's white population grew from 543 to 634, the Hannon School from 510 to 826, and the Brookmeadow School from 616 to 954.[16]

The Fanton State Department of Education's Bureau of Equal Educational Opportunities was looking to eradicate racial isolation, to enhance multicultural understanding (especially at Changeton High School, which had 764 nonwhite students), and to improve educational opportunities for everyone regardless of their background. Changeton school officials saw the Racial Imbalance Act as a source of funding, and it appears that only then did the city really make a concerted effort to work on a comprehensive desegregation/school improvement plan.

The school system developed a number of strategies to combat the unjust statistical breakdown of students in their schools, as well as the disproportionate amount of economically and racially subordinated students who were in Special Education. However,

> Despite the Changeton Special Education Department's sensitivity to the needs of minority and bilingual students and in spite of the implementation of several unique and nationally recognized program models, such as Project Mainstream and Project Open, a report issued by the Fanton Advocacy Center documented evidence that the Changeton Public Schools were denying equal educational opportunity to this population by placing them into Special Education prototypes in disproportionate numbers relative to their percentages in the school age population. (Pongonis & Malonson, 1983, p. 27)

By 1984, the racially subordinated population in the city was now 19 percent, with the Appleton School reaching 41 percent non-white enrollment and the Watertown School 47 percent (Wilson, 1985).[17] This massive segregation was in part due to the fact that the Bilingual Education Programs were housed in these particular buildings. Nonetheless, because of the statistics, the school system's accreditation

Table 2. Student Population Change: Non-white Enrollment Increases

	1978	1982	1983
Winthrop	28%	34%	39%
Appleton	18%	25%	26%
Whitman	27%	32%	closed
Watertown	30%	51%	45%
Systemwide	11%	15%	16%

status was in jeopardy, and for the next decade administrators struggled to forge a viable solution to the ever increasing problem.

On April 15, 1993, the school system received a letter from the Fanton State Department of Education. Signed by the executive director of the Office of Educational Equity, the letter spoke about a recent review of the Changeton schools and their rising segregation problem. The correspondence noted that according to the October 1, 1992, data, Changeton's number of racially imbalanced schools had increased to six. These particular schools had 51 percent or higher non-white enrollment. Improvement was politely being asked for: "We appreciate the efforts you and your staff have made this school year to improve this imbalance situation. We also wish to offer you any technical assistance we can to help in your planning to reduce the imbalance and create a desegregation plan for Changeton." By March of 1994, the Commission on Public Secondary Schools, while voting to continue Changeton's accreditation, placed the school system on official warning.

Multicultural Education in Changeton before the Formation of the Central Steering Committee

Equity Assessment

In response to a state mandate from the Fanton State Department of Education that required non-discriminatory/non-biased assessment of bilingual students, in the fall of 1979, the Bilingual Assessment Task Force was created[18] (using funds from the Civil Rights Act of 1964, P.L. 94–142) in order to address the needs of the increasing racially diverse and bilingual population. The committee was made up of administrators, teachers, counselors, and parents.

In 1981, the Changeton school system worked to develop a series of assessments for evaluating the needs of Latino/a, Portuguese, and Cape Verdean first-grade students. Kenneth Sennett (1982) argues that "tests for Hispanic populations were generally found to have been written for either Chicano or Cuban populations and did not use a vocabulary appropriate for Puerto Rican children" (p. 6). In an attempt to differentiate between learning difficulties and linguistic and cultural differences (which were so often misunderstood as cognitive deficits), "the task force was sensitizing itself to vocabulary appropriate for Puerto Rican children" (p. 6). Participants made certain that the assessors of linguistic-minority children were from the same background.

Following the regulatory mandates of P.L. 94–142 and other commonly accepted professional standards, what became known as the Changeton Battery developed a number of assessment guidelines, which included the following multicultural considerations:

> In the assurance of the right of a handicapped child to a racially or culturally non-discriminatory assessment, evaluation materials and procedures should be administered in the child's native language; test materials cannot be selected and administered in a manner that is discriminatory on the basis of race, color, sex, or national origin; Special Education programs (including assessment practices) must be equally effective for children of all cultural backgrounds; the assessor provides accurate information about the child's present levels and modes functioning within the context of his culture.

The school officials were moving into (or simply revealing more explicitly than before) Christine Sleeter and Carl Grant's (1988) description of Teaching the Exceptional and the Culturally Different approach to multicultural education. There was an impatience to mainstream as many "minority" students as possible, and educators seemed willing to try whatever culturally affirming mechanisms were necessary.[19] "Equity assessment" happened to be the buzzword of the day.

While the movement toward the democratization of assessment continued, there were other organized fronts that emerged in the name of equity and integration.

The Equal Educational Opportunity Task Force

In September of 1984, another effort toward desegregation with multicultural implications was underway. A community meeting was set to discuss issues around equal educational opportunity. As a result of this gathering, the Equal Educational Opportunity Task Force was established with the responsibility of working toward the racial integration of the schools. Holding its first meeting, members invited the chairperson of the National Committee for School Desegregation and Changeton's Public School's Task Force for the Study of Minority Students in order to get input and insight.

The Changeton Public School Task Force for the Study of Minority Students was a group of local educators who had come together as a result of Proposition Two-and-a-Half. "They believed and later proved that the legislation had a disproportionate effect on minority and poor children" (Wilson, 1985, p. 77).[20] Resembling a Human Relations approach (Sleeter & Grant, 1988), the goals of this task force were to

> examine issues which pertain to the educational well-being of minority children; interpret ethnic customs and attempt to alleviate cultural misunderstanding on all levels; review policies that specifically impact our minority students; ensure the retention of minority courses and programs that further the students' development and growth; review the Changeton public school's Affirmative Action Plan. (Wilson, 1985, p. 77)

In the meantime, the Equal Educational Opportunity Task Force selected teacher and parent representatives from each school, and sent out letters to religious organizations and other civic and cultural groups throughout the city in order to solicit participation. Translators and community representatives were to be present at all meetings in order to guarantee that input from across the district's cultures would be heard.

Gathering on a monthly basis, the task force developed into nine subcommittees, which focused on the following: "Methods of Desegregation/Magnet Schools/Alternative Choice Programs, Controlled Admissions and Transfer Policy/ Planning and Redistricting, Surveys, Parent Information Center/Rumor Control, Staffing Patterns, Multicultural Curriculum, Bilingual Education Special Needs, Teacher Sensitivity, and Re-education" (Wilson, 1985, p. 78). The state's Department of Chapter 636 provided technical support to help guide these subcommittees.[21]

By 1984, the organization developed a desegregation plan. Fitting the Human Relations approach to multicultural education, the introduction to the plan read:

> The children of Changeton are fortunate that within our public school system, the city can provide a foretaste of that diverse world they will inhabit. Our schools include children from many cultures, many nations, speaking many languages. Desegregation is the first step in a process that will enable our children to take advantage of that diversity. . . . Once we have brought our children together through desegregation, we will be better able to undertake the most important part of the process, integration. Together they will be able to learn about themselves and each other, about the world as it has been, as it is today, and as it might be in the future. Their teachers are already learning how to use the diversity of the city and its students in developing a multicultural approach to education. . . . The ultimate goal of our school system is to instill in our students a sense of pride in themselves, respect and acceptance of others as equals, and confidence in their ability to work with and get along with others, eliminating fear

and ignorance. To do less would be to fail our children, to send them out ill-prepared for their world.

As the task force was attempting to affirm diversity, they understood the importance of faculty professional development and consequently strategized how to put together multicultural in-services and conferences. Chapter 636 funds were used to hire a multicultural specialist, who, with the help of the Talented and Gifted Program (TAG) began to develop multicultural workshops for the school's faculty and staff. This new Office of the Multicultural Specialist also "aided the School Department in its evaluation of instructional materials under Chapter 622 (the state sex equity law), and disseminated guides and other equity materials to administrative staff and teachers" (Wilson, 1985, p. 75).

With additional assistance from the Multicultural Department of the Brookings Public Schools, as well as from experienced teachers from other state districts, in-service workshops were developed. "In these workshops, Changeton staff, via role playing and other devices, began to share their philosophies and feelings about race, ethnicity, and how they related to multicultural education" (Wilson, 1985, p. 75). Additional literature on cultural diversity and integration was circulated and parents got involved with the process and attended workshops and conferences.

Changeton and other area school systems also sponsored the Equity and Choice Conference with hopes of finding ways to improve the quality of urban education. Changeton's superintendent of schools was one of the hosts, and Changeton staff participated at every level.

One of the conference workshops was titled "Bilingual, Multicultural, and Special Needs Development." Apparently conflating these three categories, the group addressed staff development, parental involvement in the educational process, curriculum, and racial integration. The workshop emphasized that a model multicultural program should include a two-way bilingual component, which would involve children and parents in the process of learning a second language. "For English speaking students, this second language should be one of the native languages of other students in the school and/or school system" (Fanton State Department of Education, Bureau of Equal Educational Opportunities, 1984b, p. 31).

By the end of the meeting, the Changeton participants made some contacts with other educators interested in issues of diversity, and they entertained the idea of developing a multicultural calendar that would include school and cultural events. The calendar was eventually produced by students during art class and distributed throughout the school system on a monthly basis.

A recommendation of the Choice and Equity Report (an outcome of the conference) was that there be a "multicultural compliance specialist" on every school's Equal Educational Opportunity staff. In addition, it stated, "The basis of all curriculum development should be *multicultural*. Every subject and course offered should present its material in a way that reflects the contributions and presents the roles of the world's cultures and especially the cultures of the minority students in the schools" (Fanton State Department of Education, Bureau of Equal Educational Opportunities, 1984b, p. 31).

By 1987, regardless of years of federal, state, and local funding, special programs, and endless rhetoric to affirm diversity and integrate schools in Changeton, racial balance, let alone cultural harmony, had yet to be realized.[22]

Special Education with a Multicultural Twist

In 1990, the Kever School Initiative Program was developed in which mainstream and Special Education teachers and paraprofessionals worked as a team to provide instruction to special needs students in the mainstream classroom. These teachers used cooperative learning and whole language techniques in an attempt "to enhance the education of all students within the classroom and to increase communication between home and school" (Mascaro, 1990, p. 24). Getting parental input in planning cultural days and having them help their children at home were priorities, and parent/teacher conferences were developed for this purpose. As M. E. Mascaro (1990) describes:

> At least eight races and ethnicities are represented in this diverse classroom. One way to get parents involved is to share their culture and customs with the class. This can be done through demonstrations of dress, music, dance, and ethnic foods. Hopefully, this will help answer questions children have, such as "Who am I?" "Where do I come from?" "Where do I fit in?" (p. 25)

The idea was to have cross-cultural understanding and appreciation in the classroom, and to have those involved realize that they all have more in common than they thought. "The staff helps the students to grow and develop a respect for each other through a study of customs and cultures" (Mascaro, 1990, p. 25). Native language use was welcomed in the classrooms during instruction, and interpreters were present to assist those in need. It was the program's belief that children learn much better when racial and ethnic diversity are integrated into the educational process through cooperation rather than segregation, and when the curriculum incorporates the cultural realities of all those involved.

Attempting to work in conjunction with state and federal mandates, most pre-1993 endeavors to infuse multicultural education, though generally much more concerned with numbers rather than discriminatory practices, implicitly correlated with Sleeter and Grant's (1988) Human Relations approach. In other words, the basic philosophy underlying the majority of the multicultural actions of the past appeared to imply, in a depoliticized way, that school integration would more efficiently lead to better relations among groups and better overall academic success.

Academic Standings Leading into the 1993 Multicultural Efforts

By the 1990s, the academic standings throughout Changeton's school system continued to be bleak. In 1992, the percentage of high school seniors performing at grade-level goals in math was 25; and in science, 27 (Steinway, 1994). That year, 35 percent of seniors reported less than one hour of homework a day.

By 1994, Fanton Educational Assessment Program (FEAP), after extensive evaluations, concluded that subject proficiency levels were way down in Changeton as compared with the state averages. According to FEAP statistics, the percentage of students performing at grade level that year in the city were as shown in Table 3.

This report also showed that by 1994, 13.5 percent of the students throughout the school system were in Special Education.

In 1993, the retention rate (those held back) in Changeton High School was 11.5 percent, a number that didn't include the thirty to fifty children and teens who had moved out of the city (Hancock, 1994). By 1994, this retention number would rise to 13.3 percent (Hancock, 1994).

In 1991, 65 percent of the students in Changeton High School took the SATs. The mean combined score was 803, far below the state averages (Steinway, 1992). Thirty-seven percent of the city's student body were going on to four-year colleges. The projected dropout rate in undergraduate education for the class of 1992 was 31 percent.

In 1993, 64 percent of the students took the SATs, with an average score of 801, as compared with the state average of 903 (Parent Information Center, 1995; Steinway, 1994).

The average teacher's salary in 1989 in Changeton was $37,145, with a mean

Table 3. Students Performing at Grade Level

	4th grade	8th grade	10th grade
Reading	10%	19%	20%
Math	8%	13%	16%
Social Studies	8%	14%	19%
Writing	11%	7%	18%

(Parent Information Center, 1995).

starting salary of $19,560 (as compared with the state average starting salary of $19,739, and regular salary of $32,219) (Parent Information Center, 1995). By 1994, the average teacher salary in the city was $42,777, with a mean starting salary of $23,050 (as compared with the state's averages of $39,012, and $23,822).

From 1988 to 1989, the per pupil expenditure in Changeton was $3,880, as compared to the state's average of $4,532 (Parent Information Center, 1995). From 1989 to 1990, it was $3,997 (Steinway, 1992). In 1992, it would decline to $3,775. From 1992 to 1993, the average was $4,096, as compared to the state's $5,023; and from 1993 to 1994, the numbers were $4,672 as compared with $5,234 (Parent Information Center, 1995).[23]

From 1989 to 1990, the per pupil expenditure on textbooks was $5.86 (Steinway, 1992). From 1992 to 1994, no money was allocated to such materials (Parent Information Center, 1995).

A New High School Principal

In 1993, a new principal for Changeton High School was hired amidst controversy that he was offered the job over a woman for sexist reasons. While the superintendent of schools had made his choice for a women (Karen, the school system's coordinator of Special Projects—who the reader will meet as a member of the Multicultural Central Steering Committee), the chairman of the School Committee/city mayor (who already had revealed his racist colors in 1990, and more recently for refusing to meet with local black ministers who were concerned about the racism and police brutality in the city), cast the deciding vote. He concluded that the woman applying for the position lacked the necessary "presence" and "leadership style" to preside over the high school (Hancock, 1993a, p. 1). The mayor refuted the claim that he was anti-women.

Faced with a long history of difficult times, violence, crime, academic slumps, dropout rates, extremely high suspension rates (especially among the racially subordinated), and so on, the new principal nonetheless acted as if everything were okay. He played to conservative public support during his interview process by both praising the school and presenting an appetite for discipline. On his first visit to the potential place of business, he stated, "I thought Changeton High was a hell-hole and needed to be whipped into shape. But I've been pleasantly surprised. It wasn't what I expected. It's a lot better" (as cited in Hancock, 1993a, p. 1). The principal emphasized "the exceptional behavior of most students, the superior academic program, the outstanding and award-winning extracurricular activities, the dedication of teachers and staff members, and the pride students feel for their school" (Hancock, 1993a, p. 5). Echoing speeches from Changeton administrators of the past, he stated, "There is literally something here for every kid. . . . Any kid who goes through this high school and doesn't take advantage of everything we have, is missing out on an awful lot."

Right from the start, the new principal implemented new protocol for "unacceptable behavior," which included in-house suspensions. His basic attitude about discipline is revealed in the following statement, "The kids don't like it, so we must be doing something right" (Hancock, 1993a, p. 5).

Like those who came before him, rather than naming and demanding critical dialogue around the very real sociohistorical problems that faced students, educators, and the larger public, the new principal concluded, "I think that the image in the community needs to be polished, so I'm going to continue to stress positive things at the high school" (p. 5).[24]

The Formation of the Multicultural Central Steering Committee

With a continued history of racial imbalance and cultural tensions, in the summer of 1992, the Changeton school system, led by the superintendent, put together a multicultural in-service at a local college for seventy-five of its administrators. Two speakers were invited, and one in particular had a great deal of knowledge and experience with the community. Many of the administrators, desperate for positive change, were responsive to the guest presenters and the workshop, and this meeting led to the 1993 formation of a voluntary multicultural education committee, the focus of this book.

CHAPTER THREE

Facing Oppression

Youth Voices from the Front

Indigenous agents must speak their own realities with their own voices and not be
prevented from naming their own experiences. . . . Indigenous peoples have the
right to speak their own truth without seeking permission to narrate from
those who would continue to oppress them.
——Peter McLaren, *Che Guevara, Paulo Freire, and the Pedagogy of Revolution*

If multicultural educators truly wish to become self-reflective agents of change,
history must be embraced and engaged as a dialogue among multiple and contradicting voices. Unfortunately, youths, especially the poor and racially subordinated, are far too often left out of drafting history, describing social realities, and
debating educational policies and practices.[1] Even in the well-intentioned liberal
calls to "empower" students, young people are generally heard about and rarely
from. In actuality, the most progressive and concerned educators can't empower
students. On the contrary, it is both objectifying and patronizing to assume that
cultural workers can simply tap any given child on the shoulder with a magical
epistemological wand.

This critique also applies to the notion of "giving voice." It is presumptuous
to claim to bequeath the power of expression. Since all people already have
voices—often critical ones at that—the real challenge is, are educators and administrators willing to create dialogical spaces where all lived experiences and worldviews can be heard and addressed? In other words, will teachers allow youths of all

walks of life to reveal, analyze, and act upon the worlds that they inhabit? As Paulo Freire and Donaldo Macedo (1987) state:

> The type of critical pedagogy being proposed here is fundamentally concerned with student experience; it takes the problems and needs of the students themselves as the starting point. This suggests both confirming and legitimating the knowledge and experience through which students give meaning to their lives. Most obviously, this means replacing the authoritative discourse of imposition and recitation with a voice capable of speaking in one's own terms, a voice capable of listening, retelling, and challenging the very grounds of knowledge and power. (p. 20)

From this perspective, what educators can do is create the necessary self-empowering pedagogical conditions within which their students become theorists, meaning makers, and activists, that is, where an educator's sense of the world works through learners rather than simply on them (Cooper, 2000; Featherstone, 1999; Jenkins, 1998; Lipsitz, 1994; Martinez, 2000; Ross & Rose, 1994). In order to do so, teachers have to become ethnographers who actively gather knowledge from students and their communities of the cultural capital that emerges out of the very conditions within which youths navigate their everyday lives.

Conservatives have relentlessly worked to dismantle participatory democratic spaces that nurture the possibility for coming to voice. Pertaining to youths and public schools, Noam Chomsky (1999) elaborates:

> It starts in kindergarten: The school system tries to repress independence; it tries to teach obedience. Kids and other people are not induced to challenge and question, but the contrary. If you start questioning, you're a behavior problem or something like that; you've got to be disciplined. You're supposed to repeat, obey, follow orders. (p. 117)

An egregious example of this kind of repression is the newest wave of standardized curricula and assessment taking place across the nation. These homogenizing tools will certainly not tap the existential realities, cultural capital, and/or personal narratives of students from all backgrounds.

When young people are represented (as opposed to self-described) in the conservative press—especially the poor and racially subordinated, they are overwhelmingly depicted as dangerous and untrustworthy. However, as Henry Giroux (1996) contests:

> Of course, what the dominant media do not talk about are the social conditions that are producing a new generation of youth steeped in despair, violence, crime, poverty, and apathy. For instance, to talk about black crime without mentioning

that the unemployment rate for black youth exceeds 40 percent in many urban cities serves primarily to conceal a major cause of youth unrest. Or to talk about apathy among white youth without analyzing the junk culture, poverty, social disenfranchisement, drugs, lack of educational opportunity, and commodification that shape daily life removes responsibility from the social system that often sees youth as simply another market niche. (p. 85)

In order to expand the previous discussion of the history of Changeton and its public schools, this chapter makes use of the living personal narratives of a group of young people to expose what it is like for the most disenfranchised to live in this city. This particular facet of the research project was designed to find out from unheard voices how the city and its schools operate, and thus what the conditions have been like for many of the young and underserved. The research methodology was crafted in a way that took into consideration the tension between feeding into dominant representations of omnipresent nihilism and violence among youths, and capturing the socially sanctioned and institutionalized human suffering that this country's most vulnerable populations readily face. Rather than blaming the victims, and relying on readily available local newspapers that have had no qualms about racializing crime and creating scapegoats to account for the local troubles, the idea of this project is to capture youths' views of the present— testimonies that could tell a great deal about the past as these young people are on the receiving end, rather than the source, of an historically-based and ideologically produced set of social problems.

Gaining Trust and Access

In late May of 1993, I had a number of conversations about my research with a friend, Liz, who was at the time a team leader for a nationally renowned community organization's campaign in Changeton to help "at-risk" youths. The stories that she shared with me about the lives of the members of her team were incredibly revealing. And yet, these were histories that were not in the available literature on the area, nor were they topics of discussion in the multiple meetings with local school personnel who publicly embraced multicultural education as a way of mitigating the antagonistic social relations and violence in their community.

These were young people who had dropped out/been pushed out of school and, for many, were given the "choice" from the courts of working with the organization, going to boot camp, or getting locked up. If a portrait of the city and its schools were to be drawn, these voices would be indispensable.

With an open invitation from Liz, I decided to go to work with her on a regular basis and hang out with the young people that she had been supervising. Before my first visit, Liz told the group a bit about me and asked if it were okay with them that I be around. She said that they had voted and that the majority of the team members were "psyched" that I was coming, and that one in particular exclaimed, "We finally have a chance to speak out, and I've got a lot on my mind!"

Early in the morning, we all met in front of the Changeton courthouse, where the teams from the local youth organization regularly meet up, exercise, and leave in two vans to do various projects around town. The group was predominantly black, Latino/a, and Cape Verdean. There were also a few whites—including a person with a disability, a young overweight woman, and a gay man. In such a racist cultural climate as Changeton's, it came as no surprise that all of the core leaders were white.

The most unpopular team leader showed up late that first morning. One teen unfavorably greeted him under his breath, "Hi, shithead . . . [saying to the person next to him] he acts as if the job is about being a military drill sergeant, but the rules don't apply to him." Liz, who seemed to be the only person around that really connected with the young people, later told me that this core leader is racist, homophobic, and sexist—even with her—and talks down to all of them.

As to be expected, people were checking me out on that first day and I felt a little uncomfortable as a white researcher coming from outside the city. Having often worked with young people, I figured that it would take some time to reveal my own personal politics in order to gain enough trust among the team members to have a deep dialogue with them about the histories and realities of their lives. As I labored along side the crew, making small talk and occasionally sneaking off behind the van to share a smoke, little by little I earned the group's respect and confidence. Each day a new tragedy would headline the group's on-the-job chats. The buzz on the day of the interview that follows was that a young man whom they all knew had had battery acid poured all over his face because of a drug deal/debt gone bad.

What these youths would eventually expose (as captured in the dialogue) was a world full of crucial knowledge, a sense of social reality that cannot be ignored if educators truly hope to engage in cultural politics and address the educational shortcomings in Changeton. And yet, these are the very voices that people rarely, if ever, listen to. Rather than explore and engage such subject positions as a source of vital knowledge, these urban poor are treated as a criminalized underclass "who must be watched and contained" (Giroux, 1999a, p. 48).

On the morning of the interview, we drove through the center of Changeton in the van and the group pointed out Main Street, where they said "the action goes down." The heart of the city has a very eerie feeling to it: there are literally dozens of boarded up homes that people have been forced to abandon because of financial difficulties.[2] Many of the buildings have become crack dens or refuge for the homeless. One team member explained that after a specified period of time, these homes will be demolished by city hall, with or without the owner's consent.

Passing the high school, there was a sudden burst of laughter that rang throughout the van when a local teacher was spotted in the street. After mocking him through the vehicle's windows, the team members cynically reminisced about faculty that they had had. As I commented on the immense size of the building, Rhonda turned to me and said, "The big school, you mean the prison. . . . Changeton High, the big white lie!" As a young black woman, she had graduated two years earlier and had plans on going to college in the South. She was the only graduate on the team and she used this chip as a defense mechanism—by being a bit bossy and patronizing—against the prevalent sexist attitudes in the group. Her advice was usually sound, and although many of the others would roll their eyes when she spoke, it was apparent that most were listening.

Continuing on our way, we drove through some of the housing projects. The team wanted me to see where many of them had grown up. In the first project, the nicest of the bunch, there were bits and pieces of garbage and ransacked rusty bicycles strewn all over the place. The long-since faded paint of the project was peeling off the walls and collecting in random piles in the bars that caged in the first floor windows. As shards of broken glass glittered everywhere on the pavement, much of the group talked about ways that they had escaped from the police (whom they referred to as "Five-O") in this neighborhood.

While checking out another project, I asked the crew, "What's there to do around here?" There was an overwhelming chorus response, "Nothing!!" Rhonda elaborated, "There are so many kids from eighteen down, and they have nothing to do but get in trouble . . . drugs, guns, and reputations, that's all we got! . . . Nothing to do but screw! . . . And school, well that's boring."

We returned to work back in the park and after some long hours of painting in the hot spring sun, I offered to take the team out to lunch. We bought some smokes, played hoop, and then sat under a tree and began to talk.[3]

Not everyone on Liz's team could make it on this particular day. Some had other engagements, and Jasmine chose not to participate. Her brothers were all in prison, and understandably, she didn't want to go down that road with a racialized stranger. A few days earlier, as a group, we had discovered a notice pasted on the gate of the park that we were working in. It stated, in no uncertain terms, that if Jasmine's brothers (listed by name and description) were seen in the immediate area they would be arrested. On the afternoon of our taped discussion, she politely told me that she had to split to help out her pregnant friend.

Present on that day were: Berto, a black eighteen-year-old from Puerto Rico; Carlos, a twenty-year-old who described himself as half Puerto Rican and half African American; Dion, a twenty-year-old African American; Roland, an eighteen-year-old African American; Stevie, a twenty-year-old, mix of white and Cape Verdean; Paul, a white seventeen-year-old; and Olavo, a darker-skinned eighteen-year-old Cape Verdean. When I placed the tape recorder on the park bench, in the middle of the circle, one-by-one each person pulled it intimately close to their mouths to be sure that they would be heard and that no one would be able to deny or distort their presence.

In reading the following dialogue, one should begin to understand the real need for critical education and not simply the benign pluralism embraced by mainstream, ahistorical multicultural models. "Educators urgently need to frame the lives of youth in the United States and the culture of violence that permeates much of the U.S. society within an interdisciplinary perspective that explores the historical, sociopolitical, economic, and cultural conditions of this country, laying bare the ideologies that drive such conditions" (Leistyna, 1999, pp. 103–4). Unfortunately, in doing so, what one finds is that as a society, the United States often works against the values that its citizens publicly profess, such as the growth and health of children, the social and economic well-being of all people, and the basic tenets of democracy.

PEPI   You and school parted ways, why, what was up?

DION   I threw a chair at the teacher, yo!

PEPI   Why'd you do that?

DION   She suspended me from school.

PEPI   For what?

DION   I used to go to just three of my classes, then to all three lunches, and then take off. So I got too many demerits for missin classes and leavin school grounds. They told me that I was goin to be in detention again, and all dat. By dat point I wasn't even tryin to hear it. I ended up pickin up a chair and throwing it at her while I was walkin out.

PEPI   I talked to Rhonda this morning and she said that school was boring. Is that true?

OLAVO   It wasn't like going to school.

DION   Yeah! It wasn't for me, yo. I didn't feel like goin to class.

PEPI   Olavo, you left school close to graduation, didn't you?

OLAVO   Like three months before.

PEPI   Why?

OLAVO   I financed a car and had to keep up the payments every month. I had a job at this clothing store, but I got fired for slapping a girl. I looked for another job at night, but I couldn't find one. There wasn't too many good jobs out there. I found a morning job, so I had to quit school.

PEPI   Did anyone try and talk you out of it—teachers, counselors, parents?

OLAVO   Naaa!

PEPI   Your father didn't try to talk you out of quitting school?

OLAVO   I didn't tell him.

PEPI   He knows that you left by now, right?

OLAVO   After some months, I think it was obvious *(laughs)*. When I started working in the morning, he was like, "Why are you working at this time, aren't you going to school?" I told him "No," and he started bitchin.

PEPI   Everyone here is now working toward their G.E.D. [general education degree]?

OLAVO   Yeah. After I get my G.E.D., if I can keep clear of the criminal justice system, I'm going to college in Carlton. *(He looks around the group and asks)* Is it in Carlton?

PEPI   What's your solution to getting out of the difficult situations that you're all in?

BERTO   Move if your parents got the money, if you've got parents.

DION   You gotta wanna help yourself if you want to get out of it!

STEVIE You gotta have money!

DION   No man, it's not about money!

STEVIE I'm sorry, you gotta have money. If you don't have money, how are you gonna get outta here?

PEPI   How do you get money?

STEVIE Get a good job, get a good education.

OLAVO   There's no jobs out there!

CARLOS The ghetto is everywhere, the hood ain't no joke and there's no way out.

STEVIE There's not really that many jobs, but you have a better chance of gettin a good payin job if you have a better education than just a dropout. If you're a dropout you're gonna get a warehouse job and it's gonna suck. That's why I want to get a degree, at least associate's degree and maybe go to get a master's or somethin . . . bachelor's or whatever, and be a social worker.

PEPI   To work with kids?

STEVIE No, no! I don't want to work with kids.

PEPI   What about selling junk [drugs], a lot of people must sell junk to make money?

DION   Everybody been through that phase. We all pumped [sold] at one time, you know what I'm sayin. Either you fell into it or you were broke. I was both and got into it when I was fifteen.

PEPI   How old are most people when they get mixed up in this?

CARLOS That age.

PAUL   Twelve.

STEVIE I started sellin early, but I met a girl and had a baby, so I stopped man.

PEPI   How many of you have kids? *(All but one have children of their own.)*

OLAVO   I'm about to have one in a month.

DION   I'm not gonna have no kids, I'm too young.

PEPI   Why have kids so young? *(There's a chorus response,* "Mistake!"*)* What were you thinking, or not thinking, at the time?

STEVIE   Bustin a nut to be honest wit ya *(group laughs)*. I'm not tryin to be dirty or nothin. I had a kid on a one-night stand man.

PAUL   I didn't use condoms, I didn't know about them. We didn't have nobody tell us about AIDS, condoms, shit like that, so. . . .

STEVIE   *(Stevie jumps in.)* I knew about all that, I knew about it, but I wasn't thinkin. I was kinda drunk and it was in the dark.

PEPI   How many of you have been busted, and for what? *(The entire group responds that they have been. Some of them, three or four times—for car theft, drugs, robbery, assault, etc. As one person from among the group answered,* "For everything!"*)*

PAUL   Vandalism. I didn't do it, but I was there so I got arrested.

PEPI   What do they do with you when you're under the age of eighteen?

STEVIE   Send you to D.Y.S. [Department of Youth Services]. You laugh at the system when you're under eighteen man. That's what I did. I committed armed robbery when I was sixteen and I was in jail awaitin trial. I was livin it up. I had fun, you know what I'm sayin. You have fun when you're in D.Y.S. cause you know that ain't like adult prison man, it's cool. Dependin on who the person is, most times the advocate will try to help you. But it's just a revolvin door actually—in and out, you know what I mean.

PEPI   Carlos was telling me this morning, when we took the drive through the housing projects, that he lives in a bad neighborhood and would rather hang out with his friends than go to school. Were you guys afraid to go to school, was it uncool, what was the deal?

OLAVO   It's like all your friends don't go to school, so you try to do the same thing. You know, you'll see all your friends so you gotta. . . .They'll tell ya, "Why you goin to school man, just chill with us." You know, somethin like that.

DION   I was in seventh grade when I left.

CARLOS   If you want to leave your gang and try to do something . . .*(makes a gun with his hand and makes a bang sound)*. Now I don't care, I just want to get some education.

PEPI   All this stuff—robbing, violence, junking, having kids, leaving school—does that get you respect with the people that you're hanging with?

CARLOS   You can't make respect, you've gotta get down with respect.

DION   You know what it is man, you wanna get a reputation. That's what it is. It's all about rep—give me the money and all that shit. They see you walkin out and they say, "He's crazy y'all, I seen him the other day, man, he went in the store and did dis and did dat!" You know what I'm sayin. That's all about rep, it's all about reputation!

PEPI   What's the rep for, making people afraid of you?

DION   Yeah, exactly!

STEVIE   I had my own mother's boyfriend afraid of me. He was a heroin addict, he used to shoot up heroin and stuff, right. He knew that if I sold him a twenty, or a bundle or something, and he didn't pay me when he got the money, that I would kick his ass.

PEPI   He's living with your mom?

STEVIE   He was. It was kinda tough on my mother cause one day I went down to see her and she was sleepin in the bed. There in the other room, he was dead on the ground. He shot up a bundle and shit and died. He had jus got out of detox and he shot up a whole bundle. I don't know if you know what a bundle is—it's ten packs of heroin at twenty-five bucks a bag.

PEPI   Was he doing it to get high or did he just want out?

STEVIE   He did it cause he wanted to get high, but he wasn't sniffin, he was shootin—he was mainlinin. He shot up. . . . I went in there. I never seen a dead body until I went in there. He was all like blue. His whole body was blue. I woke up my mother and she was like, "What's the matter, what's the matter?" I said, "Stan is dead." She's like, "What!" She went in there and he was on the ground dead. He didn't have a pulse or nuttin. I checked his neck and his wrist, he didn't have a pulse or nuttin, man, so I just called the ambulance and the police came. I'll never forget that man—that was shhhhhh! I still think about that too, cause in a way I kinda think that I contributed to it. I mean, I didn't like him . . . he was ok man, he used to give me money and stuff, you know. But, I just didn't like him in a way because he was doin that around my mother and shit.

PEPI   You keep selling after that?

STEVIE   I stopped after I had the kid and shit, ya know, fuck that man!

PEPI   What about the cops, what are they like? *(There's a group response:* "Pretty fucked!" "They suck man!" "Definitely suck!" "Pigs!")

DION   Prejudice!! The system, it sucks man. You walkin on Main Street right, I see you and you walkin and you stop to talk. You stand there for like five minutes and the drug gang, the police, come around and they arrest you—they charge you with trespassin.

PEPI   What if I came through, being white and all?

OLAVO   You white so they let you go, they ask you to move on. But if you black, we black and we talkin. . . .

DION   *(Dion jumps in.)* They'd search you down, man.

OLAVO   Like three or four of them search you down.

STEVIE   You *[talking to me]* look like a clean-cut, you know, clean-cut type of guy. At worst they'll think of you like someone that's buyin, so they just be like, get outta here, take a hike, or somethin. But someone like him *(points out Roland who is the darkest)*, or even you, dog *(pointing to Dion who is lighter skinned)*. . . .

DION   *(Dion, looking at Stevie, jumps in.)* Or even you, dog, Five-O knows you, dog!

STEVIE   Yeah, they'd pat you down, they'd make you feel humiliated. They'd yell, "Open your mouth!" They'd make you take your shoes and socks off.

DION   Everythin, yo!

STEVIE   They make you feel humiliated, then they'll lay trespassin charges on you.

CARLOS   Two cops took those kids from around here, one was thirteen and one was fifteen. They took em into an ally a little down from here and beat em down. They jus put them in the car, went down North Main Street, they brung em down to that ally, and they beat em up.

PEPI   Did the kids do anything about it—press charges?

CARLOS   Can't do anything about it.

STEVIE   Look at that dude that died in *(names a city nearby)*, that Puerto Rican dude. The cops threw him down the stairs. They had him in a choke hold and he went into a comma. Now he's dead!

OLAVO   There's another guy here who got killed Rodney King style.

DION   Yeah, like Rodney King, they beat his head in. . . .

STEVIE   I've got hit with a telephone book at the police station. They do that so it wouldn't leave no bruises. They put a telephone book up to my head and they hit me.

DION   I got maced, dog.

STEVIE   I got maced three times in one night. You know what is fucked up about that! The cop that did it to me was black. I think that there's racism by both black and white cops. The cop that beat me and maced me three times was a black cop *(he names him)*. I ran and then I fell on the ground. I wasn't resistin arrest or nothin, but he hit me three times with his billy club, then he turned me over and sprayed me with mace.

PEPI   Were you at all aggressive?

STEVIE   No!! I was just layin there. He coulda already slapped the cuffs on me and brang me to the cruiser. But he had to hit me. He jus got mad cause I made him run, you know what I mean. I made him run so that's why he hit me.

PEPI   Wouldn't running be considered resisting arrest?

STEVIE   I wasn't resistin arrest, I was just layin there like that on the grass. He hit me three times and maced me. My friend, too, who has asthma. He was in the back seat of the car and he couldn't breath because of the smell of the mace. I said to the cops, "My friend needs medical treatment!" I yelled, "My friend needs medical help, he can't breath!" I kinda started goin off, I was like kickin the window and stuff so I would get their attention. Instead, they stopped the car, opened the door, and sprayed us again!

PEPI   Are most of the police white, or is the force pretty mixed? *(The group says that the majority are white.)*

DION   But there is cops out there that want to help you *(the groups mulls over a few examples, one name in particular pops up)*. Forever man! He got me with I don't know how many bags of weed, nigga. All he does is dump it out and tell you to come to church. He wants to see you in church Sunday. If you don't do it he'll get mad so that the next time he sees you he'll arrest you.

PEPI   Do the black cops beat on the black kids?

OLAVO   No.

DION   Some cops are cool. I've been pulled over in a stolen car one time. The cop jus said to ditch it, you know what I mean. He said, "I don't want to see you out and around cause I will arrest you!" He jus let me go. That wasn't a good move cause that jus made me wanna go and do even crazier shit, you know what I'm sayin.

PEPI   What do you do with the money that you make on the streets? Is it to stay alive? Is it power? What is it?

STEVIE I called it dirty money and I just blew it.

DION   Sneakers, yo! You want sneakers, you want some gear, you know what I'm sayin.

OLAVO   Buy cars, buy clothes. . . .

DION   Yo, jus as quick as that money's made, the quick it's gone.

STEVIE It's dirty money!

OLAVO   I don't have nothing that I bought with that money! The only thing left is this watch.

DION   All the money I made, I smoked it all up! Yo, cause when I was dealin I was like, damn man, what does this do, man, they be comin back every ten minutes, you know what I'm sayin. It started from an oulee [a quantity of the drug]. I smoked a oulee, then two oulees went by, and then, nigga, about three months later, I was like dis *(acts out a bony, deathly ill person). (The group laughs and one can hear,* "Exactly, yo!") I was jus dried out, yo. Dat shit ain't funny.

STEVIE I never smoked coke!

PEPI   Ok, you're twelve to fifteen, you're selling and doing junk, where's the door out of all this?

STEVIE You gotta change your environment, you gotta change your environment.

DION   I know, take it from me man, I was there, yo. Before, yo, if you woulda seen before, you ask everybody in outreach—I went there a few times, man. All messed up man, real skinny, couldn't do, you know what I'm sayin. I wanted to help myself. Then, they got me into some program and I was like no, I ain't even gonna try here, I'm gonna stop out here first. I went to jail and did a couple, few months. I got out here and ever since I haven't done it. I've been off it for a year now, since lass summer. I haven't touched it and I'm not gonna either, yo! Cause I know where it'll take me, yo! It won't take you nowhere—either six feet under or in jail. And you do a lotta shit, a lotta shit that you don't mean. I did a lotta stuff to a lotta people, yo, and it hurts when I begin to think about it.

STEVIE   Tell me you don't have to change your environment!

DION   Of course, who you hang around with, who your boys are, who they really are!

STEVIE   That's what I'm sayin!

DION   You gotta know who your boys are, man. A friend isn't a person who comes up to you and says "Yo man, you lookin good, you look diesel man. Yo, I got this rock [chunk of coke/crack], you wanna go get high?" That's notta friend . . . after he jus said you look diesel and all dat—you lookin good so let's go get high.

STEVIE   They want us to be at dat level, at his level or her level.

PEPI   Who has family here, parents or whatever?

PAUL   I've got my mom, but my father doesn't live with us.

OLAVO   I live in *(names a city in a bordering state).*

PEPI   You drive all the way here for this program?

DION   He has to!

OLAVO   I made a deal with the judge, like I've gotta stay with the program until it ends. If not, I have to spend four months in boot camp.

CARLOS   Once you get outta there you'd be twice as worse.

PEPI   Where do you go to talk about these complications and problems? Is there anybody who listens?

PAUL   I got my mother.

CARLOS   My stepfather. I wouldn't even bother my mother with my problems. She never understands. I go to my stepfather who is more of a brother.

OLAVO   I've got my grandma.

DION   I can't talk to my mother. You can't talk to my mother, yo! She be rippen, ya know, she yells a lot. So I go there and take a shower and get some clean clothes. She be mad and always say, "When you get to twenty years old, what you gonna do with yourself, I'm not gonna be here forever!" Which is true, you know, but after a while you get sick of it, man, and you wanna be like, "I get sick a hearin you bitch all the time." But you can't say nothin—she put you in this world and she can take you out.

CARLOS   As soon as you go they want you back, as soon as you go. . . .

STEVIE   My mother is still happy I left. I left when I was sixteen and she's still happy. Home was just a place you sleep at, if there's any food, which isn't often, you might have a sandwich or somethin, you know.

PEPI   At what age did most of you leave home? *(Most in their early to mid teens, but all have returned except for Stevie and Olavo.)*

CARLOS   I'm in and out all the time.

PEPI   How would you describe home, what is or was it?

DION   At that time, there was no home. You hang out on the block all night and pump, you know.

STEVIE   When you live with your mother, that's what I think of.

CARLOS   Right now, I live with my mother. Home is a place to eat and sleep. That's the only way I look at it. You can't even have a decent conversation without somebody startin a problem with you or somethin.

DION   You always get into a little beef wit your mother.

PEPI   But what are you yelling about? Is there yelling because you are in trouble a lot?

CARLOS   Cause you're tryin to say somethin and they don't wanna understand. They try to ignore it and think about it as when they were growin up— "Well, when we were growing up we weren't doing those kinds of things. . . . You shouldn't be doing that!" That's not the point. The point is we're doin it now and we're tryin to get rid of it. How can we do that? They don't wanna understand that. That's why I moved out in the first place. I started livin on my own when I was fourteen. I just came back about lass year.

BERTO   Parents really try to shelter their children. Instead of shelterin them, the children need to know the real deal. They should tell them what's up from the get go. Don't be tryin the "Oh, don't do drugs!" but they're in the bedroom at night doin drugs and drinkin their rum. "You don't do it!" that's what my mother would tell me right. My mother would tell me, "I'm grown, I can do what I wanna do." But, you're tellin me not to do it but you're gonna do it anyway. What's up wit dat? But now we're on the level, you know, everythang's jus straight out and real. That's why everythang is cool you know.

PEPI   If you are at home, do you help out, pay the rent . . . ? *(The group says yes.)*

PAUL   Yea, my mom can't work so I help her in a lot of ways.

DION   I've got a single parent, my mother. We've gotten far being out here, you know what I'm sayin. Grew up in the projects on the east side. From there she got a section eight. Now we live in our own home. I mean, it ain't her house, but it's somethin man—it's better than being in the projects. The projects ain't as bad as it was, man. Where you live now, dog *(points out Carlos)*, it ain't so bad as it was when I was livin there, it ain't nothin!

CARLOS When I moved in, there were shoot-outs every single night.

DION That shit ain't nothin compared to when I lived there, yo!

PEPI Who's shooting who?

CARLOS Different projects, different people *(the group begins to point out the turf and the gangs)*.

PEPI Can you trust people around the neighborhood?

DION You gotta know who your boys are. A boy is a person like my brother-in-law. Check dis out. My brother-in-law . . . dis is a boy to me, yo. I got arrested one time when I was wit him. He literally flattened the cop down and got arrested wit me. Now dat's a boy, you know what I'm sayin. If it were somebody else, ya know, they probably wouda jetted on me or somethin. No, he literally stopped the car and got arrested wit me. So I call him my boy, you know what I'm sayin. Wherever we go man, it's me and him, yo! If he gets into a beef I'm beefin with him, you know what I'm sayin. I'm not gonna run. Somebody gonna jump on him I'm jumpin in wit him cause I was wit him—I'm not gonna flex on nobody. See, peoples jetted on me plenty of times, yo. So many times I literally got my ass whipped and nobody did shit, yo. That's why I pick who I hang around wit and stuff like dat.

CARLOS I don't trust anybody, period! I don't trust myself.

STEVIE Damn, that's pretty bad.

DION Back then I didn't trust myself. Now, I know what I want.

PEPI How old are you now?

DION I'm twenty years old.

CARLOS You know what you want, but do you trust yourself when you get angry or somethin?

STEVIE I don't trust myself when I get angry.

DION Control yourself man, control yourself!

BERTO People mix in my project, but if you're from the outside, you're not welcome and you'll be in trouble. This town didn't use to be like this, it wasn't until the movies and shit. I mean I remember after the movie *Colors* [a Hollywood film that romanticizes gang warfare] that this dividin of the city began. Now the east side fights the west . . . it's endless. You'll beat up one of their boys and they go after you with their boys, then it's guns, and the cops come three hours later to pick up anyone who is dead or hurt. Man, the playground we call the dead ground. Two sides lined up. *(Berto has to leave for another meeting.)*

DION It was a thang about you can't pump down here, this is our territory. You try and pump down here and we gonna cap you, you know what I'm sayin. And every night it was like dat. Yo, every night you hear a gunshot or somethin. It's a territory thang, you know what I'm sayin. Like, say you get a street and you're pumpin on this street. I come down your street, what you gonna say! I don't want you on my street, you're takin my customers.

STEVIE You ever watch them nature shows and you see like lions and stuff sniffin around, and lions fightin against hyenas or somethin . . . ?

DION That's causa territory, yo.

CARLOS Territory! Survival of the fittest . . . .

PEPI If someone like myself comes into town and I don't know the territory, I don't know the boundaries . . . ?

PAUL You'd get beat up.

CARLOS You'd get fucked up!!

DION I recently got beat up and they took my hat.

OLAVO You couldn't walk with Nikes. If you have Nikes on, they'd take them off your feet.

DION That ain't nothin, yo. Remember when eight-ball jackets come out? I got beat down for mine. I was walkin down Main Street and four mother fuckas jumped out of a car. They just took my jacket and all that, yo.

PEPI They want it cause it's quality goods?

DION They want it cause they want it!

CARLOS They wanna consider it theirs.

DION It's theirs, you know what I'm sayin. If they want it they gonna take it, they gonna take it from you. And it's not really that they wanna do it, it's the reputation that they wanna get when they jump out the car and beat you down. Then people be talkin, "Yo, nigga did that shit the other night, dude beat up homeboy the other night and took his shit, dog." It's messed up ain't it *(laughs).*

PEPI What about Jasmine? She's got three brothers who are all in jail. Does she get the kind of reputation that you're talking about because of what they've done? Do people leave her alone cause they know who her brothers are?

DION Yeah, they'll never fuck wit her. But, why would you wanna fuck wit Jasmine, she's cool you know. I mean she messes around here and there, but she's cool, yo.

PEPI How many of you have dead friends from street violence? *(As I begin to count I realize that it's the entire group. They begin to talk about mutual friends who are dead.)*

DION I've seen a lotta my friends die, yo, not actually seen em die, but. . . .

CARLOS A lotta my friends were killed in drive-bys.

DION   There's another friend *(names him)*. I grew up with him in the east side, you know what I'm sayin, literally grew up with him. We was little kids growin up together, you know. He was doin good. The only thing was that he was in a mix, you know, he was dealin drugs and all dat. They ended up killin him. I think it was jealousy, yo.[4]

STEVIE   He had a record contract.

CARLOS   That's the one who got shot in front of my house.

DION   He did talk a lot of shit, yo. He used to show off a lot.

CARLOS   They got him.

DION   He used to live in the project, yo.

CARLOS   He got shot right in front of my house.

DION   He got shot in his Benz, yo, they shot him up.

CARLOS   That was like three o'clock in the mornin, somethin like that when I woke up to the blast.

DION   Jus about two months ago, this kid I grew up with robbed a bank. Before I got otta jail in March he was up there doin good, talkin about "When I get out I'm gonna do this . . . ," you know, go to school and all dat. Then, he gets outta jail two weeks later, man, and he robs a bank. They say he ended up killin himself, but I don't think he did.

STEVIE   He didn't kill himself, Five-O shot him.

PEPI   You think the cops got him?

DION   They say they heard a little gun shot right—supposedly he shot himself in the head with a .45. A .45 ain't gonna make no little gun shot, yo! Forty-five's gonna be blau-blau *(he makes very loud gun sounds)*, you know what I'm sayin. It ain't gonna be no pee-pee!

PEPI   Anybody in a gang?

OLAVO   No, I was never in a gang.

DION   I was close.

CARLOS   I used to hang with a gang, but that's about it.

STEVIE   When we were young and shit, me and my friend Joe had a little clique. It wasn't like a gang, it was just a little clique. We had jackets and hats and shit. Now, most gangs follow teams, college teams like Duke and the Kings. But, I've never been a follower, I've never followed anybody. I'm not gonna be with a buncha you know what. I mean, I got friends, but I'm not gonna like try to like hang out in a gang. To me that's kinda corny, yo.

PEPI   Now that you're older it's corny?

STEVIE   Yeah, it's corny guys.

OLAVO   Yeah, now that you see.

CARLOS   When I used to pump, I used to jus hang on the corner with my boys. They weren't makin no money, they jus watchin my back and helpin me waste the money.

PEPI At that point, you're never thinking of school, it doesn't cross your mind?

DION Hell, no!! Too much money! It's only when you get to a certain stage of bein down and out that you start thinkin.

OLAVO I think that most of the kids from Changeton get their time in when they reach like fifteen and sixteen. Ya know, they see their friends doing something and they do it. Then when you turn nineteen or twenty, you start realizing that everything is the same and you not going nowhere.

DION *(As if asking himself)* What are you gonna do now? I figured by now I'd have a car, I'd have everythang I need, you know what I'm sayin. But, it didn't work out dat way man. It's weird now cause you ride down the street, like when we were ridin in the van before, I be like damn dats messed up, dats homeboy tryin to cut yourself loose.

OLAVO A lot of my friends, that I used to sell drugs with, they see me at night and I see em selling drugs. If I go by and I don't hang out, they think, "Yo, he's a sucker!" I got a job. I'm not hanging with them. I'm hanging with different people, you know. So they think, "He's a sucker, he's not down with us no more, fuck him!"

DION They be like, "He turned on us!" or somethin like dat, cause you're not pumpin wit em.

PEPI What would happen if you had gone back to school, not a job, but back to school? Would people think that you were whimping out? ("Yeah!" *rings out among the group.*)

DION They'd be like, "Goin to school, what's up wit you!"

STEVIE They think they's badder than us. I don't care what people say!

DION I don't care what people think either, yo! I'm doin it for myself! I wanna do myself good, you know what I'm sayin!

STEVIE Yeah, that money is gonna be rollin in, but sooner or later, you're either gonna get. . . .

DION *(Dion jumps in.)* Foggy, you're gonna fall, or you're gonna be six feet under. There's only three doors that you gotta watch out for: you gotta look out for the cop door, you gotta look out for the coffin door which closes and never opens. . . . What's dat other door man?

STEVIE The exit.

DION What's dat other door, it's on the commercial, nigga? You see dat commercial wit the three doors?

STEVIE Naa.

DION Damn, what is it, man?

PEPI Is school a door?

DION School is a door, yeah.

CARLOS School is more of a window than a door, you gotta climb in, you can't walk in. You gotta climb in.

STEVIE   I've never been into school, man. When I was younger and shit, I was jus like, "Damn this is borin, man—I hate doin this." I know if I tried to put more effort into it I coulda done it, you know what I mean. I think about that now.

DION   You can do whatever you put your mind to.

OLAVO   I was doing good in school up to the twelfth-grade, and then I started fuckin up.

PEPI   Are the guidance counselors at school helpful? *(The group laughs and they hand out cigarettes to each other.)* So basically what you're saying is that you have no place to go, that you've got no one but yourself for the most part? *(There's a group* "Yup!"*)* If you had problems with your home situation and the community offered a place where you could go where they had people that you knew you could trust to talk to, would you go? Or, would you consider something like that as just another part of the system?

CARLOS   Nowadays I would go, but back then I wouldn't have.

PEPI   What about the rich people in Changeton? This city has some affluent sections. Do those people try to help the community at all?

STEVIE   Naw!! Especially not the mayor, man. The mayor is a jerk and he's an asshole—you can quote me on that too because I think he is. He doesn't want to help. They wanted to have a free health clinic in the downtown, like for low-income people, and the mayor opposed it.

DION   He also didn't meet with the local religious leaders who were concerned about all the police violence and the racism.

STEVIE   Because he doesn't want to hear it. He's racist, yo, he's racist! He's a base-head too *(they all laugh).* I sold him a joint the other day—I'm just teasin. He's a jerk though, man, you know what I mean. He tries to act like a nice guy and everythin, but he ain't, he's racist. I mean, I never had to deal really with racism and shit, but I can tell he's racist!!

PEPI   If you're poor, even if you're white, are you in the same bind?

STEVIE   If you're white and you're poor, yeah, man.

ROLAND   As long as there's niggas, there's always gonna be poor white trash. *(The group has Roland repeat this statement.)*

DION   It's true.

STEVIE   It is man. That's true. You know, cause I was a ghetto bastard.

PAUL   I was a ghetto bastard myself.

STEVIE   Runnin through the projects wit Fernandes kickers. Swear to god, yo, my mom used to buy two for three dollar sneakers at Fernandes—I didn't care! You know, as long as I had a brand new pair of sneakers.

PEPI   Stevie and Paul are white, are they outcasts among other racial groups on the street?

DION   If you down then you down, you know what I'm sayin. It's not about white or black or nothin like dat. It's jus if you down wit da gang you down wit it. You gotta show them that, yo, it's our gang and we're gonna go all out. If anybody try anything we beatin em down.

OLAVO   They [whites] do the same you know.

PEPI   How many of you have carried a piece [a gun]? *(Three of them said that they have, and two say that they've been busted with one. From the back of the group comes, "Ahhh, the guns and the knives." From beyond the park there is the haunting sound of a baby happily playing on the project grass.)*

CARLOS   At one point, I jus started sellin guns for a livin. Went to jail a couple times, moved to *(names a city in an adjacent state)*, had a kid, got tired of sellin drugs out there, came back over here, went to jail again. . . .

DION   So you used to sell guns? *(There are some giggles from the back.)*

CARLOS   I ain't gotta prove myself to nobody!

DION   I know you don't. You don't gotta prove yourself to nobody but yourself, G.

CARLOS   That's right.

DION   Dats the only person that you gotta prove yourself to, to yourself. Everybody here is supposed to be speakin the truth right *(group agrees)*. Is everybody here speakin the truth? The truth should be said out, you know what I'm sayin. You ain't foolin nobody but yourself if you lyin!

PEPI   Carlos, how old are you now?

CARLOS   Twenty. The only record that I'm proud to say I got was when I chased this dude with a hammer. He deserved it!

PAUL   I carry a knife.

STEVIE   I carried a piece, a piece of bubble gum. I never carried a gun, I never did.

DION   I like guns, yo. I do, I like guns, ya know, shootin em. I don't like shootin at people. I've shot at people, but I didn't really wanna get em. It's jus like to sting em, you know what I mean.

PEPI   You hear about violence all the time around here. . . .

STEVIE   I think that it's ridiculous, it's ridiculous!

PEPI   How many of you have been shot? *(A few speak up telling stories: one took a hit from a .22, one got stabbed twice, and another talks about a BB that is still stuck in his neck. Curious, the group touches the metal under his skin.)*

DION   Carlos, you got shot?

CARLOS   I still got the marks *(shows the group his scar)*.

PEPI   How or why did you get shot?

CARLOS   No reason at all, jus at the wrong place at the wrong time. I didn't grow up in Changeton like everybody else here. I grew up in New York. And in New York if you're passin by and there's a shoot-out, there ain't no way you're gonna get outta there cause usually there's like at least five people shootin at the same time. That's life!

STEVIE   My ex-girlfriend stabbed me. I threw a bowl of potato salad on her head *(group laughs)*. Swear to god I did, it was on one of my son's birthdays. I threw a bowl of potato salad on her head and she went crazy. She broke a bottle and stabbed me with it in my side—never forget it, it was a horrifyin experience *(group still laughing)*.

DION   Never been shot, never been stabbed, knock on wood, but I have been hit with bottles. I got scars right here *(he begins to go over his bare body like a museum, pointing them out)*. I got a scar here. . . . I was hit wit a brick twice. I had seven stitches here, I got hit wit a bottle right here. I got three stitches here and I got three stitches here, and I got. . . .

PEPI   If you walk on the street at night is somebody gonna fuck with you?

STEVIE   To be honest with you, Pepi, to be honest with you, I don't like to go into the night, man—I'm afraid, man. I swear, I'm not jokin, I'm scared to walk out.

CARLOS   If you ain't wit your boys, you gonna have that feelin that somebody is gonna jump you. The streets are jus chaos, whenever you feel like goin wild you go wild.

DION   Everybody wants to be somebody, yo!

STEVIE   It jus seems like this is like a rough generation, man.

OLAVO   Sometimes when you walking by a lot of people you like know, you walk by, right, I jus say, "What's up?" If they don't like the way you talkin, they'll fuck wit you, or they'll jump you.

CARLOS   Or the way you look at em.

OLAVO   Yeah, if you look at me, right, and I look at you and I turn my face and I look at you again, and you still staring at me, if I stare back at you, you gonna fuck with me. You gonna try to say, "What's up, man, what are you lookin at?"

DION   I don't try to make eye contact.

OLAVO   Even if you be like, "I'm sorry," or somethin like that, you know. . . .

CARLOS   *(Carlos jumps in.)* That's when they gonna start fightin because then they think you're scared, just because you apologizin and tryin to walk away.

DION   Tell you the truth *(talking to Olavo)*, I didn't think you liked me at all, dog.

OLAVO   *(jokingly)* That's true man, I don't like you man, what's up!

DION   What I ever do though, you know what I'm sayin? I never did nothin to nobody here not to like me.

PEPI   Basically what you've got is poor kids killing poor kids. Does that make any sense? ("No!" *comes from among the group*.)

STEVIE   It's jus different now, man. Like when I was a teenager, when I was fourteen, this shit first started happenin. Now, man, damn! I can't imagine what it's going to be like when my kids get older!

PEPI   You think that it's going to get worse before it gets better?

STEVIE   Hell, yeah!

DION   It's gonna get worse, yo!

OLAVO   The amount of people not gettin an education is getting worse.

DION   Drugs is a big problem with all this, but you cannot put a stop to the drugs that are comin into this country cause you know who's bringin the drugs in—the same people that claim they are tryin to get them out, they're the ones bringin it in.

STEVIE   The government's makin big money off of all of this.

DION   They're the ones bringin it in, all that CIA and all that shit. They're about makin money. They don't care. They only care about themselves. *(The group mentions a few local "reputable" people who have been known to be involved in drugs, including the former chief of police—*"He was sniffin!") You know what, one of my cases got dropped in court because of that. . . . Because the evidence was tampered with, yo.

OLAVO   So you don't know who's sellin drugs and who's dealin drugs in Changeton no more.

CARLOS   The way I look at it the cops are actually helpin. Like every single year there are more drug dealers, every year more and more dealers. Why? Cause there's more and more crackheads. There's more people gettin into crack and other drugs so there's gonna be more dealers. If the police can't stop it, all they can do is profit from it.

PEPI   You guys ever see the movie *Boys in the Hood? (Group has seen it.)* You remember when Tray's father brings them into a real rough area of South Central and he tells them, as more and more people crowd around, that rich white people are flying the drugs and booze in to promote and make a profit on racially and economically subordinated people's self-destruction. Is that what's up?

DION   That's exactly what's goin on.

CARLOS   Exactly!

DION   That movie spoke the truth, yo. Every corner you got a liquor store.

STEVIE   And what do they sell? Malt liquor!

DION   Malt liquor, all malt.

STEVIE   Saint Ives, Private Stock, O.E. [Old English]. . . .

PAUL   You don't even need an I.D. to buy.

DION   It's true what he says. I'm not even twenty-one and I can buy, nobody gets carded.

CARLOS   I look like a little kid, but no problem.

OLAVO   Most of the liquor stores in Changeton, you just walk right in. *(The group begins to point out booze stores that sell to underage kids.)*

STEVIE   I can over there *(gives the name and points it out)* anytime I want. The ghetto packy, anybody can buy there.

PEPI   Are the drugs and booze in schools? *(There is an enthusiastic group response:* "Oh, yeah!" "Everywhere!" "They're all over the place!" "Shit, yeah!")

STEVIE   There's drugs and booze in prison. You can get drugs anywhere.

OLAVO   There's a lotta dealing drugs in school.

DION   School's like a big party, man.

PAUL   That's where you go to get fucked up all day, go in the bathroom.

PEPI   We were driving by the high school this morning and I said to Rhonda, "There's Changeton High." She responded, "You mean the prison. . . . Changeton High, the big white lie!" What is she talking about?

CARLOS   It's a joke cause that ain't no high school. The whole time I was there I got one book.

OLAVO   They dictate all the rules in the high school, man.

STEVIE   It is a prison.

OLAVO   If you do something in the cafeteria, like you supposed to sit four on the table, and you sit five on the table, they'll grab you and give you three days' suspension.

DION   Because you can't be sittin in a crowd like dat.

OLAVO   Like a prison man. That's why a lot of kids do stuff like that and they get suspended and then never go back to school. They changed all the rules in the high school, man. I'm serious. I went there one day, there's one ways everywhere, man. You know how you walk around and there's like different marked buildings. It's all one way. You gotta go all the way around even if you just want to go straight ahead of you.

DION   You gotta think about it though, the kids were the ones that made it that way, the kids are the ones that made the school that way. It wasn't like someone jus came up and said let's do it this way, you know what I'm sayin. It was all the problems—I mean you have mother fuckas. . . .

OLAVO   But that's not how you solve it by doin stuff like that.

DION   I know that's true, but it's not their [the administration's] fault, I think it's the kids that go there, it's their fault cause they made it that way.

PEPI   I guess the key question is, what made the kids like this, what made you like this? Carlos just said a moment ago that while he was at the high school he only got one book. . . .

CARLOS   I got one book the whole time I was there. My sister was a straight "A" student and she used to come home with a few more books. My brother never mentioned homework. But then again, that could just be him.

STEVIE   Damn, teachers don't even care, man, you know, teachers don't care! They jus makin their money, that's how they are.

OLAVO   Yo, like that teacher we had for the G.E.D. She didn't do shit for us.

DION   She'd just give us papers, like, "Here do it."

OLAVO How do you expect to give somebody something to do like parallel lines where you don't even know what's goin on? One day I asked, "Are you gonna explain this to me?" She said, "No, just do it and then I'll explain it to you." I finished doing that shit and she was like, "Oh, it's time to go for you guys to catch the bus." She like threw us out.

PEPI The teachers in the schools, they don't care? *(Among the group, there is expressed anger about the overall apathy.)*

CARLOS They just let you hang with a paper and a pencil.

STEVIE They care about their money, man, and you always see em strikin for more and more money, but they aren't even doing shit for kids. It's obvious! Look it, look at the dropout rate man. It's obvious! . . . *(he looks around the group with a great deal of anger, he shouts)* What the fuck man!!

DION Big dropout rate, yo, big dropout rate.

STEVIE I'm serious, man. I hate that school, I hate the Changeton public school system! Somebody oughta blow it up! They're a bunch of jerks man, I swear to god!

PEPI Do you think that most students feel this way?

OLAVO I think so.

STEVIE I think they do.

CARLOS I can't speak for everybody, but I would say so.

PEPI Do kids who are good at sports get treated differently, do they get special privileges?

CARLOS Sure, they get into trouble and time and time again they get off.

DION Extra privileges and popularity, yeah, but that can work against you— you get called a jock and sporty. . . .

STEVIE You know what I notice, Pepi, I noticed when I used to go to school, if the teachers knew you came from a nice like middle-class neighborhood, they'd treat you good. They give you special attention. But if they knew you came from the projects or somethin. . . .

ROLAND *(Roland jumps in.)* If you black, the attitude is, "You dumb."

CARLOS If you come from a bad neighborhood they make sure you never make it.

STEVIE They think that you are a troublemaker.

DION Automatically, automatically!

ROLAND I was accused of a bomb scare that I didn't do. I was waiting in the principal's office for my advocate to show. I was jus sittin there waitin. After a while, I was like, I gotta go and I'm gonna go whether you say yes or no. Then she was like, "No wonder you have a fuckin tracker!" Well, she was like fat and ugly and everything, right, so I said, "It's no wonder you don't have a husband." She got pissed off and so I got suspended like my first week.

STEVIE   And, if you have problems with school they automatically think, "Oh, must be a problem at home." You know what I'm sayin. *(Dion sings in harmony with Stevie as he says "at home.")* You come in the school depressed one day, or just tired, they think, "Oh, what's the matter, is your mother beating you or something?"

PEPI   When you say you're black and you get different treatment, what do you mean?

CARLOS   I had teachers that were so prejudiced against Puerto Ricans and blacks, and I am both.

BERTO   *(Who has just returned)* I once threw a chair at a teacher who was racist against me and I made the front page—we've all made the papers.

OLAVO   They treat you different, man. I had like three classes where I was the only nigga in the room. The teacher used to teach everybody in the class but me. I used to call her, "Can you explain this to me?" She used to like ignore me.

DION   You know, like explain it but not solidly. They just rush through it.

CARLOS   Because they think that we won't be able to make it anyway.

PEPI   They think that you won't be able to make it just by the way you look, they've had you before, they know something about you, or they just look at you with the attitude that you must be from the projects and come from a poor family?

DION   All of the above. Or, sometimes they read about you in the paper, you know what I'm sayin, for gettin arrested for somethin stupit. One time I got arrested for somethin stupit y'all, what was that shit, disturbin the peace I think it was. Man, half of Changeton knew dat shit. Everybody was like, "Oh, you got arrested last night." Then I go to school and all the teachers are lookin at me like I murdered somebody or somethin. They make a big thang out of the littlest thangs.

PEPI   Do the teachers ever really try to talk with you and see what's up in your life—what's up in the street? *(There is a group chorus:* "No."; "Hell, no!"; "Nope.")

STEVIE   To be honest wit ya, I never had a cool teacher in my life. I grew up in Changeton and they've always been like kinda ignorant, or assholes.

DION   There was one teacher that I liked a lot *(he names him)*. He'd be yellin at you, yo, but he'd be teachin you no matter what you are.

STEVIE   I ended up at an alternative high school *(names it)*. That school was cool, man. I have to admit, that school was cool, man.

DION   I went there too.

STEVIE   They *(Dion chimes in and both say "individually" simultaneously)* individually come and talk to you about a particular problem.

DION   Dem teachers are cool! The alternative school is more of a school for kids who don't like school and who don't want to go to school.

STEVIE   I'm talkin about kids who are in trouble in school, you know what I mean . . . kids that like have fights in schools, and those who don't go to school.

PEPI   You guys get in fights when you were in the other schools?

STEVIE   I got in a lotta fights.

DION   Everybody into fights in school, yo—Jus for a little walkin down the hallway and a little bump like dat.

CARLOS   Either that or you're wearin somethin that looks funny to them and they start cappin on you and you don't like that—you just gotta slammmm!

DION   Yup, and that's when you bust out, yo! But it's not the same at the other school [the alternative school], they're trying to fit it so you are comfortable there.

PEPI   What is it, vocational?

STEVIE   It's like regular school.

DION   It's your five major subjects.

STEVIE   But the classes are a lot smaller, and if you need help they're there to help you, man.

DION   You got problems in court or somethin like dat, they try and work it out with you.

PEPI   So they show an interest in you? *(Stevie and Dion both respond,* "Exactly!")

DION   We'd get a break and they'd let us go to the smoke room and smoke a cigarette *(again says this in sync with Stevie).* And then you'd go back to class, no problem.

PEPI   In the Changeton school system, how many of you had a black or Latino teacher? *(Only one person responds that they had a black teacher.)*

CARLOS   The only Latino was Mr. *(names him).*

OLAVO   I had two Cape Verdean teachers like when I first came from my country, cause I didn't know how to speak. I had a bilingual program.

PEPI   Outside of these classes, when you were in the hallway speaking Creole, did people give you shit?

OLAVO   Yeah, like students, they be like, "Why don't you speak English!"

CARLOS   I get that even in the street.

OLAVO   If I don't know how to say something in English, I gotta say it in Creole. If I'm talkin to my girl in Creole, you know what I'm sayin, I'm gonna talk in Creole.

PEPI   But, now your English is strong. If you were in school, and the teacher was giving you a hard time for something, would you speak Creole—kind of a way to give shit back?

OLAVO No, I wouldn't, and I don't think that other Creole speakers do.

CARLOS I jus see it as if teachers go out their way to make an ass out of you *(Dion chimes in with Carlos and together they say)*, you go out of your way to make an ass outta dem.

PEPI Do most teachers go out of their way to make an ass out of you?

DION Yeah. . . .

OLAVO If they don't like you.

STEVIE They do, they kinda makin fun of you.

PEPI If a teacher is cool and is trying to work with you and really talk with you, does it make you more interested in school, in learning? *(There is an overwhelming "Yes" from the group.)*

DION I didn't miss one day at the alternative school.

OLAVO Yeah, you pay attention, you know what I'm sayin. You then start thinkin about it, you know.

PEPI If you go to the alternative high school, do people from the other schools in Changeton look at you like you're stupid? *(Group says yes.)*

STEVIE That's why if I had graduated from there, I wouldn't of even went to the graduation ceremony. I jus would have got my diploma and jetted.

PEPI So people want to get into this alternative high school? Or, they get in and as soon as possible they try to go to what's perceived as a "better" school?

STEVIE They want to get in and graduate from there.

PEPI Looking back on all this, if school were different, if it were to change so that you had a place where you could come in and express yourself and talk more about what's really happening in this community and in your lives—at least start there and then connect that to what's in the books and all the rest, would your response to education have been different? *(There is a group response of, "Yeah.")*

STEVIE It'd be different.

DION Way different! It would be different cause you don't be hearin about reality. You don't even be hearin Afro-Americans in the history. You also don't be hearin about the Spanish.

STEVIE All you be hearin about is American history.

DION They don't talk about what's goin on out here. They talkin the past. Alright, that's past, you know what I'm sayin. Talk about now, we're in the future. Why don't you bring up the people that doin good for us now!! Those other people are dead, let dem rest in peace.

OLAVO You gotta talk about what's going on right now.

CARLOS If you're gonna talk about the past . . . people who I don't even know or give a damn about. . . .

PAUL *(Paul jumps in.)* If you don't learn from history you're doomed to repeat it.

STEVIE I like history, I like history, man.

DION   I like history too, but they don't teach nothin. They don't teach you the real truth. Alright look, Thomas Edison, he invented the light, but who made it better? Who made the light better? A black man did, yo! Did you hear about it? I read the black almanac, yo, when I was in jail and there's a lotta thangs in there, like who came up with all kinds of medicine. A black man came up with a lotta that shit, yo! They don't teach you stuff like dat in school.

STEVIE   *(jokingly)* I don't think that's true, I don't think that's true, man, all right, I think that you're lying *(laughs)*.

ROLAND   They tell you about the people who led the country, but they don't tell you about the people that built the country.

DION   It's true, bro, it's true.

STEVIE   Can I say one thing and I don't want people to take it the wrong way. You know, I'm white, my mother's white and my father's Creole [Cape Verdean] right. . . .

OLAVO   *(jokingly)* Oh, shit, you're white *(group laughs)*.

STEVIE   No, I'm just tryin to explain something *(group still laughing)*. Forget it! *(The group encourages him to continue on.)* Like, people always complain, I don't care, man, either. They always say, "Oh, whitey did this to me, whitey did that to me." Yeah, that's not necessarily me. People talk that shit too, like, "I've been oppressed for hundreds of years." Yeah, I'm not saying you haven't, but is that me, did I have anythin to do with it? You know what I'm sayin. I didn't have shit to do with it and then people blame it on me—not necessarily me, but like you know what I mean. But you know what, though, to sum it all up *(laughs)*, no one here is an American except for the American Indians—they're the only true Americans.

ROLAND   They're not Indians, they're Native Americans.

STEVIE   Native Americans, whatever you wanna call em. . . .

DION   This is their land, yo!

STEVIE   They had it took from em.

DION   Our so-called Americans took it from em and now look at em—they ain't got no where to live.

STEVIE   They're livin in poverty conditions. I think that they should have that in school, man!

CARLOS   All they get to live by is a flag.

ROLAND   They come over here for religion and freedom to do this and that, right, but the people outside of them wanna do somethin different and they kill them or they just shut em off.

CARLOS   They took everything from the Indians, I mean Native Americans. It was the Native Americans who taught them how to survive and everything right, but they didn't appreciate it.

DION   Robbed em!

ROLAND   They just took it from em, took everythin and killed em off. It's a "I want what you got!" mentality. Kids on the streets do that nowadays and they are locked up and not celebrated—not that they should be. This whole country is a contradiction of itself.

STEVIE   I think in school they should have somethin about the Native Americans.

PEPI   Do you guys feel like you've been robbed?

DION   From a long time ago.

CARLOS   We've been robbed, yeah, slavery and colonization, like with Puerto Rico, right up to today.

PEPI   Do you feel like your youth, your education, your chance for a better future has been robbed from you?

ROLAND   They didn't have a real childhood. They never had a chance to be kids. They came from kids to being drug dealers. I had a real childhood, listen to them.

STEVIE   But there's a way to get a little bit back by gettin a G.E.D.

DION   It's true though, and stayin outta trouble, man. I mean you can go out and have a good time, you know, like last night. I was havin a good time. I ended up bustin my ankle, but I had a good time, and I didn't have ta go ta jail and I didn't have ta do drugs. I didn't have ta get high on coke to have a good time, you know what I'm sayin.

PEPI   Most of you have kids now, everybody but you, Dion. *(Dion jumps in, "I can produce, nigga, my ankle's broke but everythang else work!")* What are you going to tell your kids? What's your advice to any kid?

STEVIE   I wanna tell em to stay in school man, no matter how bad it is, jus do it, jus stay in school!

DION   Get through, yo!

Given the social, political, and economic hardships that this group of young people in Changeton faces on a daily basis (along with so many others—as one in five children, and one in four racially subordinated kids, grows up in poverty in the United States [Collins, Hartman, & Sklar, 1999]), it is only logical for educators and students in this city (nationwide and globally for that matter) to question what produces culture, social antagonisms, injustices, and identity. As argued in Chapter One, and vividly depicted throughout this dialogue, culture in general is not simply about food and fun. Rather, its production, distribution, and consumption is reflected in unequal and abusive relations of power that have produced and reproduced (via social policies, institutional practices, and media efforts to manipulate the public) epidemic levels of unemployment and poverty, crime, police brutality, home and community disintegration, illiteracy, drug addiction, and public callousness. As Chomsky (1999) points out, the obvious effects of such historical conditions are "you get violence against children and violence by children" (p. 110). And yet, despite all the national attention on violence and youth, and a growing body of literature in the social sciences documenting the unmet needs of so many young people in the United States, it is amazing how few connections are made in the mainstream national and local debates in this country between government and socially sanctioned practices that have historically hurt children and their families, and the increasing violence involving young people.

Instead of blaming youths for the world that they are caught up in, but did not create, educators and concerned citizens desperately need to forge critical partnerships with young people in order to analyze and confront the oppressive conditions and social formations that have inevitably manufactured and imposed a history of despair. The implication is not that whatever children and young adults have to say should be taken at face value, that teachers and policy makers romanticize their contributions and immediately implement their suggestions. Within a truly participatory democracy, a sign of respect and inclusion is that all voices be recognized, heard, and critically engaged for their experiential and theoretical insights and weaknesses, rather than simply affirmed (as these voices in this dialogue will be in chapters to come). As Freire (1985) insists, "We need to be subjects of history, even if we cannot totally stop being objects of history. And to be subjects, we need unquestionably to claim history critically. As active participants and real subjects, we can make history only when we are continually critical of our very lives" (p. 199).

What is being suggested here should not be misconstrued as an attempt to act as an apologist for the often violent crimes that young people of all backgrounds do commit. Even the youths from Changeton held themselves (among others) accountable for their mistakes. Ways to appropriately deal with the immediacy of an actual crime—a thirteen-year-old who shoots someone—is, to say the least, an important topic for discussion; however, the point to emphasize here is that there is a serious need to look at and preemptively eliminate the ever-increasing macro conditions within which dehumanization and its consequential microviolence are so prevalent. The society as a whole needs to call into question the larger social formations and policies that have produced a culture of survival, materialism, and deviance. However, this presupposes the ability to differentiate pathology from acts of resistance, which are legitimate (though not always conscious) responses to domination, used to help individuals or groups deal with oppressive social conditions and injustice.

From a more sociohistorical approach to understanding identity and human suffering, people can rupture and move beyond the inherently discriminatory models that equate crime with the culture of particular socioeconomic and racial groups; as if any culture exists in a vacuous space unaffected by a history of antagonistic intergroup relations and abuses of power. Educators and activists can also move beyond, without completely dismissing, psychological models that simply individualize and pathologize human behavior. They can understand and incorporate into their knowledge how the cognitive and psychological makeup of each person is a product of history and politics, and thus intimately affected by such oppressive ideologies as capitalism, racism, sexism, and heterosexism.

It is only from a more inclusive, historically situated, and critical public debate that multicultural educators can better understand the complex roots of inequality and violence in this country, and thus better inform themselves of the current sociocultural context in which students live, as well as the tools they will need to become aware, active, and responsible citizens, and critical agents of change.

CHAPTER FOUR

The Formation of the Multicultural Central Steering Committee

Its Basic Processes, Functions, and Structures

As described in Chapter Two's historical overview of the city and schools, the Multicultural Central Steering Committee (CSC) was in many ways the product of years of state and district efforts to desegregate schools. The seventeen volunteers ranged professionally from teachers of all levels, to guidance counselors, principals, and specialists. The original members, who will often be referenced throughout this book are as follows:

- Cali, white, elementary school teacher
- Giselle, Jewish, junior high school teacher
- Sara, white, director of the Adult Learning Center
- Ted, white, media specialist
- Kevin, white, assistant housemaster, high school
- Karen, white, coordinator of Special Projects
- Fred, white, elementary school principal
- Carl, black, Cape Verdean-American, high school guidance counselor
- Luis, light skinned, Puerto Rican, high school teacher
- Eva, white, administrative assistant for Curriculum and Community Schools
- Jake, African-American, high school assistant housemaster
- June, white, elementary school teacher
- Sam, white, B'Hai, chief supervisor of Attendance
- Juan, light-skinned, Cape Verdean, high school teacher
- Raul, light-skinned, Cape Verdean-American, director of Bilingual Education Program[1]
- Don, white, junior high school principal
- Melissa, white, high school Social Science Department head.[2]

Over the next three years, CSC membership would change. New voices will be introduced as the study progresses.

Granted permission from the superintendent to take the reins of conceptualizing and infusing multicultural education throughout their school district, the new committee participants wholeheartedly agreed, "Our job is to make sure people are working toward diversity." To introduce the entire school system to their efforts, in March of 1993, committee members put together an all-faculty in-service. Feeling compelled to "understand the needs in each school in their district," they distributed a "needs assessment" to the over nine hundred participants in order to get insight and advice as to where to start this enormous endeavor. After the in-service, the members of the CSC congregated at the school system's Central Administration Building, located downtown. While they would meet at a number of different sites, the administrative building provided a home base.

In a windowless room in the basement, across from the Bilingual Education Office, the group gathered around a large rectangular table. Eva, the administrative assistant for Curriculum and Community Schools, was recognized as the chair and sat at the head of the table. However, her presence did not appear to dictate the direction of the conversation, nor did it seem to inhibit the candid nature of the discussions. People joked, openly spoke negatively of colleagues, and addressed each other informally.

Through a blend of pandemonium and familiarity with committee work in general, the basic format of each monthly meeting would eventually evolve into the following. In order to keep everyone up to date, before the actual meeting all members of the committee were mailed the previous week's minutes, which were assembled by Eva. During the meeting, workshop announcements, multicultural literature, newspaper articles, survey/evaluation results, committee meeting dates, and any other pertinent documents were circulated around the table. A debriefing would occur if an in-service had taken place, if individual members had attended a workshop/conference pertaining to multicultural education, or if there were subcommittee reports (to be explained later). An attendance sheet was passed around along with the day's agenda. There was open discussion about the day's agenda. All decisions were voted on.

Going over the needs assessment data from the all-faculty in-service, which had been compiled by a voluntary task force, the group decided that as a next step a "statement of goals" should be solicited from each member of the committee. They worked together to articulate a basic format for these individual statements and rounded off their major concerns to five general areas of interest: curriculum review and change, changing staff attitudes, instructional methods, and community outreach. They also included a space in their format for a miscellaneous category—other. Each committee member was asked to come to the next meeting prepared to share his/her ideas. Individuals independently contemplated plans for the CSC, and during the subsequent gathering, the group discussed and agreed that its tasks should include:

- Based on the needs assessment, an implementation plan (with specific goals and objectives) and evaluation methods should be developed.
- A resource directory or manual should be developed and disseminated by the committee. This manual should include an overview of the data compiled from the city-wide needs assessment. In addition, it should include the specific goals and objectives of the committee, the names of members of each school's multicultural education committee (a structure that will be discussed later in this chapter), and, if available, a listing of relevant resources for teacher use or referral.
- The CSC should actively develop community coalitions. It should identify and recruit parents, local organizations, and community leaders who are culturally sensitive.
- The CSC should develop a resource library that promotes continued growth of multicultural values, is updated on a regular basis, and is available to all staff.
- The CSC should assist in the review and development of school curriculum appropriate for multicultural education. This may require the use of special consultants.

Before the committee approached any of these tasks, members discussed the need for, and immediately produced and distributed, what they referred to as a Mission Statement. This document would officially declare the group's conceptual foundation (this effort is exclusively dealt with in Chapter Five).

After a few meetings, the budding organization adopted its name to the Changeton City-wide Multicultural Central Steering Committee. With this official title the group developed and released an introductory letter to the city's schools.

Scheduling Committee Meetings

While the CSC decided to meet at least once a month for an hour and a half to two hours, it was difficult for the group to find a time that would be convenient for everyone. Although regular meetings had most often been scheduled for after school at three o'clock, there were still conflicts with those people who had children and other family responsibilities, as well as with those who were coaching sports, taking night classes, or working other jobs.

Some committee members suggested having the meetings earlier in the day. As Cali expressed, "It helps elementary teachers if we meet in the mornings from seven to eight-thirty." Others argued that, since meetings were only once a month, it could be arranged for members of the multicultural committee to be released from the regular day's responsibilities. However, the group knew that principals wouldn't be able to let teachers go. Without a viable alternative, three o'clock remained the official meeting time.

Committee Membership

The original committee began with a total of seventeen people. From the onset, members voiced an interest in recruiting new help, especially in light of the fact that many were disappointed with the racial/ethnic mix around the table. As observed by Fred, "I'm not happy with the makeup of people. Look at the seating arrangement. There isn't enough minority representation. I don't think that the makeup is right. I will leave immediately to make room for a person of color!" Grappling with ways of getting more diversified input, the group would often brainstorm in search of "people of color" that they thought would be interested and able to contribute.[3]

The actual size of the committee was also a group concern. A suggestion was made that the CSC have one representative from each school. However, they agreed that this strategy would involve far too many people, making the process unmanageable. Unable to immediately solve their dilemmas, a task force was assembled to take a look at these issues and to bring some suggestions back to the main table.

The task force decided that members of the CSC should be elected/reelected annually by consensus of the Central Steering Committee. Carl insisted that all decisions be made by consensus: "Democracy is beautiful, but consensus is the new wave. Democracy doesn't work in a revolution. One negative vote will cast them out."

The problem of how to retain the people of color remained. Kevin proposed that the two black members of the committee be exempt from any rotating membership. Others disagreed with this idea, arguing that elections were important. The group also proposed that whoever was the school system's administrative assistant for Curriculum and Community Schools would be the permanent chairperson, and that Sara be a member for three years because she was the only representative from Adult Education. In addition, there was talk of having a librarian on the committee in order to catalogue resources.

The group discussed how grade levels should be represented, and considered methods for recruiting new members. One suggestion was to have a paid committee. However, the participants immediately realized the fact that paying educators for their services would, as Don stressed, "quickly eat up the little funds that we have."

The task force understood the fact that inevitably some current members of the CSC would drop out. Knowing this, the group wanted to poll the current membership to see who wanted to stay on, and for how long. Carl asserted, "There needs to be a serious commitment, a willingness to serve. . . . We don't want deadheads to stay around forever." It was agreed that any committee member missing three meetings in a row should and would be replaced. Shooting for new membership by the end of the spring semester, the task force mailed its proposal to all CSC members for consideration.

At the subsequent meeting, the CSC debated the draft proposal. The high school would get four representatives, the elementary and junior high schools would get six apiece, central would get two, Adult Education would have one, and the remaining positions would be open to specialists. With the proposal passed, all of the issues and recommendations discussed up to that point were now policy. Volunteers began crafting a document called the Multicultural Education Committee Questionnaire for City-Wide Membership, intended to solicit information about who wished to continue with the CSC for the long road ahead.

Developing Subcommittees

Based on numerous discussions and reviews of the system-wide needs assessments, in June of the first year, the CSC agreed that subcommittees—which were also referred to as working committees—needed to be established in order to focus on specific projects and concerns. As Don stated, "This group doesn't have the time to talk out every issue!" It was decided that these sub/working committees would consist of four to seven members of the Central Steering Committee, and that meetings would be scheduled as required to perform their duties and responsibilities. As agreed earlier, four specific areas of interest needed immediate attention: professional development, curriculum and instruction, personnel issues, and community outreach.

All CSC members were asked to sign up for one of the three working/subcommittees, ranking their selections in order of preference to assist in making final appointments. There was always tension among the groups about who would volunteer to be the chairperson. A typical exchange:

CARL   Jake, you'd be great, just what we need!

JAKE   I have commitments, I don't know that I'll have the time!

CARL   That's a cop-out! We are all overburdened!

Some argued that the chairs of these working committees should be "minorities."[4] As Fred exclaimed, "Having minorities in leadership positions makes a powerful statement!" Although this particular issue loomed, further discussions led to the development of rotating co-chairs who were responsible for keeping the group motivated and focused, especially over the summer months.

Individual School/Site-Based Committees

From the beginning, the CSC discussed the importance of developing school-based committees. Jake stressed, "I want committees in every school. A lot of the administration doesn't care. With a committee in each school we can check up on the others, force them to reorganize. Changeton schools have stood still. I graduated from here in 1954, when I retire I want something to be in place!" While some individual schools had already been inspired to form their own multicultural site-based committees, the CSC gave the official word, early on, that every building would be responsible for establishing a branch. The CSC discussed ways to help site-based committees get members, and it was agreed that membership to these groups was to be no less than three and no more than seven. People on the Central Steering Committee would not be able to participate at the individual school level because of the fact that they were also expected to be on central working committees and consequently wouldn't feasibly be able to juggle their already hectic schedules.

In general terms, these school-based committees were responsible for "assessing, planning, developing, coordinating, and overseeing all multicultural activities for individual schools, and reporting the needs to working committees and the Multicultural Central Steering Committee." While it was agreed that site-based committee members would be responsible for suggesting specific changes for their own schools, there was a sense that the CSC needed to be actively engaged in these efforts. As Don exclaimed, "Site-based committees will be as active as the building principals allow them to be—it all depends on the principal. The principal forms the basis of the program for his or her school. Some principals have put committees together just to cover their backs." In order to show its support, provide guidance, and to ensure compliance, the CSC wanted to assure the school-based committees that, as Eva stated, "We will go to visit them."

The CSC then developed additional survey materials and scheduled meetings to hear what people at the elementary, junior high, and high schools had to say. Committee participants all agreed that the CSC should begin to, and eventually did, meet at the schools. As Kevin insisted, "We need to get out there!" It was also moved that the solicitation of information from faculty, students, and parents be ongoing.

To forge a more profound link between the Central Steering Committee and the developing site-based committees, members of the CSC met over the summer to develop a September multicultural in-service. This summer group also insisted that there be at least two joint meetings per year in which CSC and school-based committee members meet. The special task force proposed that the CSC stay in close contact with school principals, keeping them updated about curriculum resources, in-service training session dates, and other multicultural activities and developments. The group referred to this information as "the why, what, and where."

Upon return in the fall, the Central Steering Committee decided to provide a packet for every school, in a three-ring binder (a document that was to be continuously updated).[5] This Multicultural Information Packet, intended for every staff member, included: a message from the superintendent, a multicultural introduction and mission statement, an organizational flow chart of the committees, CSC structures/goals/timelines, an overview of past activities and resources of individual schools (taken from surveys), an activity calendar, training session/in-service dates, selected articles on multicultural education, a description of the proposed resource center and its status, and a listing of all committee members and their locations and telephone numbers. The first official report that described the basic functions and structures of the CSC (which would guide their efforts for the remainder of this three-year study) was as follows:

Multicultural Central Steering Committee

Structures, Goals, and Timelines

- To serve as an advisory board to the superintendent and Central Office staff regarding multicultural issues, policies, and procedures
- to provide support and direction to the working committees and school-based committees
- to assist site-based committees in involving their faculty in determining multicultural staff development goals and in meeting those goals
- to serve as a clearing house for multicultural materials, speakers, workshops, and activities
- to provide leadership for in-service programming on dates designated for multicultural education issues/training
- to assist with public relations and media services related to multicultural issues and training
- every Central Steering Committee member will serve on one or more of the working committees.

The organizational flow chart is as shown in Figure 4.1.

Structure of Changeton Multicultural Education Committees

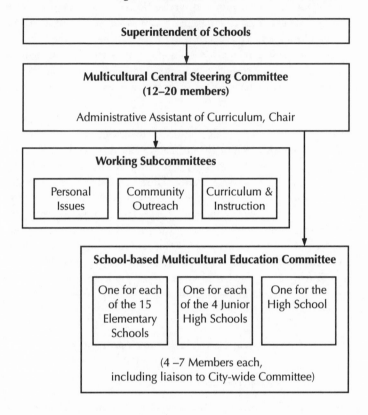

The Professional Development Subcommittee would eventually be established, taking its place in the hierarchy with the three other working committees.

Finding Funding

Virtually everything that the CSC suggested for embracing multiculturalism had a price. The committee often explored ways to access grants, and contacted such organizations as the state's Art Council, Educational Grants Alert, the National Endowment for the Humanities, and the Health Department. As Sara stated, "Their goals coincide with ours, they could set aside $2,000 for us." Some members suggested the possibility of getting grant money from recertification funds, from the statewide desegregation plan, as well as from the money that was allotted for building upgrades in the new budget. Eva was encouraging, "If the budget passes tonight, we will have money. . . . 'Inclusion' is a big word in the budget."

Others mined smaller community-based organizations. Some committee members were especially interested in targeting money from the new professional development funds that were part of the Racial Imbalance Plan. In an effort to make some arrangements with the school system's Professional Development Funds Committee (not to be confused with the CSC's professional development efforts), the group agreed that a special task force be formed to draft a proposal and a budget.

While all of these efforts generated some funding, money was always a serious obstacle for the Central Steering Committee. Not only did the lack thereof limit the possibilities of purchasing multicultural materials and hiring in-service facilitators, but it limited the committee's power within the institution itself. Faced with enormous obstacles and omnipresent reactionary attitudes, the CSC members nonetheless earnestly fought on to democratize their school system.

Part Two

The Work of the Multicultural Central Steering Committee

The Development of the Multicultural Central Steering Committee's Mission Statement

⤶

Bunched up in a basement conference room of the school system's administration building, the Multicultural Central Steering Committee was enthusiastic despite the fact that the task the group was now committed to was enormous. After hellos and some small talk about the day, the meeting commenced.

As the effort to infuse multicultural education systemwide was just under way, the topic of conversation was scattered. A plethora of underdeveloped ideas, undefined concepts, and incipient concerns were flying around the room. Carl jumped in the middle of the cacophony and insisted, "We need to show our purpose. . . . We need a clear definition of what multicultural education is, to see what we are all doing! We have got to state our goals!" Although there were a number of possible directions that this statement could have lead, the discussion immediately turned to the issue of inclusion. June argued that "kids know when teachers don't accept them . . . everyone should be included." Issues such as race, gender, disability, and self-esteem began to surface. Carl insisted that "women and the handicapped are supposed to be in the curriculum but cultures aren't." This statement was immediately met with some dissent by the women.[1]

Perhaps in an effort to temporarily avoid confrontation, Carl refocused the conversation, "We need to articulate specific goals, both long- and short-term." With this twist toward focusing on goals, the group's working definitions of diversity and multicultural education were neither elaborated, nor agreed upon.

It was decided that as a next step, a "statement of goals" be solicited from each member of the committee. Each person was asked to come to the next meeting with copies of his/her comments to share.

Two weeks later, the Central Steering Committee reconvened. The chair opened the meeting by passing around the xeroxed copies of each committee member's statement of goals and said, "Let's define ourselves and our short- and long-term goals." The subsequent discussions covered a wide range of issues and concerns, again leaving the group somewhat undefined and relatively direction-less. Melissa chose not to use the same format to express her feelings about the role and goals of the committee. She argued that the statement's format did not allow respondents to provide their own definition of multicultural education, and insisted that one "be sorted out prior to any of our goal setting." She exclaimed, "We ourselves are not in agreement about this definition."

Setting a new precedent, Melissa read from a prepared statement some ideas that defined her own "philosophy of multicultural education," which in part read:

> Multicultural education should be about ensuring that all students, especially those who come to the school system from low-income levels and from diverse ethnic and racial backgrounds, have the opportunity to develop the knowledge, skills, and attitudes necessary to participate in the workforce and in a democratic society. Multicultural education should not promote the ideologies and political goals of any specific group, including those of dominant groups, but rather, should promote a more participatory democracy.

The reading of this passage turned the committee's attention in the direction of what at that point was being referred to as "a group philosophy." Supporting this shift in focus, Luis stated, "We don't really have a philosophy on what we are trying to achieve." It was then brought to the committee's attention that one question that had frequently appeared on the original needs assessment, echoing Carl's earlier call, was, "What is multicultural education?" Sara came up with the idea of drafting "a succinct two sentence statement of what we want for Changeton." She added, "People ask me why we formed this committee, we need a statement of who we are!" As a result, they decided to have each member of the CSC draft a "multicultural philosophy," which they as a group planned to combine into a single statement and "shape until we get what we really like."

At the following meeting, Eva initiated the debate, "We need to talk about inclusion, but to what extent do we talk about inclusiveness?" A few members mentioned groups by nation and race who had been left out of the curriculum. The chair's intern, Jackie, who was white, moved the discussion beyond racial categories by making reference to "sex, age, religion, socioeconomic status, and the exceptional." In addition, she cited a piece of literature that had been handed out to the entire group, insisting that, beyond inclusion, it is also important "to challenge the social structures and the causes of oppression."[2] The dialogue about inclusion that ensued captures the tensions around the CSC's efforts to develop a unified statement about multicultural education:

JACKIE We need to replace the term "multicultural" with "diversity," "multicultural" as a term excludes others, for example the handicapped. Perhaps "diversity" is a better word to work with than "multicultural," since the latter is limited to race and ethnicity in most people's minds.

CARL No, don't the handicapped, or what do you call them — challenged, have a culture? I don't think that we need to talk about the handicapped, or sex. I know that some of us disagree on this.

CALI In working with the deaf it's different, they don't know the rules and value system. They learn the hard way or are directly taught. There are many children who just don't understand that they are out of touch.

SARA We can't exclude anyone, but we are afraid of difference.

GISELLE We should have concern for all forms of diversity, but we should give the highest priority to cultural issues in the committee's work. We need to include gender and handicap, though they are not the problem. I would like our committee to deal more specifically with cultural and ethnic diversity. The really explosive reasons that people are not getting along with one another are based on race and ethnicity, so these should be the focus of the committee's work.

JAKE When we talk about cultures, we can also talk about subcultures.[3] Cultures can be broken into Euro culture, black culture, Latino culture, etc. There's always going to be difference, but if we can achieve including all of these . . . .

JUAN The administrative workshop at the college had us deal with gender, it was important. I think that we can do all of this, but we should place our emphasis on race.

JUNE Sensitivity should not be limited to racial and ethnic differences alone, but should include gender, physical and mental challenges, and socioeconomic differences.

RAUL Bill Bradley said that the number one problem in the U.S. is racism.

CARL The Constitution implicitly includes women. You don't know oppression unless you're black.

EVA You don't know what its like to be a woman, girls are excluded from the curriculum in math and science. We would be making a mistake by excluding them.

KAREN Some people have more gender insensitivity than they may recognize, so this area should be included.

CALI Women are not empowered here at the elementary level.

GISELLE Across cultures you're still a woman. I'm a Jew, but I'm a woman whether I wear a skirt or pants.

SARA   A women is a window of many panes.

CARL   There are similar and unique problems that different people experience. If
           I value all of my students in the same way, it all goes under one umbrella.
           For example, when you say gender, does that include gays? It does for me!

GISELLE   That is not what is bothering Changeton, cultures are not living to-
           gether. I'm afraid! The papers will show how you are talking about ho-
           mosexuality, which will cover up the issue of race.

FRED   There is a risk in watering the effort down if diversity is too broadly de-
           fined. Our concern is for an equal chance for all people, but we shouldn't
           list all forms of diversity since no list can be all-inclusive.

EVA   We treat the poor kids poorly, what about them?

MELISSA   Discrimination is based on power—those who have it versus those who
           don't—and this should define the committee's work.

LUIS   We don't live in an ideal society. People who have power are excluding
           other people. I am against any form of discrimination. There is oppres-
           sion in many forms, we can't deny this, we don't have to exclude anyone.
           Martin Luther King, Jr. said that if you discriminate against any group
           you do it to all. Discrimination has nothing to do with taste, it's power.
           We do have to emphasize race but this does not mean we need to exclude
           anyone. We need to put this in an historical perspective, those who have
           historically been excluded because they don't have the power.

CARL   Who's talking about excluding!

Time was running short and Eva suggested that the starting point for the next
scheduled meeting be to look at each individual's written ideas about what she/he
felt the group's philosophy of multicultural education should entail.

At the next meeting, individual interpretations of diversity and multicultural education were presented and discussed. From the issues raised, the group
began to sketch out a draft philosophy that would serve to represent the entire
multicultural effort. The problem was, as Sara remarked, "To hammer out a philosophy will take a great amount of time." She suggested that a few people go
through the drafts of the CSC Statement of Goals, the definitions/philosophies,
the committee minutes, and the original needs assessments, and put a statement
together. This new document could then be distributed to the other members of
the CSC for comments and additional input. When the motion was passed to
approach the task as Sara had suggested, four people volunteered for the subcommittee (three men and one woman—spearheaded by Carl), and they set a date to
meet.

Drafting a Mission Statement

In May of 1993, the subcommittee convened and worked out what participants began referring to as a "mission statement"—openly discarding the idea of a philosophy or definition. Their first task was to make sure that the CSC's efforts matched the school system's ten-year Accreditation Report, as well as followed the Affirmative Action Plan that was being developed. Assured that there were no conflicts of interest in the work that they were proposing, the group began forging a rough draft.

The subcommittee had worked through various phrases before they came up with what the participants felt was a strong opening line: "Multicultural education is a process designed to enrich us all." While crafting the next sentence, those present changed "it is the creation of a learning environment" to "our goal is to create a learning environment that reflects an understanding, acceptance, and appreciation of all cultures." The group agreed that "acceptance" should follow "understanding," and completely rejected the idea of using "tolerance," feeling that the term carried with it negative rather than inviting connotations. The next consolidated idea held that "it [multicultural education] crosses all disciplines, is inclusive of all peoples, and promotes a sense of unity and common purpose for all. The committee believes that we are all enriched by the study of other cultures and that the understanding, appreciation, and celebration of our diversity promotes unity." The general consensus of the subcommittee was, "The statement is simple, but it covers everything." Grounded in a language that implicitly embraced a Human Relations approach to multicultural education, the document was copied and distributed to the CSC members by mail.

The Central Steering Committee grappled with the subcommittee's draft statement and rehashed the debate of whether or not to specifically address all groups. Carl explained that he consciously chose not to "label things by age, race, and sex," claiming that there was general concern that a list of descriptors along these lines would inevitably exclude some groups: "You'll leave someone out then, you'll offend someone. In order to make it all-inclusive we need to make it broad. . . . It is clear that we are saying cultures." Raul contended, "Those others, gays for example, belong to a culture." Juan agreed, insisting that the committee "stay away from group identification . . . gays are part of a culture, we are including everyone." Carl then contradicted his previous statement, arguing that by using the descriptor "all," "We'll be taking on every small group whether or not we feel it's important. Before you know it, AIDS advocates and on and on." Fred reinforced Carl's position, asking, "Are we going to get involved with every group that comes along?" There appeared to be general agreement amongst the committee members that all the bases were covered and that the Mission Statement "creates a sense of unity and a human purpose." The chair then asked to take a vote, and the subcommittee's draft was accepted. It was also moved that the CSC would "reform this document as we grow." The Multicultural Central Steering Committee's Mission Statement read:

Changeton Public Schools

Multicultural Committee's Mission Statement

> The mission of multicultural education is to promote a process designed to enrich us all. The goal is to create a learning environment that reflects understanding, acceptance, and appreciation of all cultures. Multicultural education crosses all disciplines, is inclusive of all peoples, and promotes a sense of unity and common purpose. The Multicultural Committee believes that we are all enriched by the study of other cultures and that the understanding, appreciation, and celebration of our diversities promotes unity.

A formal letter (also written, edited, and printed by the CSC), called "An Introduction" (which included the Mission Statement), was then distributed throughout the Changeton schools in order to inform people about the committee's efforts. In part, the letter read:

> The Multicultural Central Steering Committee has reviewed the recently adopted Changeton School Department's Affirmative Action Plan that recognizes that students and staff will benefit from being exposed to people of different backgrounds who are serving the school system in a variety of roles; and the philosophy statement of the Accreditation Committee which indicates Changeton High School strives to promote cultural awareness.

Critical Interpretation and Discussion

In the awesome endeavor of conceptualizing and infusing multicultural education, it is crucial to have a document that formally articulates and situates such efforts, not only for the group itself, but also for the community of schools and the general public.

What was especially important about the CSC's group process in developing an official statement is that the members made a concerted effort to solicit the input of each individual participant. However, there are some serious problems that occurred in the conceptualization and drafting of the final version of the document.

If the Central Steering Committee itself had ideological differences as to what words like "diversity," "multicultural education," and "inclusion" meant, then how would the ambiguous terminology used in the Mission Statement clearly say anything to the public that it was intended for? What tends to happen when there is not a critical understanding of the ideological nature of language is that people assume a face-value treatment of concepts like democracy, as if everyone were talking about the same thing. However, without really defining the words, people communicate through assumptions of understanding—assumptions that are usually inaccurate. For example, George W. Bush and Noam Chomsky can both be talking about good education, but they are ideologically situating themselves in these apparently simple terms in drastically different ways. Perhaps the most important word that was readily used but never defined by the committee was "culture."

Throughout the three years of observations in Changeton, especially during the development of the Mission Statement, the meaning of "culture" proved to be a major point of ambiguity for the Multicultural Central Steering Committee. While "culture" appeared to have different meanings among committee participants (many of whom, as Sleeter and Grant [1988] foreshadowed, seemed to equate the word with race and ethnicity), individual definitions were never clearly articulated and there was consequently never an agreed upon group definition of the term. Without at least a clear understanding of individual conceptual differences, it would inevitably be confusing for the group to move into an elaboration of multi*cultural* education. In fact, as a result of the lack of semantic clarification, the committee had a hard time categorizing what would and would not be considered a cultural group and thus who to include in its efforts. Witness Carl's contradicting comments "don't the handicapped, or what do you call them—challenged, have a culture?" and, "women and the handicapped are supposed to be in the curriculum but cultures aren't." Giselle added to this entanglement by stating:

> We should have concerns for all forms of diversity, but we should give the highest priority to cultural issues. . . . We need to include gender and handicap, though they are not the problem—I would like our committee to deal more specifically with cultural and ethnic diversity. The really explosive reasons that people are not getting along with one another are based on race and ethnicity, so these should be the focus.

After Carl mentioned gays, Giselle insisted, "That is not what is bothering Changeton, cultures are not living together."

When the Central Steering Committee argued that the Mission Statement was all-inclusive by insisting that "it is clear that we are saying 'cultures,'" what the group needed to work to understand is that the very lack of an agreed upon definition means that saying the word in and of itself can't explicitly signify anything. Perhaps the only thread that unified most of the uses of culture in the committee's Human Relations approach and discussions was a consistently depoliticized and ahistorical understanding of the word.

As discussed in Chapter One, within mainstream multicultural models, such as Teaching the Exceptional and the Culturally Different, Human Relations, and Multicultural Education, the term "culture" is usually used to refer to group practices and material artifacts decoupled from the sociohistorical, economic, and political conditions that have given rise to such phenomena. The Central Steering Committee fell into this very trap in that the group had yet to adequately explore culture as being produced and reproduced within socially sanctioned and institutional abuses of power. The committee members need to struggle together to acknowledge and confront the reality that so many people in their very community are forced to deal with a society in which they are stripped of their voices and relegated to the margins of political and economic power. The voices in Chapter Three, "Facing Oppression: Youth Voices from the Front," are a good source for understanding this dynamic. But power and abuse are not only limited to the cultures of the oppressed. How white youths become racist, how the wealthy become callous to poverty, and how most of what all people learn as they are socialized into cultural groups are generally imposed and not negotiated. In other words, cultural politics implicates everyone in society and vice versa. The CSC would then be better able to understand how culture is significantly shaped within the sociohistorical antagonisms of everyday life in Changeton.

During the committee's initial developments, even the focus and discussion of race and ethnicity did not engage the realities of racism and white supremacy. Instead, the idea of culture was being cleansed and romanticized, and, as illustrated in one of the Mission Statement's clauses, reduced to a "celebration of our diversities." (This issue of the limitations of affirmation will be dealt with in great detail in the next chapter.)

Jackie and Melissa attempted to use critical language that implicated unequal relations of power in the production of culture: Early on, Jackie insisted that beyond inclusion, it is also important "to challenge the social structures and the causes of oppression"; and Melissa stated, "Discrimination is based on power— those who have it versus those who don't—and this should define the committee's work." Luis's comment was also potentially effective in approaching the historical realities of what constitutes cultural politics: "If you discriminate against any group, you do it to all. Discrimination has nothing to do with taste, it's power. . . . We need to put this in historical perspective, those who have historically been excluded because they don't have the power." Unfortunately, these words of wisdom were virtually ignored. In fact, they were erased from the CSC's public statements and overall intragroup and public persona. As such, the issues were never adequately named and engaged.[4]

It is unclear how the Central Steering Committee felt that this new statement of purpose, which reflected basically the same use of language and intent as the school system's earlier efforts at infusing multiculturalism (as discussed in Chapter Two), as well as the Affirmative Action Plan and the Accreditation Report, would make any substantial difference. These earlier efforts, which also did not name the cultural realities of oppression, were unsuccessful in bringing about change. In fact, if they had brought about significant social transformation, there would be no urgent need for the CSC at the present time.

It could be argued that the use of overly general language, as in the Mission Statement, is strategic in that it leaves the contents of the document open to interpretation, and/or it avoids controversial issues and thus the possibility of intimidating and scaring potential supporters away. Nonetheless, not explicitly naming oppression of all kinds leads to the virtual exclusion of certain crucial issues necessary for understanding how culture is actually produced, circulated, consumed, and resisted, and consequently negates the possibility for substantive social change.

Essentializing Group Identities

Mainstream models of multicultural education generally fail to acknowledge the complex diversity that exists within groups. Not only are there intergroup differences, but there are also intragroup cultural realities that need to be addressed so as to not essentialize group identity. As discussed in Chapter One, essentialism ascribes a fundamental nature or a biological determinism to humans.

During the development of the CSC's Mission Statement, the committee often approached various groups (whether or not they considered them cultures) in a way that greatly risked bunching people together, disconnecting them from the complexities of intragroup diversity across social class, race, religion, age, gender, health, sexuality, and so forth. For example, when talking about sexual orientation, there was reference to "a" culture, implying that all gays are the same. This form of essentialism also emerged in the group's discussion of gender: Giselle commented, "Across cultures you're still a women." This comment may imply that across cultures, women occupy a lower status than men do; however, without more elaboration it risks supporting the idea that there is some biological essence to women that places them beyond the social, historical, ideological, and political. Such an homogenizing notion completely disregards the multiplicity of cultural realities that diverse women around the world face (Anzaldua, 1990b; Minh-ha, 1989; Mohanty, Russo, & Torres, 1991). Sara's poetic statement captures this diversity, "A women is a window of many panes."

Essentialism was also evident in the following comment: "Cultures can be broken into Euro culture, black culture, Latino culture. . . ." The assumption in this case, conscious or unconscious, was perhaps that race predisposes people to particular cultural realities. An open and critical recognition of the ways in which racialization and racism play a significant role in shaping everyday practices and identities would have been extremely helpful in expanding the committee's understanding of cultural politics. Instead, what these overgeneralized categories can serve to do is negate the fact that "Latino/a," for example, does not capture the diverse and complex geographies, histories, and social realities of the great many groups that are reduced to such a general point of analysis. In other words, "There are no guarantees of identity or effects outside of the determinations of particular contexts" (Grossberg, 1996, p. 165).

As discussed in Chapter One, Critical Multiculturalism, unlike the more mainstream models, is concerned with the multiple and interconnecting relationships of race, class, gender, sexual orientation, health, religion, and so forth, and how these ideologically constructed categories work to produce particular kinds of experience. The cultural patterns that are the result of hegemony (the dialectic of domination and resistance) and the concomitant unequal distribution of power among these categories need to be addressed by the Central Steering Committee and not pushed aside. In this way, a number of what are significant markers of identity won't get excluded from defining the group's agenda.

Inclusion or Exclusion?

The key to a critical model of multicultural education would be to take into serious theoretical and practical consideration how all different life experiences and worldviews emerge. Although the final draft of the Mission Statement used phrases such as "understanding, acceptance, and appreciation of all cultures," "is inclusive of all peoples," and "we are all enriched by the study of other cultures," was the committee really taking about everyone? In the name of fairness, Carl insisted that a list of descriptors would inevitably exclude some groups and thus preferred using the phrase "all cultures." However, in his next statement, he argued that by using the word "all," "we'll be taking on every small group whether or not we feel it's important."

Fred also revealed the exclusionary ideology embedded in the word "all." He stated, "Our concern is for an equal chance for all people," but later inquired (subsequent to a comment about AIDS advocates), "Are we going to get involved with every group that comes along?" When it came to a politics of identity and difference, the Central Steering Committee should have avoided the use of the ambiguous language of inclusion in its Mission Statement so that the realities of exclusionary practices can be named, deconstructed, and transformed. This critical process should have been implemented in the CSC's early treatment of persons with disabilities, gender, and sexual orientation. (The treatment of social class will be elaborated in Chapter Six.)

Of the limited references to "disabilities" (which is disconcerting in and of itself), there were two comments in particular, by Carl and by Cali, that were representative of the kinds of stigmatizing symbolic violence that works to shape how people with disabilities are perceived and treated in society:

> don't the handicapped, or what do you call them, challenged, have a culture? I don't think that we need to talk about the handicapped . . . the handicapped are supposed to be in the curriculum but cultures aren't.

> In working with the deaf it's different, they don't know the rules and value system. They learn the hard way or are directly taught. There are many children who just don't understand that they are out of touch.

The first quote's reference to "them" ("what do you call them"), embodies the kind of division that exists in mainstream society. The dichotomy of "us" and "them" not only serves to legitimate the unequal power relations that relegate "them" to a subordinated status, but it also works to confirm the "us" as the norm. Them in this sense carries with it derogatory connotations—"not normal" or "you people over there." The reference to students not knowing that "they are out of touch" also serves this dichotomous and dehumanizing role—"in touch" and "out of touch."

The ideology that informs the above comments went unchallenged in the CSC's work. Melissa, June, and Jackie all spoke of the importance of including the disabled; however, the distinction "disability" (and all of its intragroup complexity) dropped out of sight in the Mission Statement. Some members justified not having to deal with the disabled by claiming that "they are already covered in existing school policy." As such, the mainstream antagonistic social relations that persons with disabilities deal with on a daily basis went, and would continue to go, uncontested.

During the development of the Mission Statement, the issue of gender also exposed ideological divisions in the Central Steering Committee—divisions that are representative of the larger society. As with the concept "disability," gender was disarticulated from its ideological/cultural roots. In fact, the CSC never really engaged the complexities of the relationship between gender and culture; in other words, how sex-role socialization and the concomitant discourses that situate how men and women are supposed to speak, act, walk, and so forth, went unexplored. Some members actually chose not to see the category as cultural at all.

One strongly supported viewpoint (by most of the women around the table) concerned whether or not to replace the descriptor "multicultural" with "diversity" when describing the work of the committee. Jackie voiced, "Perhaps 'diversity' is a better word to work with than 'multicultural,' since the latter is limited to race and ethnicity in most people's minds." However, the call to name discrimination against women (let alone patriarchal domination) as an essential part of their multicultural efforts was met with resistance by a number of men on the committee.[5]

Virtually dismissing the importance of understanding gender politics and the production of gendered identities, Carl insisted, "The Constitution implicitly includes women, you don't know oppression unless you're black!" Not only did this stance create a decontextualized hierarchy of oppression that prioritized issues of race, but it also neglected to engage the multiple and interconnecting relationships of language, gender, race, class, sexuality, and so on. Pitting different groups against each other and creating a hierarchy of oppression, rather than creative multicultural communities of solidarity, is counterproductive. Instead of reproducing such a hierarchy, the CSC should embrace feminist struggles while challenging the women, who were predominantly white, to address their own racism. White women often hide behind gender issues so as not to have to deal with their own discriminatory beliefs and actions (Frankenburg, 1997; hooks, 1981; Minh-ha, 1989; Mohanty, Russo, & Torres, 1991; Wallace, 1990).

Some women on the committee responded to the comment about not knowing oppression: "You don't know what its like to be a woman, girls are excluded from the curriculum in math and science!" "Women are not empowered here at the elementary level!" "Some people have more gender insensitivity than they may recognize, so this area should be included!" This last statement by Karen is of special importance in that she had just been denied the position of high school principal for what many citizens interpreted as sexist reasons. As revealed in Chapter Two, the mayor, who cast the deciding vote, concluded that she lacked the necessary "presence" and "leadership style" to preside over the high school. Nonetheless, such dissent fell by the wayside of the finalized language of the Mission Statement. In fact, the issue of gender would rarely if ever again surface in the committee's work.[6]

The welcoming language that was used in the CSC's official Mission Statement reveals little about the group's position on the issue of heterosexism—that is, personally or institutionally discriminating against someone because of their sexual orientation (Abelove, Barale, & Halperin, 1993; Muños, 1999; Sedgwick, 1990). Throughout their discussions the committee members seemed to avoid this controversial and complex topic. However, it was unclear if they were doing so because they honestly believed that race and ethnicity not only defined culture, but were the central issues that demanded their immediate and undivided attention, or if they were strategically (though perhaps unconsciously) avoiding the issue because of their own discriminatory dispositions.

Throughout the committee's discussions, it appeared as if many members were trying to minimize the importance of sexual politics so that they could justify not having to deal with them (also perhaps a strategy used to ignore disabilities and gender). Sexual orientation at one point was reduced to a matter of gender—"When you say gender, does that include gays? . . . It does for me." Two other CSC members argued that gays in fact have a culture: "Those others, gays for example, belong to a culture."[7] "Stay away from group identification—gays are part of a culture, we are including everyone." However, instead of elaborating on the relationship between sexuality and culture, it appeared as if Raul and Juan simply used avoiding "group identification" to object to naming sexuality in the committee's written statement. Immediately after, Carl interjected, "Before you know it, AIDS advocates. . . . " It is important to note how "AIDS advocates" risks reinforcing an ideologically coded phrase to imply gays. This is precisely where Fred declared that he was reluctant to get involved "with every group that comes along."

At another juncture, working with gay and lesbian concerns in the Mission Statement was considered a risk for the CSC because "the papers will show how you are talking about homosexuality, which will cover up the issue of race." This statement was perhaps being made so as to use fear of a media backlash to dissuade the committee members from confronting their own assumptions about sexuality. The media would most certainly have made a great deal of disparaging noise if the group had chosen to publicly confront homophobia. In fact, there had already been negative assaults by the Changeton press when other less contentious multicultural issues were raised in the community and schools. However, the key for the CSC is to be strategic while at the same time honest about the values and beliefs that inform one's/the group's position on an issue. In other words, the committee should anticipate the press's response and work it to the group's advantage; but, participants shouldn't simply erase the realities of sexual politics because of the fierce debates that may emerge. In fact, instigating such polemics would be extremely helpful in educating and including the public in these culture wars. (The issue of sexual orientation will be revisited in Chapter Six in order to see if this analysis is on target.)

The daunting question lingers—was there more here inside the Mission Statement's ambiguous language than simply a creative and productive strategy to keep the committee's efforts moving forward? Would such neglect foreshadow the next three years to come? Perhaps the Mission Statement subcommittee's claim that "the statement is simple, but it covers everything" risks being restated as "the statement is simple and covers up everything." Carl's rhetorical question—"Who's talking about excluding!"—though not intended to solicit a reply, in fact merits further exploration by the group. Unfortunately, the Mission Statement was never revisited or altered over the three-year period.

CHAPTER SIX

Professional Development

Raising Consciousness among the Faculty and Staff

As with the majority of attempts to develop multicultural programs across the country, the Changeton Central Steering Committee put a great deal of emphasis on professional development. In fact, the group's first in-service, "Working with Diversity," was a concerted effort to begin to "sensitize" the school system's over nine hundred teachers and administrators to the concerns of a multicultural world.

In order to jump-start their movement, members of the CSC consulted with two professors of education from area colleges and, with their help, began the production of a video called *Comments on Multicultural Education*. The video, which consisted of Changeton teachers and administrators explaining why they supported the idea of celebrating diversity, was a strategic way of showing the in-service participants that a number of people within the school system were dedicated to the infusion of multicultural education. Through the use of familiar faces, the video also served the purpose of personalizing the district-wide transformation process in a way that would be inviting and less threatening to others.

After viewing the video, the superintendent of schools addressed the large audience. He stated that in Changeton there were "repeated unwelcome verbalisms across the board from teachers, administrators, and staff to students from different backgrounds." He also explained that many educators expressed frustration at not being able to understand the needs of all of their students.

After a speech from a parent about discrimination, Eva introduced another video, *The Eye of the Storm*, better known as *Brown Eyes, Blue Eyes* (in which the teacher separates the class by eye color and discriminates against one group while glorifying the other). As the film rolled, there was whispering and laughter throughout the audience. Perhaps the response was incited by the dated clothing and beehive hairdo of the video's central figure. Maybe some of the over nine hundred people present were nervously reacting out of their discomfort with the in-service setting and implications. It may have been the apparent homogeneity of the classroom on the screen (all young, white, working-class kids), as compared with the demographic reality of Changeton. In a very different tone from laughter, two white women commented to each other, in response to the obvious implications of the video: "It doesn't carry over, we don't see that. . . . It's not racial, they like you or they don't."

The Call for Sensitivity Training

Gathering their forces after the in-service, the CSC participants met at the Central Administration Building. The focus of the group's discussion centered around the attitudes and beliefs of the faculty and staff in the city. Committee members expressed disgust at the reactions of colleagues, a number of whom left the workshop during the *Brown Eyes Blue Eyes* video. Fred exclaimed, "People were reading, others were laughing, it was a waste of time . . . disgraceful!" Jake insisted, "Our main goal is to change the attitudes of those people who think that many of these children don't belong here—older staff that have never dealt with this in the past lily-white schools." Carl shared with the group how, mistakenly, a Thai translator had been brought into his office to act as an interpreter for a Vietnamese student. Carl was disturbed by what he referred to as the "you've seen one, you've seen them all" syndrome. Kevin offered the following story: "It was a snowy day and a black woman was stuck in a snow bank. The custodian helped her and replied: 'Give those niggers a drivers license, but they'll never learn how to drive!'"

The committee agreed that the process of "culturally sensitizing" people should be implemented throughout the school system, "including cafeteria workers, custodians, and office managers." The participants also realized that in-service training was essential in that "you can't just change people's minds simply by telling them to change." Instead, members of the CSC wanted to expose participants to certain issues and actively involve them in raising awareness. The pressing question for the group was how to transform the faculty and staff's attitudes when "they may not know the depth of the problem." "Teachers in Changeton have no idea what baggage these kids are bringing to school," exclaimed Kevin. Giselle added, "I saw a staff person who said, 'Now Giselle, how did your mother bring you up?' It was obvious that he had no idea about the lives of these students, some who may not have parents at all. We need to sensitize teachers, which goes together with raising the students' egos."

Sara insisted that the CSC find ways to make teachers deal with youths "not as culturally disadvantaged, but as different." Jake agreed, telling the story of a teacher who upon hearing the accent of a new student, wanted him out of the class. The evicted youth was an honors student in math and social studies. Understanding the immediate implications of and reactions to such abusive treatment, Raul insisted that "crime and economics are all tied to this, these are the people that drop out, they are the ones in the parking lot. . . .We need to teach these kids to work and keep the system going."

The committee understood the fact that teachers' discriminatory attitudes have an enormous impact on students' perceptions of schooling and themselves, as well as on their academic outcomes—"Teachers have tremendous influence on students in the messages that are transferred down." Jake summed up the situation, "Some don't know, some don't care, and some are truly racist."

Emerging Goals for Professional Development

To help the committee focus in on individual members' concerns, as revealed in Chapters Four and Five, the group drafted and distributed amongst its membership a questionnaire, the Multicultural Committee Draft of Goals. As "Changing Staff Attitudes" was one of the categories (and central goals), the following issues and insights, were mentioned in the responses:

- Provide training day(s) for at least two members of each school's multicultural committee. Focus on dealing with differences, prejudice reduction, and teaching for confronting issues of prejudice and discrimination.
- Work with school-based committees in order to develop an action plan, for example, school-based workshops that deal with issues of race and social inequality.
- We need experiential activities and opportunities to recognize and evaluate the ideological influences that shape our thinking about schooling, society, ourselves, and diverse others.
- Teaching culturally different groups requires more sensitivity, it requires placing equal value on all students. The committee should be involved in providing training to all staff; that is, sensitivity workshops, in-service training, and more educational incentives for continued education.
- We need to heighten the importance of staff sensitivity toward the diverse backgrounds of students and their families, sponsor in-service training that promotes respect and sensitivity, and develop a resource bank of presenters that could be used by other groups in the system offering in-service training.

- Allow teachers more input in decision-making procedures in individual buildings; staff will be more positive and enthusiastic if it is their school and not the administrators'.
- All else will fall into place once educators' visions are expanded. Start with sensitivity workshops and cultural awareness sessions to get teachers to confront their suppressed feelings, especially regarding racism. Then, work with teachers to help them view everyone as innately equal; that is, the concept of oneness.
- All staff must be involved, not just portions of it.
- Pay for the teachers to take multicultural courses and give them credit for this toward pay increases.
- Have non-bilingual teachers attend bilingual workshops and the bilingual convention.

Looking to the Greater Community for Professional Development

The group brainstormed about programs that could help in their efforts to sensitize colleagues. CSC members would attend professional development meetings whenever possible in order to gain insights about potential future in-services. As Eva stated, "If you go out, we need people to bring back to this table as much information as you can." Each time that the group would assemble, participants would share news about upcoming, or previously attended, multicultural workshops in the area. Carl informed the group that an anti-violence organization was holding a meeting and that the CSC should attend in order to "volunteer our expertise."

The committee agreed that it would be good to have parents and the public at large see teachers and administrators showing a deep level of commitment to embracing diversity by involving themselves in activities outside of the schools. However, a common problem with many of these workshops was the price. For example, one popular institute's in-service ranged anywhere from a three hour presentation for $1,100 to a two-and-a-half-day in-service at a cost of $6,600.

By June of 1993, the CSC dedicated itself to developing its own "multicultural training activity for central, working, and school-based committee members," with the hopes that it would be ready to go as early as September. Having received $1,200 from the state desegregation plan to provide for the in-service and some extra funds needed to pay for substitute teachers, the Central Steering Committee's plan of attack was to find an organization that could help shape and facilitate the group's multicultural efforts. September 30, 1993, was the chosen day, and there was little time to waste.

In August, a volunteer subcommittee took on the responsibility for organizing the upcoming in-service. In search of facilitators, the group first approached Facing History, an organization that links the Holocaust, discrimination, and public schooling. However, the spokesperson for this organization recommended that before the CSC utilize their services, they should provide some introductory activities to help lay a foundation. He suggested that this include exposure to "an expert on urban settings."

Through word of mouth, the subcommittee contacted Sandy Bur (a white man), as well as Lesley Warner (a white woman) and Mandy Roberts (a black woman), from two area colleges. The subcommittee met with Bur, who was a professor of Urban Studies (and who had also worked with the Nobel Public Schools), to help prepare for the upcoming event. Sara suggested that the CSC broadcast the in-service to all the schools. This way, teachers could call in for questions and create discussions in their classrooms. Sam agreed with the idea, citing George Washington University, which had done something similar. However, because of the complicated scheduling problems that this idea presented, let alone the enormous expense, the motion died.

The subcommittee didn't want to make the same mistakes that the CSC had made at its first all-faculty in-service. According to the needs assessment results, a great many participants didn't like the original workshop, claiming that it was too big and didn't allow for interpersonal interaction. This time around, the committee also wanted the facilitators to give people practical information that they could bring back to their schools. Kevin expressed the need for people "to meet, look at materials, and learn about what to look for and what to do."

With very little input from Bur, and virtually none from Warner and Roberts, the in-service was set to take place. Attendance would include all members of the Central Steering Committee, plus two multicultural representatives from each school. In theory, the workshop was designed "to give staff a voice through leadership training and skills building" and "to empower them to help other teachers who may be in the middle and will come over to our side."

Volunteers prepared an information packet for all of the in-service participants. They solicited the information that they needed from individual schools (for example, what multicultural ideas each building had already put into practice and lists of site-based committee members), collected some literature on multicultural education, and prepared an in-service evaluation form. The group wanted to have ongoing evaluations/questionnaires for gaining insight from the greater educational community.

The In-Service

On September 30, the Central Steering Committee and two representatives from each school met at a local college (fifty people all together). Eva set up the tables for registration and distributed name tags. There were billboards that exhibited what schools had done so far to support multiculturalism. Each participant received a red binder (which CSC volunteers had assembled) that included a list of the Central Steering Committee members, a list of site-based multicultural committees and their chairs, a letter of welcome from the superintendent, a CSC status report with a copy of the Mission Statement, a tentative schedule for future in-services, complied needs assessment data from the March all-faculty in-service, a list of multicultural activities taking place in the schools (by building), and a chart describing the command structure of the school-wide multicultural education committees. It also included journal articles which presented a variety of perspectives on anti-racist, multicultural education (most notable authors being Gloria Ladson-Billings, James Banks, and Peggy McIntosh).[1]

Sandy Bur opened the workshop with an overview of the racial/ethnic history of Changeton. He spent most of his time describing the exploitation that the majority of working-class immigrants had faced over the years in such communities. Describing the demographic shifts of Nobel and Changeton from the 1960s through the 1980s, Bur anticipated a continued shift in a direction in which "whites will eventually be the minority," and he stressed the importance of teaching "all kids that they have a lot to offer."

Warner and Roberts then took the floor, echoing the importance of dealing with the changes that the first presenter had detailed. However, instead of lecturing from center stage, the two facilitators put the people into a large circle and suggested that during the exercises they were about to undergo, everyone keep track of their feelings.

The two women began to separate the large group with descriptive binarisms: right handed and left handed, height (over/under six feet tall), age, eye color, field of study, those who have traveled internationally, those who served in the military, those who have participated in the Nobel Marathon, those who live here in Changeton, marital status, and parental/grandparental status. They continued this process by dividing the group by language abilities, socioeconomic status ("middle to upper middle class, blue collar"), private or public education, gender, and finally by sending "the non-whites" to the other side of the room, asking for the "WASPs" (perhaps erroneously assuming that all whites are Anglo-Saxon Protestants) to "stay over here."

After this extensive process, the facilitators had everyone sit down and discuss what they "saw, said, felt, and experienced." Random comments from the group began to surface: "Manipulated!" "We moved around too much!" "I began to anticipate the exercise!" "Segregated!" "I didn't like to be white or non-white." Roberts asked if the participants felt labeled. One white male claimed, "It made everyone feel like a minority." When asked to identify with a particular social class, many participants agreed that it made them feel uncomfortable. The general consensus in the group was that people "felt good about some categories, and bad about others."

Some participants challenged the membership of certain groups. For example, it was argued that Jamaicans and Haitians do not necessarily fall under the descriptor black. To this, Roberts responded, "What do you call a nigger with a Ph.D.?" "A nigger!," she answered laughingly to a silent room—implicitly asserting that all racially subordinated people are discriminated against regardless of their national origin or accomplishments.

There were also people who didn't know where they racially/ethnically stood. One woman sat down in the middle of the floor, later explaining to the larger group, "I was born in the U.S. My family is from Cape Verde. They originated in Europe (Italy). Where am I? When I changed my descriptor, they changed my minority status." One white man, addressing the two facilitators, inquired, "What would happen if you asked who is racist and who isn't?" He added, "We need to talk openly and honestly about racism." With this, the group began discussing the differences between "racist" and "prejudice." Most people seemed to be participating enthusiastically, though no clear definitions emanated from the brief interaction.

Jake encouraged everyone to get back into a big circle to get people as close together as possible. Alluding to the previous exercise, he stated, "We all mixed in the differences and belonged with each other at one point, we all have differences and commonalities."

Roberts made reference to the Peggy McIntosh article (on white privilege) in the red binder that was handed out. She then read the article aloud and talked of her experiences of being followed and harassed by sales people in stores. On a tight schedule, the group, without much engagement with the literature, viewed three video clips of stereotyping in the classroom. The idea of presenting these scenarios was to have people begin to talk about how they would handle such situations. However, just as the discussion was getting warmed up, time ran out. In the remaining few moments, the facilitators handed out the CSC's in-service evaluation.

Debriefing the September In-Service

At the next Central Steering Committee meeting, the members present immediately focused on what had taken place at the previous workshop. Carl stated: "Bur was atrocious—he was only going to speak for ten minutes. He talked more about the blue collar stuff, and not about different populations—total irrelevance!" The committee agreed that the first speaker "was a bomb." Kevin noted,

"They [some participants] spoke positively in the staff meeting and are developing ideas." The quantitative results of the in-service evaluations also indicated a positive response: the overwhelming majority rated the workshop as "good" to "excellent." Some members found the experience to be "thought provoking," but were left with the feeling of "now where do we go?" Sara was disappointed; "I wanted to go to the back of the room and call a time-out—my agenda was not fulfilled!" Melissa was completely dissatisfied: "We raced back and forth for no reason!" Jake expressed the sentiment that too much had been crammed in: "There was no time to interact with others." June felt, "It was a good start for newcomers, but for people who had already dealt deeply with these issues, it was a letdown." Raul and Juan supported this point. Sam insisted that the meeting wasn't for members of the CSC, that "it was intended for the inexperienced." In general, the committee members were in agreement that they wanted a lot more dialogue. As Fred concluded, "The speakers were too long."

Inspired by the in-service's first exercise, the CSC discussed the realities of categorical separation. Jake insisted, "Until we say that these children are ours, we will not begin to solve the problem, but we shouldn't pigeonhole them as black or brown." The group talked about how students are registered in the schools by race. Jake added, "Right away, you are asking people to separate themselves." Arguing that Cape Verdean is a mixed race, Raul stated, "America wants you to come here and fit into categories that are already established and millions of people are marked 'other.'" Some of the CSC in-service participants admitted that they felt uncomfortable when the facilitators asked the group to separate by race. Without exploring these potentially edifying issues, the CSC mulled over what to do for its next in-service.

Preparing for a Second In-Service

For their next workshop, the Central Steering Committee discussed the possibilities of bringing in Globe of Human Differences (GHD).[2] Some teachers had already participated in "cultural sensitivity training" with this organization, and they provided positive feedback about the experience—"With GHD, you really had to self-explore and ask yourself questions." Jake mentioned the Globe of Human Differences workshop that he and some colleagues had attended "that really made the participants feel class conscious." Making reference to the markers of high socioeconomic status, as well as to the discomfort that often occurs when educators in positions of privilege are challenged to self-reflect, he added, "The people from Borton in their Brooks Brothers suits were embarrassed." Sam insisted that, "We need to feel uncomfortable, we need to get to the root!"

Committee members explored having a daylong workshop for the same individuals who had attended the September in-service. They wanted to keep away from working with the entire staff, agreeing that, "It's too big, the smaller the group the better the dynamic." Carl insisted that a vanguard needed to be created and that the in-service participants would be in charge of making something happen in their individual schools—"The site-based committees are the catalyst for change at the building level."

The Central Steering Committee problematized what needed to be accomplished at the next in-service. This time around, the group felt that it would be crucial to work much more closely with the facilitators in shaping the workshop agenda. The members also recognized the importance of asking the other school representatives what they thought should be covered. Initially the committee wanted to arrange two or three meetings with the elementary, junior high, and high schools in order to hear what these teachers had to say; however, scheduling proved to be far too complicated to gather such insight.

In November of 1993, a new volunteer subcommittee met to prepare for the upcoming workshop. The CSC had decided to collaborate with the same people who had attended the September in-service, whom they hadn't interacted with in some time. The task force discussed the virtues of working with smaller groups; however, because of the small representation from each school (two people) the CSC would be unable to break participants up to focus on their individual school needs.

The subcommittee went over a number of possible strategies for shaping the upcoming in-service. Sara proposed that there be one hour of discussion around pertinent issues; with a second hour dedicated to study circles for troubleshooting common problems. The group also discussed the possibilities of having an exhibit area where people could spend as much time as they wanted at the different academic levels. There was mention that the local Expo Center had had a multicultural education fair where participants received their own passport, giving them access to the different countries and activities that were being presented. The main problem with this particular model was that the cost was well over a million dollars. Without getting discouraged, the subcommittee members felt that they could mine the unique resources that they had available to them in their own school system and immediate community in order to make something like this work.

While there was overall agreement that it was crucial to have some form of curricula displays at the in-service, and to allow the representatives to voice their concerns and provide insight, the role of the facilitators of Globe of Human Differences was unclear. It was time for the two organizations to meet.

By December of that year, the CSC had contacted Globe of Human Differences, requesting the presence of a spokesperson at one of its meetings. Sue

Kara, a black woman, granted the committee's wishes and brought with her a large brochure containing a list with the goals and objectives of the program to combat prejudice and discrimination.

Eva introduced Kara to the members of the CSC and told her about the committee's Mission Statement, multicultural goals, and previous in-service experiences. She explained that the group had decided to use the date set in January as a follow-up session to September's efforts, only this time with a greater emphasis on getting feedback from the entire group and providing practical applications.

Checking to see how many people had already attended a GHD workshop, so as not to repeat anything, Kara explained that her program was developmental by nature—"We can tailor the workshop to make everyone feel good." The GHD representative then explained that "teachers' biases are based on a lack of information," and that her organization was about "self-examination, awareness, and sensitivity. . . . We have ways of bringing out issues and questions just for this purpose." She revealed that Globe of Human Differences had some action planning exercises (which she preferred not to call "activities") that required a minimum of nine hours to properly work through. "These issues are confrontational," she said laughingly.

Understanding the Central Steering Committee's desire for interpersonal interaction, Kara emphasized the point that "the wisdom, far beyond that of the two facilitators, is in the dialogue of the group." In terms of practical tools, the woman explained that GHD had an agenda and a study guide, but not an actual curriculum. She suggested having a different in-service session for integrating the basic tenets of the guide into Changeton's existing classroom content.

In contemplating what should be the basic components of the workshop, some CSC members emphasized the need to know more about the different cultures in the community and recommended having group presentations. While Kara agreed that it was important to have an update on the populations that were attending their schools, she warned of the dangers of essentializing identities:

> The Latino/Hispanic communities are seen as one when they have many differences, Asians are also lumped together. We need to approach different people in different ways, we need to recognize what we don't know. . . . We talk of individual European countries, but not when it comes to Africa.

Feeding off this point, Carl revealed that there are ten different islands in Cape Verde alone. He continued by saying that he wanted to be able to talk about all groups and issues without emphasizing the negative—"nothing negative, no violence, we are working on that." Giselle agreed, "We shouldn't deal with all the negatives such as lynchings, rather, we need to accentuate the contributions of different groups." Melissa immediately rejected this position:

The bottom line is that we have an aging white staff and we need to talk about the negative. They [teachers] think that these kids are from Nobel. We go out to the bus stop to show people that these kids live here, these issues are serious. I'm tired of dancing around with food and simple curriculum changes, and I don't like the idea of a fair, it trivializes multicultural education, as do Black History and Martin Luther King, Jr. Month!

June agreed, arguing that "we need to ask hard questions today to get at reality."

Kara assured the group that there was going to be conflict, opposition, and challenges to deal with in their infusion of multicultural education. She stressed the need to help educators digest new information about human diversity into something positive. Questions about an action plan came pouring out of some members of the CSC. For example, Fred inquired, "I want to know strategies that teachers can respond with if they hear a racist remark in the teachers' lounge!"

In January of 1994, the CSC was ironing out the details of a two-workshop contract with Globe of Human Differences. The committee was trying to decide if they should have small groups for better interaction, or to have the whole group meet together (all fifty participants). The GHD representative suggested that the large group could be used for initial introductions so that no one would be a stranger, and that they could then break into smaller units. In troubleshooting what to do in the first of what would now be two workshops, Kara told the committee, "There are some things that you don't want in the first session; some issues are difficult for the people that are in denial of living in a multicultural world." However, the general consensus among members of the CSC was that, "That's not your audience, these people have taken a step forward." Arguing in favor of more consciousness raising, Melissa exclaimed, "I like small group discussion, it's less flashy, but good for examining biases and teaching people to recognize prejudice, so kids can do the same . . . it is important for kids to question what they've learned—'maybe grandpa is wrong, I think I need to check this out.'" Carl added, "We should sensitize teachers and raise them to a level of consciousness, but there has to be a place for sharing what they are doing." For the second part of the in-service, scheduled for March, he wanted to break up the participants by departments (for example, history, math, science). Emphasizing the need for an interdisciplinary approach, rather than one of fragmentation, Melissa countered, "We have talked to each other, and not others, for over twenty years. We don't even sit together in the teachers' lounge. The Cape Verdeans are in one corner . . . how can they [teachers] do it [develop community] in the classroom?"

The CSC was pressed with time to make a decision about the two up-coming in-services with Globe of Human Differences. The superintendent wanted an official statement of what the committee was going to do, as well as a proposed budget, by eleven o'clock the next day. Kara confirmed that the CSC wanted GHD for two three-hour sessions and requested that the committee solicit questions from participants so that she and her colleagues could consider their concerns and needs in structuring the workshop. Unfortunately, Mother Nature stepped in and the anticipated January in-service was snowed out and not rescheduled until March 16th.

First In-Service with Globe of Human Differences

In March of 1994, the rescheduled in-service was under way. The local museum was open to the Changeton school system at no cost. The two GHD facilitators, Kara, who had helped the CSC organize the workshop, and Sandra Casey, also a black woman, distributed the following handouts: a GHD workshop evaluation called "What I Expected? What I Got? What I Valued? What I Want?"; a list of definitions; GHD "Goals of the Program and Objectives"; Peggy McIntosh's article, "White Privilege: Unpacking the Invisible Knapsack"; "Guidelines for Challenging Racism and Other Forms of Oppression"; "Guidelines for Achieving Communication Free of Racial and Ethnic Bias"; and a GHD newsletter and calendar.

The day began with a very brief introduction to the Globe of Human Differences, which included a short video. The two facilitators stated that the objective of their organization was "to enhance self-esteem, to develop critical thinking skills, to counter stereotypes, to build empathy, and to encourage educators and young people to take steps to change the world." Kara explained that it was important that the group in attendance wanted to be at the workshop, pointing out that her organization "is usually brought in as a form of punishment."

The two facilitators openly embraced the active participation of the group, encouraging them to voice their individual opinions: "We need to share and speak with 'I' statements, from our own personal experience—'I believe,' 'I think'—so we can get out of the practice of generalizing." After reviewing the day's agenda, Kara spoke very briefly about the ways in which people learn stereotypes through the media, social interaction, stories, and the perspectives of others. She stated that the goal of the type of training that the group was about to undergo was to challenge and "unlearn unconscious stereotyping." With that in mind, the two facilitators began with their "action plan."

The first activity consisted of playing a game called Ropes. Words beginning with the letters in "ropes" were solicited from the audience, starting from the letter "R"—"respect," "refrain" ("from statements that are insulting")—to "O" words—"open-minded," "order," "opinion" ("that students know the difference between fact and opinion")—to "P" words: "peace," "patience," "perspective"—to

"E" words: "enrichment," "enlightened," "emotion"—to "S" words—"sensitivity," "sympathy," "social science" ("people who are in the profession of making excuses for other people's behavior").

With little to no substantive interaction or semantic/ideological analysis, Casey introduced herself and the Name Game. The basic idea of the exercise was to share a story about your name. The facilitator talked for awhile about being African American and having a Euro/Irish name. After going around the room, Casey stated that, "Identity to children is extremely important, as is spelling and pronouncing their names properly." She then asked the entire group how this exercise could be used in class. Some participants mentioned the importance of showing respect toward students. Others commented on the need of starting the learning process from what students bring—"You have to take them from where they are and build on this." One teacher exclaimed, "The kids know that they know a hell of a lot more about Puerto Rico than I do . . . teachers need to be learners."

One respondent was concerned that "many students don't know what their background is, nor do they always know who their father is." Jake (a CSC member) argued that this type of exercise can be dangerous: "What about those kids who don't have a heritage to fall back on, blacks, for example? Some youngsters would feel embarrassed. 'Mommy, where did we come from?'" Without challenging Jake's assertion, the two facilitators, short of time, quickly moved to the next activity called Name Five, which they explained could be used with various age groups. Equipped with a pencil and paper, each participant had sixty seconds to name five people in the following categories: prominent (male and female) African, Latino/a, Asian, Native, Jewish, and Catholic Americans.

With time up, the group was asked how the activity made them feel? One participant replied, "Stupid!" Casey discussed the importance of finding role models from peoples' own groups that they could look up to. Perhaps missing the point, one teacher of Irish descent, responded, "I agree, put Kennedy in all the groups." During this discussion of role models, a white woman mentioned the need for gay and lesbian representation (a category not mentioned in the instructions of the GHD exercise). The group began to talk about the West Nobel Parade and the controversy over whether or not to allow gays and lesbians to march. A white woman of Irish descent described the event as "a parade to celebrate Irish history." She claimed that because "they insisted upon participating, now everyone is hurt because there is no parade at all." Instead of using this particular pedagogical moment to discuss heterosexism (a word that is used in the literature and definition list of Globe of Human Differences), the facilitator cut this conversation short in the name of time.

Moving on, the next activity consisted of forging what the facilitators described as "a common language." They had small groups each explore one of the terms on the definition list that they had handed out: "stereotypes, prejudice, discrimination, racism, religious bigotry, anti-Semitism, sexist, heterosexism," and "scapegoating." Unfortunately, all of the discussions around these definitions were bereft of any profound theoretical analysis of what constitutes oppressive ideologies and practices. The dialogue among the group stayed at a level of descriptive experiential stories, with no sense of why the incidents described took place. It wasn't as if there were no provocative comments throughout the discussions, comments that could have been used to invoke a more critical analysis of the sociohistorical nature of oppression. For example, there was mention of "intergenerational racism," there was a reference to "tracking as a form of stereotyping—'stupid kids' are tracked down," there was recognition that "kids grow up with the myth that whites are superior and that's why they are in the gifted program," and there was reference to the fact that the gifted program was suddenly diversified when it was in serious jeopardy of being dropped because it was made up of all white students. However, none of these issues were targeted for elaboration or profound engagement.

Instead, the facilitators chose to redirect the area of inquiry into issues of Bilingual Education. Without defining the concept, Casey asked the entire group, "Is there tension between mainstream and bilingual children?" One participant responded that "A student came to me crying and said that someone called him a bad name, a 'bilingual,' and asked what this meant." Some of the larger group giggled, "We have a new swear word." A white, male, foreign language teacher, when asked if he felt that being bilingual was a plus or a minus, responded without elaboration "a minus." Again, as this conversation was warming up, it was cut short "because of time constraints." People needed to fill out evaluations. Part two of this in-service was arranged to take place the following week and all participants were asked to read for homework the Peggy McIntosh article, "White Privilege: Unpacking the Invisible Knapsack."

The second session with Globe of Human Differences took place in much the same way as the first. Kara and Casey distributed the following: GHD workshop evaluation; "Sample questions for multicultural training," from the Administration Office of the Nobel Public Schools; "No One is Born Prejudiced, Prejudice is Learned and Can Be Unlearned, What You Can Do"; an action plan sheet; "Guidelines for Establishing a Multicultural Education Environment"; and a multicultural checklist.

Kara opened the day's discussion with some words about "the need for safety and feeling comfortable" when dealing with multicultural issues. She then had the entire group read aloud the McIntosh list of white privileges, asking for responses to the ideas being expressed. A Latina emphasized the article's central point, "These are more than individual acts of meanness, it took a long time for it to become systemic. In reverse, it will take a long time to get back to individuals." Fred (from the CSC) commented, "Things have changed since 1989 [when the article was written]. Things are not as bad as then. For example, there are more races represented in the media, and more different newscasters." With no critical interrogation of this assumption, the facilitators asked, "How does privilege manifest in the classroom, how do you see it?" One person replied, "Department heads, principals, and teachers are mostly white males." Giselle (of the CSC) shared that she sees this kind of discrimination more in the adult community than in the classroom, explaining that "confidence comes from long-term privilege."

There was resistance among many members of the group to the notions of white privilege and oppressive pedagogical practices. One white woman argued, "I have a student who thinks that I gave him a bad grade because he is black!" Kara responded, "I can't deal with the fact that people will say that being black is an excuse—that's a cop-out, people hide behind it." Carl chorused in, "Kids know that they've got you, they say that you are a racist." Another white woman shared that she and some of her colleagues had done a statistical analysis which revealed that "students of color had the lower grades." She exclaimed, "Why is it racism if students' expectations are that they are supposed to do poorly?" Fred jumped in the conversation, "We don't want to shift the blame to white males in multicultural education." There was general agreement among the group that this was a "point well taken." Some whites at the in-service voiced the opinion that they didn't think that their position was necessarily one of privilege. One man even said that he wasn't going to give up anything, even if it were a privilege. June, who had made a number of comments throughout Central Steering Committee meetings that difficult issues needed to be confronted, suddenly had a change of heart. She argued, "There is a backlash against the white male. I have three sons, we have to work through privilege, but we also need to appreciate others. What is the purpose of this in-service and the CSC? I think it's tolerance. . . . Math, science, and language have no color. . . . We need concrete strategies to go back with." Mentioning that this was "not simply a white/black thing" and that "gender, class, and sex are also important issues," Kara took the floor pointing out how the literature evoked "feelings of anger, confusion, and uncomfortableness." She argued that these feelings need to be dealt with, especially when working with students—"We want students to be comfortable, then they will do better."

Casey took the floor and read aloud the definition sheet that the entire group had briefly discussed during the previous meeting. When "stereotyping minorities" was mentioned, one Latina made the point that "'minority' is a negative term, it's 'non-white'. . . . It's a stereotype in itself, it means smaller than, less than." Without acknowledging the comment, Giselle presented what she thought was an example of a positive stereotype—"nice Italian yards." Kara worked with this second comment, making the point that, "Positive or negative, we cannot use your example to represent a whole group." Another Latina argued that with stereotypes or generalizations, "You take away the individuality of the person." Jackie (of the CSC) brought up Asian stereotypes of science and math wiz-kids. She argued that such images were "good for those that succeed, but bad for those who don't." A Portuguese man agreed, stating that "stereotypes create expectations and burdens." June insisted that "stereotypes always have negative connotations."

Moving on, the facilitators introduced a new exercise to the entire group: "Name a situation where you felt you were the favored/unfavored." The participants provided a number of different examples, including a Cape Verdean man being greeted with respect because he was a teacher "and not a peasant," and a woman who had to ask her husband in order to leave the country. Eva, the chair of the Central Steering Committee, shared the following anecdote: "I was in a local liquor store and I wanted to cash a check. The white man behind the counter told me that I couldn't write a check from [names the distant town that she lives in]. 'But,' he said, 'you look familiar so we will cash it.' I'd never been in that store before." At this point, one white woman expressing frustration with the in-service, exclaimed, "I don't feel that I'm getting anything here that I can use! I can't know everything about all groups, religions, or cultures. All students need certain things. Let's talk about that and their similarities." Kara responded, "Would you agree that with more personal awareness that you'd be better prepared for the classroom and curriculum development?" With no response from the woman, the facilitator added, "We will get to materials and practical solutions." She then moved on to the next activity.

The new exercise consisted of a list of sample questions that had been solicited from Changeton teachers. Two groups were given fifteen minutes to address any one of the issues raised. The first team addressed the problem of racist jokes in the teacher's lounge. The general consensus was that offensive behavior of any kind should not be tolerated. The participants discussed how such acts should not necessarily be challenged "in a combative way," but rather strategically. For example, "Ask the perpetrator if they would say that in front of someone of the race attacked."

The other group discussed whether or not multiculturalism was separatist. The participants all felt that "balkanization was a real danger." There was talk of developing team activities that could help create more interactive conditions. One white woman recommended reading Arthur Schlesinger's book, *The Disuniting of America*, for "its important insights." Another person mentioned that, "We don't need to announce that an activity is multicultural, we should just do it."

The facilitators then went over a checklist entitled, How Effective Is Your School in Creating a Multicultural Environment? Still in groups, the participants had five minutes to respond to the questions. After some discussion of the daily school greeting in various languages; recognition of different racial/ethnic groups; the presence of ethnic art; cultural fairs; food and dance; multicultural storytelling, plays, and concerts; and foreign language teaching, the general consensus was that, in terms of affirming diversity, "things are getting better." Out of time, the facilitators asked the people to fill out the GHD in-service evaluation.

In the Central Steering Committee's post-in-service discussion, most members felt that the workshop was "nonthreatening," "comfortable," "inclusive," and "built on our sensitivity and camaraderie." Jake concluded, "We recognized that we do have a problem and not to simply place blame. There are things that you have to be aware of, that came out in the exercises." Fred informed the group that some people were upset because they felt that the European groups were not mentioned at all. He also brought up the issue of white-male bashing, pointing out that "many people don't support multiculturalism because they feel that it's against white males and females." He added, "Their concern is that we should not shift the blame from one group to another." The committee was aware of the fact that gossip was circulating around the schools that there was an exercise at the in-service that had supposedly led to white-male bashing. Luis, stated that he didn't get that impression at the workshop and countered, "The purpose was to show that everything is centered around white people as if they are the center of the universe. That needs to change. We need to start to teach the cultures of all of the students." Melissa jumped in, "I missed a good fight, I'm all for male bashing, the history of 'he' has got to go." Giselle concluded, "It [the in-service] was excellent, I enjoyed it . . . if we can speak to each other, we can certainly speak with our children." The committee agreed that the efforts had an impact on the participants and that they "sent out a message." A comment was made that "the high school is now selling T-shirts that say, 'Be color blind.'"

Eva expressed concern about whether or not "these sensitized people" [in-service participants] will be able to help people during faculty meetings—what took us six hours?" The CSC felt that the best way to help school-based committees was to continue to provide support and materials. Raul stated:

> There are some people who will never be sensitized. We will only make an impact by bringing in more people . . . having role models here, for example, blacks, Asians, etc. Asians are role models for all of us, even white kids. Certain minds are made up, if you change 10 percent you'll be lucky. We need more people.

In April of 1994, the Central Steering Committee received the compiled in-service evaluations from Globe of Human Differences. The report included the facilitator's description of the two days and responses from the participants about what they expected, what they got, what they valued, and what they wanted.[3] The majority of comments embraced the in-service efforts, pointing to the benefits of "openness" and "sharing experiences." The overwhelming request was to provide more "how-tos."

The CSC continued to attend workshops and gather materials that could be helpful in raising consciousness among colleagues. In October of 1994, the committee was made aware of an upcoming conference presented by the Center for Training and Health Education: part one was titled "Working and Living in Culturally Diverse Environments," and part two, "Making Schools Safe for Gay, Lesbian, and Bisexual Youth." While some members volunteered to attend the first part of the in-service on cultural diversity, not a single person voiced an interest in issues of sexual orientation. In fact, when talking about advertising the event and writing a proposal to request the necessary funds to secure some seats, the group consciously tailored its public statements by omitting the gay/lesbian section.

The Central Steering Committee Meets with a Representative from the Racial Imbalance Professional Development Committee

By the third year of the life of the Central Steering Committee, the entire Changeton school system, because of the Racial Imbalance Plan (the attempt to desegregate schools), was now working on issues of professional development. On top of their own independent projects, the members of the CSC felt that it was important to get more involved with these mainstream district efforts in order to make recommendations and have an influence on the decisions that would be made. As such, they invited a representative from the school-wide Restructuring Committee to attend one of their meetings. The representative, Jill, informed the CSC that the Restructuring Committee had recently changed its name to Professional Development Committee, and that the executive committee was made up of administrators. She expressed a desire to get teachers involved and explained that she had recently visited the Math and Guidance Departments in search of ideas and input.

The CSC understood that there was still a good deal of money available through the Racial Imbalance Plan that could continue to be used to promote its multicultural agenda. Helping the Central Steering Committee find ways to effectively use the available professional development funds, and to assist teachers in earning PDPs (professional development points), Jill proposed ideas such as taking graduate courses, attending workshops/conferences, forming study and focus groups, getting involved with peer coaching/mentoring, doing committee work, developing educational projects, working with student teachers, and developing curricula. She also informed the group that speakers from several colleges were coming to talk—"We have a specialist from California coming to discuss cooperative learning and cooperative discipline for working with problem students." On her way out, she left the official professional development activities calendar.

After the representative from the Racial Imbalance Committee departed, the CSC was eager to get some proposals on the table. The participants felt that in order to more cohesively direct their efforts they would need to form a permanent professional development working committee (instead of the ad hoc committees of 1994), much as they had with curriculum and instruction, personnel issues, and community outreach.

When the subcommittee was officially established, the members worked to develop on-site multiculturally oriented courses that educators could take to expand their knowledge and earn PDPs. Their first major plan was to bring in Dr. James Steele, the black president of a local community college, to speak to the Central Steering Committee about educating "men of color." The group wanted to see what he had to offer in order to make an informed decision about whether or not to have him return and work with local faculty and staff.

In June of 1995, Steele met with the Central Steering Committee. Asking the group about some of the issues that they had been wrestling with, he listened intently to criticisms of having a predominantly white staff and concerns about "behavior problems" with certain youth. Maria (Latina, principal, and new member of the CSC) cited that "in the Behavioral Adjustment Program, it's all boys and mostly minorities—especially black males." She asked: "Is this an issue of poor parenting skills or what? It's not an issue of racism! I'm the principal and I see that these kids can't control themselves. What are some ways to deal with this?" Steele drew a brief autobiographical sketch and then elaborated on the history of problems faced by racially subordinated men. Arguing that it takes a long time to change a culture, he pointed out that "it has only been 130 years since America's apartheid and only since 1954 that we've actually had racial integration." He stated that "400 years of slavery has had an impact on the consciousness of whites and people of color" and insisted that people, especially educators, "need to understand how we are related historically."

Citing the fact that the number of racially subordinated people between the ages of eighteen and twenty-four in prison exceeds the number in higher education, Steele said: "Internal rage and human waste is astronomical. They are bright and talented, but they turn outside rather than inside the system." The purpose of his work, he explained, was to help organizations such as Changeton's Central Steering Committee "inculcate certain strategies to prevent this from happening." He insisted that "educators need to examine the values that shape our society." He commented on how white male property owners had a major impact on the "beginning of society," as well as how "white male values informed the framing of the Constitution." The black speaker then threw in the disclaimer, "I'm not blaming anyone for that today," arguing that people in present-day society "have inherited such conditions." The problem as he saw it was that "people don't talk honestly about these issues."

Steele insisted that the "vision of America has never been one of multiculturalism," but rather "one of ethnocentrism." He made reference to segregated housing and schools, pointing out how society is stratified "by color, class, and cast." Arguing that "the mission and vision of schools have not been multicultural," the speaker commented on how "culture has not even been addressed in schools" and how "only 20 percent of students are now catered to." Steele continued on by mentioning how "students of color are called on less in class." To combat such destructive forces, he highlighted the importance of "the ecology of the school": the name of the building, what's on the walls, and treating diversity not just as a month here and there, but rather, as a ongoing issue that needs to be dealt with all the time.

Exposing the CSC to his ideas about student motivation, and alluding to Maria's original question, Steele stated, "Motivation is both internal and external. For black male students, boredom is the greatest problem. They are more physical than whites. This is not taken into consideration in schools." The speaker argued that instead of being supportive and rewarding, schools deal with young black men in a containing and controlling fashion. He said that this was also a problem in the black community where "mothers restrict their sons and support their daughters—minority families do this." Steele's basic point was that "this destructive control by families" had to be dealt with, and that "acceptance" is what teachers need to work toward. Dismissing traditional forms of assessment, he insisted, "For behavior adjustment, we need some clinical work with each individual child," and added, "There is high trauma among kids of color, a fact of prenatal care."

The committee wanted to know if Steele could come back and offer a class for teachers. He responded that everything that he did was adjustable and not canned, and that he would be delighted to pay another visit to Changeton. They made tentative plans for the fall.

Critical Interpretation and Discussion

As professional development should be a major component in any model of multicultural education (Banks, 2000; Bennett, 1998; Gay, 2000; May, 1999; Pang, 2000), it's admirable that the Multicultural Central Steering Committee was willing to go through so much trouble, with no pay and an almost nonexistent budget, to attempt to educate the Changeton school system's faculty and staff in the area of cultural diversity.[4] As "sensitivity training" and "the affirmation of diversity" were viewed with the utmost importance—"Teaching culturally different groups requires more sensitivity, it requires placing equal value on all students"—the group diligently labored to conceptualize and implement workshops.

While creating a caring and safe educational/community environment is extremely important, working from a theoretical model limited to issues of sensitivity and affirmation, as argued in Chapter One, can create three fundamental problems. First of all, such a model can work against social theory by individualizing and thus psychologizing discrimination and oppressive practices, disconnecting identity from its ideological, sociohistorical, and institutional construction. Second, a sensitivity model often functions through a lens of cultural relativism, from which all cultures are valued equally and uncritically. Third, an exclusive focus on sensitivity and affirmation has the propensity to restrict awareness of the complexities of cultural politics.

The Personality Vacuum: Abstracting the Social from the Psychological

> Psychology with its notion of the isolated, developing individual allows for the interpretation that all societal problems can be ultimately located at the door of the individual actor. This allows for an interpretation of society as an aggregate of individuals rather than a totality that is much greater than its individual parts. (Sullivan, 1990, p. xii)

Caught within a Human Relations approach to professional development, which focuses on nurturing positive interpersonal and intergroup interactions in schools by encouraging respect and unity, the Changeton Multicultural Central Steering Committee concentrated on transforming individual psyches, and thus directed its professional development energies toward "changing attitudes," "self-reflection," "asking yourself questions," "self exploration," and "addressing personal prejudice." Most multiculturalists would agree that self-actualization and prejudice reduction are essential to social change, and that educators need to critically reflect on the assumptions that they carry about themselves, learning, and different cultures. However, discrimination was being dealt with by the CSC as if the abusive treatment of students and their poor academic performance were the end result of an educator's ignorance, personal affective character, or individual values and beliefs, rather than the product of historically and socially sanctioned practices and conditions that produce such dispositions and subjectivities. Epitomizing the tendency to individualize discrimination and the extraction of the psychological from the social in the CSC's deliberations, Jake stated, "Some don't know, some don't care, and some are truly racist."

The central problem/limitation with pathologizing individual behavior is that self-actualization and prejudice reduction do not necessarily point out where the self or the discriminatory tendencies come from. The committee needs to more deeply examine how schools, the media, and other institutions nationwide function to legitimate particular experiences and worldviews at the expense and distortion of others. Developing a strong sense of the social and political realities that shape people's lives shouldn't be limited to "unlearning" what individuals have come to know. It is also imperative to identify how such values and beliefs were produced, legitimated, distributed, and consumed. Focusing on individual attitudes and affect, Kara, the facilitator from Globe of Human Differences, explained to the CSC that "teachers' biases are based on a lack of information," and that her organization was about "self-examination, awareness, and sensitivity." Placing an emphasis on the self, she stated during the actual in-service that the goal of the type of "training that the group was about to undergo was to challenge and unlearn unconscious stereotyping." However, a contradiction had just been created between "a lack of information" and "unlearning unconscious stereotyping."

To argue that "biases" and the perpetuation of oppression are the result of a lack of information runs the risk of implying that humans are biologically predisposed to do the things that they do, driven by some innate fear and disdain of the unknown. The reality is that teachers are well informed. The problem is that the information that most people have received, consciously or not, through their own formal education, the media, and social interactions (which the facilitator briefly mentioned in passing) serves to perpetuate values, beliefs, and actions that are psychologically, socially, symbolically, and physically oppressive. As Guy Debord (1988) states, "Thus the spectacle's instruction and the spectators' ignorance are wrongly seen as antagonistic factors when in fact they give birth to each other" (p. 28). The serious misgiving is that a great deal of the information that the general public uncritically assimilates serves to divert it away from the real issues and pedagogical sites that shape their very lives. Ignorance is thus not the lack of experience and knowledge, it is the very product of that experience and knowledge.

The CSC and in-service facilitators need to provide adequate theories of and actions against the producers of inequality and social injustice prevalent in both the process of schooling and the larger society. As suggested in the CSC's draft of goals, "We need experiential activities and opportunities to recognize and evaluate the ideological influences that shape our thinking about schooling, society, ourselves, and diverse others." Melissa also argued in favor of consciousness raising and interrogating the sources of discriminatory behavior—"it is important for kids to question what they've learned—'maybe grandpa is wrong, I think I need to check this out'. . . ." In this sense, "critical thinking skills," which the committee embraces, are not just about higher-order cognitive processing, but rather ideological analysis—an examination of the values and beliefs that inform the knowledge that shapes human behavior.

The CSC has to develop a deeper understanding of the historical, institutional, and socially sanctioned character of oppression in place of its individualized notions. In a well-intentioned response to a teacher's mistreatment of a linguistic-minority honors student, Raul insisted, "Crime and economics are all tied to this, these are the people that drop out, they are the ones in the parking lot. We need to teach these kids to work and keep the system going." Similarly, Steele later commented, "They [young black males] are bright and talented, but they turn outside rather than inside the system." What these statements risk communicating is that the society is systemically structured to accommodate everyone if educators could just get individual obstacles and the resulting student resistance out of the way of the existing educational process. In other words, if people were given the opportunity to learn in an environment that is welcoming, then everyone would stay in school and eventually succeed in the larger society.

Raul's observation could easily be misinterpreted in a way in which crime and economic difficulties are the products of nasty teachers whose inappropriate behavior results ultimately in schools failing to adequately serve students. From this limited view, racism, crime, poverty, illiteracy, unemployment, and all other kinds of social injustice and discrimination are reduced, not to the logic of capitalism and of institutionalized and socially sanctioned oppression, but rather to interpersonal social relations—as if they exist in a vacuum. Critical pedagogues should examine how abusive macro social and economic conditions produce poverty and a great deal of crime.

Raul's statement also is in danger of implying that educators of all backgrounds are basically reformers and functionaries of the state, responsible for keeping the system going. In Jurgen Habermas's (1962) sense of the public sphere—civic sites that are as free as possible of coercive political and economic influences—teachers should be openly recognized as public intellectuals and cultural workers who should teach in a way that keeps the state honest. The point isn't that educators can completely work outside of the system, or that educational institutions are the all-encompassing panaceas to social change. However, a foot-in-foot-out philosophy can be useful: the idea being to use the margins of society as a place for group solidarity and consciousness raising, while at the same time working within the core of the system itself (for example, in the classroom) to decenter and eradicate dominant oppressive practices within institutions. In doing so, educators must simultaneously provide ways in which students can effectively ally themselves with other public movements and spheres in order to change the larger social order that positions public education in the first place.

Institutionalized discrimination was mentioned in the Globe of Human Differences' literature, on its list of definitions, as well as when a Latina at one of the in-services tried to emphasize the importance of engaging the socially sanctioned industries of values and beliefs: "These are more than individual acts of meanness, it took a long time for it to become systemic. In reverse, it will take a long time to get back to individuals." In addition, near the end of the third year, Steele pointed out to the CSC that "educators need to examine the values and the institutions such as slavery that shape our society." The committee should work to articulate the interconnecting linkages among micro-level political, economic, and social variables; the formation of identities (including their own); and subordinated groups' academic performance at the micro-level classroom. In other words, the entire educational community should explore the ways in which schools reflect the larger social order and "the ways in which powerful institutions and groups influence knowledge, social relations, and modes of evaluation" (Giroux, 1983, p. 55). In this way the majority of CSC members can move beyond their original premise that the institutions that structure society are okay, including their own school system, and it is simply the people who need changing. But this requires the ability to theorize.

Theory is how people interpret, critique, and draw generalizations about why the social world spins the economic, cultural, and political webs that it spins. It is the ability to make sense of the everyday, that is, the why and how of what has been happening. Psychologizing beliefs and practices, rather than deconstructing their sociohistorical formation, actually works against the possibilities of understanding and producing critical social theory. If the world is reduced to the internal workings of the individual, then, beyond their own personal experiences, it is virtually impossible to make generalizations about what socially takes place around them—the very conditions within which those experiences are produced. As such, "culture" becomes a vacuous term.

The Central Steering Committee, and the workshop facilitators and participants, for the most part, limited themselves to the sharing of individual stories and "documenting feelings." The Globe of Human Differences in-service encouraged the CSC and the representatives from the school-based committees to voice their individual opinions: "We need to share and speak with 'I' statements, from our own personal experience—'I believe,' 'I think'—so we can get out of the practice of generalizing." While it is extremely important for individuals to come to voice around their own life histories, and to avoid any perpetuation of stereotypes, people nonetheless need a language with which they can examine and establish social patterns. Educators who embrace what the GHD facilitators were calling for in the individualization of experience and history make it virtually impossible to analyze what it means to be exposed to a particular cultural reality or group history. As such, it is impossible to understand how "I" is more often than not an intersubjective form, that is, the product rather than the creator of meaning. There needs to be theoretical engagement with the ideological and material context that generated such narratives or affective states of mind, rather than individualizing voices away from their sociohistorical significance.

In order to affirm and engage the complexity of diverse human histories and perceptions, a fundamental tenet of Critical Multicultural Education, when it comes to professional development and/or teaching, is the inclusion of facilitators' and in-service participants' (both teachers and students') voices in the learning process. This type of democratic participation calls into question everyone's location (subject position), experiences, and assumptions. Such histories can provide profound examples for grounding social theory, rather than being relegated to vacuous, descriptive "I" statements. As discussed in Chapter One, in listening to and engaging opinions and values that are made public, the idea is not for in-service facilitators or teachers to be disparaging or censorious. Rather, the dialogical interaction is meant to leave people ill at ease to a point that everyone acknowledge and take responsibility for their complicity in reproducing forms of discrimination. If the CSC truly hopes to bring about significant social change through professional development, the organization desperately needs to make the structural connections between the personal and the political in greater depth by grappling with the dialectical tension between the individual and the social. As Paulo Freire (1996) states, "I engage in dialogue because I recognize the social and not merely the individualistic character of the process of knowing" (p. 202).

Without critical social theory, the group is likely to conclude that the central goal of professional development should be to look for mechanical strategies for responding to discriminatory incidents. For example, Fred, eager to confront the harsh behavior from some members of his staff, inquired, "I want to know strategies that teachers can respond with if they hear a racist remark in the teachers' lounge!" Before searching for an efficient response, which is an important step, educators should first learn how to theorize about oppressive behavior and then act upon such injustices from an informed rather than robotic position.

Avoiding the Pitfalls of Cultural Relativism

As argued in Chapter Five, it is difficult to address multi*cultural* education without a working sense of culture—how is it produced within particular relations of power and what in turn does it work to create and maintain. Overall, the committee was working toward solutions to enhance educational success by embracing cultural relativism—in which, for the most part, all differences are equally acceptable. It spoke of "acceptance," "appreciation of all cultures," "a celebration of diversities promotes unity," "equal value on all students," and "staff respect for and sensitivity toward the diverse backgrounds of students and their families." The affirmation of diversity is extremely important if multicultural education of any kind hopes to gain the initial trust and participation of all groups in society.

However, the face-value celebration of diversity can create an interactive process within which it is virtually impossible to engage all cultures for their strengths and shortcomings. In talking to the multiracial youths in Chapter Three, Carlos described his predicament: "At one point, I jus started sellin guns for a livin. Went to jail a couple times, moved to (a nearby city in an adjacent state), had a kid, got tired of sellin drugs out there, came back over here, went to jail again." Trapped in a language of affirmation, the liberal multicultural educator would be compelled to romanticize this worldview. There is no room for critique, cultural analysis, and ethical intervention. As stated earlier, a Human Relations approach openly avoids such exploration, arguing that it creates tensions and antagonisms, rather than harmony. In fact, what usually happens in mainstream multicultural classrooms is that students never get a breath of this harsh reality in formal learning because teachers rarely investigate the existential realities that shape many young people's lives and self-concept. Success in raising students' self-esteem is not the byproduct of some pedagogical narcissism in which the students miraculously and momentarily find peace with the world around them. Multicultural education should be used as a way to prepare learners with what exactly they will need in order to excavate their history/cultural roots, and consequently the discursive nature of the self. It is only then that real substantive personal transformation and social agency can occur.

When professional development is based on in-service games, role plays, or ideas such as cultural fairs, all of which are generally sanitized of any engagement with the core of sociohistorical abuses of power, it can never achieve any kind of critical awareness among educators or students. So when the CSC mentioned developing a convention that would use passports to move from one national exhibit to another, advocates of this creative and potentially informative idea should also propose visiting the homes where people actually live. As the Social Studies Department chair stated, "They [teachers] think that these kids come from Nobel [the capital of the state]. . . . We go out to the bus stop to show people that these kids live here." Giselle also spoke to this issue—"It was obvious that he [a teacher] had no idea about the lives of these students."

In order to encourage them to theorize culture, the facilitators of the workshop with passports should ask educators what it is like to survive in a dilapidated housing project where drugs, violence, and hunger are everyday realties. They should explore what it means to take care of sick parents, how it feels to have no school books, what are the inevitable ramifications of not trusting public education, what it's like to have your imprisoned brothers' pictures posted around the city, what's it like to see battery acid poured all over someone's face because of a drug deal gone bad, how it feels to wake up to gunshots outside the bedroom window or to lose friends to street violence or to find your mother's boyfriend dead in your house from an overdose of drugs, what it feels like to get stabbed or shot, or what it's like to be beaten by the police—all social realities described by the local youths interviewed. In other words, what would be crucial here is to develop a deeper understanding of what defines culture so as to be able to move beyond an ahistorical sense of values, beliefs, group ethos, language, and practices, and to understand how these elements are produced within abuses of power and antagonistic social relations. As Carlos describes, "The ghetto is everywhere, the hood ain't no joke and there's no way out." Tricia Rose (1994) observes that "the ghetto exists for millions of young black and other people of color—it is a profoundly significant location" (p. 12). It is within the clashes of cultural capital (which would include different language, cognitive, and learning styles, literacies, knowledge, and so on) that educators as ethnographers can begin to understand the communities they are intended to serve and what their students are bringing to the arena of formal learning. This would be much more informative than simply internationalizing multiculturalism by exoticizing life back in some other country that many children have never even seen. In addition, even if the focus were on different nations, the facilitators of such a fair should point out the reality that globally cultures exist hierarchically in U.S. international policy, and that within neoliberalism and globalization not all people have equal opportunities to cross over or are treated with the same kinds of integrity when they do emigrate.

Different from What?

Throughout their work, members of the CSC often made reference to difference (for example, "we are afraid of difference"; "we should see these kids not as culturally disadvantaged, but as different"; "focus on dealing with differences"; "schools should embrace difference"; "we are all different"). As with the concept of culture, the committee has to work to define what exactly "difference" implies. Cultural relativism and an emphasis on affirmation won't permit members to recognize the fact that difference only exists in relationship to a referent. The critical question is, what are the defining parameters of that referent, that is, of the person/group who is speaking?

As discussed in Chapter One, the concept of difference in the United States is generally not examined in ways that name and call into question the dominant referent group—the invisible norm of the white, upper-middle-class, heterosexual, healthy, Christian male by which all others are evaluated and positioned. Educators need to recognize the fact that they are not simply individuals making random comparisons in the world. In reality, they are marked by group membership, whether or not they understand or perceive themselves as such. Whites, for example, are marked by membership to a category that has historically been used as the referent for negatively evaluating racialized others (Allen, 1994; Fusco, 1988; Hill, 1997; hooks, 1992; Leistyna, 1999; McIntyre, 1997; McClintock, Mufti, & Shohat, 1997; McLaren, 1994; Morisson, 1992; Roediger, 1994; Winant, 1995). It is precisely these social markings, which shape identities and points of reference, that are far too often taken for granted or seen as universal/human.

The first three multicultural in-services that the CSC developed and participated in should have provided such an analysis of "difference." At the first workshop, one of the facilitators, after categorically separating the group, asked if the participants felt labeled. One white male claimed, "It made everyone feel like a minority." Others made reference to feeling "manipulated," "segregated," and that they "didn't like to be white or non-white." Some people were uncomfortable with the social class differentiation. The general consensus among the in-service participants was that "I felt good about some categories and bad about others." In order for this exercise to be more productive, there needs to be a substantive discussion of how these divisions among groups are legitimated in society, thus moving the experience into something more than just psychologically driven sensations (racing "back and forth for no reason!") and beyond Jake's relativistic stance—"We all mixed in the differences and belonged with each other at one point, we all have differences and commonalities." As Lawrence Grossberg (1996) warns, "A theory that celebrates otherness fails to acknowledge the difference between experiences, real historical tendencies and cultural discourses and meanings, as well as the complex relations that exist between them" (p. 169).

There were a number of opportunities during this first workshop to elaborate on some crucial points about the politics of identity and difference. For example, when a woman sat down in the middle of the floor, explaining to the larger group, "I was born in the U.S. My family is from Cape Verde. They originated in Europe (Italy). Where am I? When I changed my descriptor, they changed my minority status." Or, while debriefing the in-service back at the Central Administration Building, Raul explained to the CSC that, "America wants you to come here and fit into categories that are already established and millions of people are marked other." These types of voiced experience provide ample room to explore the history of socially and institutionally sanctioned racist and segregationist practices in the United States. Taking advantage of these pedagogical moments and analyzing the sociopolitical system that gives rise to those differences is crucial for educators, students, and citizens.

As the word "difference" is embedded in GHD's name, Kara and Casey should have taken the in-service participants to a critical level of understanding the dynamic concept. Kara did warn of the dangers of essentializing identities; "The Latino/Hispanic communities are seen as one when they have many differences." However, she should also have situated intragroup and intergroup differences in relation to power.

Moving beyond the Comfort Zone

The inherent flaw with any theoretical paradigm that relies solely on cultural relativism, sensitivity, and affirming diversity is that it generally functions within a depoliticized comfort zone that does not allow for critical analysis of people's assumptions and values. As Donaldo Macedo (1996) states, "I am reminded of how
educators who embrace your [speaking to Freire] notion of dialogue mechanisti-
cally reduce the epistemological relationship of dialogue to a vacuous, feel-good
comfort zone" (p. 202).

In developing in-services for faculty and staff from throughout the school
system, the committee talked about comfort and feeling free to speak and share
experiences. At one point during workshop preparations, Carl informed the
Globe of Human Differences facilitator that he wanted to be able to talk about all
groups and issues without emphasizing the negative—"nothing negative, no violence, we are working on that." Giselle agreed, "We shouldn't deal with all the negatives such as lynchings, rather, we need to accentuate the contributions of different groups." It is important to note that Melissa, who would soon resign from the
CSC, immediately rejected this position, "The bottom line is that we have an
aging white staff, and we need to talk about the negative. . . . I'm tired of dancing
around with food and simple curriculum changes." There were a few other calls
throughout the years for critical engagement. June argued, "We need to ask hard
questions today to get at reality." Sam insisted, "We need to feel uncomfortable,
we need to get to the root!" In addition, a workshop participant stated, "We need
to talk openly and honestly about racism." However none of these demands were
actually fulfilled.

The facilitator from GHD, in troubleshooting with the committee on what
to do in the first in-service, stated that "we can tailor the workshop to make everyone feel good." Kara told the CSC, "There are some things that you don't want in
the first session; some issues are difficult for the people that are in denial of living
in a multicultural world." This assurance of comfort was again reiterated when the
same facilitator opened the in-service discussion with some words about "the need
for safety and feeling comfortable" when dealing with diversity. This strategy of
interaction resulted in a variety of issues and tensions going unaddressed and thus
uncontested.

Subsequent to Kara's opening statement about safety and comfort, she introduced the Peggy McIntosh article on white privilege, and the group read it aloud.
Instead of really examining the issues raised therein, and reflecting on in-service
participants' own subject positions in society, there were comments that revealed a
denial of unearned privilege; as witnessed in Fred's response: "Things have
changed since 1989. Things are not as bad as then. . . . For example, there are more

races represented in the media, and more different newscasters." There was general agreement among the group that "we don't want to shift the blame to white males in multicultural education." Some whites at the in-service voiced the opinion that they didn't think that their position was necessarily a privilege. June, a white woman, who often made the comment that the CSC needed to confront difficult issues, redirected her focus when it came to discussing the realities of whiteness. She argued, "There is a backlash against the white male. I have three sons, we have to work through privilege, but we also need to appreciate others. What is the purpose of this in-service and the CSC? I think it's tolerance. . . . Math, science, and language have no color. . . . We need concrete strategies to go back with." If given the opportunity, in-service participants who were challenged and felt under attack tried to move, whether consciously or not, away from the object of knowledge/ analysis. This movement was often done in a call for practical solutions and materials. Unwilling to engage the ideological construction of whiteness, this particular individual (from the above quote), not only requests "concrete strategies," but also wants to move out of the political and into what she erroneously believes to be neutral and objective ground—"Math, science, and language have no color." Beyond a call for "tolerance" (a word that the drafters of the Mission Statement rejected as uninviting), educators need to question the privilege that whites have: Being in a position to decide who and what will and will not be tolerated.

Along these same lines, confronted with issues of white supremacy, one white woman expressing frustration with the in-service, exclaimed, "I don't feel that I'm getting anything here that I can use! I can't know everything about all groups, religions, or cultures. All students need certain things. Let's talk about that and their similarities." A call for harmony and not engagement, this comment translates as, "I am not comfortable with where this is going, let's talk about something else—abstract educational needs and materials, for example." If all youths have certain (apparently universal for the speaker) needs, and those needs are empathy, respect, encouragement, and to be treated with integrity, then that requires naming and engaging their experiences across racism, sexism, homophobia, classism, linguicism, and so forth. The above comment risks implying that students' needs have nothing to do with cultural politics. Perhaps using her position of privilege to avoid an analysis of the harsh realities that many people face, the speaker wants to turn to a discussion of "similarities," which risks translating into, "Let's only talk about what you have in common with me so that I am not uncomfortable."[5]

After June's statement, Kara took the floor pointing out how the literature on privilege evoked "feelings of anger, confusion, and uncomfortableness." She added that this was "not simply a white/black thing," and that "gender, class, and sex are also important issues." What appeared to be an opportunity to discuss how a politics of identity and difference cuts across individual categories disappeared after this statement. It was as if the facilitator were using other categories to divert the group away from the tensions that were building around racial issues. Referring to the temporary discomfort, she argued that these feelings need to be dealt with, especially when working with students—"We want students to be comfortable, then they will do better." However, in leaving the in-service participants' discriminatory comments untouched, she herself neglected to confront the assumptions and potential prejudices of the people directly in front of her. In this sense, the facilitator seemed to be "falling prey to a laissez-faire practice" (Freire & Macedo, 1996, p. 202). In other words, whatever the group wants it gets, and in this case, it is to avoid the volatile issues. As Freire elaborates:

> In the end, the facilitator is renouncing his or her duty to teach—which is a dialogical duty. In truth, the teacher turned facilitator rejects the fantastic work of placing an object as a mediator between him or her and the students. That is, the facilitator fails to assume his or her role as a dialogical educator who can illustrate the object of study. (p. 202)

Instead of assuming this dialogical duty, Casey (the other facilitator) chose to read aloud a definition sheet (which included the word "racism" on the list) that the entire group had briefly discussed during the previous session. Shifting to the abstract level of text, rather than using the living breathing examples in front or her, was perhaps a strategy to get the group to take another look at racism—to temporarily make participants feel more comfortable by not focusing the discussion on them as individuals (which would contradict the earlier call for "I" statements). However, the list of terms was never linked back to the comments that had previously been made by the in-service participants about whiteness, nor was it linked to the socially sanctioned and institutional practices in Changeton's schools and other public agencies.[6]

If comfort were a strategy for keeping everyone open-minded and listening at the in-service, then the members of the CSC should have at least challenged each other's (and their colleagues') assumptions and statements once the group was back at the Central Office debriefing the workshops. In support of what they had just experienced with Globe of Human Differences, and avoiding confrontation altogether, Jake exclaimed, "We recognized that we do have a problem and not to simply place blame. There are things that you have to be aware of, that came out in the exercises." Consistent with this theme of blame, Fred brought up the issue of white-male bashing, pointing out that "many people don't support multiculturalism because they feel that it's against white males and females. . . . Their concern is that we should not shift the blame from one group to another." He also informed the group that some people were upset because they felt that the Europeans were not mentioned at all during the workshop. As denial was

154 | *The Work of the Multicultural Central Steering Committee*

prevalent among the committee members, there would be no discussion about the continued effects of white supremacy.

Denial may have very well been what informed the CSC's eventual acceptance of James Steele. At the end of the third year of their work, the committee wanted to know if Steele could come back and offer a professional development training session for teachers. However, it wasn't clear if they wanted him to return to Changeton because he was black, because he pushed the level of critical multicultural theory beyond what the previous in-service facilitators had done, or because the committee felt good that he wasn't pointing fingers at the white community. During his speech, the black speaker threw in the disclaimer, "I'm not blaming anyone for that [discrimination] today," arguing that people in present-day society "have inherited such conditions."

The willingness to embrace a culpritless world invoked a huge contradiction in the committee's logic: up until this point, it seemed as if the social institutions were functional, and once negative teacher attitudes were changed, schools would cater to all students. Suddenly it sounded like no one was to blame because people are the products of what they have inherited from history and institutions. The majority of the committee should work to recognize the fact that dialectically people breath life into existing institutions and socially sanctioned practices, which in turn breath life into people. Insisting that there is no one to blame risks shifting the power of human agency to historical determinism. In this uncritical sense, people become objects of history (passive recipients) and not subjects (shapers) capable of engaging and transforming both themselves and the world around them (Freire, 1970).

Comfort zones also allow people to blame the victims for their own predicaments. At this same in-service, there were statements that could be misinterpreted, if unelaborated, as arguing the cultural and/or genetic inferiority of racially subordinated students. For example, a white woman shared the story that she and some of her colleagues had done a statistical analysis which revealed that "students of color had the lower grades." If this observation were suggesting that the tools for assessment and classroom curricula and pedagogy need to be scrutinized for any discriminatory practices, that's a step in the right direction. On the other hand, if the person is using this "research finding" to justify why racially subordinated students are tracked down, thus excusing himself or herself, or the institution, from any responsibility therein, then the only viable alternative for explaining such a pattern of failure (or lack of intelligence) is cultural deprivation and/or genetics. Antonia Darder (1991) adds, "Further, this view supports an assimilation bias held by the majority of teachers that fails to perceive the racism inherent in consistently judging and comparing bicultural students' success to that of students from the dominant culture, and in expecting bicultural students to incorporate dominant cultural values as their own" (p. 39).

The white woman who made this problematic statement about research and lower grades also exclaimed, "Why is it racism if students' expectations are that they are supposed to do poorly?" Never questioning the internalization of oppression through the preponderance of negative representations, stigma, and mistreatment (which can lead to learned helplessness or oppositional behavior), this comment served the purpose of taking any responsibility away from society or the teacher, blaming the victim for her or his predicament. It was unclear why Kara had brought up the issue of internalization in the presession for the in-service when she stated, "Some of this is the internalization of negative stereotypes . . . ," but not here. (Steele does bring up this issue further down the road.)

Blaming the victim was also the potential message embedded in Kara and Carl's statements to the in-service participants, made after the defensive remarks (with tones of reverse discrimination) of a white woman who exclaimed, "I have a student who thinks that I gave him a bad grade because he is black!"

————

KARA   I can't deal with the fact that people will say that being black is an excuse—that's a cop-out, people hide behind it.

CARL   Kids know that they've got you, they say that you are a racist.

————

While confronting someone who is unjustifiably pulling the race card is crucial, having two black people make these statements to a predominantly white audience is extremely dangerous. Without carefully and deeply situating the discussion within the realities of discrimination, the two speakers risk the possibility of reducing all incidents of racism to racially subordinated peoples' excuses and acts of manipulation. Their comments feed into the mentality of the white teacher at the in-service who defined the social sciences as, "people who are in the profession for making excuses for other people's behavior." Not only is this a callous accusation of guilt cast toward the victim, it is also an outright rejection of social theory: in some existential twist, it assumes that people are all individually responsible for their actions and that researchers shouldn't be "making excuses" (that is, theories of explanation of events) for everyone.

After the professional development in-services, most committee members felt that the workshops were "nonthreatening," "comfortable," "inclusive," and "built on our sensitivity and camaraderie." Perhaps the participants were comfortable because of the tendency to avoid the real, difficult issues and tensions among the group, as well as those in the schools, city, state, nation, and world. It would surely have been different if, as one white man, addressing the two facilitators after the separation exercise, inquired, "What would happen if you asked who is racist and who isn't?"

The argument could be made that comfort can be strategically used in order to maintain participant attention—keeping the defensive fists down and minds open to the material being covered. However, if professional development doesn't at some point guide the group into what is disconcerting, uncertain, and dark, the obvious consequence will be that oppressive identities and practices will remain unchallenged. For example, by disregarding the source of racism in this country, and denying the realities of white supremacy, race relations disappear from the discussion altogether, and whiteness becomes invisible and evasive.

Color-Blindness

Whiteness has played a significant role in shaping ethnic patterns, social identities, and institutions in the United States. However, whiteness has paradoxically been able to mask itself as a category—it is simultaneously "everything and nothing" (Dyer, 1988). The underlying evasive ideology that informs the social construction of whiteness is strategically infused such that those who for whatever reason buy into its logic are unable, or simply unwilling, to see and thus name its oppressive nature.

By not recognizing whiteness as a racial identity, most whites see themselves as race free and less ethnic than "others," and consequently take for granted the privileges they secure by such an ideologically charged racial marker (MacCannel, 1992). Francis FitzGerald's (1986) data reveals that white, upper-middle-class professionals don't identify themselves as "ethnic, cultural, or powerful" (p. 218). Ruth Frankenburg's research (1993), which consisted of interviews with white women, showed that whiteness is "difficult for white people to name . . . those that are securely housed within its borders usually do not examine it" (pp. 228–29).

Limited to a multicultural discourse of relativism, sensitivity, affirmation, and comfort, it's no wonder members of the CSC embraced such ideas as "unity and common purpose," "working with teachers to help them view everyone as innately equal," "the concept of oneness," "we are all the same under the skin," and "not pigeonholing them [racially subordinated students] as black or brown." The CSC also celebrated the fact that the high school was selling T-shirts that said, "Be Color-Blind." Although such efforts are meant with the best intentions, not naming and working with the ideological markers of difference across race, class, gender, sexuality, and so forth, can have detrimental results. As argued in Chapter One, educators can't value "all" students if they deny any engagement with their diverse life experiences that are the very products of those socially constructed categories. Because of the fact that the process of racialization begins at such an early age, by no means should experiences be denied or artificially homogenized in the name of equal treatment.[7] Educators shouldn't hide behind what appears to be an objective and just way of dealing with all students—the idea that "I value all people as human beings"—if they truly hope to work toward significant social change.

What is ironic is that in the very article that the in-service participants were required to read twice, the author Peggy McIntosh (1990) asserts, "I think that whites are carefully taught not to recognize white privilege. . . . My schooling gave me no training in seeing myself as an oppressor, as an unfairly advantaged person, or as a participant in a damaged culture" (p. 31). This social construction of not seeing, or complicity through denial, is embodied in the laughter of the two white women at the all-faculty in-service who commented to each other in response to the obvious implications of the *Browns Eyes, Blue Eyes* video: "It doesn't carry over, we don't see that. . . . It's not racial, they like you or they don't." Such attitudes completely disregard the realities of discrimination as expressed by the youths in Chapter Three:

ROLAND If you black, the attitude is, "You dumb." . . .

OLAVO They treat you different, man. I had like three classes where I was the only nigga in the room. The teacher used to teach everybody in the class but me. I used to call her, "Can you explain this to me?" She used to like ignore me.

Any depoliticized and ahistorical approaches to multicultural education can provide window-dressing-type reforms, but simply acknowledging peoples' differences, or avoiding them altogether in a color-blind approach, will not lead to an eradication of the abusive ideological and structural patterns of schools and society in the United States. If real substantive change in going to take place, then systems of domination and their invisible dimensions need to be marked and eradicated.

The long-term goal of any political project should be to achieve a world in which biological features such as color, gender, and sexual orientation have no negative social significance or unethical meaning. However, such an immediate transition is impossible in that these categories play a major role in the production of social identities, interactions, and experience in the United States.

Encouraging Ongoing Reflection and Action

The Central Steering Committee members worked diligently to conceptualize and implement professional development in-services as they themselves assumed that they were prepared to "culturally sensitize" others. For example, Maria, when asked if she wanted to participate in a workshop stated, "I don't need to go to these meetings, maybe some of the others do, but I don't." This confident sense of political awareness was also the case when Carl, after he informed the group that a local anti-violence organization was holding a meeting, said that the CSC should attend in order to "volunteer our expertise." Along these same lines, while debriefing one of their in-services, some members argued that the workshop "was a good start for newcomers, but for people who had already dealt deeply with these issues, it was a let down"; "it was intended for the inexperienced."

There was recognition among the Central Steering Committee that the rest of the Changeton school system needed help—"They may not know the depth of the problem. . . . Teachers in Changeton have no idea what baggage these kids are bringing to school." However, the committee itself never really asked about "the baggage" that its participants were bringing to school, or to the infusion of multicultural education.[8]

There appeared to be a de facto acceptance among the CSC members that an individual's subject position (for example, one's race, gender, experience as a teacher) predisposes him or her to theoretical awareness. Carl, during an interview, referred to Jake as "Mr. Black Changeton." Within this depoliticized stance, skin color, for example, somehow implied multicultural education, that is, multicultural education exists by virtue of the presence of diverse people. However, as Christine Sleeter (1993) states: "Some teachers of color who have successfully entered the middle class accept much about the social class structure that ought to be questioned. Further, there are bodies of content knowledge and pedagogical practice that teachers of color often find very useful but do not simply know without being taught" (p. 169).

The two black male members shaped a great deal of the direction of the CSC. In fact, there was a good deal of neglect in engaging and confronting these men's assumptions (with the exception of Melissa). In part, this was a result of a lack of overall political awareness on the group's part, on gender, and on the trap of political correctness in which whites (the majority of the CSC) hesitated to engage/contest the assumptions of the people that they are ostensibly trying to support in the infusion of multiculturalism. The point here is not to solely blame certain individuals for the committee's shortcomings and depoliticized positions on multicultural issues. It is simply to question whether or not at times the group members were able to justify some of their own discriminatory practices by standing behind the voice(s) of a non-white person.

Ideologically, the committee members didn't support just any racially subordinated voice, otherwise the CSC would have seriously considered the insight in Luis's words. However, within race relations in the United States, the hierarchy based on whiteness has also historically created skin tone tensions among racially subordinated groups. Lighter-skinned blacks and Latino/as, within the dominant paradigm have often been given more prestige. Because of the tensions caused by such differentiation, darker-skinned people may not consider those individuals with lighter skin with the same kind of solidarity. Caught in the racialized trap— in the struggle over identity and respect—it's common to hear, as a sign of indigence, that "Chincano/as or Asians are the next best thing to being white!" This ideology is perhaps reversed in a model based on political correctness. In other words, Luis, as a light-skinned Latino junior faculty, is perceived as less legitimate when juxtaposed to blackness.

Luis's thick Puerto Rican accent could have also played a role in his virtual silencing. Linguicism—discrimination by language, especially racialized languages in the United States—is very common. This is illustrated in the children on the playground who used "bilingual" as a swear word. It was also clear in the experiences of the youths in Chapter Three—"Why don't you speak English!" (linguicism will also be evident in Chapter Ten).

Another basic example of the need for ongoing professional development for the members of the CSC can be seen after the in-service in which it was clearly revealed that stereotypes are always negative, a burden, and objectifying. Back at the Central office, Eva expressed concern about whether or not "these sensitized people [in-service participants] will be able to help people during faculty meetings— what took us six hours?" The CSC felt that the best way to help school-based committees was to continue to provide support and materials. Raul commented that more people needed to be brought in—"Asians are role models for all of us, even white kids."

Perhaps unaware of the implications of his statement, Raul's comment risked feeding into the perpetuation of a new form of racism embedded in model-minority stereotypes. These stereotypes depict the youth of the multifarious populations that fall under the gross generalization "Asian" (or more pejoratively, "Oriental") as predisposed to be academically successful, especially as "science and math whiz-kids." These essentializing images not only monolithically bunch together the enormous complexity of the peoples/cultures that fall into this category, but they also misrepresent the history of exploitation of Asians in the United States. In addition, such representations strategically function to disregard the harsh realities of "the other side of the Asian-American success story" (Walker-Mofatt, 1995), that is, they ignore the great many Hmong, Laotions, Cambodians, Filipinos, and Pacific Islanders, among others, who actually live in abject poverty, readily experience social injustice, and find refuge in youth gangs.

The preponderance of these exaggerated positive images simply serves to perpetuate intergroup antagonistic relations (for example, one of the messages being, "Why can't you blacks and Latino/as be like them—so hard working with such good family values?") and acts as a justification for cutting federal support for those in need. As Wendy Walker-Moffat (1995) states, "It is in the vested interests of those who want to avoid the costs of educational reform to maintain the "success" of Asian Americans as evidence that ethnic minorities can succeed in existing schools without Affirmative Action, in-service teacher education, or special program support" (p. 5). Raul risks feeding into this ideological manipulation. Hopefully, continued professional development will help eliminate such representational risks.

As location does not predispose critical consciousness, Critical Multicultural Education invites everyone to further explore the relationship among their own identities and individual experiences—and society's larger historic, economic, and ideological constructs—and their inextricable connection to power. Part of this awareness for the Central Steering Committee presupposes an examination of social class, sexuality, and cultural resistance in the United States.

Addressing Social Class

The significance of social class emerged early on in the Multicultural Central Steering Committee's work. The issue arose during the drafting of the Mission Statement—"We treat poor kids poorly, what about them?" and "Sensitivity should not be limited to racial and ethnic differences alone, but should include gender, physical and mental challenges, and socioeconomic differences." It also came up in the preparation for the first in-service: "We had a workshop that really made the participants feel class conscious. . . . The people from Borton in their Brooks Brothers suits were embarrassed." In the first small in-service, when asked to separate themselves by social class, many individuals agreed that it made them feel uncomfortable. Steele also commented about how society is stratified "by color, class, and cast." However, the CSC needs to develop a deeper theoretical understanding as to how socioeconomic status (beyond the mere quantity of money a person possesses) in part shapes the values, beliefs, worldviews, discourse styles, social relations, and actions of people.

The first in-service facilitator, Sandy Burr, included in his speech the history of exploitation of the poor in Changeton. But, his contributions were considered by the CSC to be "a bomb." In the CSC's debriefing of that day, Carl stated, "Bur was atrocious—he was only going to speak for ten minutes. He talked more about the blue-collar stuff, and not about different populations—total irrelevance!" Capitalism and socioeconomic status should be considered significant issues when dealing with raising consciousness about multiculturalism. The committee needs to engage the interpenetrating relationship among power, economic resources, and social control, as well as how schools function as major socializing influences in preparing students for their place in a hierarchically divided labor force (Anyon, 1980; Apple, 1990; Bourdieu & Passeron, 1977; Bowles & Gintis, 1976; Giroux, 1983). In this way, the members will develop a clear understanding of the historical materialism that has in large part shaped the city's past, as well as the ways in which class warfare has been used to incite racism and other forms of oppression (Allen, 1994; DuBois, 1935; Feagn & Vera, 1995; Goldfield, 1992; Roediger, 1991). Understanding the diversion of the poor and working-class whites away from issues of racism and solidarity, Roland, a young black man from Chapter Three, stated, "As long as there's niggas, there's always gonna be poor white trash."

Throughout the three years, there was no mention of the fact that the affluent, white minority in Changeton run the schools (as they have historically controlled the city), and that many of the faculty and administrators don't actually live in the predominantly blue-collar community. In addition, there needs to be a discussion of how the CSC members' own social-class lenses shape the ways in which they see their students (and vice versa), the kinds of expectations that they have of them, and the ways in which they have been approaching the entire debate over multiculturalism. The youths in Chapter Three recognized the problem of social class and education:

STEVIE   You know what I notice, Pepi, I noticed when I used to go to school, if the teachers knew you came from a nice like middle-class neighborhood, they'd treat you good. They give you special attention. But if they knew you came from the projects or somethin. . . .

CARLOS   If you come from a bad neighborhood they make sure you never make it.

STEVIE   They think that you are a troublemaker.

DION   Automatically, automatically!

The neglect of issues of class and capitalism (and the interconnecting relations with race) is disconcerting given that in the year in which the committee got its start, the average household income was extremely low, and locally there were 13,000 people living in poverty (Information Publications, 1994).

Revisiting Sexual Orientation

As was foreshadowed in Chapter Five, indifference toward sexual politics (which should be interpreted as a form of heterosexism and homophobia) would resurface in the CSC's work. During the discussion of role models at the Globe of Human Differences in-service, a white woman noted the need for gay and lesbian representation. The group began to talk about the West Nobel Parade and the controversy over whether or not gays and lesbians should be allowed to march. A white woman, of Irish descent, described the event as "a parade to celebrate Irish history." She claimed that because "they insisted upon participating, now everyone is hurt because there is no parade at all" (another example of the binarism of "us" and "them"). Instead of using this particular pedagogical moment to discuss heterosexism (a word on the definition list in the literature from Globe of Human Differences), the facilitator cut this conversation short in the name of time. The brief controversy over the West Nobel Parade was never again mentioned in the CSC's discussions.

Another egregious example of this neglect manifested during the registration process for an in-service being provided by the Center for Training and Health Education. Not a single member of the committee expressed the need to better inform themselves about the topic "Making Schools Safe for gay, lesbian, and Bisexual Youth." Instead, the CSC strategically eliminated any mention of the gay/lesbian section of the workshop advertisement when they went in search of public funds that would support their attendance of the first part of the conference. It thus comes as no surprise that the committee never actively, or even rhetorically, sought out the membership of an openly gay or lesbian person (or a disabled person for that matter), as they had done with the various racial groups.

There was a poster on the wall of the guidance office supporting the gay/lesbian organization—CRAGLY: Changeton Regional Alliance of Gay and Lesbian Youth. The poster explained that CRAGLY was "a safe non-exploitive youth group." It also provided a helpline phone number. As multicultural educators should develop an approach for honestly addressing sexuality and exploring the connections between sexual orientation and the cultural realities of everyday life, the CSC needs to forge an active coalition with such organizations. Future efforts shouldn't ignore the tangible reality of people like the young man that I interviewed, a student who had dropped out of Changeton High School, turned to drugs, and attempted suicide because of his public mistreatment for being gay.

Developing a Theory of Resistance

As defined in Chapter One, and witnessed in Chapter Three, resistance is a legitimate (though not always conscious) response to domination, used to help individuals or groups deal with oppressive social conditions and injustices (Austin & Willard, 1998; de Certeau, 1984; Hall & Jefferson, 1975; Scott, 1990; Willis, 1977). Such a concept could assist the CSC a great deal in understanding a number of the predicaments faced by educators in the everyday life of Changeton's classrooms, hallways, and streets. But the group was rarely encouraged to make linkages between student behavior and broader oppressive social practices and institutions. Perhaps the most striking example of the CSC's lack of political awareness, in terms of resistance theory, came when Maria cited the fact that "in the Behavior Adjustment Program, it's all boys and mostly minorities—especially black males." She asked James Steele, the last of the in-service facilitators, "Is this an issue of poor parenting skills or what? It's not an issue of racism! I'm the principal and I see that these kids can't control themselves. What are some ways to deal with this?"

This comment, from a non-white woman, who had previously stated that she was not in need of in-service workshops, not only risks blaming the victims for their predicament—"poor parenting skills or what"—but it does so with biological implications—"These kids can't control themselves." There needs to be a theoretical search to make sense of why these students, a majority of whom are poor and racially subordinated (and stigmatized for being in the Special Education, Bilingual Education, and Free Lunch Programs) are reacting the ways that they do. Consider the feelings of Carlos, Stevie, and Roberto about discrimination in local schools:

CARLOS They just let you hang out with a paper and a pencil. . . .

STEVIE Damn, teachers don't care, man. . . . I hate the Changeton public school system! Somebody oughta blow it up! The're a bunch of jerks. . . . They kinda make fun of you.

CARLOS I had teachers that were so prejudiced against Puerto Ricans and blacks, and I am both.

ROBERTO I once threw a chair at a teacher who was racist against me and I made the front page—we've all made the papers. . . .

CARLOS I jus see it as if teachers go out their way to make an ass out of you *(Dion chimes in with Carlos and together they say)*, you go out of your way to make an ass outta dem. . . .

Instead of making sense of these kinds of attitudes and/or behaviors, there is generally the desire by mainstream educators to "deal with this"—implying finding efficient ways to get this type of behavior (which is interpreted as deviance rather than resistance/opposition) to stop. This is why these students are so often referred to as "problem students," as articulated by the representative from the Racial Imbalance Committee.

Steele responded by attempting to make some critical connections between institutionalized racism and the present predicament that many people are facing in society and in schools. He stated that "400 years of slavery has had an impact on the consciousness of whites and people of color," and insisted that people, especially educators, "need to understand how we are related historically." He briefly presented the need to question dominant values in the United States, and made references to "internal rage," deficit-model orientation, internalized oppression, and stereotypes, thus raising some key theoretical issues that shape cultural politics.

To combat such destructive forces, Steele highlighted the importance of "the ecology of the school": the name of the building, what's on the walls, and treating diversity not just as a month here and there, but rather as a ongoing theme. However, there was still no explicit discussion of resistance theory as a possible answer to Maria's question about behavior. Instead, Steele presented a biological and cultural model that, in the end, also risked blaming the victim. He stated, "Motivation is both internal and external. For black male students, boredom is the greatest problem. They are more physical than whites. This is not taken into consideration in schools." Essentializing blackness, by relegating all black males to being more physical, Steele argued that instead of being supportive and rewarding, schools dealt with young black men in a containing and controlling fashion. The use of "physical" here is problematic in that the current stereotype of racially subordinated peoples, especially blacks and Latino/as, is that they are innately aggressive and violent.

Steele seemed to be working from an Afrocentric biocultural model that was very popular in the 1970s and 1980s. The basic logic is that blacks (more specifically West Africans) are not passive like whites.[9] He said that this issue of constraint was also a problem in the black community, where "mothers restrict their sons and support their daughters—minority families do this." Not realizing the fundamental contradictions in his logic, Steele's basic point was that "this destructive control by families" has to be dealt with, and that "acceptance" (not critical engagement) is what teachers need to work toward. In addition, he insisted that "for behavior adjustment, we need some clinical work with each individual child," because "there is high trauma among kids of color, a fact of prenatal care." Embodying a major contradiction, it seems that he had simultaneously bought into the dominant cultural deficit model of blacks and an ambiguous form of Afrocentrism.

The CSC should be encouraged to inquire into the history of the learner and the immediate context of youths in the Behavioral Adjustment Program in Changeton, and avoid objectifying and essentializing the students, that is, the racist idea that all blacks are the same. The committee should be encouraged to problematize the deficit/remediation model implicit in the name of the program itself—"Behavior Adjustment Program". Steele did recognize the problematic patterns in these programs in the fact that "it's all boys and mostly minorities—

especially black males." However, he should have responded to Maria's question by elaborating more intently and specifically on the connections between institutionalized racism and the present predicament that many people are facing in society and in schools. He should have made clear to the group in attendance that social identity (that is, how we are perceived and consequently treated by others) is what in part shapes resistant behavior—why they "turn outside rather than inside the system"—and not some mystical, essentialist connection to Africa that blacks in the United States, in fact, have never had. Take, for example, Roland's unwillingness to sit still:

> I was accused of a bomb scare that I didn't do. I was waiting in the principal's office for my advocate to show. I was jus sittin there waitin. After a while, I was like, I gotta go and I'm gonna go whether you say yes or no. Then she was like, "No wonder you have a fuckin tracker!" Well, she was like fat and ugly and everything, right, so I said, "It's no wonder you don't have a husband." She got pissed off and so I got suspended like my first week.

As Bonny Norton-Pierce (1993) argues, "We need a theory of social identity that integrates the learner and the learning context, and how relations of power in the social world affect social interaction between learners and teachers and among peers" (p. 7).

Resistance theory was also implicitly neglected in the following statement by Jake, who argued that the Globe of Human Differences' Name Game could be dangerous: "What about those kids who don't have a heritage to fall back on, blacks, for example? Some youngsters would feel embarrassed. 'Mommy, where did we come from?'" Educators need to work against a cultural deprivation interpretation of the African-American experience, which has been disseminated throughout this country since their enslavement. By not promoting the cultural importance of resistance to domination as a positive force, educators will be unable to celebrate the positive cultural realities of blacks in the United States. For example, African Americans, by reinventing the dominant communicative form of English into counter-discourses to fight white supremacy, were able to forge a culture of rebellion out of the oppressive nature of slavery and were thus able to work toward the political solidarity necessary for avoiding total domination. These new languages created the "space for alternative cultural production and alternative epistemologies—different ways of thinking and knowing that were crucial to creating counter-hegemonic world views" (hooks, 1994, p. 171). Educators must recognize this incredible history of resistance; a history that would be extremely insightful and motivational to black students who have been told time and time again that they have done nothing. If in fact schools were doing their jobs, then students wouldn't have to go home "and ask Mommy" because her participation and life story, as well as the long history of enslavement in this country, would already be a part of the school curriculum. These anecdotes and testimonies could then be linked to students' current experiences, predicaments, and active theorizing about the world around and within them.

The in-service discussion of whether or not multiculturalism provoked separatism among racial and ethnic communities also reveals the need for CSC members and school-based representatives to understand the dialectic of domination and resistance. The group overwhelmingly felt that balkanization of racial and ethnic groups in the United States was "a real danger." One white woman recommended reading Arthur Schlesinger's book *The Disuniting of America* for "its important insights" on this problem. This position on separatism runs the serious risk of falling into the conservative ideological trap that misinterprets and misrepresents efforts by subordinated groups to survive within the racial/cultural hierarchy in the United States. For example, linguistic minorities and racially subordinated peoples' attempts to combat oppression, resist the forces of domination, and transform the status quo through group solidarity are summarily dismissed as a form of cultural separatism/anti-Americanism. As Schlesinger (1991) wrongly asserts, "The cult of ethnicity exaggerates differences, intensifies resentments and antagonisms, drives ever deeper the awful wedges between races and nationalities. The end game is self-pity and self-ghettoization" (p. 29). It is made to appear that what is referred to as an unwillingness to join the mainstream, and not the imposed ghettoization of many groups by the dominant society (including schools, which are profoundly segregated), is the central reason for their poor living conditions. Historians and educators such as Schlesinger reduce the complexity of capitalist social relations, sexism, homophobia, and white supremacy to a simple response, "Why don't you just join us?" However, this superficial invitation is merely a victim-blaming mechanism that obfuscates the realities of discrimination and those responsible, consciously or not, for its perpetuation. While it can't be assumed that the CSC and the in-service's site-based committee participants had read Schlesinger's work, their position on separatism risks pointing in the same direction, as not a single person voiced a concern about imposed segregation.

Future Challenges

In their efforts to conceptualize and implement professional development for their colleagues, the Central Steering Committee members worked tirelessly to build a foundation on which multicultural education could become a fundamental part of the overall process of public schooling. The CSC should certainly continue with its noble job of introducing multicultural education—avoiding the paralysis of activists who can't move together until they've solved their ideological differences. However, they need to be openly honest, and insistent, about naming to the public (in hopes of a larger debate) the very content and detail of the discrepancies that are left on the table.

CHAPTER SEVEN

Curriculum Development
and Instruction

⌒

From the onset, the Multicultural Central Steering Committee was concerned with the nature of curricula used throughout the school system. The superintendent of the district, in an eloquent speech to the over nine hundred teachers and administrators at the first all-faculty in-service, insisted that "the celebration of the Chinese New Year and black history be continued and expanded upon," and that the schools should embrace difference by first discarding the melting pot metaphor—a reality that he argued was nonexistent. The superintendent also stressed that "Contributions from different groups benefit all students. The curriculum needs to be inclusive of different groups existing as their own entities." In addition, he addressed the need to "emphasize the darker side of history in the classroom: Indians, stereotypes, and slavery," and he encouraged people to participate in a May/June seminar on race superiority and prejudice at a local college. The superintendent also stressed the importance of embracing multiple perspectives, having children identify with their past, and the absolute necessity to prepare them "for their future roles in a democratic society."

At the close of the all-faculty in-service, the Central Steering Committee distributed a needs assessment to the participants. The topics of two of the questions related directly to the curriculum: the ways in which multicultural curricula provide a positive experience and ways in which curriculum development can be improved in this respect.

A volunteer subcommittee met before the next official CSC meeting in order to compile the survey data. Kevin noticed that "people want curricula, check out the research." The mountain of information collected made it impossible, within the time constraints, to synthesize the open-ended questions. However, after quickly scanning the pages, word was passed on to the larger committee that a great many of the responding teachers requested multicultural materials.

At the next CSC meeting, the group talked of the need to get access to, and duplicate, materials so that they could be shared throughout the school system. They also discussed how some members of the school community were already familiar with multicultural practices in the classroom and thus could help to get others involved. Jackie mentioned the existence of multicultural crayons that match the various human skin tones, and she recommended that they be purchased for the Art Department. There was also a reference made to various multicultural computer programs available at a nearby museum. Raul (who was in charge of a video committee for the Bilingual Education Program) informed the CSC that "there are seventy-five tapes available dealing with issues of diversity."

A general sentiment that ran throughout the committee's discussions was that special days, such as Cinco de Mayo, were not enough—that diversity should be present throughout the curriculum and that any approach to introducing multicultural materials "should be interdisciplinary." The committee deliberated and settled on two basic points: the CSC should "develop a resource library that promotes continued growth of multicultural values that is updated on a regular basis and available to all staff," and the committee should "assist in the review and development of school curricula appropriate for multicultural education, which may require the use of special consultants."

At the subsequent meeting, Raul initiated a discussion about classroom content and inclusion by stating that "the Eurocentric curriculum in Changeton has left out many people: Chinese, Chicanos, and blacks; it is as if they have contributed nothing." He added, "Teaching a Eurocentric curriculum when such a large percent of the population is not Euro is ridiculous—it is not important to them! We need something that is going to build self-esteem." Jackie added that people receive different kinds of education around the world and maintain very different concepts of schooling. She felt that it was extremely important that educators "draw out of people, not just put information in them. . . . We need to draw out of everyone—teachers and students, by identifying their location . . . who they are."

As the CSC was in the midst of struggle to define multicultural education, as well as its own philosophy therein, the members voted to distribute a questionnaire amongst the group in order to solicit individual perspectives on more detailed goals around the issue of curriculum and instruction. Insights and concerns raised from this survey consisted of having "learning experiences throughout students' school careers that reflect positive portrayals of and attitudes toward all people," and "to provide the conditions for all children to feel better about themselves and to reach their educational and vocational potential."

The CSC wanted to review the existing curricula for biases "keeping the concept of oneness in mind." Some members felt that the "ethics and values in the K-12 curriculum should be reviewed, modified, and added to." There was also mention of disseminating "information about instructional methods that are effective with diverse groups of students" and providing "workshops on participatory learning; for example, cooperative learning activities, and critical, emancipatory, liberatory educational methods and strategies." One respondent stated that instructional methods are "best left to the individual teacher."

At the May 12 session, members of the CSC distributed and discussed a recent article from the local newspaper entitled "Talks Seen as Bridge to Racial Understanding." The committee was inspired by the public debate over multiculturalism that had just taken place during the town meeting. The article spoke of one white parent, who asked, "Why should such a heavy emphasis be placed on black history?" A youth worker from a local community-based organization immediately responded:

> You can't keep perpetrating a fraud. Current history textbooks depict blacks only as slaves and ignore their accomplishments, such as founding colleges and making medical breakthroughs. Children of all ages are left with the impression that blacks were slaves, from slaves we went on welfare, and we have never made a contribution. The books have to change. My generation grew up learning to suck up to racism and was erred by telling its children that racism was a thing of the past.

The CSC agreed that "the content of the curriculum would make a big difference." Don exclaimed, "When Mexicans learn that they were responsible for many things, it will raise their self-esteem." Raul added, "I don't think that we are conscious of the European overdose in schools to a population that gets the feeling that they've contributed nothing. . . . The Chinese have had a sophisticated culture for thousands of years and we know very little about it."

Overall, the committee's concerns centered on including other voices and experiences in the classroom content. Sara proposed having an activity in which kids create scenarios where people who have experienced discrimination act out what it is like to be alienated. She argued that this type of project "gets right down to the human level." She also thought that it would be helpful for the students "to create a kit that reveals their cultural background . . . and give the staff time to look through it." Melissa talked of a "world or global approach to education, which includes the West," but she argued that "Western legionaries want to separate the two."

By the end of June, the Central Steering Committee had conceptualized, debated, voted, drafted, and released a document entitled "The Multicultural

Committee: Structures, Goals, and Timelines." Included in this statement were considerations for curriculum and instruction:

- Establish a multicultural resource center/library.
- Interface the Multicultural Central Steering Committee with the school system's City-wide Curriculum Committee on all activities and recommendations.
- Assist in the review and development of school curriculum appropriate for multicultural education.
- Create a baseline inventory of courses, units, texts, materials, and activities across all disciplines, schools, and grades that reflect a multicultural approach; to be updated annually.
- Use the baseline to identify gaps and areas of weakness, and work with appropriate administrators to address these issues.
- Collect and disseminate information about instructional methods that are effective with diverse groups.
- Recommend staff training activities and resources for instructional strategies like cooperative learning.

The committee anticipated having all of these elements in place by the fall semester. Faced with this awesome task, the CSC worked to conceptualize a Curriculum and Instruction Subcommittee that would take the responsibility for dealing with these areas.

At the July meeting, the CSC agreed that they should tap any and all available resources: film libraries, public schools and their various departments, a new multicultural bookstore in the city, and organizations such as Art Reach, the Bureau of Equity and Language Services of the Fanton State Department of Education, and a local anti-violence group. Some members requested slide shows about Puerto Rico and countries represented in their schools. Giselle made the suggestion that the high school's Social Studies Department put together a history book on Changeton and its cultures. In addition, she thought that graffiti should be recognized as "a mosaic of multicultural achievement."

In preparation for the September in-service, it was agreed that developing and providing curricular strategies for teachers, "especially those who are on the fence," was extremely important. June demanded that the in-service provide practical materials: "I don't just want talk. When all is said and done, more is said than done. I want concrete tools that can be taken back." Kevin felt strongly that, before the actual in-service, the CSC "go around and check what curricular changes are being made in Changeton schools." In agreement, Don added, "Before we go out as a missionary, we need to know what is already in place." The group decided to draft a questionnaire, "The Multicultural Survey," in order to research what schools had actually been doing up to that point.

Having collected and synthesized this new data, the CSC, at their first small in-service, provided a display of all the activities that the schools in Changeton had been participating in. This list was also reproduced in a spiral-bound book that was distributed to all the workshop participants. The following is a sample, from each educational level, of schools that were participating the most in the infusion process:

Appleton Elementary School

- bilingual and regular education for grade three were integrated to study Puerto Rican geography, history, art, music, customs, food, and literature
- students made passports that highlighted the countries where children were born, this was integrated into writing and language arts classes
- a unit was developed and taught on the continent of Africa, El Salvador, Guatemala, China, Eskimos, and Native Americans—geography, languages, cultures, art, music, life styles, and foods were discussed
- celebrated holidays around the world
- had a sale of multicultural books
- planned a multicultural celebration
- a unit taught called "We Are All Alike, We Are All Different"
- displayed map of the world labeling the origins of the children
- the owner of the local multicultural bookstore came and read to the children
- celebrated Chinese New Year
- a vision statement for the school states as one of its goals to celebrate multiculturalism and diversity
- had Japanese Doll Day

Swell Junior High

- posters celebrating multiculturalism displayed in every classroom and throughout the building
- showcases hold displays celebrating multiculturalism
- the diversity of the cultures of the student population is shown through photographs displayed throughout the school
- a thematic unit, "We Are the Same under the Skin," to be developed

Changeton High School

- minority literature class offered to seniors
- a new curriculum offered emphasizing a multicultural perspective on literature
- the Social Studies Department in-service featured the following programs and videos: *Facing Our Nation and Ourselves, Inclusion and Racism,* and *Eye of the Storm*
- units celebrating Black History Month and Women's History Month taught
- a guest speaker spoke about the contributions of black female writers to American history
- the Tuskegee Airmen were guest speakers
- a Harvard University, black psychologist spoke to staff

- a guest speaker spoke to the staff concerning the role of teachers and administrators in schools that have changing demographics—a tape was made and shown to selected students
- 500 students took a field trip to view the movie *Malcolm X*
- Project My Turn held a food festival
- Chinese New Year celebrated
- committee established to address the *hows* of celebrating multiculturalism
- African American club reestablished
- multicultural food program and cookbook produced in the Home Economics Department
- field trip to John Hancock Hall to participate in a Spanish cultural program
- students visited a Spanish restaurant
- Language Week celebrated, morning announcements done in different languages
- *Eyes on the Prize* shown
- tapes entitled "Destinos" are being used in conjunction with the Spanish classes
- twelve foreign exchange students from Spain at a local high school join our Spanish language students in after-school activities
- college field trips for Cape Verdean, Haitian, Asian, and other students
- some colleges have visited Changeton High School to speak specifically to linguistic-minority students.

Regardless of these lists of activities, the actual in-service dealt primarily with sensitizing the group to issues of diversity. As a result, none of these practical applications were discussed among the participants. While the workshop was generally seen as a success in terms of raising cultural awareness among faculty, it fell short in the eyes of many of the CSC members in providing hands-on classroom activities. Kevin wanted "more how-to, nuts and bolts, rather than theory." Fred commented, "I walked away with very little for my staff."

Preparing for the Second In-Service

The Multicultural Central Steering Committee prepared somewhat differently for its next multicultural faculty in-service. Brainstorming with the workshop facilitator from Globe of Human Differences, the CSC talked about the possibility of having different display areas. Carl made the point, "What teachers hear doesn't beat when they see a room full of materials." Don stated, "After the central needs of schools are identified, then it's our job to scramble around and find out what's available." In response to this idea, and in reference to the earlier discussions of multicultural fairs and material exhibits, Eva voiced the concern that while they could very easily present commercial materials at the in-service (including those provided by GHD), they were encouraging false hopes because the CSC would not be able to afford to make such purchases—"We are tantalizing them with what we cannot afford." Kara understood this predicament and encouraged the committee to put the call out to teachers to invite them to bring their own knowledge and materials with them to share with the others.

Wanting to address some more difficult issues, Giselle asked, "Boys are throwing condoms at the girls, how do we deal with such disrespect?" Kevin wondered, "What about people that use bad names to describe their own group? . . . When you try to stop them from using such derogatory remarks, they say, 'You can't tell me what to do, it's my group.'" Kevin added, "Do you see how insidious this is, if a black calls another black a nigger then a white sees it as okay!" Carl exclaimed, "Look at TV rap programs, what we are doing to each other is awful. . . . What we are fighting against, the media is doing the opposite!" Kara took on Kevin's comments by arguing that "some of this is the internalization of negative stereotypes." She summed up by stating that "unacceptable behavior is unacceptable." Carl agreed and insisted that there be "a single standard for all students."

The discussion turned to sharing materials, strategies, and knowledge, and then to the concern of where to house these and any other multicultural resources. A few members of the committee offered their schools as possible locations. It was first suggested that the Bilingual Office be the resource center. However, Carl was worried that "people may avoid this spot." He immediately retracted this statement by saying that housing the resource center there "would take away the stigma of what Bilingual Education really is—it's not just Puerto Ricans." Fred, recalling the school system's earlier attempts at desegregation, suggested hiring a full-time multicultural specialist to run a center—"kind of like Jackie Robinson's old job."[1] While some participants supported the idea, others preferred a "committee" rather than an "individual coordinator." Eva intervened, declaring that finding such a home would be the job of the Curriculum and Instruction Subcommittee.

Curriculum Concerns at the March In-Service

At the next in-service, the Globe of Human Differences facilitators discussed possibilities for "affirming diversity in the classroom curriculum." For example, they mentioned the use of family trees and world maps. The basic premise was that students really need to learn about each other and that identity to children is extremely important. Carl suggested, "Ask the students, let them teach us." The participants (again, the CSC and two members from each site-based subcommittee) came up with the following practical ideas and strategies, many of which echoed the long lists of multicultural ideas provided at the previous gathering: "there should be school/classroom recognition of all ethnic groups; have a daily greeting over the school P.A. in various languages; develop cultural fairs, multicultural storytelling sessions, plays, and concerts; include ethnic art, food, and dance"; and "have teachers meet together across departments to form ideas for the curriculum."

At the close of the in-service, Globe of Human Differences offered the CSC a thirty-five dollar curriculum study guide called "Educating for Tolerance." Eva purchased a couple of copies for the Central Steering Committee to examine.

At the next committee meeting, Eva informed the group that the materials from Globe of Human Differences would cost about a thousand dollars for the entire Changeton school system. While money was always an issue (taking what they could from the Racial Imbalance Plan Funds and from organizations interested in fighting violence and discrimination in their local community), the CSC was aware of the fact that there was pressure from schools to get hands-on materials. Juan declared, "It's time to get to the classroom, to show that everything is not centered around white people." Contemplating pedagogical approaches, Raul alluded to the importance of embracing multiple perspectives:

> Teaching about Vietnam, the Vietnamese will have a very different story. The white kids would respect the others more if they knew more about them, and at the same time, the others would feel part of the exclusive fraternity that invented and discovered.

Carl added:

> There is a lot of ignorance about multicultural education, about who's getting excluded. We all know that it's [the curriculum] Eurocentric. We have historically been excluded. Where are the black and Latino cowboys? How much would that do for the esteem of black kids—the history of the cattle movement. Cowboys are everyone's heroes—buffalo soldiers. The other kids feel excluded, as if they have done nothing. Whoever writes the history writes it in the way they want.

Keeping with the CSC's earlier commitment to solicit, review, coordinate, and summarize the voluminous multicultural materials that were being implemented across all grade levels, schools were again surveyed to see what exactly they were doing to extend their efforts to infuse multiculturalism. The Central Steering Committee set a specific date and waited to receive the data. In the meantime, members were finally selected for the Curriculum and Instruction Subcommittee.

Curriculum and Instruction Subcommittee Is Mobilized

The subcommittee met for the first time in April of 1994. After some discussion of the Curriculum and Instruction Subcommittee's purpose, Melissa presented the group with a piece of literature from a nearby school system, entitled "Goals and Objectives: Character Education." Respect and responsibility were the central values stressed in this document. Melissa expressed that they had a theme that Changeton could and should evaluate and build on. Contesting the idea of universal values, Luis argued, "We need to incorporate values in our classrooms . . . but, if we want inclusion, how do we include everyone's values? We need to hear from the community and not just the committees. Let's make sure it's inclusive." Without engaging the issues of "whose values," it was agreed by the other subcommittee members that emphasis on the "two major universal moral values" of respect and responsibility would be excellent to introduce to Changeton teachers and their classrooms.

Some members of the Curriculum and Instruction Subcommittee suggested compiling resource lists in order to inform teachers systemwide about bulletin board ideas, speakers, videos, biographies of teachers, recent library purchases in the various schools, and so forth. Interested in writing proposals to obtain the necessary funds to be able to purchase materials, Don made the point that when searching for resources the CSC should look beyond what was labeled multicultural education, in that other organizations such as the Health Department were doing important work that applied. It was unanimously agreed that any listings of resources would have to be cross-referenced by grade levels and cultures, and that there should also be emphasis on an interdisciplinary approach to multicultural education. As a central goal, this working committee felt strongly that in order "to assist teachers in becoming aware of the predominant cultures in Changeton, staff development training should be offered that focuses on learning about and understanding the social, cultural, political, religious, and economic aspects of Changeton's largest immigrant populations: Cape Verdean, Hispanic, Haitian, and Asian."

When the CSC reconvened, the Curriculum and Instruction Subcommittee presented some of the issues that the participants had discussed during their recent meeting. Carl began the post-presentation discussion, asserting that "black history is the same for Cape Verdeans, Haitians, and African Americans. We all came along the same pipeline where this is now our national heritage. I want something in the curriculum guide to include this when talking about world history. We also need to include everyone!" Melissa responded, "You have to look at history more than simply black and white. . . . Your statement is broad and dangerous—Africa is not all black!" Carl agreed, but he insisted that general knowledge of the diaspora of African people around the world be recognized. In response to the idea of "including everyone," Melissa retorted, "We can't include everyone. What do students need to know? We are trying to find common points, but Eurocentrism is not it!" A suggestion was made for the CSC to visit those Changeton schools (and their site-based multicultural committees) that were considered to be doing a great deal in terms of infusing multicultural education. As a result, the next CSC meeting was scheduled to meet at the Parson School.

The Parson School was an old, classic building, and a number of the CSC members had either taught or been educated there. Upon entering the school, flags were everywhere and there were showcase booths that represented different countries: Haiti, Cape Verde, Laos, among others. One teacher handed out sugarcane, and others told stories about how it is produced. There was a "Save Our Planet" display on the wall with different animals, as well as an anti-drug poster with the logo, "Pulling Your Strings." Almost every inch of the school's walls was covered with global motifs, including a beautiful rain forest. Fred, the principal, told the CSC that Changeton Fights Back had helped fund the efforts and that the school was in the process of looking for other forms of support. He exclaimed, "Different grades are doing different cultures. We did the same thing last year, but it was rushed. This is a one-month multicultural program. There will be Asian dances and steel drums playing. The flags were purchased with grant money. Bring people from your schools to come and see!"

Even before the group visit, Carl was invited to the Parson School to be a spokesperson on the history and culture of Cape Verde. He revealed to the committee, "Students knew the folk tales, and I was going to show them places on the maps, but they already knew them too. They taught me. Kids were excited to share what they knew about their cultures. I came to give and I received more than I ever could have given." Rhonda, a new CSC member from the Dominican Republic, added that these multicultural efforts hadn't taken away from academic programs—"It is woven into the curriculum across science, math, writing, reading, and art." Fred confirmed that the Parson School teachers (guided by members of the site-based multicultural subcommittee) had developed this all on their own and that there was "no one way to do it, no road map." These types of efforts, the CSC agreed, should nonetheless be shared among Changeton schools. While not a recipe, they were considered important resources for inspiring other such curricular activities. The Central Steering Committee members all acquiesced to the importance of starting to infuse a positive model of multiculturalism at the elementary level and to teach young students to respect diversity. As Carl exclaimed, "This is where it begins!" Sam added that the Parson School "embodies our idea of a multicultural fair and we should recommend that a representative from each school come see this." Juan agreed, but explained that creating multicultural courses at the high school level was more difficult—"They stick to the curriculum, don't stress geography, and students don't learn much about other cultures." He suggested that "Social Studies should provide a course where students learn to share across cultures."

In the meantime, the data from the Multicultural Survey came pouring in. It was diligently compiled by a volunteer group and mailed to all members of the Central Steering Committee. Unfortunately the information was not substantially different from the original list of activities that had been circulated at the September in-service. Participants in the survey mentioned multicultural activities around literature, holiday celebrations, bulletin boards, posters and murals, music, fairs, and costumes. They also included lessons around what were ambiguously referred to as "the following cultures: African, Jewish, Cape Verdean, Chinese, black American, European, Mexican, Native American, Japanese, Puerto Rican, and Hispanic."

The faculty of the Physical Education Department, denying the inherently political nature of their work, stated that "activities are coeducational with no significance attached to color, race, sex, or national origin." In a similar fashion, the Mathematics Department, hiding behind the objectivity and neutrality that has been historically associated with this area of study, responded to the survey in the following way: "There have been no activities as those described in the CSC memo which have been initiated by members of the Changeton Mathematics Department."

The Central Steering Committee discussed the implications of this new list of multicultural activities. The main concern was not the uncritical nature of these efforts, but rather that the enumeration did not capture all of the multicultural work that was taking place. "My school is doing more than this!" was a common response. Because of the "incompleteness" of the data, the committee debated whether or not to distribute the information district-wide, eventually deciding not to.

Back from Summer Break

In September, when the Central Steering Committee met again, there was a feeling that the momentum of the previous school year had been broken—"It seems so far away, we need subcommittee update reports." The CSC discussed the idea of each school making a large map to show where all the parents in the school were from. The group also talked about holding a multicultural logo contest that would represent the entire school system's celebration of diversity. The Curriculum and Instruction Subcommittee stated that it was in the process of working with the Social Studies Committee. Eva pointed out that "in terms of the curriculum, the Social Studies Committee, which has different goals than ours, nonetheless has a subcommittee whose goal is to do some of what we have talked about. They hope to come out with a system-wide document." CSC members wanted to know if they could see the curriculum guide developed by the Social Studies Department before it went into print. Melissa informed them, "We [the multicultural committee] have no authority to do that."

The last substantial reference to curricula came at the end of the third year when James Steele gave his first professional development talk in Changeton. He spoke of the deficit model that racially diverse people are subjected to:

> We have inherited a mind-set that color is a cultural and intellectual deficiency. The TV shows this, the stereotypical roles blacks play as secondary to whites. Blacks have also internalized a great deal of this—it's even in our folklore. In schools, the curriculum doesn't take this into account—look at the Dick and Jane texts. This creates in the minds a sense of inferiority and inadequacy.

While looking to find time to contemplate Steele's insights, the Curriculum and Instruction Subcommittee was having internal problems. Members had been unable to continue participating or had joined other committees. They also needed a chairperson since theirs had resigned. This type of turmoil was not uncommon at this stage in the Central Steering Committee's growth. For the entire third year of the study, efforts at expanding curriculum and instruction were stagnant. By that time, the Central Steering Committee was preoccupied with diversifying the faculty and staff and the general sentiment was that the school-based multicultural committees were now more than prepared to deal with specific classroom issues.

Critical Interpretation and Discussion

> You will never make colonialism blush for shame by spreading out little known cultural treasures under its eyes. (Fanon, 1961, pp. 179–180)

The Multicultural Central Steering Committee worked extremely hard as they surveyed the needs of Changeton educators and assembled and distributed lists of the types of activities that local schools were enacting in order to affirm diversity. The CSC also scrambled to gather together community resources, and they struggled to develop a home for such materials, one that the group hoped would be updated on a regular basis and available to everyone. The committee wanted especially to boost interdepartmental diversification of the curriculum throughout the system. However, a few obstacles limited the possibilities for substantive curricular and pedagogical growth in Changeton Public Schools.

The Divorce of Theory from Practice

As argued in Chapter One, a major obstacle of critical transformative education in the United States is that theory is often devalued among educators and consequently disarticulated from the actual practice of teaching. This divorce of theory from practice is reflected in a great many mainstream multicultural education models that inspire a search for materials and methods, with little exploration of the conceptual framework or the sociohistorical and cultural realities that inform such practices. One of the major dichotomies that readily surfaced in the Central Steering Committee's work, eventually becoming an obvious point of contention, centered around personal awareness versus prioritizing practical materials. Some members commented on the importance of developing "our own self-consciousness before we go into the classroom"; others wanted more "how-tos."

Figuring either that theory was irrelevant or that the Human Relations approach to multiculturalism could remedy educational and social problems, the emphasis on classroom applications for the CSC became evident. Kevin insisted that "people want curricula, check out the research." Other members argued: "What teachers hear doesn't beat when they see a room full of materials"; "We need more how to nuts and bolts rather than theory!"; "I walked away with very little for my staff"; "We need curricular strategies for those people who are on the fence"; "I don't just want talk. . . . When all is said and done, more is said than done. . . . I want concrete tools that can be taken back!" Don stated, "After the central needs of schools are identified, then it's our job to scramble around and find out what's available." The problem is that needs, and not political awareness, are the impetus for searching out appropriate materials. The critical question is how can you know what you're lacking, or even understand the specific problems within a particular context, without deep theoretical analysis? Theorizing is intended to assist administrators, teachers, students, and the public in better making sense of the educational process, the world that shapes such a social dynamic, and their interactions therein. The Central Steering Committee needs to explore in more depth the idea of praxis—the ongoing process of reflection and action/theory and practice. Otherwise, the group's emphasis on practice/action risks turning teachers into efficient multicultural technicians rather than creative and critically engaged public intellectuals attempting to understand and confront the predicaments that they face on a daily basis.

The Inextricable Link between Knowledge and Power

Examining schooling as a form of cultural politics, Critical Multicultural Education argues the impossibility of objective inquiry and absolute truth. Rebutting modernist claims to a universal foundation for truth, reason, and culture, critical educators strive to demonstrate to students how classroom content and pedagogical practices are the very products of particular historical, social, and economic conditions. In order for this learning process to be interactive—a pedagogy of exposition rather than one of imposition—educators need to provide spaces for students to explore the contingency of knowledge (that meaning emerges out of specific social contexts and not out of some fixed essence in nature). The idea is not to simply turn people into uncritical sponges of theory. Rather, the goal of strategic teaching, in which students begin to take ownership of their own learning and metacognitive awareness, is to nurture them into being active theorizers. In this sense, theory works through students and not simply on them. Young people are more than able to come up with solutions to problems in schools and the larger society and to recognize and acknowledge their own accountability for discrimination and violence.

A constructivist sense of knowledge presupposes multiple readings of the world. Beyond the call for a "bias free" classroom and curriculum, the committee needs to more profoundly confront the subjective nature of both perspective and history. Some members of the CSC did grapple briefly with the idea of multiple perspectives—as did Raul when he said, "Teaching about Vietnam, the Vietnamese will have a different story." Some participants did raise the issue that no history is innocent of the intents of its authors—Carl stated that "whoever writes the history writes it the way they want."

Rebutting objectivity and neutrality, the committee could confront the Math and Science Departments, which made no effort to infuse multiculturalism. For example, these educators should acknowledge the significance of one of the Changeton school's "interdisciplinary unit in which cooperative reading groups explored the lives and work of scientists and mathematicians from various ethnic/racial groups." There is a great deal of literature and research on critical multicultural math that could be enlightening in the public school classroom (Alberts, 1994; D'Ambrosio, 1990; Gerdes, 1999; Knijnik, 1992; Powell & Frankenstein, 1997). This is also true of literature and research that addresses the inherently ideological nature of science and technological developments (Bell & Kennedy, 2000; Bender & Druckrey, 1994; Biagioli, 1999; Conley, 1993; Gould, 1981; Harding, 1994; Lyotard, 1994; Roberts, 1999; Robinson, 1994; Ross, 1996).

With a more postmodern understanding of knowledge, the CSC could also contest the Physical Education Department's refusal to change their approach to gym class. The committee should encourage faculty and students to dialogue about the dangers of popular representations of black athletes, the essentialized predispositions of black rhythm and dance, the sexist treatment of women in sports, the racial and gender makeup of cheerleading, how social class limits certain people/groups from participating in a number of sports, or the discriminatory images of sexual orientation (for example, calling names such as "sissy" or "fag" on the field of play, the stereotype that all female athletes and gym teachers are lesbian, and the idea that only gays become male dancers or ice skaters). Also, as Christine Sleeter and Carl Grant (1988) argue, "Physical education programs that fail even to alert young people to the existence of wheelchair sports are perpetuating a limited conception of American athletics" (p. 148).

If Changeton educators want to universalize anything, it should be a belief in the ideal of unity in diversity; that is, they should use the heterogeneous experiences, which includes the counter-discourses of oppressed groups, in the curriculum to contest the homogenized Eurocentric foundations that schools are built upon.

Avoiding the Pitfalls of a Depoliticized Approach to Curricula

As has been argued, knowledge, which is the product of interpretation, guides the ways in which people understand and interact with society and nature. Because knowledge is always a product of representation (Barthes, 1972; Foucault, 1972; Hall, 1997; Said, 1993), it is crucial within a critical multicultural model of education, to excavate whose values, understandings, and agendas are at the core of public schooling: who chooses textbooks, assessment instruments, faculty, etcetera. Changeton educators need to understand, name, and eradicate the ways in which mainstream schooling so often systematically (rather than arbitrarily) turns a blind eye to the realities of so many people. Instead of simply adding elements of diversity to existing classroom content, the Central Steering Committee needs to question the underlying logic that gives shape to the institutionalized relationship among power, knowledge, and classroom protocol. The CSC basically understood that people of particular backgrounds were being excluded, but such systematic silencing was simply being treated as an omission that could easily be remedied by adding new materials to the old. Arguing for inclusion, at the exclusion of any in-depth analysis of society's unequal power relationships and long history of institutional and socially sanctioned oppressive practices, Raul's comment reflects the group's direction: "The white kids would respect the others if they knew more about them, and at the same time, the others would feel part of the exclusive fraternity that invented and discovered." This vision of cultural harmony can invite simple social and educational reforms, but by attempting to get the "culturally different" to fit in ("to feel part of the exclusive fraternity"), Raul risks coming across as accepting whites as the norm and looking to them for ultimate approval. Progressive educators shouldn't embrace a paradigm of content addition that does not question the basic structures of society and schooling and how they are so deeply implicated in shaping particular kinds of identity, situating difference, and reinforcing forms of control.

Instead, the CSC should have followed the lead of the youth worker from a local community-based organization, who when asked by a white parent, "Why should such a heavy emphasis be placed on black history?" immediately responded: "You can't keep [perpetrating] a fraud." What makes this position critical, rather than merely supplemental, is the understanding of the role of systematic silencing and historical engineering in distorting the ways in which so many people are seen in the present day. The CSC needs to embrace a system-wide analysis of exclusion and negative representations in texts and other classroom content (Loewen, 1995; Zinn, 1990). The youths in Chapter Three were calling for this type of critical pedagogy. They answered eagerly when asked how they would have responded to a different type of schooling:

PEPI   Looking back on all this, if school were different, if it were to change so that you had a place where you could come in and express yourself and talk more about what's really happening in this community and in your lives—at least start there and then connect that to what's in the books and all the rest, would your response to education have been different? . . .

DION   Way different! It would be different cause you don't be hearin about reality. You don't even be hearin Afro-Americans in the history. You also don't be hearin about the Spanish. . . .

OLAVO   You gotta talk about what's going on right now. . . .

DION   I like history too, but they don't teach nothin. They don't teach you the real truth. Alright look, Thomas Edison, he invented the light, but who made it better? Who made the light better? A black man did, yo! Did you hear about it? I read the black almanac, yo, when I was in jail and there's a lotta thangs in there, like who came up with all kinds of medicine. A black man came up with a lotta that shit, yo! They don't teach you stuff like dat in school. . . .

STEVIE   [Native Americans are] livin in poverty conditions. I think that they should have that in school, man!

As the solicited lists of multicultural themes and activities in Changeton public schools pointed out, there were lessons on African Americans, Latino/as, and Native Americans. However, these explorations and discussions need to move beyond simply food, dance, costumes, and uncritical approaches to understanding Thanksgiving. One important suggestion was Giselle's call for the high school Social Studies Department to put together a history book on Changeton and its cultures. If teachers, students, and the public were exposed to a critical history, concerned Changetonians would have a much deeper understanding of the problems that they are facing.

Moving beyond Exoticizing and Romanticizing Cultural Realities

The solicited multicultural lists of site-based activities were loaded with lessons and events that recognized and celebrated cultures from abroad. There were curricular activities centered around such aspects as "passports that highlight where children were born," the study of various nations and their holidays, Japanese Doll Day, and flag displays. It seemed that a great many of those educators who participated in adding to these lists were equating national origin with culture—reducing all the intranational diversity to one homogenized portrait. This assumption not only reduces the multiplicity of cultural realities within a nation to one portrait, but geopolitical borders also separate groups of people by extracting culture out of international and transnational relational developments.

What these nation-focused approaches speak to is the trend in multiculturalism to concentrate predominantly on "immigrant experiences." For example, the Frankfurt School had as a multicultural activity "a multidisciplinary approach towards a research report examining immigration and customs of students' ancestors," and the Curriculum and Instruction Subcommittee prioritized providing workshops in which the focus would be on "understanding the social, cultural, political, religious, and economic aspects of Changeton's largest immigrant populations." While such workshops around the formative aspects of students' lives should come to fruition, the focus on immigrants should not obfuscate the reality that many of the people that face extreme obstacles in public schools in the United States have been here for generations—blacks, Native Americans, Native Hawaiians, Chicano/as, Puerto Ricans, women, gays and lesbians, the poor, the disabled, and so forth. These are not histories of immigration, but rather they are the products of such engineered forces as enslavement, conquest, exploitation, and systematic exclusion. Many of these voices can rupture the simplistic notion of pluralism and the liberal demands to satisfy the needs of so-called newcomers. As argued in the previous chapter, if well-intentioned teachers want to create culturally responsive models, that link the home life to schooling, they are compelled to engage in the actual conditions within which people live, rather than some romanticized version of culture elsewhere.

Affirming aspects of international cultures is one step in the right direction, but this is by no means enough. For example, handing out sugar cane and discussing its production without an historical analysis of colonization and slavery will not give learners a sense of the complexities of culture, and in this case, the bittersweet realities of the cane itself. Nonetheless, mainstream multicultural educators have a tendency to stick with the sweet. Such efforts, while a good start, are limited. As Carl revealed to the CSC after he had visited the Parson School to be a spokesperson on the history and culture of Cape Verde, students were well aware of the material, to a point where he admitted that they actually taught him. The children already knew the songs and folktales that the CSC member anticipated would bring them joy. However, in addition to joy, what students need to develop are the critical literacy skills that will enable them to read, make sense of, and participate in or protect themselves from the world around them.

If educators are to address immigration, as they should, it is important that they problematize their understanding of this phenomenon. Teachers need to develop historical clarity as to why people come to this country. In this way, they can better understand the relative insignificance of the nice things that are often superficially used to define culture, and delve into the traumatic realities of what many of their students have experienced—war, starvation, displacement, culture shock, discrimination, and so on. Educators committed to Critical Multiculturalism need to use the existential realities of their students as building blocks to learning, but not in a romanticized way that obfuscates the suffering behind the identity. Carl's emphasis on the Afro-diaspora in the curriculum—"we [blacks] all came along the same pipeline where this is now our national heritage"—could bring these issues to the surface for students. However, this suggestion would need to take into consideration the differences in skin tone and how black immigrants from countries such as Cuba, the Dominican Republic, Jamaica, and Cape Verde, for example, do not necessarily have the same sense of history or point of identification as African Americans. It would also need to confront the reality that, in the United States, immigrants and subordinated groups frequently experience intergroup antagonisms: on the one hand, immigrants often do not want to be associated with the stigmatized social identity imposed on African Americans, and on the other hand, African Americans do not want to be camped with the negative representations of immigrants. Carl, in a post-resignation interview, acknowledged this very problem:

> Take one Afro-American kid—I'm not meaning to stereotype, but let's take one Afro-American kid walking down the street and he sees other people of color speaking in different languages. He doesn't identify with them. He sees the color from a distance, but as he comes closer he doesn't really identify with them. As a matter of fact, he may or she may say, "Ahh, it's them.". . . It's no different from when you walk in a corridor in school and you see those divisions.

Unlike the superintendent's call at the original all-faculty in-service for the need to "emphasize the darker side of history in the classroom: Indians, stereotypes, and slavery" and to make people more aware of issues such as "race superiority and prejudice," the overwhelming majority of activities on the established lists of multicultural lessons and events consisted of superficial add-ons to the existing curriculum (with no engagement with the ideological makeup of the traditional body of knowledge), and scant looks at history and culture (with no substantive analysis of social class discrimination, racism, sexism, homophobia, and such).

There were some creative activities that held promise: studying the historical contributions to society that women have made, black history, the civil rights movement, and Puerto Rico. However, as argued in Chapter One, the study of Puerto Rico, for example, disconnected from the history and current state of colonization, can't be expected to reveal the cultural experiences, discourses, cognitive and learning styles, literacies, and foundations of knowledge, which are the products of the antagonistic social relations within which real people live and grow up. It is only through actual existential analysis that people can begin to understand cultural realities. It is then that they can see into the social forces that, for example, racialize Bilingual Education—"it's not just Puerto Ricans."

However, this does not imply that only historical periods of oppression should be evaluated, for example, the Abolitionist movement, the Holocaust. The point here is that if young people are to understand dehumanization—such as what the Nazis did to Jews, gypsies, gays and lesbians, and the disabled, among others—educators need to start with where people are, what they themselves have experienced. It is then that teachers and students can begin to build bridges to the horrors of slavery, the Holocaust, and other such atrocities, and in return, better understand the historical present.

The multicultural lists contained work with AIDS and drugs—"the Health Department translated Drug/Alcohol and AIDS Policies into Creole and Spanish." While it is crucial to inform the public, and especially youth of all backgrounds, about sexuality and sexually transmitted diseases, it is nonetheless dangerous to simply mention concerns about AIDS as a multicultural activity without problematizing the ideology embedded in the dominant media representations in which only gays, the poor and racially subordinated, and drug addicts contract and are responsible for spreading the disease (Ludwig, 1997; Mercer, 1994). At the same time, "drugs" has become a code word for inner-city racialized youths. It is as if rich white children and young adults don't struggle with substance abuse, and as if whites do not represent the largest percentage of users and abusers (Ferrell & Sanders, 1995). The local and state health departments risk perpetuating these destructive stereotypes and distortions by describing their multicultural activity as "a family-centered substance abuse prevention program targeted the needs of African-American, Cape Verdean, Haitian, and Hispanic communities." As such images are used to discriminate and perpetuate antagonistic social relations, the actual implementation of this curricular activity in Changeton should problematize these issues.

One of the most potentially critical activities listed in the Changeton survey data was the World Food Day Awareness Project. The teacher responsible for this event described it as "students through problem solving were made aware of racism and prejudice and its effects on world hunger." From a strategically depoliticized perspective that didn't mention "racism and prejudice," the local paper depicted the interdisciplinary project involving math, food, and geography as "students gathered in the computer lab to learn about the challenges facing citizens of farflung lands trying to survive drought and poverty so they can put food on their family's table" (Hancock, 1993b, p. 6). As about four hundred transnational corporations control two-thirds of the earth's fixed assets and 70 percent of the world trade, and organizations like the World Bank, the International Monetary Fund, GATT, the World Trade Organization, NAFTA, and the G-8 are shaping the "New World Order," forging what Peter McLaren (2000) refers to as the "globalization of misery," students in a course on world hunger should be encouraged to explore how neoliberalism (that is, transnational corporate exploitation), globalization, and U.S. foreign policy contribute greatly to the very poverty that countries around the planet experience—that they are not as distant as newspaper articles would like people to believe (Amin, 1998; Castells, 1996; Laclau & Mouffe, 1985; Lash & Urry, 1987; Prazniak & Dirlik, 2001; Bauman, 1998; Jameson & Miyoshi, 1999). This is even more urgent given the events of 9/11 (Chomsky, 2001). They should also examine related environmental issues and pollution (The Group of Green Economists, 1992), biotechnology, genetic engineering, agribusiness, sweat shops (Shaw, 1999), fast food (Schlosser, 2001), and so forth. In addition, such lessons need to interrogate the United States's racialized policies of working with different countries around the world. For example, the disparate ways in which the crisis in Rwanda was treated as compared to that of Kosovo—an African nation versus a European nation. It should also examine the poverty and hunger in the United States, and more specifically in Changeton. As almost a quarter of the population in the United States experiences poverty everyday (Collins, 1996; Collins, Hartman, & Sklar, 1999), it is by no means "farflung."

The CSC should embrace the call for critical literacy—"Provide workshops on participatory learning; e.g., cooperative learning activities, and critical, emancipatory, liberatory educational methods and strategies." Some members did mention the importance of not treating superficially such events as Martin Luther King, Jr. Day. Nonetheless, there was little effort by the group or the working and site-based communities to recognize and insist upon utilizing the very political nature of these historical figures and events to generate discussions among learners and teachers about oppression in society, as well as in schools.

The CSC should also encourage faculty and staff to avoid limiting the dialogue to central personalities and cultural icons, at the exclusion of local everyday people who have been making a positive difference in people's lives. As Stanley Aronowitz (2000) argues:

> The actions of ordinary people are just as significant in structuring societies. The antebellum slave revolts, struggles for women's rights, working-class upsurge and resistance to corporate power in the nineteenth and twentieth centuries—in short, the culture and politics of the everyday lives of subordinate groups—are crucial to the configuration of social relations. Their movements and their cultures alter the strategies of dominant groups and, in the twentieth century, have radically altered the nature of economic, political, and cultural power. (p. 130)

The Multicultural Central Steering Committee needs to work to move the schools and their respective practices beyond the nice and the neat, the fun and affirming, and into the more critical terrain of examining the realities of asymmetrical relations of power. It is only then that the faculty and staff will able to avoid the pitfalls of liberal multiculturalism and move into more liberatory and transformative curricula and pedagogies.

Some educators may argue that the reason that the majority of multicultural activities offered in public schools across the nation are about food and fun is that they are being served up to children: the idea being that elementary school children are far too young to be exposed to hard and painful issues such as discrimination and poverty. However, the reality is that many youths already know what it's like to hear about a six-year-old shooting a classmate. As Roberto testified in Chapter Three, "Man, the playground we call the dead ground." Many children have experienced what it's like to be ignored because they don't yet speak English, not to be invited to birthday parties and sleep-overs because of the color of their skin or their religion, to witness domestic violence, to be evicted from their home, to be hungry, to lose a family member or friend to illness, murder, drinking and driving, suicide, or a drug overdose. Many youths have an experiential *sense* of being sexually molested, bullied, rolling the halls alone in a wheelchair, being called a freak because they don't fit in, being considered ugly or overweight, walking grounds littered with trash, or seeing violence and sex on TV—including in cartoons. The sad reality is that children at a very early age are racialized, sexualized, gendered, marked by social class, and commodified. In the past few years, here are just a few of the names that young people, K–5, use to address each other in the Changeton hallways and on the playgrounds: spic, nigger, wop, Jew boy, towel head, camel jocky, slope, chink, cracker, poor white trash, fag, lesbo, butt fucker, that's so gay, blow me, pussy, hoochie mama, slut, stupid ass bitch, nappy hoe, four eyes, twitchy (to a boy with Tourette's), butt ugly, gimp, and project rat.

The CSC was right to insist that the schools get to students in their early years. As Carl exclaimed, "This is where it begins!" In order to effectively achieve consciousness among the very young, educators need to move away from the idea that children exist in an abstract age of innocence, and instead, actually engage them, with appropriate discourses, in exploring and examining the social relations and texts (such as cartoons and Disney images) that they are readily exposed to (Giroux, 1999b; Jenkins, 1998). Being well-informed and instilling civic responsibility at an early age would be a crucial step in the direction of preparing students for democratic participation in a complex world.

Addressing Eurocentrism

Some on the Central Steering Committee were skeptical of the grand narratives of Eurocentric teachings. As Raul stated, "I don't think that we are conscious of the European overdose in schools to a population that gets the feeling that they've contributed nothing." However, the group's superficial reach into the depths of the problem proved to draw little satiating water. For example, the few times that Eurocentrism was addressed by the committee, it was not engaged in a way that named white supremacy. Instead, in a relativistic manner, the term functioned as a measuring cup to quantify curriculum use in terms of how often a certain worldview is or isn't mentioned.

During meetings and in-services, there were opportunities to confront the ideological construction of whiteness and its effects on classroom content and student interactions—"It's time to get to the classroom, to show that everything is not centered around white people." Nonetheless, the conversation would always be rerouted into a debate over inclusion. On this particular occasion, Carl (consciously or not) redirected the group by making the argument that

> There is a lot of ignorance about multicultural education, about who's getting excluded. We all know that it's [the curriculum] Eurocentric. We have historically been excluded. Where are the black and Latino cowboys? How much would that do for the esteem of black kids—the history of the cattle movement. Cowboys are everyone's heroes—buffalo soldiers.

It is important to contest any romanticization or distortion of the exploitation of Native Americans, blacks, and Latino/as (especially Chicano/as) during the conquering of the West. Joseph Suina (1988), in his essay, "Epilogue: And Then I Went to School," in which he talks about his experiences as a Native-American child and dealing with internalized oppression, mentions how few of the Native children, because of the stigma attached to their identities, wanted to act as themselves in the game cowboys and Indians. In a process of decolonizing the mind, Suina grew to resist the cultural invasion and symbolic violence that his people were experiencing. Contrary to the idea that "cowboys are everyone's heroes," one can be quite certain that there are few if any pictures of John Wayne on the bedroom walls of the 269 Native Americans living in Changeton. Given the racial stereotypes, objectification, and commodification in sports, posters of black Dallas Cowboys are problematic enough.

Buffalo soldiers were freed slaves who had found employment in the U.S. Cavalry. Their job was to lead the way for mostly white settlers to usurp the lands of the West. Buying into the myth of what it means to be American, and the respect that was supposed to come with wearing a uniform, buffalo soldiers participated in their own exploitation and the destruction of other racially subordinated peoples. Unfortunately, in Carl's call for cowboys, there is no focus on the historical significance of whiteness in the production of identities and discrimination. Instead, inclusion, regardless of the consequences, is the ultimate goal.

Melissa attempted to target the knowledge/power relationship that informs Eurocentrism when she talked of a "world or global approach to education." She made reference to "Western legionaries" who "want to separate the two", and alluded to the ways in which certain bodies of knowledge are legitimized, usually at the expense of others. This insight is enormously significant if the CSC hopes to critically engage the process of standardization and the hierarchical nature of traditional approaches to curricula. What Melissa's point also reveals is that it is in fact the "Western legionaries"—the E. D. Hirsches, Lynn Cheneys, William Bennetts, Chester Finns, Diane Ravitches, and Harold Blooms, among others, that support standardization and canonization of knowledge, who are actually advocating a form of separatism (which they readily accuse multiculturalists of doing). In other words, categories like "Western," and canons by their very nature, exclude. Juan understood this problem when he explained that creating multicultural courses at the high school level was more difficult—"They stick to the curriculum, don't stress geography, and students don't learn much about other cultures."

In addition, the problem with using "Western" when identifying a particular view of the world, is that the struggles and forms of resistance by African Americans and other racially subordinated groups are also part of Western history. As Steele stated in the previous chapter, "400 years of slavery has had an impact on the consciousness of whites and people of color." He insisted that people, especially educators, "need to understand how we are related historically." It is this relational history and its concomitant cultural manifestations and social formations that need to be engaged. Otherwise, the use of "Western" creates a reductionistic binarism that obfuscates the complex interrelationships that constitute a politics of identity and difference. For example, insisting that teaching a "Eurocentric curriculum when such a large percent of the population is not Euro is ridiculous—it is not important to them!" risks abstracting the traditional body of knowledge reinforced throughout society from the realities of oppressed students. In fact, it is this very body of knowledge that in part shapes and works to insure the reproduction of dominant culture that in turn produces subordinated lives both here and abroad.

The dialectic of Raul's logic that non-Euro students won't be interested in the existing curriculum is that because affluent whites may be able to identify with Euro traditions, then these traditions are necessarily healthy. Within current social relations, including the process of public education, white students are not encouraged to recognize the fact that they are also racialized, gendered, sexualized, historical, and thus ideologically driven—and that they are so often dehumanized in the process. Recognizing the need to also expose dominant groups to the realities of diversity, Jake stated during a post-resignation interview, "I'm basically talking about mainstream education. I would like to have a person of color [as a teacher] so that the white kids in this school would have that experience along with the others." If multicultural education is to be more than a mere slogan, teachers/learners should be encouraged to make connections between the sociopolitical realities that shape their lives and interests, and the body of knowledge that is in part implicated in the formation and maintenance of those realities.

There are endless opportunities in all classrooms to engage in critical dialogue around relational histories and cultural production. For example, from 1985 to 1990 the Changeton High School Jazz Ensemble won five gold medals in international competition and has ever since been highly touted by the local press. As an interdisciplinary approach to multiculturalism, this particular course should explore the history of the African diaspora, enslavement, social struggles and creative resistance to racism, unemployment, and poverty that come with the kinds of economic oppression, deindustrialization, and disenfranchisement that have and continue to produce the music in the first place (Chernoff, 1979; Gilroy, 1987; Hebdige, 1987; Jones, 1963; Ogren, 1989; Rose, 1994). In this way, the class could explore the links among blues, jazz, and rap/hip hop culture, and connect such musical forms not only to their roots, but also to the realities of contemporary popular culture in the United States. Exploring music's role in mass movements toward social justice (Garofalo, 1992) should be an integral part of public education. This doesn't mean that such art forms should be decoupled from pleasure. On the contrary, as African-American choreographer Leni Sloan (1986) states:

> There is nothing wrong with tap dancing. There is nothing wrong with using your voice and your body as a musical instrument. It is the laughter and the music and the dancing at the exclusion of dramatic images . . . of realistic images which is at fault, and it is this exclusion that we hope to dissolve.

Such an approach to education would require a critical understanding of popular culture and its role in shaping meaning and identity.

The Role of Popular Culture in the Classroom

The images embedded in the media (for example, newspapers, music, film, radio, magazines, television, video games, and everything else that carries meaning), largely shape people's sense of self and the world around them (Boyd-Barrett & Newbold, 1995; Dines & Humez, 1995; Hall, 1997; Morley, 1992; Strinati, 1995). The Central Steering Committee members need to take seriously the pedagogical implications of popular culture in a way that would compel them to insist that such issues and materials play a significant role in classroom curricula and instruction.[2]

Disregarding this cultural impact is a major oversight in that young people generally get more from these pedagogical images and sounds then they do from formal schooling. According to the 1994 Fanton Educational Assessment Program (FEAP) survey, the percentage of students at various grade levels with less than one hour of homework was as follows: fourth grade, 55 percent; eighth, 34 percent; tenth, 30 percent. At the same time, the percentage of students who watch four or more hours of television was: fourth grade, 43 percent; eighth, 39 percent; tenth, 25 percent (Parent Information Center, 1995). Carl opened the door to discussing the importance and dangers of popular culture, "Look at TV rap programs, what we are doing to each other is awful—What we are fighting against, the media is doing the opposite." This statement, one of the few by the CSC that targets representational politics, should be extended to a call for a great deal more analysis on the committee's part in terms of understanding how discrimination and resistance are shaped by larger media practices. Otherwise, without naming and discussing the ways in which white corporate interest co-opts the anti-colonial political projects embedded in such cultural expressions, Carl risks insinuating an outright rejection of hip hop culture. As Ewuare Osayande (1996) argues:

> As far as hip hop culture is concerned, all current media outlets that define and promote hip hop are controlled by whites—rich, upper-crust whites at that. (p. 14)

> Our anger must be focused on those persons, companies and government agencies that are behind the wholesale slaughter of our community, using our miseducated youth to achieve their ends. (p. 31)

Understanding the ostensible political project of hip hop culture and its role in personal and social agency, Tricia Rose (1994) argues that "a large and significant element in rap's discursive territory is engaged in symbolic and ideological warfare with institutions and groups that symbolically, ideologically, and materially oppress African Americans" (p. 101). Michael Eric Dyson (1993) observes that rap artists "were creating their own aesthetic of survival, generated from the raw material of their immediate reality, the black ghetto" (p. 191). As an object of knowledge in the classroom, this type of political project can open the doors to an interdisciplinary view of the world—crossing economics, political science, art, sociology, media studies, ethics, and history.

Theories of popular culture could also have been elaborated and encouraged when Kevin exclaimed to the Globe of Human Differences facilitator, "Do you see how insidious this is, if a black calls another black a nigger then a white sees it as okay!" Kara alluded to "the internalization of negative stereotypes." But, she concluded that, "Unacceptable behavior is unacceptable." "Unacceptable" in this sense seems to imply that deviance is the central reason for such language and actions.[3] Carl agreed with Kara and insisted that there be "a single standard of behavior established for students."

Negotiating standards should be a crucial part of the process of Critical Multicultural Education, a process in which everyone should be included, but generally are not. The youths in Chapter Three spoke to this very problem:

_____

OLAVO   They dictate all the rules in the high school, man.

STEVIE   It is a prison.

OLAVO   If you do something in the cafeteria, like you supposed to sit four on the table, and you sit five on the table, they'll grab you and give you three day's suspension.

DION   Because you can't be sittin in a crowd like dat.

OLAVO   Like a prison man. That's why a lot of kids do stuff like that and they get suspended and then never go back to school. They changed all the rules in the high school, man. I'm serious. I went there one day, there's one ways everywhere, man. You know how you walk around and there's like different marked buildings. It's all one way. You gotta go all the way around even if you just want to go straight ahead of you.

_____

If the idea is simply to maintain the unnegotiated standards that are currently in place without student and public input, then the resistance/oppositional identities that they insight will no doubt persist.

As for Kevin's concerns over the use of certain language in schools, the term "nigger" has had its racist social meaning recoded in the word "nigga." Tommy Lott (1994) explains:

> When used in black vernacular culture, such a reversal of meaning allows this term to function as a source of pride rather than denigration. . . . The appropriated use by gangsta rappers adds an ambiguity that shifts, depending on whether

the term is used in a white racist discourse or whether it is connected as an idiom of a resistive mode of African-American cultural expression. (p. 246)

The word was readily used by the youths in Chapter Three:

DION   What's dat other door, it's on the commercial, nigga? You see dat commercial wit the three doors?[4]

Recognizing what may have been cultural resistance embedded in the act of using the word "nigga" is important for effective communications between students and teachers. Kevin's well-intentioned position risks serving the purpose of blaming the victim for reproducing racism. It also creates a problematic dynamic when a white man tells a black student how he can and can't refer to himself. This very issue should also be an object of knowledge that is openly explored in the classroom.

The idea here is not to romanticize popular culture and to assume that all of its manifestations are clearly forms of cultural resistance. Inevitably, within the stronghold of white supremacy, capitalist social relations, and corporate directed media (Bourdieu, 1996; Carey, 1995; McChesney, 1997; Phillips, 2001), expressive forms such as rap are easily co-opted in ways that are antithetical and destructive of their ostensible purposes (Dyson, 1996; James, 1995; Ro, 1996). In fact, most of what people see in popular culture is embedded with forms of ideological domination, whether it's oppressive messages against women, gays and lesbians, racially subordinated groups, and religions other than Christianity (Said, 1981; Shaheen, 1997), or capitalist materialist logic that works to promote uncritical consumption. All the more reason to publicly expose and rupture its intent.

In Chapter Three, the young men mentioned the formative dangers of popular culture. For example, Berto stated, "This town didn't use to be like this, it wasn't until the movies and shit. I mean I remember after the movie *Colors* that this dividin of the city began. Now the east side fights the west . . . it's endless." They also alluded to pop culture's junk mentality, and its commodifying powers within capitalist social relations:

OLAVO   You couldn't walk with Nikes. If you have Nikes on, they'd take them off your feet.

DION   That ain't nothin, yo. Remember when eight-ball jackets come out? I got beat down for mine.

When asked, "What do you do with the money that you make on the streets?" Dion responded, "Sneakers, yo! You want sneakers, you want some gear, you know what I'm sayin." Olavo added, "Buy cars, buy clothes. . . ." Addressing the commodification of identities within the logic of capital-embedded popular culture, Noam Chomsky (Chomsky, Leistyna, & Sherblom, 1999), talking about an eleven-year-old who kills another child for a pair of sneakers (to the disbelief of the general population), states:

> Why not? We're telling this eleven-year-old through television, "You're not a real man unless you wear the sneakers that some basketball hero wears." And you also look around and see who gets ahead—the guys who play by the rules of "get for yourself as much as you can"—so, here's the easy way to do it. Kids notice everybody else is robbing too, including the guys in the rich penthouses, so why shouldn't they. (p. 112)

Corroborating this point, Roland (from Chapter Three) remarks in disgust about the treatment of Native Americans:

> They just took it [the land] from em, took everythin and killed em off. It's a "I want what you got!" mentality. Kids on the streets do that nowadays and they are locked up and not celebrated—not that they should be. This whole country is a contradiction of itself.

Steele, in the company of the CSC, made the most extensive analysis of representational politics:

> We have inherited a mind-set that color is a cultural and intellectual deficiency. The TV shows this, the stereotypical roles blacks play as secondary to whites. Blacks have also internalized a great deal of this—it's even in our folklore. In schools, the curriculum doesn't take this into account—look at the Dick and Jane texts. This creates in the minds a sense of inferiority and inadequacy.

The CSC should be encouraged to extend this insight by having young people develop critical media skills (critical literacy) so as to be able to analyze the values, beliefs, and agenda buried in the images that they are constantly subjected to, and to realize that these aren't really reflective of what their lives are or should be measured by. Critical Multicultural Education requires that educators create classrooms within which students analyze the history of representations in popular culture, and the ways in which such discursive formations come to life and shape people's sense of reality. With more of a cultural studies approach to the curriculum, students develop the ability to recognize and confront their own cultural assumptions that have developed as a result of the vicarious teachings of the media.

Educators and youths should participate in the kinds of classroom questioning that leads to a deeper understanding of the sociopolitical realities and signifying systems that shape their tastes, desires, sense of self, and views of the world. It is only then that they can begin to see how people are turned into atoms of consumption, how prestige gets inscribed on things like the Nike symbol, and how other such signs take on significance for society, especially for those who are relegated to severely limited access to far more important kinds of status. Through such analyses, people can also begin to see how it becomes possible to reposition themselves in the world. Sut Jhally's Media Education Foundation offers a wide range of videos that critique popular culture, repressive state politics, and corporate colonization of public space (www.mediaed.org).

This engagement with popular culture would require major pedagogical changes to traditional approaches to formal education. That is, it would demand a restructuring of the current social relations and interactions among students and teachers in the classroom.

The Importance of Pedagogy

Unfortunately, pedagogy was not a central issue in the three years of work conducted by the Central Steering Committee. When it came to methods and strategies that teachers could use to democratize the classroom, there were very few recommendations and concerns. Even the sparse suggestions about cooperative learning went unexplored. As such, the CSC never really engaged the importance of not only what is taught (curriculum), but how it is taught (pedagogy).

Educators who are trapped within traditional ways of teaching, in which the teacher is at the front of the room dispatching what's deemed official knowledge to what are perceived as passive tabula rasas, work to reconfirm dominant views of identity, meaning, authority, and interaction, whether they are aware of it or not. Such a process has proved to silence many students who do not match the cultural capital of the school or that of the teacher. Or, this type of restrictive interaction creates a pedagogical battlefield on which participants fight over not only whose values and portraits of the past will be voiced in the educational process, but also how they will be included.

A real danger for teachers, even well-intentioned ones who do a great deal of research, is objectifying their students by using literature and existing theory to situate people in the classroom, not allowing them to present themselves. The key to theorizing and anticipating what a teacher may face is recognizing that there is a fine line between generalizing and stereotyping, which is precisely why people need to be critical of all of their assumptions, regardless of any empirical justifications.

As Jackie stated to the Central Steering Committee, "We need to draw out of people, not just put information in them . . . by identifying their location . . . who they are." One woman argued at the GHD workshop, "Teachers need to be learners," and Carl insisted, "Ask the students, let them teach us."

The Central Steering Committee was moving into understanding that approaches to multicultural education are not recipes that can be mechanically followed. Fred alluded to this when he explained to the CSC that the Parson School teachers had paved the multicultural transformation of their school all on their own, and that there was "no one way to do it, no road map." Methods and content can only be generated when teachers create pedagogical spaces in which they have access to their students' realities and needs.

With the goal of drawing out of the students, Critical Multicultural Education relies on dialogue and creating the self-empowering conditions within which all participants in the learning process—students, teachers, parents/caregivers, and the public—come to voice. In this way educators can move beyond the realities of speaking through fictitious identities, for example, teachers speaking to the assumptions that they carry about students, and students doing the same with the teachers in front of them. Critical multicultural curricula and pedagogies are intended to facilitate deep interactions between teachers and students in a way that focuses on ideological analyses and political actions capable of eradicating oppressive practices and institutions both in schools and society. As Paulo Freire (Freire & Leistyna, 1999) argued, the concept of dialogue is not simply about having a conversation with students:

> The teacher who seeks to dialogue has to be very reflective, constantly refining his or her view of the world. Educators can't merely repeat information. For a real dialogue to take place, the teacher also needs to engage the students in epistemological uneasiness in a way that inspires them to revisit the knowledge that they already possess in order to get a better understanding of, expand upon, or rewrite, it. (p. 48)

One way to include more voices in the educational process would be to diversify the faculty and staff, which was exactly what the CSC was trying to accomplish. The following chapter explores the committee's efforts to do so.

CHAPTER EIGHT

Diversifying the Faculty and Staff

From its inception, the Multicultural Central Steering Committee voiced concerns about the makeup of the faculty and staff throughout Changeton Public Schools. The general sentiment was that there was an obvious pattern of exclusion for hiring, resulting in the department heads, principals, and other positions of influence being occupied mostly by white males. Countering this historical trend, the CSC argued that role models were needed to enrich all students' lives, including Euro-Americans. As Jake stated, "Students need to see people that are from their communities. They need to see people in successful positions. Otherwise, forget it!" Carl added, "Without equitable staffing, multicultural education can be set aside as a passing fad."

At the original all-faculty in-service, the superintendent of schools pointed out the importance of diversifying the faculty and staff. Changeton had over nine hundred teachers systemwide; however, of that large number, there were fewer than ten racially diverse faculty members outside of the Bilingual Program. He told the audience that the School Committee had a new and extensive Affirmative Action Plan, and that the school system was in the process of advertising at seventy colleges on the East Coast "to attract more candidates of color."

In the CSC's first questionnaire, committee participants were asked to list possible objectives under staff diversification. The central point that readily surfaced was that "the committee should be involved with the affirmative action process of interviewing and making recommendations in the hiring of new teachers." During their discussion, Fred revealed that the most recent faculty/staff replacements were all white. He also exclaimed, "We should just forget the other applicants. . . . The whites are qualified, but we need blacks." Raul stated, "I interview people all the time that are more than qualified in a mainstream classroom, but with my kids they fall short." Carl interjected, "This works two ways. A person who is black, brown, or yellow may not be qualified. I don't want blacks in the position if they are not qualified."

The committee made certain that any efforts that it was going to embark upon in order to get more people of color on staff were in line with the school's Affirmative Action Plan. The group talked about how to actively recruit, and they wanted that at least one of their members be included on the school's search and interview team. In fact the CSC argued that any system-wide issues and decisions that dealt with multicultural education should have its input—"It would be negligent if we were excluded." Searching for an open door to getting more deeply involved, the group supported the idea of developing a proposal with the CSC's recommendations regarding outreach, recruiting, and retention of racially diverse candidates under the Affirmative Action Plan.

Personnel Issues Subcommittee Is Formed

In order to deal with the overwhelming task that it faced, the Central Steering Committee appointed a group from within to be in charge of personnel issues. The subcommittee knew that by March of 1994, a window of opportunity in the hiring process would arise. Personnel Issues Subcommittee members began visiting teacher education programs at local colleges to inquire if they had any candidates. The specialist at one university recommended sending teams down South "where they could definitely get people." Inspired, Giselle contacted the Placement Office at Tuskegee and obtained the names and contact information of some qualified students.

In addition, the committee brainstormed over former substitute teachers who might be suitable for teaching full time, and the group also looked for a list of Changeton High School alumni to encourage them to come back and work in their hometown. However, beyond class reunions, the CSC soon came to realize that the overwhelming majority of graduates had very little, if any, contact with Changeton Public Schools.

Refusing to give up, Jake visited the University of Fanton for recruitment. He discovered that "there were only twelve minorities and very few were qualified through certification." The placement representative at the university felt that because of the prestige of other careers, students were going elsewhere for employment. She also mentioned the fact that the competition among schools to hire candidates of color was fierce.

Creating Incentives to Work and Live in Changeton

Jake informed the committee that qualified candidates were more interested in going elsewhere "because they have a better financial package than we do." "Why come here when they can make $10,000 more in Nobel or Bingham!," he exclaimed. Luis added, "My cousin makes more in Nobel, but I prefer to stay here." Kevin rebutted, "Money is one of the pieces to our problem, but there are many others." The committee members were convinced that educators would like to come to their city if they could see the benefits. Jake stated, "I'm not going to give up on this school system, we can market this city as a great place to live."

Eva suggested a more aggressive recruiting campaign for students of education to come and do their practicum in Changeton. The committee understood that if they could get a number of racially subordinated student-teachers they could then hire them if they were good. The idea was to give potential educators a chance to see the schools and the community, which would hopefully result in their wanting to stay. It would also give the school personnel a chance to evaluate the candidates' potential. The CSC needed more publicity and contemplated "a glossy brochure of why people would want to come to Changeton."

Knowing that it would probably take three years to negotiate anything with the local teachers union, the CSC discussed the ambitious idea of developing its own teacher education programs, what the group referred to as "growing their own," and "a farm team." With such a large number of racially diverse children in Changeton classrooms, it was suggested that homeroom teachers ask their students if they are interested in teaching in the future. The subcommittee figured that those young people who expressed such a desire could be counseled/nurtured to work with a hired member of the school community. The group also discussed having the guidance counselors talk up the need for teachers as well as emphasize the value and merit of the job. Giselle stated, "I tell kids that they should be educators, that we are going to retire and there are going to be jobs."

Melissa revealed that a grant already existed that supported the idea of youths picking an educator of their choice and shadowing them. Students who participated in this program also put together portraits of special teachers and attended a teacher appreciation dinner at a local college. The Personnel Issues Subcommittee wanted to expand these efforts. As career day was being planned at one of the junior highs, Eva asked and secured that the field of education be included as one of the offerings.

Another idea was to select interested students and offer to pay for their higher education if they invested one to four years of their time to teaching in the city. The group searched for possible ways of enticing "rich people and local colleges to provide the necessary funding." The subcommittee also worked to establish a recruitment team to go beyond colleges of education and reach out to local organizations such as the African American Club and recruitment collaboratives in the Nobel area.

Regardless of all these ideas and efforts to diversify the faculty and staff, the CSC quickly realized that the critical issue was whether or not there would be secure jobs for recruits. As Jake asked, "How can we attract someone for a position that is not there? We're leading the charge, but we need to have something to back it up with; otherwise, it's embarrassing!" Feeling a need to touch base with the school system's mainstream efforts to recruit faculty and staff, the Personnel Issues Subcommittee decided to meet with John Stills, the administrative assistant for personnel in the Human Resources Office of the Changeton schools. Anticipating the get-together, the group developed some questions and assembled an information packet about what it had already accomplished and how it could help in any efforts to diversify the faculty and staff.

After the meeting, the working committee reported back to the CSC. They went over some of the ideas that Stills had suggested about how to get applicants. Most of the ideas echoed the committee's previous discussions. Committee members were nonetheless encouraged by Stills's agreement that the Multicultural Central Steering Committee form a search committee that could work in coordination with the Human Resources Office. Desperate, the subcommittee planned on meeting over the summer months in order to put together a presentation and proposal for the administration and the teachers union.

Revving up for the Fall Hirings

Due to natural attrition and early retirement, there was an unusual number of new job openings—sixty to eighty—coming up in the fall in the city's schools. Members of the working committee were in agreement that there was "a crisis in Changeton and a moral imperative to do more than simply advertise job openings." Encouraged by Stills to set up recruitment teams, which in the committee's eyes would include the school system's affirmative action officer, a teacher, a principal, parent representatives, and active members of diverse communities at large. The subcommittee wanted to establish this task force as an adjunct to the Personnel Department to accomplish the following:

- Make frequent contact (four or five times per year) with minority recruiters at colleges in Fanton, and other states.
- Survey staff for names of qualified candidates of color and linguistic minorities.
- Make presentations to college student groups marketing Changeton and teaching opportunities in the Changeton Public Schools.

- Establish a Future Teachers of America Club at Changeton High School for students interested in entering the field of education, encouraging minority students to join.
- Make presentations to agencies and associations that service people of color and linguistic minorities (civic, cultural, religious, etc.).
- Find ways to aggressively recruit and advise college students of color interested in teaching in Changeton.
- Investigate the possibility of establishing scholarships at local colleges for students of color who are willing to teach in Changeton after graduation.
- Investigate various sources of funding, such as Reebok and the Ford Foundation, for possible scholarships and loans.
- Investigate recruitment strategies used in other school districts.
- Find ways to incorporate a commitment to recruitment, hiring, and retaining minority staff in any future bargaining packages.

CSC members agreed that the administration's backing would be key to their efforts, but they thought that they should first approach the teachers union and then take that information to the administration. Eva made the arrangements for the subcommittee to talk to the head of the union. When asked if the meeting would be on school property, Melissa responded, "We'll meet them in the middle of the streets if need be!"

The Personnel Issues Subcommittee wanted to find out from the union what exactly it could do to help find appropriate recruits and to create structures to keep them employed. The committee had already faced the realities of layoffs and the problematic nature of seniority. Ben exclaimed, "Nobel can keep their people when the cuts come, we can't offer that kind of job security."[1] Jake told the group that Changeton High School had nine minority educators, but they were all laid off because of financial crises. He added, "We risk losing them again once we get them because they do not have seniority, these minority teachers need some kind of assurance. There are teachers that want to come here, but are afraid of not having job security." The group wanted to know if it could grant waivers to teachers of color who didn't have certification, or who had yet to finish their degrees. The Bilingual Education Department had a waiver system to get people in and the CSC wanted to make the same kinds of concessions. Don mentioned a graduate of Changeton schools who was now a counselor in another system. He wanted to come back to his hometown to work, but he said that he needed assurance that he would not be laid off as had happened to him in the past.

The CSC wondered if the school system could offer "recruits of color" tenure as a form of job security. Jake noted that tenured teachers had also lost their jobs in the past to seniority—"We had two black women and lost them both." Fred had a problem with fast-track tenure and wanted at least a one-year trial period. He stated, "There is a student teacher now who is an undesirable candidate of color." With these concerns, the committee approached the teachers union.

The CSC representatives explained to the head of the teachers union that they wanted to have an impact on the hiring process and that they were not proposing that any present union members be displaced. The committee insisted that this was the optimum time to get involved in this effort at staff diversification due to the fact that Changeton was involved in a desegregation plan and that there would be an influx of money as a result. The head of the teachers union responded by providing a couple of sources for recruitment. He gave some reasons for the lack of candidates, one of which was the low salary that the school system offered. He also said that most people don't stay in teaching longer than seven years. When pressed for a statement of commitment, the union leader supported the hierarchy of faculty and staff recalls, but said that he was willing to look into some of the contractual language in other systems that have dealt with this issue. After the meeting, Jake insisted, "It was a waste of time to meet with the union because of the issue of seniority." Fred agreed, "The union refused to bargain."

Back to the Drawing Board

The Central Steering Committee members realized that they would need the support of the School Committee and the superintendent if they were going to make any significant changes in existing policy. They wondered if the administration could put forth a proposal even if the union chose not to. Kevin stated, "We need to push from two sides . . . if the administration doesn't push then it makes it more difficult for us to push within the union." The Central Steering Committee wanted to see the administration take a stand and to publicize the union's actions. The idea was that the combination of pressures from the administration and the local media would push the union to comply.

The CSC realized at this point, given the upcoming fall hirings, that they would need to take the initiative around the issue of hiring without the union's consent. Eva informed the group that restructuring money provided by the Racial Imbalance Plan wouldn't be sufficient to pay for a full-time search committee. But CSC members insisted that there was enough money to pay for a few of them, by the hour, to accomplish some of proposed tasks. For example, the committee could explore other local public school systems to see what they were doing about diversifying their faculty and staff. The group also felt that they should actually be going into schools and finding/encouraging people to go into education.

After discussing the development of a recruiting team and tactics, the committee decided to write up a presentation and send/bring it out to colleges/schools to recruit. With the drafting and submission of a proposal, restructuring money was provided in order to hire substitutes for those Personnel Issues Subcommittee

204 | *The Work of the Multicultural Central Steering Committee*

members who were already doing this leg work. Predicting events to come, Carl was extremely concerned that all of the suggested ideas were long range and that the Central Steering Committee had to do something about taking advantage of the new hirings in September.

Black Members Resign as a Result of Fall Hirings

In September of 1994, there were seventy-five newly hired faculty and staff in the Changeton Public Schools: 12 percent were black and 6 percent were Latino/a. However, few of the positions filled by people of color were in the mainstream. According to the New England Desegregation Assistance Center (1995), "As of October 1, 1994, more than 19% of the newly employed certified teachers were individuals of color, as were 52% of newly employed support staff" (p. 35). Jake voiced some deep concerns with what had transpired, "This is educational reform? . . . When will we have this opportunity again?" With a great deal of anger, he stated:

> It was a crisis situation, we had a window of opportunity and we dropped the ball at the high school. The high school has no African-American teachers in the mainstream. Why could we not have done something to influence the powers that be? We need a special commission to address that if it is going to be effective. We need change. If the commitment is not there, then we need to take another avenue. There was a large number of teachers hired in the mainstream, and we missed the opportunity. Enough said!

Fred told the group that he had an opening and wanted a minority person, but no one came up—"I don't think that there are people available." However, some members of the committee contested this notion that there were simply no candidates—"We are sick and tired of listening to that, that no one has applied."

A few weeks later, when the CSC was rehashing the troubles with personnel, they received a letter of resignation from Carl and Jake. The two educators were extremely disappointed with what they described as the failure of the School Department to hire people of color in mainstream programs. They felt that a window of opportunity had been lost, one that would have shown a long-term commitment to change. In the letter, the two concluded: "We don't believe in false hopes and therefore we cannot be part of this. We do not doubt the CSC's commitment and sincerity. This resignation is seen as a positive act. We are still committed to our community."

Eva met with the two men in order to discuss the problems. In the meantime, the Central Steering Committee strategized about ways to get them back—"We need them, we are losing their much needed perspectives!" Sam argued that Jake and Carl were giving a stronger message by leaving than by staying. Giselle disagreed, "Why leave, what can you do from the outside?" Sam replied, " It's all talk, we need to do more than we are saying." "But we are in infancy," she rebutted. Maria, the chair of the Personnel Issues Subcommittee, insisted that the group had good ideas—"At the National Association of Bilingual Education Conference, we saw methods for recruiting that we could use"—but it didn't have the power to bring them to fruition.

Regardless of the letdown after the fall hirings, the resignations, and the lack of support from the teachers union, the Personnel Issues Subcommittee was pushing on and in the process of developing a presentation for the school system's administration. The members met with a representative from the Task Force on Staff Diversity (an adjunct of the Human Resources Office working in compliance with the Racial Imbalance Plan). Stills also attended the meeting to help guide their efforts. He again attempted to explain how difficult it is to find such candidates of color, and he distributed amongst the group a data sheet which gave the numbers of education majors who graduated in May of 1994 from area colleges—a total of 24 out of 1,061. A percentage of .0226 were African American. At the same time, Stills dismissed the idea of recruiting out of state. He informed those present that Changeton had been part of a consortium that recruits in the South (which costs as much as a thousand dollars), but that such attempts had not produced a single candidate. He insisted that, "statistically speaking, people find employment within thirty-five miles of where they live." He also mentioned that Human Resources was trying to encourage prepracticum students in the area to come to Changeton.

Stills called for more networking, suggesting that the CSC contact an organization that deals with twenty to thirty public school systems, as well as the Urban Teachers Program at a local college. He also promised to put in a request for some money from the desegregation budget to support these efforts and said that he would present some difficult questions to the teachers union.

Working Committee Meets with a Recruiting Organization

In November of 1994, the working committee met with a representative from a teacher recruitment organization. This outreach program was sponsored by the Council of the Great City Colleges of Education (a consortium of teacher education programs located in the nation's largest cities), and the Council of the

Great City Schools (representing the nation's forty-seven largest urban school districts). This nonprofit organization, endeavoring to build a more capable and diverse teacher workforce for the nation's schools, stood by the motto: "Why teach: you can make a difference, more jobs in the 1990s, responsibility and leadership, money for college, salaries are rising, and teachers have the power to change lives." The representative provided the CSC with information in the following areas: how to begin a pre-collegiate teacher training program, teacher recruitment, alternative licensing, and scholarships and loan forgiveness. The representative first discussed the possibility of creating a pre-collegiate fifth year program at Changeton High School and getting local colleges to support or underwrite such efforts. She also mentioned developing a summer bridge program, which would sponsor college students to teach during the summer with Changeton educators, stating that "there are twelve locations doing this now and we could have a program here." Other suggestions included contacting Phi Delta Kappa's Future Educators of America for advice, encouraging the growth of after-school programs/clubs that focused on teaching, developing an education program as an integral part of the curriculum at the high school, creating a magnet program at the high school level (for example, a math/science module with a teaching component), and looking to other schools in the country that are doing so. The representative also suggested making linkages with colleges in order to provide a scholarship for students to pursue teaching as a career. In addition, she emphasized exploring, for developmental insight, work being done in South Carolina and North Carolina in state-wide summer and cadet programs that start in junior high.

The representative explained to the committee that any recruitment efforts down South would be ineffective because "Fanton is perceived to be the most racist state. . . . Professionally this is not a pleasant place to be." She suggested contacting black churches in Nobel, explaining that "they know which students have gone to college." She also encouraged contacting the Fanton Teachers Association (giving a name and phone number) to research the option of alternative licensing.

When talking about scholarships and "loan forgiveness" (that is, funding students' higher education in return for their teaching services), the representative informed the group that there were resources available, such as Dodge Grants, and money from the Reader's Digest/Dewitt Wallace Foundation. She cited two books— *Teaching's Next Generation: A National Study of Pre-collegiate Teacher Recruitment*, and *Careers in Teaching Handbook*—that she felt were informative on these issues. She also recommended that a statement of purpose be sent to the teachers union, regardless of earlier unsuccessful efforts. To prepare the CSC for drafting a letter to the union, the representative gave the committee a couple of sources for appropriate contractual language.

Central Steering Committee Moves Forward

As a result of their meetings with various organizations, Multicultural Central Steering Committee members began contacting black churches in Nobel and sending memos to school principals so they could help to look for potential recruitments at any conferences that they were attending. The group also began to draft a letter asking to be part of the core of the Racial Balance Hiring Board. Such suggestions began to bear fruit. For example, Fred contacted a nearby college and recruited a Special Education minority person. He insisted, "Our efforts are not falling on deaf ears." Giselle exclaimed, "See, we didn't miss the opportunity, it's ongoing!"

In January of 1995, the Personnel Issues Subcommittee gave the CSC a list of activities that members had discussed and were developing. This included a copy of a letter that was designed to help recruit teachers. Maria had recently read the two books that the representative from the recruiting organization had left behind. For two days during winter vacation she outlined the texts, organized what she thought would be valuable, and drafted a report that would be sent out pending the CSC's approval. Maria also prepared for the Central Steering Committee a brief description of specialized magnet programs. She informed the group that she was in the process of preparing a summary description of summer institute programs. In addition, she was preparing a letter and a list of addresses to be sent out to teacher preparation programs.

In February, the letter was sent to the directors of Lehmen College (Walton/Lehman Pre-Teaching Academy) in Bronx, New York; Lincoln High School Pre-Teaching Magnet Program in Yonkers, New York; Richard Green High School of Teaching in New York; Westchester's Putnam School Board Association (Teaching: The Profession of Choice) in Scarsdale, New York; Langley High School (Langley Teaching Academy) in Pittsburgh; Austin High School (Austin High School for the Teaching Profession) in Houston; and Riverside University High School (Education/Human Service Specialty) in Milwaukee. Maria updated everyone on what was being done and shared the unfortunate news that she had only received one response—the Langley Teaching Academy sent an information packet.

The Personnel Issues Subcommittee members discussed adding "education" to the Career Pathways Program and "teaching" into the School to Work Program. They planned to invite the directors of these organizations to their next meeting. They also contacted the Future Teachers of America Club. Another immediate action was to look into "the interest inventories" done by the students to find out if there are any questions/answers that had to do with the teaching profession. The committee offered to meet with anyone who expressed an interest in education. The group decided to develop a letter to be sent out on a regular basis to Changeton High School graduates attending college. The working committee also began serious talks with a local university about getting an internship going where students would take classes on local campuses and get high school credits.

The next topic for the working committee was to revisit a clause in the contract for retaining minority teachers in case of layoffs. The participants stressed that the protective clause would only apply to new hires. Hoping to get full support, the group worked to draft a proposal to be submitted to the union, and the members prepared a statement to the director of Human Resources and the superintendent of schools.

Round Two with the Teachers Union

The Central Steering Committee wanted to meet again with the teachers union. The group discussed new approaches to dealing with what the membership described as a "recalcitrant organization." Tensions rose when Maria exclaimed, "This dinosaur system of seniority has got to go. If we are talking about new hires, the system has to change. It's not moral, it's not right. The system is going to perpetuate itself!" Cali, who was well connected with the union, exclaimed, "There shouldn't be a free ride for minorities, they need to be qualified—we simply can't lower standards!" Raul responded, "We have to watch this talk of lowering standards, they [future teachers] wouldn't want that either." Cali asked the people present how they wanted to explain to the public that minorities have an advantage over others? She stated, "We cut by seniority, so we have an older staff. . . . We can't give two guarantees." Feeling that they had little voice and power, many members of the CSC openly expressed hope that the courts would do what they had done in Nobel and compel Changeton to "match our populations." Cali requested that the group draft some recommendations for the teachers union that she could bring to the next meeting.

In September of 1995, the Personnel Issues Subcommittee chair made two speeches to the teachers union, both of which addressed what she described as "an area of major concern to our school system, and that is the lack of minority staff members among our faculty." Maria gave a brief overview of the committee's goals and progress. She expressed the dire need for backing from both the administration and the union in order "to recruit minority faculty members, and to keep them once we do get them." She emphasized that the multicultural committee was not suggesting keeping any teachers who could not do the job—"That does no one any good; we are not suggesting playing a numbers game."[2] She added, "We plan to put forth a major effort to find minority candidates. What we want is some kind of commitment from the union that the thrust will not be in vain. We need to keep these people once we get them. What can you do to help?" The head of the union said that he would contact other schools with Affirmative Action and Desegregation Plans to see what was being done; however, he also reiterated that "the hierarchy recalls can't be changed."

Nonetheless, the Personnel Issues Subcommittee continued to take action to diversify the school system's faculty and staff. The group assembled and distributed handouts about teacher recruitment to all of the local schools. In addition, members of the committee became very visible in the search for a new superintendent. They met with the School Committee to develop focus groups to help search for a qualified person. These efforts would lead to the temporary employment of an African-American man.

In late September, the issue of staff diversification became the official project of the Task Force on Staff Diversity, which was developed under the Desegregation Act by the Personnel Department. Because of this, the Central Steering Committee voted unanimously to disband the Personnel Issues Subcommittee with the hope that CSC would be kept informed as to what exactly was being done.

Critical Interpretation and Discussion

Virtually all models of multicultural education embrace the idea of providing role models for students by having faculty that match their backgrounds who can hopefully diversify perspectives in the curriculum, challenge stereotypes, and create a welcoming environment to parents/caregivers. The Changeton Central Steering Committee, recognizing the crisis in local schools—having fewer than ten racially diverse teachers/administrators (outside of the Bilingual Program) in the entire school system—struggled in good faith to expand its faculty and staff. Unfortunately, even after committing an enormous amount of energy and hope, the Central Steering Committee ran up against a number of obstacles, the most challenging of which proved to be the teachers union.

Labor unions are political interest groups. The critical question is, what interests, forms of worker protection, and ideals do they serve? The issue at hand isn't whether or not labor unions enhance educational performance of teachers and students. There is plenty of research to show that a strong union presence in schools contributes to educational success (Grimes & Register, 1991; Institute for Wisconsin's Future, 1996; Kleiner & Petree, 1988; Zwerling & Thomason, 1994). Such success includes curbing dropout rates among males; producing higher SAT, ACT, and NAEP fourth grade reading test scores; better graduation rates; enhanced performance among African-American students; and a more stable school environment.

Nevertheless, one centralized organization with generic provisions can't effectively deal with the complex political realities and the diverse range of needs inherent in the process of public schooling. As Richard Clark (1994) argues:

> By its very nature, the union contract with the district is a centralized force. To the extent that it determines processes for staffing, identifies leadership roles such as department heads, or defines teacher responsibilities, the contract removes such decisions from the hands of the school governance councils and impinges on the daily life of teachers. (p. 39)

By not making it a priority to forge a decision-making process in schools that is more contingent and participatory, teachers and especially diverse students' interests are often unheard, or simply unaddressed. In fact, research has shown that monolithic solutions to the contextual complexities of daily life in schools—specific city, building, teacher, family, and student interests and needs—move teachers away from their commitment and participation in teacher unions (Johnson, 1990; Louis, 1990; Metz, 1990; Siskin, 1994). This provides ample fodder for right-wing think tanks, media, and politicians to demonize unions.

Conservatives claim that their goal in improving public education is that of forging reforms for the good of children. For example, Myron Lieberman (1997), in his book *The Teachers' Union: How the NEA and the AFT Sabotage Reform and Hold Students, Parents, Teachers, and Taxpayers Hostage to Bueaucracy*, makes the argument that the principal obstacle to all educational reform in the United States is the well-entrenched teachers unions, which he argues are filled with corrupt, overfed bureaucrats who overpower and quell dissent among the ranks. Likewise, Charlene Haar (1998), president of the Education Policy Institute, states, "From the school house to the White House, the teacher unions are the most formidable foes of meaningful education reforms—reforms which I believe are necessary to achieve superior educational outcomes for children at lower costs to parents and other taxpayers through competition" (p. 39).

It is a legitimate claim that one of the major problems with unions and their contract provisions is that they may have certain interests of teachers in mind, but they also focus on the priorities of labor and district leaders who generally don't work or live in the immediate area. However, such critiques should by no means act as a call to dismantle labor unions altogether—on the contrary, these crucial institutions have proved in many respects to be a democratizing force that educators can rely on, even though they are rampant with corruption and nepotism, and block important transformations in public education. Instead of throwing the baby out with the bathwater as conservatives propose, the idea should be to restructure and reface organized labor so that its interests are expanded and more inclusive. This is certainly not the conservative goal of complete and unquestionable control in the privatization of public education, standardized curricula and assessment, and the dismantling of unions altogether (Saltman, 2000).

Countering this trend of union rejection, activists must also redirect teacher unions' focus into democratizing their own bodies and the very schools and workers that they were ostensibly designed to support. Thus if unions are going to respect the needs of public schools, they have to develop less hierarchical structures and more collaborative work environments. Nina Bascia (1994) argues that: "Teacher union strategies are likely to be more salient where they match the patterns and connections of a particular professional community. . . . A teacher union may serve as a general locus for community membership where it encounters and interacts with community characteristics" (p. 8).

Unions need to help provide new educational resources and assist schools in renegotiating relationships with students, faculty, and communities at large. If regulating working conditions is one of the top priorities among teacher unions, then as part of meeting the needs of a particular professional community, the diversification of the faculty and staff must play a role. In the case of Changeton, the teachers and the union need to work in collaboration with the Multicultural Central Steering Committee in order to attempt to acknowledge and subsequently address the needs of all people involved in the educational process.

Unfortunately, teacher unions have historically paid more attention to economic issues and struggles for power with the administration, often at the expense of developing more effective school programs (Bascia, 1994; Kerchner & Mitchell, 1986; Louis, 1990). What ends up happening to policy initiatives is a ping-pong match between the union and the administration, when both reactionary bodies, as an avoidance technique, are simply blaming the other for the lack of concrete strategies and decisions. As Jake describes, in his interaction with the school system's head of personnel:

> We just signed a contract where your side could have insisted upon putting that [diversifying the faculty and staff] in. There are two sides: the union side and there's the administrative side, which the superintendent and all of the others have control of if they think that that's important. Why don't they put it in the contract, why don't they put in on the table, and why don't they fight for that till the end? Instead they just keep shifting it back and forth and say, "Why don't you go back to . . . ?"

Jake and Carl didn't believe in the sincerity of the claims of existing leadership to support their multicultural efforts. In talking about a volunteer task force that they had assembled, which included "a couple of dedicated Anglo adjustment counselors," Carl asserted:

One of the adjustment counselors came to me after the first in-service that inspired the development of the Multicultural Central Steering Committee. He said to me, "It's gonna blow, I can't hold it together!" So we call a meeting with the principals of the schools. One thing led to another and the superintendent came to our meeting and listened to our cause. It wasn't just a movement coming from the dark side, ya know, it was problems. So anyway, we reached a point where the superintendent made a commitment. I don't believe that that commitment would have been reached unless there was a threat of potential racial problems in the schools, and so it was done not because they liked what we had to say, but it had to be done and suddenly.

Upon resignation from the CSC, Jake and Carl were immediately encouraged to rejoin the group by Eva and the head of Personnel. Jake describes the invite as:

It was a dog and pony show of statistics. . . . In other words, Eva put that whole thing on to try to soothe us so that we would not let the letter [of complaint against the system] go forth. Her whole meeting was to try to convince us not to leave the committee and for her not to have to present the letter of resignation. I really wanted to tell her that I wasn't impressed.

Like other labor unions, the Changeton teachers union worried that empowering individual educators and programs might detrimentally affect its ability to care for its membership. However, in the city's schools, the union was basically excusing itself, in the name of seniority, from dealing with the politics of difference and representation—a common practice across the country.

Teachers should expect unions to serve as protection against excessive interference by others, but such organizations should also provide an option for representative participation in decision making, secure instructional resources and personal economic benefits, and ensure the recognition and respect of others for the realities of teaching. But, more importantly, instead of pitting teachers of different backgrounds against each other over meager and diminishing resources, activists need to collaboratively focus their energies on why schools don't have the necessary support and funding in an age of budget surpluses, an overfinanced Pentagon, and endless waves of corporate welfare. The ramifications of creating intergroup tensions is captured by Khalil Hassan (2000): "A reactionary program, in turn, plays itself out here where there are all sorts of interethnic and interunion rivalries, and can lead to a 'cut the best deal' mentality in which it is acceptable for one group of workers to gain at the expense of others" (p. 66).

Unfortunately, there is a long history of this in labor unions in the United States. Many of these predominantly white, male organizations have been known to exacerbate the struggles of women, racially subordinated populations, gays and lesbians, linguistic minorities, and the poor. For example, as discussed in Chapter Two, labor struggles have historically adopted racially exclusive forms of organization. As Howard Winant (1995) notes: "Race was already present in the way white workers recognized themselves in the 19th century. . . . Why else would they have been more threatened by emancipated black labor (or conquered Mexican labor or immigrant Asian labor) than by the flood of European immigrants in the later 19th century" (p. 33)? Hassan (2000) observes of labor unions:

> Generally, "exclusion" has been in the context of skilled or craft employment, but it has also been based upon race, ethnicity, religion, nationality, gender, or even bargaining units. Here the notion has been that by narrowing the labor market, the price of the labor power of those who are organized can increase. (p. 61)

When it came to organized labor and teaching, Michele Foster (1993) notes:

> Despite the fact that the teaching profession was open to blacks, historians have amply documented that the careers of black teachers have, nonetheless, been sharply circumscribed by racism. Over the years, black teachers were paid less than white teachers, rarely hired except to instruct black pupils, discriminated against by largely white unions. (p. 274)

In present-day politics, unequal power relationships built around race, gender, class, sexuality, and so on, continue to play a critical role in public school labor and social relations. As Jake stated in a post-resignation interview:

> I said to the head of Personnel, with all due respect, I think that it's a waste of time going to the union because the union is going to protect the majority, and the majority happens to be white. I know that it's a waste of time for us to go back to the union, absolutely positively it's a waste of time because here's what they're gonna do. If they even took it up as an issue, they'll put it on the floor where ya have all white teachers. . . . Now are you going to tell me that they're gonna vote to put a knee to the system!

Carl shared that he was almost forced out by the teachers union during the peak of Proposition Two-and-a-Half ("My union did all they could to remove me [as a bilingual counselor] and place mainstream people into that position, but the city backed me and I was hired and we beat that particular grievance").

As working-class demographics have changed, especially in color and gender, one cannot help but wonder whether or not the inability to democratize the teaching force in the name of seniority, or simply the lack of attention to the problem of diversifying the faculty and staff (with the exception of the CSC), is in fact a concerted effort to maintain power among the white constituency. The contradiction of a protective but exclusive labor organization is far too glaring to simply pass over because of an existing tenure policy. As Hassan (2000) points out:

> The fight for membership control, in certain cases, takes on the character of the struggle against national oppression and patriarchy, and becomes extremely complicated when the largely white leadership of a union organization defines itself as leftist or progressive and the opposition (based within an emerging demographics group) does not necessarily have the same politics . . . the failure of a supposedly progressive or leftist leadership to raise the issue of member control (as well as the matter of leadership reflecting membership) will almost inevitably lead to internal strife and the undermining of a left/progressive agenda. (p. 71)

Or in the case of Changeton, the simple unwillingness to develop more flexible structures that would facilitate the diversification of its faculty and staff—its future union membership—is out of fear of a power shift. Hassan continues:

> It must be added that the issue of member control has racial, ethnic, and gender dimensions. Specifically, as membership changes in composition and character, the failure of the leadership to reflect the membership more appropriately has an almost colonial taint to it. (p. 71)

This taint can be strongly felt in the following anecdote. In an informal interview, one elementary bilingual teacher shared a story of how her teachers union representative openly stated, after hearing the low scores of racially subordinated, linguistic-minority, and poor students on the state's standardized tests, "We should condemn the gene pool in Changeton!" When she noticed that the two teachers in front of her looked appalled, she added, "Are you going to tell me that Richton [the name of a well-known, affluent, predominantly white town] doesn't have a better gene pool!" This type of response is not surprising given the current sociopolitical climate in which Richard Herrnstein and Charles Murray's (1994) publication of *The Bell Curve,* or perhaps more importantly the popular reaction to the book, has worked to legitimate, through empirical studies, the idea that blacks and other socially subordinated groups are intellectually limited.

Democratizing Teacher Unions

Instead of becoming disinterested with unions, as teachers have when their daily lives and best interests are not acknowledged (Johnson, 1984; McDonnell & Pascal, 1988), educators, students, and concerned citizens need to call for the development of unrelenting and shifting forms of collaboration through networks, partnerships and alliances within and beyond the school. Dennis Carlson (1992) is worth quoting at length here:

> it is clear that if teacher unionism is to serve a pivotal role in support of demo-cratic agendas in the schools, it will need to change in significant ways. Perhaps most importantly, teacher unions will need to become more democratic them-selves and find better ways of ensuring that oligarchic and patriarchal tendencies are countered so that the voices of rank-and-file teachers are heard and listened to. It will also need to do a better job of building coalitions of interest in urban communities with poor and working-class white, black, and Hispanic groups so that its power base extends beyond the school system and the professional educa-tional establishment. (p. 247)

Not only can educators learn from exemplary practices of some teachers un-ions (Peterson & Charney, 1999), but they can also take advantage of the strategies of Immigrant Worker Centers across the country and internationally (Gordon, 2000; Levin, 1996), the New Directions Movement and its Solidarity Schools, as well as other labor struggles to deracialize unions (Bacon, 2000; Kuhn, 1998) such as Black Workers for Justice, in order to reinvent their own organizations. In addi-tion, critical multicultural teachers can create union-like alternatives while work-ing to change the official union, such as faculty advisory counsels, unit building committees, teacher representation at the state and district level on curriculum committees, and liaisons to the administration (Bascia, 1994).

The Central Steering Committee was in the process of working toward alter-natives that could create the necessary political push to change the hierarchical structure of the existing union. In order to secure resources, the CSC attempted to apply pressure on the union with the help of the administration (the superinten-dent, the Human Resources Office, the Fanton Teachers Association, and the School Committee). The CSC also wanted to resort to legal pressure on the ad-ministration and on the union. In addition, the group discussed publicizing any actions that worked against their democratizing efforts.

The CSC wanted to create alternative structures to ensure staff diversifica-tion, but not at the expense of colleagues who had already shown years of commit-ment to the educational community; that is, such creativity in Changeton in the name of diversification was not intended as an assault on seniority. Not wanting to be complicit in pitting groups of teachers with different backgrounds against each other, the committee was simply looking to develop flexibility for hiring and hold-ing on to diversified faculty. At the same time, many educators would like to be certain that seniority does not mean that teachers are not held to some degree of accountability for quality and ever improving pedagogy. It is also important to note that experience is not simply about the number of years that a person has taught. If a Puerto Rican educator, for example, effectively connects with the realities and cultural capital of a particular body of students because their lived experiences are similar, but has only a few years of teaching behind him or her, that educator is in many ways more qualified to teach in that setting.[3]

A helpful illustration of alternative organizing for Changeton can be seen in the actions of the National Coalition of Education Activists (NCEA), which, as Stan Karp (2000) argues, "has been putting this idea to the test by attempting to build a multi-racial, grassroots network of parents, teachers and community activists working in many different ways for school change across the country (p. 3). This organization has been promoting an anti-racist agenda, an understanding of the realities of everyday schooling, a sincere commitment to establishing profound relationships with grassroots multi-constituency organizing, and a desire for larger social change. Karp adds:

> The result was a vision of what "social justice unionism" could accomplish in education summed up in a draft statement to be circulated in anticipation of a larger institute next year. The draft calls on education unions to adopt a "broader conception of the interests of teachers and of teaching," "a better partnership with the parents and communities that need public education most," "a new vision of schooling that raises the expectations of our students and the standards of our own profession," and "a new model of unionism that revives debate and democracy internally, and projects an inspiring social vision and agenda externally." (p. 3)

In the fight for concrete policies like staff diversification, teachers unions should promote intergroup coalitions—including across social class borders (Rose, 2000). As part of coalition building, what the Changeton Multicultural Central Steering Committee absolutely needs to do is get the support of the largest population in their schools, the students.

Where Are the Students' Voices?

A significant group of workers who are readily ignored in the educational process is students. Carlson (1992) asks, "Should our objective be to organize students into their own trade unions to negotiate with school management over adequate compensation for their labor in the classroom, or to change the way students' work is organized so that it is less alienating and more motivating" (p. 249)? The CSC should work to not only include students in the infusion process of multicultural education, but it should also help mobilize them into an organized political bodies so that they are able to voice their concerns and realize their own goals.[4] As Howard Zinn (1999) argues in the book *Transforming Teacher Unions: Fighting for*

Better Schools and Social Justice, "If teacher unions want to be strong and well-supported, it's essential they not only be teacher unionists but teacher of unionism . . . to create a generation of students who support teachers and the movement of teachers for their rights" (p. 46). Students need to learn about organizing and voicing their concerns through community meetings.[5]

Mobilizing students is especially important because of the fact that they, unlike the overall makeup of the Changeton faculty, are extremely diverse in backgrounds, cultures, and experiences. Thus if the majority of educators in the schools, who are overwhelmingly white, middle class to upper middle class, heterosexual, and Christian, choose not to push the union to make democratic changes, then the students can.

Changeton had already witnessed some of the potential powers of student voices in the 1960s and 1970s when the student senate and the student council served as a grievance board and service organization that investigated some of the school system's problems with gym uniforms, grade-point-average determination, ten o'clock homeroom, classroom content, and students' rights. Their actions set the groundwork for curriculum restructuring (which included both student and administration review teams), new methods of disciplinary action, and so forth. In essence, these student-based organizations acted as a vehicle for bringing important educational issues before the administration.

Youth movements nationally and internationally also provide insight (Castillo, 2000; Childs, 1996; Cooper, 2000; Featherstone, 1999; Lakes, 1996; Martinez, 2000; Ponvert, 1998; Reddy, 2000; Temple, 1999). There is always the lesson to be learned in the Chicano/a public school student uprisings in Los Angeles. In what were referred to as "brown outs," the students went on strike in order to voice their dissent over the history of oppression against racially diverse peoples. Their efforts bore the fruit of a Chicano/a Studies Program and the diversification of faculty and staff.

Local student organizations such as Changeton Regional Alliance of Gay and Lesbian Youth, ACTION (Achieving Community Involvement in Organizing—an activist group that combats educational, social, and economic oppression), Teens as Community Resources, Project Hip Hop (Murray, 2000), the African American Club, the Cape Verdean Club, LASO (Latin American Student Organization), the participants in the Peer Mediation Program (where students resolve conflicts among themselves), the Teen Empowerment Program, Our Positive Posse (whose motto is "Youth Want Peace On Changeton Streets"), and the Teen Council (an organization set up to advise the City Council about issues of youth violence and racism) need to be included in this political process. As the teacher-advisor to LASO stated, "We want to create an organization to serve as an instrument for positive action for Changeton students." In the early 1990s, the Latino/a students were in the process of forming a potentially influential multimedia group with a bilingual newspaper and a cable-access TV program. Even in its early stages, LASO is symbolic of the transformative powers of students' voices—the Changeton High School principal had "trepidations about a separate club instead of the multi-cultural club he envisions in the future, but he supports LASO because of the response of the 80 students who signed a petition to create the club" (Koch, 1994, p. 17).

It would have been enlightening for the CSC if they had spoken with the youths in Chapter Three. Unfortunately, neither the students, nor their parents for that matter, were invited to participate as members of the Multicultural Central Steering Committee. Both groups were talked about, but never with.

Labor unions can, as they have in the past with certain important issues, play a significant role in the reversal of acts of social injustice, but only if their internal politics are refaced—not simply by plastic surgery in a postmodern world of imagery and business as usual, but by a real participatory transformative movement. Such new political movements need to develop coalitions with the public at large. The CSC was engaged in a process of developing community outreach services, which is the focus of the following chapter.

CHAPTER NINE

Efforts to Create a Partnership between the School and the Public

It was clear from the words of the speakers at the Multicultural Central Steering Committee's first all-faculty in-service that the role of parents and the communities at large would be significant in the current and future plans for multicultural education in Changeton. In fact, as part of the conference put together by the CSC, a presentation entitled "Multicultural Issues from a Parent's Perspective" was given by a young black mother of a 1992 graduate of Changeton High School.

The woman argued that regardless of the fact that her son was "academically successful" the "schools were not user friendly." Sharing with the audience the story of how her son's dyslexia was not diagnosed until the fifth grade, she demanded to know why this condition had not been recognized earlier by local educators. Her questions not only pointed to the institution's possible neglect of its children, but also to racism. In addition, the concerned parent spoke about the role caregivers and the educational staff should play in helping each student to "broaden his or her perspective," and in creating a safe community and "a sense of belonging . . . to feel a part of the whole."

At the CSC meeting that followed, the committee reviewed the roughly compiled results of the needs assessment that had been circulated at the in-service. The data clearly indicated that faculty systemwide wanted more "parent programs." Kevin shared his experience with the group:

I had a problem with a Haitian student, and I had no idea where to go for help! How do you deal with the individual child across cultural differences? We need to find a way to pull parents in to explain these differences. It becomes our neighborhood. I can destroy a child if not!

Carl revealed:

> A Vietnamese girl came in with serious neck scars. The student said that she did it to herself "spooning." It is part of their culture for dealing with certain illnesses. They [school officials] thought that they were going to have to 51A [state removal of a child from a home] her. We can't jump to such conclusions! Teachers hold 51As over parents' heads. We have put kids in foster homes which is unheard of in their countries.

The CSC was committed to the inclusion of parents, local organizations, and citizens in the school system's multicultural transformations. In the early stages of the Central Steering Committee's work, a document was developed that asked all members to list possible objectives under "community outreach." Karen argued, "The school should reflect the community, therefore the committee should strive to provide community representation and input on all decision-making bodies in the school." She insisted that the CSC recommend and promote open classrooms that encourage parental involvement, and recruit volunteers who could be used as teacher aids, storytellers, and paraprofessionals. It was then asked whether or not parents would be invited to join the Central Steering Committee? The group agreed that such participation would be important. In the committee's initial discussions, the members acquiesced: "Our role should be to provide leadership, advice, and access to resources which reflect the diversity of the community. The CSC should actively develop community coalitions, and identify and recruit parents, organizations, and community leaders who are culturally sensitive."

The CSC's discussions of parental involvement probed the possibility of having their input in the hiring process in the schools. Raul suggested that both parents and teachers should sit in on the interviews to screen faculty candidates in order to find the most qualified individuals. Melissa agreed, but added, "That's a nice process but not a common practice in our school system." The group realized that the bottom line was that the superintendent, the teachers union, and the Personnel Office were in charge of making actual decisions.

The committee also recognized the importance of having representatives from the community who could assist in the academic assessment and placement of newly arrived linguistic-minority children. The CSC was concerned that too many children were being placed in Special Education because the relationship between language proficiency and cognitive performance was not properly weighed in the evaluation process.

It was generally understood by the Central Steering Committee members that they would need to develop a resource bank of individuals representing different cultural and ethnic realities who would be willing to come into the school to be speakers, tutors, mentors, and adult role models for students, or to serve in other capacities in which they could provide positive insight for educators. Eva told the committee that teachers were approaching her about a Cape Verdean storyteller who had come to the school and captured the hearts of students. She stated, "The kids are still talking about it."

Some members proposed having a forum for community leaders with representatives from various ethnic communities—"with a focus on diversity, self-esteem, and what we want for our children." Others concentrated their thoughts on ways to diversify the curricula and school activities so that students would be inspired to ask parents/caregivers questions about their studies at home—"starting conversation with the family." As Fred stated, "Parents love to be included!" Eva was concerned that bilingual children were losing touch with their family culture.

The CSC was cognizant of the fact that parent-teacher conferences in the traditional sense were not sufficient interaction with the community. Kevin exclaimed, "It's comical to parents, two hours to go through sixty kids isn't enough. Parents want more conferences!" June suggested, "At the parent meetings tonight, we should bring up and discuss issues of multicultural education. If we can get parents involved with school councils, this will get the ball rolling." More generally, Kara, from Globe of Human Differences, asserted:

> This is not just a school issue, but a community and society issue. The school is part of the larger community, everything is connected. I work with the PTA and it is warming to hear that parents want to make a difference in their children's lives. Treat the parents like educators. They are the best kind of volunteer. I highly recommend any participation in any way that you can get them involved.

The CSC continuously brainstormed for ways to let people know where there were resources in the community, encourage participation, and to have the public get to know the multicultural committee members. In coordination with other school groups and community organizations, the Central Steering Committee members agreed that they needed to sponsor events where school staff and local citizens and organizations could interact, share information, and "work on projects of mutual interest." They wanted to encourage parents to attend workshops where diversity would be the focus of what they called a "community curriculum."

Fred argued that one of the major obstacles to parent participation was the lack of "minority representation in the schools." He explained, "My school only has two black teachers. . . . My families don't want to come to a school that is all white." Karen insisted that parents would want to come in and express themselves if they were represented. While the Personnel Issues Working Committee was in the process of finding ways to diversify the faculty and staff, the CSC understood that in the meantime it would need to go out and recruit parents.

With these goals in mind, members of the multicultural committee continued to involve themselves with public meetings. For example, some individuals, including Eva, joined about three dozen educators, parents, and law enforcement officials who were opening a dialogue on racism one Wednesday night—the first of three meetings. "We want to bring those things that are normally said in private out in the open," said the chairperson of the Minority Parents Coalition, a racially mixed group trying to build bridges between racial and ethnic groups throughout the city. Eva informed the audience that the school system had recently begun an organized effort to make its programs more multicultural.

The CSC also began making contacts with professors at some of the nearby colleges, people at city hall, and local businesses. Eva mentioned to the committee that the Foster Museum had changed its approach to exhibiting in order to bring in more multicultural art. It was also providing grants where artists would go into schools and make clay masks with students. Concerned about parent professional development, Sara informed the group that a connection between the multicultural education committees and the Changeton Adult Education Program would be crucial. She was working on a proposal requesting grant money for this very purpose.

In order to realize the unique resources that they had available to them, and to show the faculty, most of whom did not live in Changeton, where their students were from, some committee members wanted to set up a tour of the neighborhoods. The group also suggested having "a night at Changeton High School with parents and kids," as well as a student in-service day where "cultural enrichment could be stressed through the presentation of cultural artifacts, music, dress, and foods."

Local religious organizations showed a vested interest in working with the CSC. They wanted to learn from the committee about how to deal with diversity in their own houses of faith. Giselle stated, "I would like to have a tour of every church in town! We don't know each other's religions. . . . We should sit down with the theologians and discuss." After consulting with CSC members, the superintendent, who had been meeting with this interfaith coalition, agreed to invite representatives from the multicultural committee to their next get-together. It was understood that such religious leaders knew their constituencies and thus could help the CSC identify speakers and resources, and co-sponsor multicultural programs in the community.

As the new education reform bill was being designed to get parents more involved with schools, the Central Steering Committee decided to meet with a representative from the School Committee. The CSC members explained that when they surveyed the elementary schools to better understand what they had been doing to infuse multiculturalism, they discovered that very few parents had been involved. The representative insisted that parents appreciate seeing teachers in a different format—"outside these four walls." However, she expressed a concern that the parents who would get involved with outreach efforts would be the ones who were already participating. "We need to reach the more difficult ones!," she exclaimed.

Community Outreach Subcommittee Takes the Reins

Focusing in on the details of creating a partnership with the public at large, the Central Steering Committee laid out specific plans for a Community Outreach Subcommittee. In its official report, entitled "Multicultural Committee Structures/Goals/Timelines," the CSC declared that this group would be responsible for the following:

- to recruit and develop a resource bank of individuals who are willing to visit classrooms and speak with students on issues of diversity
- to encourage parents and other volunteers to work in the schools
- to sponsor events at which school staff and community members can interact, share information, and work on projects of mutual interest
- to establish "street captains" (community liaisons) to keep others informed of what is going on.

The subcommittee worked to establish a list of people from various fields who could come for no fee and speak in the schools. Carl argued that participants didn't need to be professionals and could simply be a friend or family member. He concluded, "They are the keepers of the keys to culture, and they can help us." Sam, as chief supervisor of Attendance, and Raul, as director of the Bilingual Education Department, were able to provide student lists that could and would be used to determine local cultural pockets. This working committee also suggested that a letter be developed and sent to all school principals and site-based committee chairs as an example of the type of letter that schools should send to the homes of all students. This proposed document was intended to inform the public as to what the committee was doing and to inquire about anything local people could offer as a resource to help with the school system's multicultural efforts. Sam told the group of a questionnaire that had already been used in one of the Changeton schools. In it, parents were requested to indicate their desire to speak about or demonstrate activities in their native culture. He added as a caveat, "Forms are intimidating!," and insisted that the committee not come on too strong. Feeling that such an instrument would mesh with what was occurring in the greater city-wide outreach program (which will be discussed later), the working committee debated what the contents should be.

224 | *The Work of the Multicultural Central Steering Committee*

A draft School Voluntary Questionnaire was conceived in order to solicit information from parents and families. The group debated whether or not there should be a question that deals directly with "clashes with American culture." In order to encourage respondents to come into the school and participate on some level, it was suggested and approved that the survey be done in different languages. The group also agreed how effective it would be to have the resources identified at all of the schools, and to keep track of them on some type of database.

The Community Outreach Subcommittee felt that one obvious way to connect the school to the home would be to develop more effective registration student orientation packages, which were handed out at school registration. The participants requested that the Changeton High School Multicultural Committee prepare an addendum to the Student/Parent Handbook. In addition, they requested that the superintendent prepare a welcome letter emphasizing the school system's commitment to diversity. Any such correspondence would be included in all orientation information for parents and caregivers (which would be available in Spanish, Cape Verdean Creole, Haitian, and Vietnamese translations, as well as in English). Raul was recruited for help with the translations.

Taking sections from the CSC Mission Statement, the final letter from the superintendent included the following passage: "Every school is involved in this multicultural effort. I invite you to become actively involved at your child's school and to contribute to our continuing effort to provide for Changeton Public School students."

Some schools were beginning to show a healthy response to the outreach efforts. By May of 1994, the Parson Elementary School, with the hard work of the school-based multicultural committee, set the pace of what could initially be done to raise awareness, embrace diversity, and get the public involved in the educational process. The idea was built around the banner "School Celebrates Cultural Awareness." The faculty and staff involved in this project developed a brochure that invited parents and the general public into the school (for an open house) to see their children's work. Fred, the building principal, exclaimed, "We want to show off our school. We sent out invitations for the open house. Parents are bringing in food and are getting involved—it sparks conversation in the home!" He added, "Tomorrow, visitors were informed, there will be food tasting."

Public Relations

In the face of bad press from the local media, and resistance from some faculty who were not in favor of multicultural education, the Central Steering Committee members realized that a major part of their work would not simply be to find support, but also to confront the negative messages that were going around to dissuade people from embracing multiculturalism. Melissa stated, "We have not done a good job with public relations. . . . There are parents down the street who don't know what we are doing, or what multicultural education is."

In an effort to "hit the ground running," the Community Outreach Subcommittee participants shared ideas with each other regarding a possible "media blitz" with all the local news agencies. The group met with Ted, the school district's media specialist and a CSC member, who had produced the committee's original introductory video and had strong community connections. They discussed the possibilities of radio public service announcements, spots on cable television, creating a new video on diversity, as well as working with the local Student Community Service Project.

Providing names and phone numbers, Ted also recommended that the group revisit the organization that had helped Changeton schools produce public service announcements in the past. The basic strategy was that members of the multicultural committee could appear on television and radio shows, and could arrange coverage of multicultural events taking place in the schools and throughout the city. Ted recommended that the committee touch base with the editors of local ethnic newspapers and suggested developing a listing of the local multilingual/ethnic programs. In addition, the media specialist encouraged the CSC to "take some pictures of multicultural displays in schools and put them in the paper."

Working with the school system's liaison to the local media, the subcommittee prepared a press release introducing the CSC, its mission, current activities, and future plans. The task force also considered, for the following year, a multicultural education activity calendar and a multicultural newsletter, intended to publicize events and outreach activities. In addition, some members seriously contemplated the idea of developing a multicultural logo.

Coming up with a Multicultural Logo

In search of strategies to create a positive backdrop, draw the public into the schools, and thus widen the system's human resource base, Giselle suggested that the Central Steering Committee consider challenging its students in a city-wide contest to design a multicultural education logo to represent Changeton's celebration of diversity. The subcommittee discussed the possibilities of presenting the winning logo on rented billboard space in front of the high school and having the local media cover the event. The general idea was that a billboard with the winning logo would be a big invitation to the public to come and visit the schools.

The CSC also decided that the logos could be used for letterheads, calendars, and any official information that went out from the multicultural committee.

Giselle contacted the director of Art in Changeton schools in order to inquire about what would be involved in sponsoring a contest for school children to develop a multicultural logo. She gathered information for contest guidelines and procedures and began to plan for the following year. The School Community Advisory Board (part of the Adult Education Program) was targeted as a source for the $300 necessary to fund such an event. The contest was publicized throughout the schools (especially in the art classes) and during parent/teacher conferences. Art teachers worked together with the school-based multicultural chairpersons in order to get things underway. The date for final entries was set.

On April 26, 1995, there was a multicultural logo awards ceremony in one of the high school conference rooms. To a full house—jammed with the local media, Eva introduced the audience to the CSC's efforts "to celebrate diversity." She discussed the importance of multicultural art and talked briefly about the screening process of the contest.

There were prizes for the three different levels: elementary, junior high, and high school. Members of the Art Department and the Central Steering Committee had acted as the final judges. As planned, the winning logo was placed in front of the high school on a billboard. One participant also had his artwork painted on the wall of his elementary school. As Sam exclaimed, "The logo is permanent!" Family members took pictures and the press circulated the room collecting stories and names.

Developing a Parent Information Center

In the first year of the CSC's efforts, the group spoke of the need to more actively include parents in the school registration process and to have a more elaborate orientation for new arrivals. In order to do so, Eva briefly mentioned developing what she referred to as "a parent access center"—"an information center that would provide support for families." The idea for a parent center was actually the result of efforts that were growing out of the Racial Balance Plan that had recently been passed by the state.

A representative from the Racial Imbalance Committee met with the CSC. She informed the group that her organization was in the process of meeting with teachers and parents in order to collect data on the school system's needs. The original goal for this center was to develop a site that could assist in placing students and to ensure that classrooms did not exceed twenty-eight people. It was understood by the Racial Imbalance Committee that it would need to strategize in order to deal with the yearly transitional nature (moving from one school to another or moving outside of the system) of about one-third of the student population. They would also have to decide which schools had openings, to collect records (for example, health, behavior, and transcripts) on each individual student, to assist in academic assessment, and to provide parent professional development. The center could thus assist parents in informing themselves about the educational system, as well as in choosing where they wanted their children to attend school. Such services would also take the pressure off the guidance counselors during registration so that they could do their jobs more effectively.

The Racial Imbalance Committee's representative informed the CSC that coordinator, secretarial, and multilingual parent liaison positions were being created and advertised. She stated that there would eventually be ten such liaisons in place to help parents make choices—"to call people, deal with translations and interpreting, assist the principals, whatever is needed."

As the center would be the place for school registration, and thus the first stop for many newcomers, it was proposed that it provide tours of the schools. Each school would have its own brochure, and principals would introduce themselves through video tapes. The center also developed displays and a library of materials. Parents would have one month to shop around. The representative added, "Of the 1,400 kindergarten students, we hope that 90 percent will get their first, second, or third choice. We will track with an optional survey what/why schools are popular." The Parent Information/Access Center was set to be open by November 1. The city took over the third and fourth floors (over four thousand square feet) of 36 Main Street. The building was being renovated and the allotted area was described by Sara as, "beautiful, with ample private space for meetings with parents and for children to play."

Eva told the CSC members that they could have "major input in this project," but they needed to give the Racial Imbalance Committee a proposal of ideas and to update them as to some of the multicultural materials that they had gathered that could be useful to the center. Sara got heavily involved with this particular project and spearheaded an effort to influence the Racial Imbalance Committee's decisions pertaining to the parent center.

The Community Outreach Subcommittee wanted to ensure that multiculturalism was a central theme and that all cultures be represented at the center. Sam stated, "It's a good time to hand out to parents the multicultural information and surveys—a welcome kit, and to ask them if they would like to get involved." All the information about and from the Parent Information/Access Center was being translated into Spanish, French, and Portuguese. The chair of the subcommittee drafted a proposal asking for approval to develop a survey to identify staff people with facility in languages other than English who could assist in communication with individual parents and groups. The CSC granted the request, as the group understood the importance of publishing all multicultural messages in various languages that represented the local ethnic makeup. Raul described the possibility of placing some of his community relations facilitators at the center on a rotating basis—"The facilitators could help clients by translating procedures and forms." He also mentioned how the Changeton Bilingual Department had drawn big groups by throwing parties with food.

The working committee made a calendar of parent meetings and workshops so that such information could be readily accessible to the public. It was also suggested that the center contact local realtors and ask them to inform new home owners of the existence of such an organization. Members of the subcommittee, looking to develop a proposal that would ensure a multicultural component to the parent center, visited six other towns that had put together similar facilities to see what they had done. The subcommittee felt that the new center would need something special to help draw and later recruit ethnolinguistically diverse parents. Sara insisted, "We need to see what the parents want." Both Sara and Eva attended the superintendent's Parent Information Center meeting and solicited advice from school principals and parents.

The outreach subcommittee was especially concerned with making sure that the Parent Information Center could effectively disseminate information to the public. The representative from the Racial Imbalance Plan agreed to help the CSC's Community Outreach Subcommittee organize announcements so that they would fit on the Changeton Community Cable, Changeton Public Schools, and Continental Cablevision video bulletin boards. The schedule that they strategically worked out allowed for sufficient public promotion in advance for the kindergarten registration.

Critical Interpretation and Discussion

We need to understand and learn to live productive, satisfying lives in communities as small as the family and as large as the universe. (Goodlad, 1994, p. 4)

The Changeton Multicultural Central Steering Committee made a concerted effort to understand the complexities involved in public/school relations so as to be able to develop more productive partnerships. The CSC understood the need to move beyond traditional PTA/PTO meetings and parent-generated bake sales. As Kevin exclaimed, "It's comical to parents, two hours to go through sixty kids isn't enough. Parents want more conferences!"

It was clear to the committee members that there were enormous resources outside of the four walls where they worked, resources that school personnel would be foolish to ignore if they truly wished to improve the educational conditions for all of their students. The group wanted to take advantage of what parents/caregivers could contribute to the educational process, especially in communicating to faculty and staff the values and beliefs that inform the ways in which students approach the world around them. As Kevin stated, "How do you deal with the individual child across cultural differences? We need to find a way to pull parents in to explain these differences. It becomes our neighborhood. I can destroy a child if not!"

Carl added, "They [parents] are the keepers of the keys to culture, and can help us." In essence, the committee wanted to treat parents like educators. This is essential if such a collaboration is to eventually lead to what Malcolm Levin (1987) describes as:

> Parents and teachers are coming together to know each other better, to better understand each others' life situations and concerns and to develop shared activities and interests. . . . Little by little they are beginning to relate as partners rather than competitors, in promoting the educational and social welfare of the children they hold in joint custody, so to speak. (p. 287)

A significant part of creating a real bond between schools and parents/caregivers is to dismantle the barriers that block people from entering public educational institutions. The CSC explored some of the multiple reasons why more people are not involved in school life. Their conversations were beginning to probe the skepticism and lack of participation on the part of parents by acknowledging the reality that large numbers of people work overtime to keep food on the table, don't have the educational skills to bridge the relationship between their children and the classroom, have little to no familiarity with the institution, and feel that their ideas about learning are not deemed adequate. The CSC wanted to avoid reproducing the conditions within which stories like the following from a former Changeton student occur:

> My parents encouraged the three of us to continue in school. My father would constantly remind us that dropping out of school was not an option in his household. As best they knew how, my parents tried to encourage the value of education at home. However, they could only go so far in their encouragement because they themselves struggled with the English language and felt disconnected from the Changeton school system. The majority of the teachers were not friendly and the school system was not willing to share resources and helpful information with parents.

Research (Miramontes, Nadeau, & Commins, 1997) shows that "many low-income and working-class families do not have the resources and confidence about the educational process that many middle-class parents take for granted" (p. 205). Parents are also discouraged because there is virtually no representation on the faculty for the great majority of backgrounds and experiences. Recognizing the low racially subordinated representation in the schools, Fred observed, "My families don't want to come to a school that is all white."

The Central Steering Committee was moving away from the victim-blaming stereotypes held by a great many educators—that parents/caregivers are simply disinterested and unresponsive to their children. The group became more aware of apathetic school personnel. For example, one Changeton teacher shared the following incident: After school, a Haitian elementary student wanted to change his bus route. The bilingual teacher wanted to call home to ask the parents if they were aware of this. The building principal said that such a phone call was unnecessary because "parents on that side of town don't care about their kids . . . now if it were the west side, we should call." In addition, the CSC understood that a myriad of parents have had unpleasant experiences with schools—as one mother of a young black student told the group, "schools are not user friendly." They had heard that two bilingual graduates, coming back to visit their former teachers at the high school, were turned back for no apparent reason—other than perhaps their age, race, and accent—by the security at the door.

Hoping to transform such callousness and discrimination, and move away from the traditional lip service that most educational institutions have paid to parental/caregiver involvement, the CSC discussed ways of sharing power by having members of various ethnic and racial communities actively participate on decision-making bodies, such as school councils, personnel search committees (for example, sitting in on interviews during the hiring process), and the curriculum committee (for example, in the academic assessment of linguistic-minority students). As Karen stated, "The school should reflect the community, therefore the committee should strive to provide community representation or input on all decision-making bodies in the school." Kara, the facilitator for Globe of Human Differences insisted, "Ask for help and allow it to come in."

In order to break the ice and get parents involved, the Changeton Multicultural Central Steering Committee developed outreach information packets, often in the form of what they called "welcome kits," which were translated into the major community languages and sent to all homes. The CSC worked to develop better student registration and orientation packages, and parent/student handbooks. They wanted people "who represent different cultural and ethnic realities" to come in and contribute their knowledge and talents as tutors, mentors, guest speakers, role models, teacher aids, storytellers, and paraprofessionals. Letters and questionnaires were designed and sent to all homes in order to tap information from parents and families.

The CSC wanted to make parents and caregivers understand that schools were now on their side. However, in order to do this, the Changeton schools need to be encouraged to move away from simply embracing people's physical presence and their superficial contributions—as in the Frankfurt School's activity (which was representative of the overwhelming majority of committee-generated multicultural practices) in which "parents volunteered to explain/show classes their native dress, customs, and cuisine." While such schools, including the Parson School, were moving in the right direction by opening the building to parents/caregivers and cultural diversity, this presence shouldn't just be for show. More importantly, but not mutually exclusive, parent participation should also be about real political inclusion (as the CSC hoped for) in the basic processes and decisions of everyday school life. It should consist of profound dialogue around understanding the often antagonistic relations that parents face in schools and within the public at large. In order to initially include the parents/caregivers in such positions of power, a question that was originally part of the committee's community survey, but was eventually edited out, should have been kept—inquiring about "clashes with American culture." It is only when parents/caregivers are part of the school life that educators can get at the real issues that concern them, and how they can actively and appropriately contribute to bettering educational institutions and practices.

Which Communities?

Mainstream multicultural efforts to create a partnership with communities rarely supply an adequate definition of "community." Are people referring to particular racial/ethnic groups, neighborhoods, socioeconomic strata, women, gay and lesbian populations, local businesses, and so forth? "There is the geographical community that physically surrounds the school; there are the ethnolinguistic communities that comprise the student population; and there are the institutions, services, leisure activities, and commercial enterprises that constitute the life of the broader civic community" (Miramontes, Nadeau, & Commins, 1997, p. 202). Arguing in favor of the term "public" in place of "community," Nancy Fraser (1994) states:

> The concept of a public differs from that of community. "Community" suggests a bounded and fairly homogenous group, and it often connotes consensus. "Public," in contrast, emphasizes discursive interaction that is in principle unbounded and open-ended, and this in turn implies a plurality of perspectives. Thus the idea of a public, better than that of a community, can accommodate internal differences, antagonisms, and debates. (p. 97)

It is crucial to recognize the multiplicity of groups and issues that are present in every town and city. Otherwise, a false and reductionistic binarism of "us" (the public), against "them" (the schools) is created. In other words, within the politics of education, it can produce the misconception that there are only two competing interest groups and agendas (Szkudlarek, 1993). Without being open to all differences of opinion and perspective, the idea of community involvement and public deliberation collapses into a paradigm of containment. Emphasizing John Dewey's conception of the "Great Community," Elizabeth Kelly (1995) insists that political life should be interpreted "not as a process that could be preordained, but rather as necessarily resulting from the constant interaction of human beings with each other in day-to-day life" (p. 49).

The Central Steering Committee wanted to take advantage of the local area's individual, cultural, commercial, political, and industrial resources. In part, the CSC seemed to understand that the idea of community can be defined along several dimensions. The group endeavored to develop collaborative relationships with some of the local agencies and institutions—the area's ecosystem—perceiving them as potential resources for contributing to the educational success of students in the schools. Taking the advice of a multicultural in-service facilitator, who insisted that "this is not just a school issue, but a community and society issue," the CSC wanted to develop what they referred to as a "community curriculum." The group wanted to sponsor events where school staff and community members could "interact, share information, and work on projects of mutual interest."

Such efforts are undoubtedly invaluable to creating coalitions; however, the idea of "mutual interest" immediately sends up red flags. Who is in the position of power to decide core interests and whether or not a concern or focal point is mutual? Throughout their efforts (as revealed in Chapters Five and Six), the CSC greatly risked excluding particular groups and issues. The Central Steering Committee, and more importantly other powerful school agencies, hold the power to decide what interests are capital in this infusion process. If the participants truly hope to create democratic conditions—conditions that should be based on participation and dissent, rather than conformity, they need to struggle against the generally held belief of the committee that "democracy is beautiful, but consensus is the new wave. . . . Democracy doesn't work in a revolution." Acknowledging the reality of multiple communities, Dennis Carlson (1997) concludes that the goal of critical inclusive participation "is not so much to achieve consensus on one 'true' or 'objective' depiction of reality, but rather to clarify differences and agreements, work toward coalition building across difference when possible, and build relationships based on caring and equity" (pp. 117–18). Preclusion and the disdain for "difference" fall into what Carlson calls a "normalizing community":

Throughout much of this century, the dominant idea of community in America was represented by what I will call the normalizing community. Within normalizing communities, some individuals and subject positions (i.e., white, middle class, male, heterosexual, etc.) are privileged and represented as "normal," while other individuals and subject positions (i.e., black, working class, female, homosexual, etc.) are disempowered and represented as deviant, sick, neurotic, criminal, lazy, lacking in intelligence, and in other ways "abnormal." (p. 99)

Public institutions of education have historically promulgated "normalizing" conceptualizations of community, and in doing so, they have reproduced an exclusionary model of participation in the name of public good and cultural commonality. Educators and activists must "eradicate the underlying assumption that the institutional confinement of public life to a single, overarching public sphere is a positive and desirable state of affairs, whereas the proliferation of a multiplicity of publics represents a departure from, rather than an advance toward, democracy" (Fraser, 1994, p. 83). Strongly in favor of using the imposed margins as sites of possibility, withdrawal, and recruitment, bell hooks (1990) insists that such a space "offers to one the possibility of radical perspective from which to see and create, to imagine alternatives, new worlds" (p. 150). As a positive sign, research shows that when outreach is organized specifically to engage parents from low-income and traditionally marginalized groups, their levels of involvement and participation in school affairs increase (Brandt, 1989; McCaleb, 1994).

Another important insight around creating public spheres that are inclusive of all voices is not to essentialize the idea of community. As Maxine Greene (1996) argues:

Wherever we are trying to build a democratic community, we cannot settle for conditioning or merely imposing uniform behaviors from without. Nor can we ascribe fixed essences to people or treat them as "representative" of given groups, cultures, or even genders. Treating them as various and situated, we have to take into account a diversity of perspectives and realities. (p. 28)

As discussed in previous chapters, the CSC had a propensity to essentialize groups. This was again a risk in their community outreach efforts to find individuals "who represent different cultural and ethnic realities."

Democratizing Language

If including the public (multiple communities) in the educational process, and vice versa, is to be realized, critical dialogue needs to be at the center of political participation and deliberation. In order to achieve such dialogue, people need to be literate in multiple ways of perceiving and speaking about reality. Engaging a full range of perspectives is not an argument for a particular position or ideology, but rather, it leads people to recognize that there are multiple audiences, and demands a willingness to strive to understand and make themselves understood in speaking and acting across differences (Leistyna & Woodrum, 1996). Those educators who hope to engage in critical dialogue (so as to reclaim the past and create opportunities for communities to participate in the transformation of present realities) need to include the multiple languages and their diverse worldviews as part of the process of bringing the public into the schools and the schools into the public.

Rather than emphasizing the need to interact with a diversity of perspectives and modes of expression, many progressive educators in the United States unfortunately assume that multicultural education can take place solely in standard English. What's even more ironic is that teachers and administrators will invite translators for parents/caregivers at events like PTA/PTO meetings, while the children of these parents are, as one Changeton teacher described (as did the youths in Chapter Three), "reprimanded and humiliated for speaking Spanish or Creole in the hallways and in the classroom." The parents are meant to be role models of cultural and linguistic diversity, but the reality is that the administration, as the teacher added, "will let you know when you can and cannot speak."

Teachers and administrators who abide by an English-only ideology so often discount the insights, contributions, and legitimacy of experience of all those who do not speak or write in a particular fashion, and they ignore the way language may either confirm or deny the life histories and experience of the people who use it. This has devastating consequences. As Gloria Anzaldua (1990a) attests:

> If you really want to hurt me, talk badly about my language. Ethnic identity is twin skin to linguistic identity—I am my language. Until I can take pride in my language, I cannot take pride in myself . . . as long as I have to accommodate the English speakers rather than having them accommodate me, my tongue will be illegitimate. (p. 207)

Support for multilingual education among the CSC was for the most part unclear, regardless of the presence of Raul (the Bilingual Program's director). There was concern about the relationship between parents and bilingual children, and interest in proper assessment of linguistic-minority youths so that they don't end up in Special Education; however, there were very few proposals to form coalitions between "mainstream" teachers and bilingual educators, and some committee members openly rejected such language programs.[1]

Systems of communication other than English were generally referred to by the committee as "foreign". The use of the adjective "foreign" when describing language in the United States is extremely problematic. It assumes that there is a national standard, which contradicts the protection of linguistic diversity in the Constitution. It also places any language outside of English into the realm of otherness, disregarding the fact that Spanish (the language of the Southwest and the commonwealth/colony of Puerto Rico), Native-American tongues, and Native Hawaiian, by definition, are not of other nations.

Trying to work against the kinds of language that discourage participation from those people not familiar with school protocol, the Multicultural Central Steering Committee did develop surveys to identify staff with facility in languages other than English who could assist in communication with individual parents and groups.[2] In order to break the language and cultural barrier, the committee wanted to place what were coined "community relations facilitators" (faculty from the Bilingual Department) at the Parent Information/Access Center. However, even though the CSC was translating the materials into other languages, such systems of communication were equated with monolithic standards—Spanish, Portuguese (when the local population speaks Cape Verdean Creole), and French—as if languages were universal and neutral bodies. As Jim Gee (1996) argues, the idea of a standard is problematic:

> We need to be clear that any language—English, for example—is not one monolithic thing. Rather, each and every language is composed of many sublanguages, which I will call social languages. . . . This sounds simple, but it is not. First, we are all, despite our common illusions about the matter, not a single who, but a great many, different whos in different contexts. . . . We accomplish different whos and whats through using different social languages. (p. 66)

Uncritical approaches to language neglect to engage the very social and historical conditions within which codes of communication develop, and within which individuals are apprenticed. Consequently, the inherent relationship among locale, experience, ideology, power, language, and identity is insufficiently explored (Anzaldua, 1990a; Bakhtin, 1981; Halliday, 1976; Heath, 1983; Voloshinov, 1986; Vygotsky, 1978). Homogenizing definitions of language also abstract systems of communication from issues of sexism, classism, racism, and heterosexism, which in part shape the discourse styles that people use. Educators should never ignore the way that systems of communication, which are all social and historical constructions informed by particular ideologies, play a significant role in shaping (rather than simply reflecting) human perceptions and worldviews.

The committee should also be encouraged to recognize the imposed protocol in school communications—accent, clothes, communicative competence, pragmatics, prosodics, body language (eye contact, touch, spatial relationships, and so

236 | The Work of the Multicultural Central Steering Committee

on), technical jargon, job prestige, and knowledge—that can only come from particular socializing experiences. All of these important aspects of effective communication can lead to severe misunderstandings and limited interaction. For example, concerned with the packages that were being sent to all homes, Sam insisted that "forms are intimidating!," and he encouraged the committee not to come on too strong with parents and caregivers. While the CSC didn't want to make any written communications with parents and caregivers "intimidating," the group never really addressed why such sentiments exist. On a larger scale, the CSC also must engage the debates over Ebonics (not to assume that black English is a single language). If the goal is to embrace linguistic diversity, CSC members need to develop a deep theoretical understanding of the relationship among language, ideology, power, culture, and identity, and recognize the reality that none of them speaks a standard—each has an accent and a particular take on language that surely represents the communities and contexts in which they have been apprenticed.

Bringing the Schools into the Homes

As exemplified in Changeton schools, part of what keeps this type of learning (in the dialectic of teacher as learner so as to be able to teach) from coming to fruition is that a great many educators don't actually live in the cities and towns in which they teach. The physical distance between teachers' and students' communities means that educators are probably unaware of (or even worse, indifferent to) parents/students realities (Torres-Guzman, 1995). One of the Multicultural Central Steering Committee's goals in forging a school/community partnership was to bring the schools into local homes. A basic strategy was to provide homework activities that would inspire students to ask parents/caregivers questions about school life and society. This connection is crucial, given the FEAP (Fanton Educational Assessment Program) statistics concerning the percentage of students talking to a family member about school work once or less a month: fourth grade, 17 percent; eighth grade, 25 percent (Parent Information Center, 1995).

The CSC should also participate in what was proposed as a tour of the neighborhoods and houses of faith that local students inhabit, and the possibility of having students do histories of their neighborhoods. Jay Macleod (1991) provides educators, interested in extending the walls of schools, with pedagogical insight for bridging the classroom with the street. He developed strategies for high school students to study the local culture and history of their community. In doing so, they were able to understand the economic and sociopolitical realities that shape their lives. It is this kind of political awareness that can successfully guide social agency. Part of experiencing a living history of the city would require deep dialogue with the elderly of Changeton. The activity "Call a Nursing Home," posted in the high school's guidance office, is a step in the right direction; however, such an action needs more attention and promotion.

The committee was also concerned with proactively helping parents cope with the inevitable cultural changes their kids are facing. This is a positive step in that, as Christian Faltis (1995) argues, "The key to involving parents within the joint fostering framework, therefore, is to strike a balance between learning about the home environments of your students while the parents of your students learn about school-oriented activities and programs" (p. 248). As encouraged by Sara, as well as the subcommittee members, those involved in the development of the Parent Information/Access Center need to work on more effective ways for the CSC to connect with the Changeton Adult Education Program in order to help conceptualize and provide parent professional development. Miramontes, Nadeau, and Commins (1997) argue:

> A parent education program should be a central feature of any community outreach program. . . . Classes may include anything ranging from 2-hour hands-on workshops, to family literacy and family math programs, to citizenship classes. . . . These educational opportunities, in turn, can provide a springboard for community renewal. (p. 20)

This particular focus is extremely important if school personnel hope to open up their doors to parents/caregivers who may not possess the necessary tools to critically navigate the institution.

Bringing the Schools into the Community

A fundamental tenet of Critical Multiculturalism, one that the Central Steering Committee needs to more fully engage in their discussions of community outreach, is having students and teachers actively involved in community service. By linking the traditional classroom to other public sites and issues, schools can participate in the process of teaching outside of the formal walls of public education. Schools absolutely need to play a more dynamic role in community development and renewal. Maria Torres-Guzman, Carmen Mercado, Ana Helvia Quintero, and Diana Rivera Viera (1994) stress the importance of linking classroom learning with community action. They describe a typical class:

> The learner had to apply what was learned in the classroom to what happened in the community, and their community action informed and gave meaning to the classroom learning. The students' actions were embedded in the passion, morality,

and caring they felt for what happened to their family and friends in the community. Reflecting on the significance of what occurred permitted the students to distance themselves sufficiently so as to gain understanding of the political, social, and scientific complexity of their work . . . students themselves were creating change within the school and in the community. (p. 114)

If all contingencies in the community, such as businesses, houses of faith, and so forth, also worked to provide forms of public education, beyond their own self-interests, they too could participate in rebuilding the local communities. This participation is not meant to imply a move toward the privatization of public education, nor does it support creating public pedagogical spaces where the capitalist and Christian story can be beaten into the heads of youths. Unfortunately, many businesses use the idea of community outreach in order to solicit free labor and to train these volunteer workers as potential future staff (Saltman, 2000).

Democratizing Schools

In order to forge productive community outreach partnerships, educators need to deeply understand the social relations of their schools within the larger sociopolitical context. The Central Steering Committee should discuss and address in greater detail the power differentials and economic realities that shape the environment in which they work, and in which their students live—including the particular issues and identities that the group valued or prioritized. Otherwise, parental and community participation will be minimal. Over the years in which this research was conducted, other than the visits of some outside speakers, visitors from a local Baptist church, and some collaboration among schools, there was very little connection with the public, and very few parents/caregivers, beyond the regular lot, got involved in school life.

If collective deliberation is to become a reality, then critical educators and other public intellectuals need to work toward recognizing disparate discourses, bringing them together, "creating bridge discourses and in opening new hybrid publics and arenas of struggle" (Fraser, 1989, p. 11). Rather than arguing that "democracy doesn't work in a revolution," the point is that democracy is the revolution—it is the very process and not the end result. Without collapsing into the tyranny of the majority, it is what makes a true partnership with "communities as small as the family and as large as the universe" possible.

Part Three

*The Impact of the Multicultural
Central Steering Committee
in Changeton over the Years*

CHAPTER TEN

In the Aftermath

A Dialogue with Changeton Teachers in the Trenches

Regardless of the Central Steering committee's three years of dedication and hard work, without deep theoretical awareness of cultural politics necessary to conceptualize social and educational change, the social antagonisms and inequities within the Changeton Public Schools and the city at large persisted. Schools didn't seem to be bearing the fruit of the committee's theories and labors. Racially diverse representation on the teaching staff was 7 percent (New England Desegregation Assistance Center [NEDAC], 1995, p. 35). That same year, the Fanton Educational Assessment Program's test scores indicated that over 60 percent of the students in the city could not read at grade level (Williams Associates, 1996, p. 9). And, in the 1995–96 school year, dropout rates remained high.

The high school principal, who had raved about the educational system in the city four years earlier when he was initially hired, now pointed a finger of blame at the parents for unrest in the schools and the streets: "We as parents are sending confusing messages. I question whether we've been good role models for them. That's the biggest problem in American education today, the lack of direction from adults" (Reardon, 1995, p. 17). As with the national conservative, ahistorical rhetoric, what are fundamentally socially sanctioned, institutional, and economic problems get brushed off as a "family values" concern. The principal also argued that kids "need to know the limits. . . . They need to know right from wrong. . . . But, they're mixed up, they're confused" (p. 24). In the 1994–95 school year, when this principal "decided a student was causing too many disruptions to stay in the regular day program, he had little choice other than 'to put him in the streets'" (Yarmalovicz, 1998a, p. 1). This tougher stance was echoed throughout the

| 241 |

public schools. "As a consequence, 39 students were expelled from the Changeton School System during the academic year" (p. 1). Racial, social class, and linguistic segregation throughout the school district remained a serious problem within the educational community. The implication here is not that the Central Steering Committee stands alone in perpetuating the school system's horrific state. In fact, even if the committee had conceptualized the multicultural infusion process with a progressive agenda, as suggested throughout the critical interpretation and discussion sections of Chapters Five through Nine of this book, the group was bereft (at least at that point) of the necessary economic and institutional power to turn such ideas into actions. A series of sanctioned outside audits of the school system's organizational structures reveal the limited and limiting political realities that the CSC faced.

In 1994, under pressure by state and local agencies to meet the requirements of the Fanton Racial Imbalance Act of 1974, a report entitled "A Long-Range Voluntary Desegregation and Educational Equity Plan for the Changeton Public Schools" was commissioned by the Changeton School Committee and the interim superintendent (who was an African-American man), and assembled by the New England Desegregation Assistance Center (NEDAC) at Brown University. In 1995, the report was compiled and released.

When local citizens were interviewed by the research team about desegregation and a politics of difference, much like the CSC, they mentioned such goals as:

• Increase the diversity of the faculty and staff of the public school system so that it reflects the diversity of the student body.
• Implement staff-development programs in multicultural education and the management of diversity.[1]
• Improve support services for minority students for the purpose of reducing the disproportionate number in basic tracks or programs.
• Allow greater involvement of parents in educational policy issues.
• Better distribute the number and location of Bilingual Education Programs in schools to avoid bilingual ghetto schools.

The use of the descriptor "ghetto schools" in this last statement points not only to the realities of linguistic ghettos where language-minority students are relegated and overly concentrated, but it also begs questions of the material conditions of such schools. The researchers not only documented the fact that there was a serious problem with discrimination and segregation in the Changeton Public School System, but they also discovered that the schools that were in the worst physical condition in the city "are also the most racially imbalanced."[2] Given the racism prevalent historically and currently throughout the city, it is no surprise that these dilapidated buildings house the Bilingual Programs where the overwhelming majority of linguistic-minority children reside during the school day.[3]

These schools, in which up to 53 percent of the elementary students enrolled were receiving free or reduced-cost lunch (NEDAC, 1995), were described by the desegregation planning team. Some of the most horrific details from the various schools include

- most of the windows are in extremely poor condition—opaque
- students have had to move to other classes or wear coats and gloves
- they have a very small book collection
- improvements to this facility would include repointing the bricks, reroofing the entire building, and adding a smoke detection system
- the building needs painting throughout after significant plastering repairs take place
- the electrical system is inadequate
- water constantly infiltrates into corner classrooms
- there is no ventilation system
- the playground is unsafe
- there are staff concerns regarding slightly elevated radon levels
- the faculty and students are unable to take full advantage of basic audiovisual instruction equipment because each classroom has just one duplex outlet near the classroom clock, which leads to unsafe use of extension cords
- lighting in the classrooms is extremely poor and needs to be completely replaced . . . the lighting system is also unsafe due to occasional ballast failures . . . the pungent PCB-laden fumes from failed ballasts have led the fire department to call for evacuation of the school during the removal process
- most classrooms contain exposed cast-iron steam radiators . . . this creates a safety problem for children who sit nearby
- one school lacks a gymnasium, an adequate library, and functional office space . . . most importantly there is no cafeteria; children eat lunches at their desks in the classroom
- students eat their lunch in the basement within fifty feet of the lavatories and boiler room
- replace the 100-year old chalkboards and the green shades
- the library also serves for music instruction
- the hot water/steam pipes and valves are showing deterioration to the point of imminent failure.

While the list goes on, this is enough to clearly depict the actual material conditions within which teachers and racially subordinated, linguistic-minority, and economically oppressed students work. In fact, the NEDAC (1995) concluded, "Over time almost all public school facilities in the City of Changeton have begun to exhibit shortcomings in their mission of supporting quality education" (p. 39). With the Fanton Educational Reform Act of 1993, it was unclear as to why the renovations of these schools (all schools for that matter) had not been undertaken, especially given that "Changeton may apply for up to 90% reimbursement of the costs for new school construction and renovation projects if these costs are essential in implementing a comprehensive school desegregation program" (p.4).

To remedy some of the social and educational inequities, and to address the parents' concerns and insights, as part of their report the research organization recommended that a Task Force for Diversity Planning be established and that the CSC be "an important resource for the task force" (p. 36). It is interesting to note that the stated goals of such a task force were very much the same as those of the Multicultural Central Steering Committee. Instead of addressing why the CSC did not have the power to implement some of its own suggestions, by simply creating an additional organization, the NEDAC greatly risked facilitating the administration's use of the passing-the-ball technique, that the CSC had already experienced with the teachers union when trying to diversify the faculty and staff.

Demographics continued to shift in the city. By the 1996–97 school year, the student population was as follows: Asian: 3.3 percent, black: 35.3 percent, Latino/a: 12.4 percent, Native American: 0.5 percent, and white: 48.6 percent (Fanton State Department of Education, 1997b). Of the students, 13.8 percent were in Special Education; 6.9 percent were limited English proficient; and 28.5 percent of students' first language was not English (Fanton State Department of Education, 1997b).[4] The incoming first-grade class was expected to be 48 percent racially diverse, with many bilingual, poor, and single-parent children (Blotcher Guerrero, 1996c).[5] Meanwhile, the CSC and site-based committees continued to meet and develop multicultural ideas; however, regardless of the extremity of the actual problems in Changeton, for the most part, diversity continued to be defined along the lines of a trivia contest about the flag display in the cafeteria and visits to a Mexican-Spanish restaurant in another town (Boone, McGrath, & Dupuy, 1996).

Under pressure to abide by the state Education Reform Act of 1993, in 1996, a major research project called the Central Office Assessment, Reorganization Option and Recommendations, costing $50,000, was conducted in Changeton.[6] The report consisted of interviews with 115 people at the Central Office—including all its administrators and support staff. In addition, all school principals and curriculum personnel were interviewed in small groups. The assessment team concluded that, in large part, Changeton school officials were "out of touch," and that the "Central Office is not perceived as providing the leadership the system needs, but rather, as creating barriers and protecting turf" (Williams Associates, 1996, p. 4). The consultants found that "the way power and control are used by some individuals in the system angers and distances many, and inhibits the effective functioning of the system as a whole" (p. 4).

Irrespective of the three years of work by the CSC, according to the researchers, "We received multiple disturbing reports that there are teachers in the system who believe some children can't learn, who behave in ways that encourage truancy, and who discriminate against children of different races or socio-economic class" (Williams Associates, 1996, p. 9). They noted that "in the process of creating system-wide values, some schools could not agree on a value which embraced, honored, and respected diversity" (p. 15). Experiencing first hand the high rates of suspension and the permanent removal of some students from school, the team added, "We were distressed that people identified the expulsion process as something that was working well in the system" (p. 9).

In terms of educational reform, the Williams Associates concluded:

> Educational Reform seems to be optional in Changeton. Some are wondering when it will affect the city. Some believe it is not possible to implement here. Some are ignoring it. Many others believe that educational reform would make a significant difference. This all speaks to the issue of site-based management which uniformly people feel is not in place, regardless of what education reform has directed. (p. 4)

In reference to the "Special Projects" taking place throughout the school system, the drafters of the report observed that "the authority of Special Projects people is often unclear. They have responsibility for making things happen in the system but no authority to follow up or sanction non-performance, or non-compliance with requests" (p. 5). The Williams Associates observed that "principals and curriculum administrators report much resistance to curriculum changes, that teachers do not feel involved, and the perception is that curriculum is dictated by the Central Office" (p. 9). The researchers were concerned that "the process for the development and implementation of curriculum is at best not understood and at worst non-existent" (p. 4), that professional development is not linked to curriculum development, and that "there does not seem to be an overall educational philosophy or theory base about grouping, strategies, methodologies, multiple intelligences, etc." (p. 10). The research in 1996 also revealed, "There appears to be very little accountability in the system at any level" (p. 6). To counter this laissez-faire attitude, the Williams Associates suggested that in Changeton, "each individual should have job expectations, be held accountable for their performance, receive regular supervision and performance coaching. Failure to perform should be followed by the establishment of a professional improvement plan. Failure to improve on that plan results in the non-renewal of the contract" (p. 13). The consultants also suggested developing a long-term action plan to implement the desegregation plan, which the organization felt was not being treated as a priority. The consultants agreed that, "given the student population of Changeton, and the intent of desegregation, this is a serious issue and demonstrates the need for diversity training throughout the system" (p. 15).

When it came to diversifying the faculty and staff, the Williams Associates (1996) noticed that for the teachers and principals who are known to do a poor job, "the system waits for their retirement" (p. 7). But retirement alone couldn't solve the problem in Changeton, in that, as witnessed by the CSC in Chapter Eight, the hiring process was rigged. Corroborating this earlier claim, this new research found that:

> Interviewees did not report anything positive about the functions of Personnel. Every stage of the personnel process, including identification of needs, establishment of criteria, advertising, recruitment, screening, interviews, selection, orientation, and record keeping was seriously critiqued and criticized. There is a strong cry for the staff to be more reflective of the diversity of the community and of the student body. There is a consistent concern about who has the final say about who is hired, both process and outcomes. There is inconsistency in the system in the hiring process, which may be based on personality rather than clear procedure. (pp. 7–8)

The report pointed out, "In general, the system does not seem to want to take on the underperformance issues which exist at every level" (p. 9), and it recognized that a good deal of these problems would be difficult to rectify:

> It is difficult to change the culture of a system. The change process always engages denial and resistance. Systemic change requires leadership from the top. Someone must hold the vision of creating a system that meets the needs of the children of Changeton and creates the opportunities for success that they deserve. (p. 12)

While no mention was made in the report of the Multicultural Central Steering Committee's efforts, it's obvious that for three years this activist organization was paralyzed within these very unequal power relations. After asking Jake and Carl, "Do you consider the Multicultural Central Steering Committee complicit in the neglect?", both men responded, "They have been powerless." Carl added, "Let me say this, they have yet to seize power, they have yet to take power. At this moment they have no power, but there is potential for them to seize and grasp power around the issues that they present."

As history repeats itself, there was a good deal of denial of the sanctioned research's articulation of the cultural problems in Changeton. The president of the teachers union found some of the claims of the systemic assessment "questionable." He stated, "It's destructive criticism, not constructive criticism. . . . I don't feel that the school system is trying to preserve the status quo" (Blotcher Guerrero, 1996b, p. 2). He concluded that budget cuts were the heart of the problem. In fact, many critics of the report seemed to avoid the ideological issues by pointing their fingers at the economic crisis in the city.

Complaining that the report did not take into consideration the history of budget cuts that the school system has undergone, the president of the Changeton High School Parent Advisory Council downplayed the criticisms: "I'm very suspicious of anything done by consultants. . . . Anyone can come up with negative criticisms, I want to see the recommendations to solve the perceived problems" (Blotcher Guerrero, 1996b, p. 2). The president of this city-wide council also felt that the underlying problem was a lack of funding (Blotcher Guerrero, 1996b). However, contradicting this position, one parent rebutted, "It's not a money issue. . . . It's an issue of putting the right people in the right places and having open communications systemwide. . . . The problems that exist can be cured without a lot of money" (Blotcher Geurrero, 1996b, p. 2). General parental reaction to the report's conclusions and implications was muted.

Under continued pressure, in 1997, a new report entitled "Administrative Reorganization of the Central Office" was compiled and released by the New England School Development Council (NESDC). By interviewing all Central Office administrators and School Committee members—as well as conducting two multihour focus group sessions with principals, observations, and an analysis of administrators' logs—this study also sought to identify areas that were not being adequately addressed throughout the school system. The researchers concluded that the problems in Changeton's schools were "systematic and organizational in nature" (p. 3). It was recognized that absolute power and control seemed to be concentrated at the superintendent's door.[7]

In terms of personnel, the consultants observed, "There appears to have been a history of 'promotion from within' as opposed to a balanced administrative personnel approach that bases administrative staffing on the needs of the school system and appropriate qualifications of the individuals" (p. 7).

The research team also argued that reevaluation of the curriculum should be ongoing. The consultants agreed that "there needs to be a seamless flow of support services for all pupils and especially effective coordination between regular and Bilingual Programs" (p. 10). In addition, they suggested that "alternative educational programs need to be developed more fully, especially in response to drop out prevention, chronic absenteeism, or as an alternative to suspension/dismissal" (p. 6). NESDC insisted that "School Committee members must be advocates for all of the city's children and should create and foster an atmosphere which emphasizes what is best for the entire system without allegiances to specific wards. . . . This is especially important when one considers the demographic diversity evident in Changeton schools" (p. 13).

The report also contended that the "overall culture of the system is not conducive to higher pupil achievement and elevating the overall performance level of this demographically diverse system" (p. 12). The New England School Development Council believed that "there may be a need to re-examine and adequately publicize the overall mission of Changeton Public Schools. . . . The task should be accomplished under the leadership of the School Committee, with assistance and guidance from the superintendent and appropriate input from school staff, parents, students, and other citizens" (p. 12).

A Dialogue with Teachers in the Trenches

In 1997, two Bilingual Education teachers from the Changeton Public Schools were interviewed about the problems they face and potential solutions. They both teach first grade Cape Verdean students. Susan is white and U.S. born. Ally is of Cape Verdean descent, but was born in the United States and raised here for most of her life. Their school, at the time of the dialogue, was made up of more than 75 percent racially subordinated students (NEDAC, 1995).[8]

PEPI   Are you both working in the same school?

ALLY   Yes, but there are three schools for Cape Verdean bilingual students who number in the six to seven hundreds. We are the largest of the three Bilingual Programs in the city. What's interesting is that in this city the minority is really the majority. But the powers that be don't want to release this fact. They skew the data by not counting the Cape Verdean population as "minority"—they are seen as white. Consequently, a great number of bilingual kids are not accurately depicted in the school census. I think that in part they are afraid of white flight. The Cape Verdean program is potentially a large force, but it is difficult to have an effect on schooling when teachers are constantly uprooted from the schools that they work in. This makes it very difficult for us to establish ourselves. You become part of the school and then you're moved. We are constantly having to reestablish ourselves. It's not easy going into a mainstream—or "regular" if you may—school: they don't know who you are or where you've come from. You're considered subordinate in that most think that you don't speak English. For example, Susan would get all the messages from the mainstream teachers who had something to tell the bilingual faculty. As one teacher said, "I'll put your name [Susan's] at the top of the telephone tree . . . I want to make sure I'll reach an English speaker." This is crazy, the majority of bilingual educators are born here in the States. Trying just to become a part of the mainstream staff and to have such educators acknowledge that we are professionals is no easy task—it's like we are outcasts. People simply don't want to understand that what we do is work hard to educate kids by using the native language to facilitate the learning of English, and to raise their self-esteem.

PEPI   Are you treated differently Susan because you are white, because you are seen as the "real American?"

ALLY   We think so. But then mainstream teachers also use race to their advantage—I was almost not hired because I didn't look Cape Verdean enough—whatever that means.

SUSAN   But most educators and staff talk down to all of us. We are typically referred to as "you bilinguals," or "that's the bilinguals." The department office is in the basement of the administration building—that's indicative of our status right there. Bilingual and Special Education are not even written in to the school system's handbook in terms of the hierarchy-of-power chart. We are definitely treated differently.

PEPI   Are you and your children openly excluded?

SUSAN   Sure, for example, the head of reading does not want to order materials for the bilingual classes. Students in the monolingual program receive handwriting books while my students get copies of the page to be done. These kinds of incidents of inequity and racism are numerous. I remember when the bilingual teachers were not invited to a party that was being held for the assistant principal—we were the only ones left out. When we are invited to such events, it is as if it is an act of charity. At one picnic for the sixth grade, the Cape Verdean teachers and their kids were assigned to pick up the trash.

ALLY   When the mayor's wife asked if she could come to the school and sing for the children, only the second grade monolingual students were invited. When I found out about this injustice, I approached the vice principal who was in charge of this special activity and asked why my students were not allowed to participate. I was told that she thought that "they would not be able to handle this musical event." After I picked myself off the floor where I had fallen in stunned disbelief, I asked her what kind of music was played. They were incredibly complicated musical "masterpieces" such as "Old MacDonald Had a Farm" and "Bingo." Although I tried to explain to her that all children, including bilingual children, love and enjoy music and that to not include us was a slap in the face, I was brushed aside with a "We'll make sure that you are included next time." Of course, there never was a next time, at least not one that I actually knew about. These injustices just reaffirm for my students that they are not part of the dominant culture and that the power structure in the school really does not want them to become participating members— certainly not to transform it in any significant way.

SUSAN   We've had a lot of trouble with the lunch people. When our kids went through the line the lunch ladies wouldn't give them vegetables. My teacher aid was very active and she would be there with the students, trying to demand that such foods be served. But staff would dismiss her demands, rebutting, "You are just an aid." One day she came and got me, saying, "I can't take this any longer! . . . Our kids are not being fed!" So I went down to the cafeteria and asked, "Is there a problem here with feeding all kids?" The lunch lady responded, "The bilinguals don't eat vegetables!" I asked if there was a menu and she pointed to the posted notice. I then inquired, "These things on the menu, do all the children get everything?" "Yes," she said, "But they eat it!" I demanded an explanation as to how the service could possibly know what the kids do and don't eat when they are not at the table with them? I informed them that I am going to stand here from now on and make sure that everything on the menu is put on their plates.

ALLY   I take my class to lunch and I stand there and tell the kids what is offered. If I don't see it on their tray, I make sure that I ask them, "Do you want . . .? Did you forget your . . .?" But the harassment is nonetheless ongoing. One time a little Cape Verdean boy forgot to get his milk when going through the line. When he returned, a lunch lady refused him access to the fridge. She said to him, "If you forgot your milk the first time, then tough luck, those are the rules!" As I was approaching this woman to reprimand her for such harsh behavior, I saw a young white boy, who had just returned to the line, being given a bag of potato chips by the very same person. I not only go down to the lunch room to protect my kids from the food service, but also from the large room full of behavioral problems that are inadequately addressed. I don't want my children to pick up the bad behaviors of the mainstream students. Bilingual students are already stigmatized as being the deviant kids. I remember at the class picnic, the Cape Verdeans were accused of eating all of the hamburgers.

PEPI   Were all the servers in the cafeteria white? *(Both say:* "Yes, all white.")

ALLY   The only time that you see a so-called minority in this school, other than the few of us in the Bilingual Program, is with the Spanish-speaking substitute teachers that come. They abuse them with great ease.

PEPI   So what you describe is common practice?

SUSAN   Yes! It's common! Take the gym teacher for example. She is very prejudice and lets people know that from day one. She'll come to us on a regular basis, demanding, "I want an aid in there because those bilinguals, they don't understand. . . . I spend my whole time giving them directions." Once, I responded, "Don't you think that it has to do with the fact that children are young (these kids are six and seven-years-old), that they just want to play—it's a gym?" "No," she screamed, and continued yelling at us. Some of the bilingual classes only have English-speaking aids. If it's really an issue of language, which it isn't, it doesn't make any sense that she wants these assistants in there to help give directions.

ALLY   Such teachers are just paranoid. They are afraid of dealing with some children. They think that linguistically-diverse children don't understand, but the reality is that they just don't give people a chance. They have a bad attitude towards our kids. What is the big deal? If a child is less proficient, use another term. There are different ways that you can express something. Just be a little more patient and sensitive. It might just take one little effort where you adapt and change your ways, the child will pick it up. Isn't that what teaching is supposed to be all about? A lot of times the mainstream faculty don't want to go that little extra road. You wonder with the way things are going with the national attitudes towards Bilingual Education, and the desire to cut such programs down—maybe eliminate them altogether, what are they going to do with these diverse children? What are they going to do when they have a number of these linguistically-diverse kids in their classrooms?

PEPI   How do you think that all this stigma affects the kids? Do you see forms of internalized oppression, learned-helplessness, resistance, or reaction? I realize that they are very young, but do [you] notice the signs of such behavior?

ALLY   The kids are young, but they feel it. They are treated as if they have a defect or something, that they are less than the other children in the mainstream. The mainstream teachers use very aggressive body language and talk loudly with our children—very different than with the other kids. Just recently, a black student, who was in the Bilingual Program, graduated and received a college scholarship. Teachers were mumbling under their breath that he probably got the award because he is black. These kinds of attitudes have a dramatic affect on the kids' self-esteem and confidence, on how they see themselves and learning—especially in learning English as a second language. Some block out the harsh treatment, but most can't.

SUSAN   The mainstream teachers don't even want to deal with the bilingual children that are in the mainstream now. If the child is a behavior problem they send him or her back to us and say that it has to be a language proficiency problem. I had a student who was mainstreamed and the teacher called me almost everyday, "This child's behavior is outrageous!," she would say. Teachers like this never question the uninviting atmosphere in their classroom that may insight such behavior, or inspire a lack of English language usage. I try to explain this correlation to them, but I can never get through.

PEPI   Is there any effort on the school's part to communicate with the various ethnic communities, to use diverse languages, and to make sense of diverse cultural realities?

ALLY   There are, but too often what appears to be well-intentioned in principle turns into bad practice. I was asked to serve as an interpreter at a core meeting. It was a review of a particular child—a Spanish-speaking child who was in the mainstream in the fifth grade. First of all, it is disturbing that a native Spanish speaker was not present, they forgot to put in for an interpreter.

PEPI   Is the assumption that you are all the same—you've seen one bilingual, you've seen them all?

SUSAN   They put the Cape Verdean and Haitian kids together in the same language classroom because as one teacher put it, "It's Creole, isn't it!"

ALLY   It certainly seems that way. The attitude of the white facilitator with the Puerto Rican family was really insensitive. She could not deal with the fact that this family was traveling to the island in the summer and returning in November. She was making the parents feel so uncomfortable and uptight about the issue, which she herself could not have understood in that she had not asked them about why they were traveling. She didn't ask if there was someone sick in the family back home, or something like that. She just assumed that it was for a vacation—they are just on vacation again. "We can't have this, we just cannot have this!," she said, throwing her arms up in the air—"There is nothing that we can do for this child!" I was so frustrated because I felt that she did not do her job by breaking communication with the parents. The parents remained civil. The mother could be heard saying to the father, "See, I told you that we can't go to Puerto Rico." Just the threat, just the threat of not being able to be themselves. If someone told you that you couldn't go back to your home state, how would you feel? The facilitator did not try to reach out to them in the least bit. And then I hear from teachers all the time about bilingual parents, "They should always attend parent/teacher conferences, don't they care what their child is doing!" But really, who would want to go willingly into this hostile environment!

SUSAN   The general attitude is that "if they are leaving the school system for any extended period of time, then we don't have to deal with them." "Why should we waste our money and write up this education plan, and all this stuff, if they are not going to be around?" I've heard this said many times. The faculty and administration kind of float along with such children until they go.

ALLY   When the facilitator superficially researched this particular Puerto Rican child's educational history, she noticed that at one point he had been in the Bilingual Program. All of the sudden the focus of attention and blame shifted. The facilitator blurted out, "I don't know why the Bilingual Program let him out!" It was sadly obvious that she didn't want to have to deal with the situation. In fact, she conducted no real research/ investigation into the child's academic track record—she didn't even look at his report cards or teacher comments. "I don't know why, I don't understand why!," was all that the facilitator could repeat. I'm sitting there as a bilingual teacher listening to all this. Apparently it must have dawned on her [the facilitator]. After I left the room and was walking down the hallway, she called me back and said, "I hope that you don't take it the wrong way, what I said about Bilingual Education." I responded that: All programs have their pros and cons, but I really wish that you would understand how the Bilingual Program functions. . . . If that child was mainstreamed, there was a reason. He must have reached a certain level of competency or proficiency. It's not that we just send these kids out. These decisions of who and when to mainstream are crucial, they are very hard to make. That's probably the hardest choice that I have. You feel like a mother hen—should I let the child out, is he or she going to survive among these wolves?

SUSAN   Then you have the other extreme. I have a child who just came here from Cape Verde at the end of October. He's trying so hard to speak English, and he's so proud of what he has learned and everything. When the reading teacher comes in to read a story to the kids, the child will say things like "Good afternoon, how are you?" The teacher said to me, "What is he doing here, he's already speaking English." I instantly responded, "Wait a minute, when you read to the students, do you ask him specifically to tell the story in English, or to answer some questions . . . ? Ask him next week." Well, it was funny because I never heard from her again.

PEPI   There is obviously a level of theoretical ignorance around language acquisition and literacy. It is totally inappropriate to use communication skills—talking—to assess literacy development.

SUSAN   No doubt! Another little kid, who had never been in a formal classroom in the States, or back home in Cape Verde for that matter, was experiencing culture shock from the transition. In response to her behavior, the teacher wanted the child tested for learning disabilities. It is no wonder that the Special Education classes are full of kids of color, immigrants, and other linguistic-minority students. But in reality, these are issues of language, culture, and abuse and not some cognitive deficit or pathology. You can't expect children to come from another country and sit down and act like robots.

PEPI   It sounds like there are those faculty and staff who are not aware of the real issues at hand here, and there are those who don't really care about the well-being of these children.

ALLY   There are both, but how long can we survive in this society, in the United States? I mean you can go from microcosm to macrocosm, how long can we survive like this? How long can a community, a city like this, not start to educate from top to bottom? We want to educate the children, we want them to acculturate by learning English, and to be productive members of society, but the process of doing that has got to be humanizing. We need to reeducate teachers, this is what needs to be mandated. We need to prepare teachers for the children who are in front of us. I used to watch the class lines go by. You always knew, even if you didn't see the teacher, that that was a bilingual group. Now you see a line go by and if you don't catch a glimpse of the teacher, you can't tell if it's a mainstream or bilingual class. There are so many faces, non-white faces, it's just so diverse. Are teachers in the mainstream prepared for this? Mainstream teachers question our professional preparation and if we are qualified to teach. I think that it's time that they started to question themselves, are they prepared? This one teacher they hired for ESL thought that it stood for "early special learner" and not "English as a second language."

SUSAN   We really need to start in teacher colleges because educators across the board need to learn how to introduce multiculturalism. Multicultural education in this city is seen as a separate course, that's what I hear on these committees all the time. Some faculty can be heard saying in a disgruntled tone, "Oh, we've got to teach that now!" Or, it's like, "Put a block in your plan book for multiculturalism." So they pick a country and they tell a few facts and they've done multiculturalism.

PEPI   How do such educators see culture and understand cultural politics? Do they recognize and address sociohistorical tensions and antagonisms that produce social relations, cultural realities, and attitudes towards learning English?

ALLY   Not even close! The multicultural committee that I'm currently on [the most recent version of the CSC] wants to explore the fifty states. Now, when you hear the fifty states, it doesn't conjure up thoughts of multiculturalism—you think geography. I finally got to a point where I went to the last meeting and said, "I can't deal with this concept of multicultural education—under this theme." A lot of them put their heads down. They didn't even want to look at me saying such things. They just looked through their papers or somewhere else. It's very interesting to watch the reaction when you ask teachers to do something different, especially critical thinking around these issues—you run into some serious resistance on their part. There are those that perhaps felt the same way that I did, but were afraid to say it. I had one teacher, after the meeting, who said, "I'm glad that you spoke up because that's exactly how I felt."

PEPI I found this very problem in my three-year study of your city's schools and their developing concepts of multicultural education. They had Japanese Doll Day, flag ceremonies, and the likes, but very little that would really help all those involved deal with the racism, discrimination, and violence that are omnipresent throughout this city and country.

SUSAN Which is a problem because there is an awful lot of prejudice in the school that I'm in, and the overwhelming majority of teachers, including those in the Bilingual Program, don't stand up and challenge the oppressive acts that are taking place all around them. I say to my colleagues, "These are the things that need to be challenged, why are you people sitting back!" They often respond, "Because we don't want to make any waves." Well, sometimes you have to! The more that I think about this the angrier I get. You begin to understand why some of these kids, especially the black kids, get up and are violent: it's like water torture and they incessantly drip on you. At a certain point you've got to let it go— explode! While this is happening all around us we have people saying, in the name of multiculturalism, "We are dressing up for character day at the end of the month and everybody has to be a character from their favorite book." This one women looks over at the bilingual teachers and says, "Well you colored people should dress up to be like the folks from black history." We just had Black History Month. And everyone just sits there. She comes out with this "colored" thing, and we just sit there. We have to challenge this because when you don't, people think that you agree with them. You've got to let them know somehow that what they are saying is not appropriate.

ALLY Sometimes we are our own worst enemies because we don't stand up. A few years ago I wouldn't have either, but the more that you recognize and theorize these problems and injustices, you get to a point where you come to voice on such issues no matter what the consequences. I can't keep it in anymore and I think that a lot of us need to come to voice, to have a voice. Until we do, all those suppressive and oppressive things will just continue on. This makes learning very difficult for children, especially when the subject is the language of the group that is treating you so poorly.

SUSAN The best way to teach is to watch your students' faces. You know if they are getting the point of the lesson or not. If you're teaching it one way, and they are not getting it, then why bother, it's just a waste of time and breath to me. Your purpose is for children to learn no matter what

country, background, or language they come from. If they're not learning, then you are not doing your job!

———

Faced with the conservative public contention that the problems that these
two bilingual teachers describe has to do with the language of instruction, and
that an all-English environment will lead to academic success and social harmony,
it became necessary to dialogue with an English as a second language teacher, in
the very same school system, to see what she had to say. Beth is a white ESL instructor for low-incidence populations, grades one through six.[9] She opened the
discussion with a story of how she nurtured the interests of her students by having
them conduct research on the history of explorers from their countries.

———

BETH   We were all happy and brought our list of explorers to their main
teacher. She didn't say anything, no teacher stuff that you say to make
students feel good. She just couldn't deal with it. It was like, "Why are
you bothering me with this?" or something. She made it seem as though
this exercise had no importance. To me, affirmation is something that
you have to do to acknowledge that all kinds of kids are here, that they
exist, that their cultures and languages are valid. As a teacher, I feel embarrassed that she wasn't able to see the need to bring the students in
from where they are coming from. It was a major failure on her part. I
connect with kids because I believe that the only way to reach them and
make them feel included is to get them started talking about what they
know. Tell me about you . . . I need to know, because if you start talking
then I can take you somewhere.

PEPI   Is apathy among the faculty the norm?

BETH   We are not doing as much for these linguistically-diverse kids as we
could. As ESL teachers, we are in such a hostile environment. Number
one, mainstream teachers don't want our kids in their room, period!! We
have a kid from Angola, a second grader. He is a nice little boy who
smiles and says, "Good morning" and "How are you?" when he sees you.
He is obviously really well brought up, from a good family—not that the
school knows anything about his background. He's black. Well, in the
second grade, there is no one who is tolerant, let alone enlightened. He
ended up in this ESL classroom and the teacher has made no secret
about the fact that she does not want him there. In order to get rid of
him, she got him into a first-grade math class even though he can do
math. She claims that he can't. So he leaves her room for math. When
the math teacher sent him back because the class was not an appropriate

level, the teacher complained to the school principal. She's doing anything that she can to get rid of this child. Again, when the first grade went on a field trip they wouldn't let him stay in the room with the teacher who had complained, so they sent him to me in the middle of my class lesson. Does he really make them that uncomfortable? When I asked the principal if she was aware of what's going on, she told me to go down and address the issue. I said, "No, it's not my place!" When I petitioned a third time that the student was being mistreated, she said, "Yes, I understand what you are saying, but I'm telling you that the best thing for this kid is to keep him in the first grade math class." Basically what she was saying is that this teacher is a problem, she is near retirement, and there's nothing that I can do at this point. This was seen as the best solution for the kid because we cannot protect him from this teacher, or from teachers like her for that matter.

PEPI   You showed me some pictures of some seriously violent scenes, such as shootings and police beatings, that your students drew in class. Are there teachers who take the social conditions in which many kids often grow up in seriously, using their experiences in the classroom to develop further learning and understanding?

BETH   In response to the pictures, their regular teacher said to me, "Oh, they are just making that stuff up, they are exaggerating." How does she know, she drives away each day from school in a Mercedes or a Lincoln. . . . With this teacher you go into the classroom and there are two reading groups, the high reading group and the low reading group. There are no non-white students in the high reading group. You should see how kids are segregated in this school. When the class goes to the library for example, all the kids of color sit together. I couldn't have this in my classroom. I would mix the students up.

PEPI   I'm sure that the kids find some comfort in the solidarity that is generated from a common experience within such oppressive conditions.

BETH   I can understand why they would want to sit together, but you can't have such segregation, you need to develop some kind of relationship-building activities. To not do so is a glaring omission on the part of the teacher. I think that she is a very, very racist woman. Such teachers don't have good social skills with adults either. Her husband is on the School Committee. This is the type of people that you are dealing with.

PEPI   Does anyone work to understand non-mainstream students?

BETH   There is one guy in the school who is brand new. This is his first year. He is twenty-two years old and is both a Special Education and mainstream teacher. They gave him every problem kid at the fifth-grade level, he's got a class like you wouldn't believe.

PEPI   The class acts as a holding tank for kids that the school is unwilling to work with?

BETH   Yes! It's so transparent some of the stuff that goes on in the school—cause he's like six-foot-five. However, he is good, he's understanding. But for most teachers I can't say the same. We had a kid come from Jamaica. They put him in the ESL Program and I had a fit. I said, "You can't take a kid from an English-speaking country and put him in an ESL track. . . . I don't care if he has an accent or speaks a dialect." They did, they railroaded it through when the director was out sick. Why? Because he couldn't read and no one wanted to teach him so they put him in ESL. Everybody in the school was saying that they couldn't understand when the Jamaican child talks. He does speak differently from how you and I do, but if you have half a brain you can follow and detect language patterns to work from and on. The principal of the school that he was supposed to go to didn't want him because, as she said, "We've had Jamaican kids before and they haven't done well." It's like saying so let's solve the problem by bouncing him into ESL. I went nuts and said, "Do you know that this is illegal!" But, they did it anyway. The first-grade teacher that got him, she is young with all kinds of methods, but she is also racist like you wouldn't believe. She made no attempt to use the kid's background to enhance her own understanding and teaching, and would say things in the teacher lounge like, "Oh, yaa, mon, let's light up some ghanga."—mocking a Jamaican accent and demonstrating stereotypical attitudes. I said to her, "This is a first-grade kid, you can't look at him like you might look at a Reggae singer from Jamaica—you are talking about a little boy!" As a responsible teacher, you make an effort to find out about a child's culture, but don't bring your stereotypes to it.

PEPI   What was the rest of the faculty's reaction to her racist jokes?

BETH   They all laughed. The kid is very dark skinned. If he were a little kid with a Scottish accent and red hair I just don't think that people would react in the same way. The only big concern that the school community had with this kid, revealing their deep-seated, coded racism, was his smell—a huge issue was made about his body odor.

PEPI   Is there any kind of support against such racism from above?

BETH   The new superintendent doesn't have a clue. His big initiative is to have multilingual teachers volunteer our language abilities for translation purposes. He needs this because the institution refuses to provide adequate bilingual services outside of the classroom.

PEPI   It makes you wonder what they are going to do when Bilingual Education is completely dismantled.

BETH   Why should we provide our services for free? It's not that I'm against giving my time, but rather, this makes me complicit in the dismantling of support services altogether. Somehow speaking another language is not seen as a special skill, I'm not even recognized as a professional. It's a "let's use the janitor to translate for the court" kind of attitude. We are referred to as "you ESL instructors," or "you bilinguals." I have more education than most of the other teachers in this building, and yet they think that I am not a real teacher. They don't know anything about my background, they have not seen my resume, but their erroneous perception is that I'm not a real teacher, nor are my students real students. Case in point: ESL classes are canceled when they need a substitute teacher for a regular class—this happens to me all the time. Why? Are our ESL students less important? One day I was asked to sub for a sixth-grade teacher. She left me a list of things to accomplish while she was gone, which I did. The next day she was amazed, as if I wouldn't be able to do all this. I wanted to tell her that her job is not that difficult. She has a text that she follows, anybody can do that. My job is much more difficult, but they think that we don't do much. They wouldn't have a clue as to how to do my job.

PEPI   Is there any collaboration between the ESL and the mainstream teachers?

BETH   We can't collaborate with mainstream teachers, they won't do it. They are not interested in what I do. They don't see that what we do has any relevance or application to what they do. Two colleagues of mine and I have offered, like five different times, a workshop on working with second language learners in your classroom. We have never had anybody, not a single person, interested in coming. People's general attitudes and responses are that "it's not interesting, not relevant, not important," and/ or "not a concern." This is all very insulting.

PEPI   Dedicated teachers must burn out beating their heads against the wall constantly.

BETH   Uggg! I've had such an awful, awful year. I can't stand to even go there anymore. I don't even eat lunch with the teachers. It's like turning over a rock and seeing what's underneath. I've seen what these people are really like, so have other ESL teachers, but they have a lot more invested here in terms of retirement and such.

PEPI   Aren't there policies in place to protect against these kinds of injustices?

BETH   Rhetoric perhaps, but practice is a different ballgame. Before, there was no written policy for assessing who of the low-incidence populations was going to go into the ESL classes. They were just selecting all the kids who didn't speak English at home and putting them in ESL. Well, a lot of these children can read and write as well as I can. There is this one ESL teacher who is a Neanderthal, a real throwback. He took all the advanced courses for ESL teachers and learned absolutely nothing from them—in one ear and out the other. He is still deciding whether or not it's true that you can't require the ESL students speak perfect, grammatically correct English before before they are mainstreamed. We finally developed a policy for screening first graders for the ESL Program. This same guy wasn't doing his job. He was supposed to test the kids in the fall and then again in the spring. He was testing them only in October for the following year's placement. The progress that they made during the year was totally discounted.

PEPI   Do these types of incidents—overt and more subtle forms of manipulation of policy and mandates—happen a lot?

BETH   Definitely, or they create progressive reforms that are never intended to succeed. The Haitian Bilingual Program was placed in an all-white school in an attempt to appear on paper as though the school system was complying with the desegregation laws. They put this Haitian program in this all-white, racist school. Imagine what it has been like for the Haitian kids and teachers—I mean, these black kids in a sea of white. There are no other minority people in the school except for this one health teacher. These kids are isolated, and they are readily picked on by the mainstream students. Naturally, as anyone would, they react to such unwarranted abuse. Well, guess what; the Haitian students are getting suspended from school all the time by an assistant principal who is a real S.O.B. Every week they have been getting suspended.

PEPI   Don't teachers, including those in the mainstream, get involved in order to defend the children and to develop better intergroup social relations in the building?

BETH   One of the Haitian teachers went to the principal and said, "I cannot allow you to suspend any more of my students." However, it's the director of Bilingual Education's job to implement language policy, to protect against this, but he doesn't. Just today they were bunching first and third graders. Even if you can't read, there is a lot of difference between these two age groups. We discovered this year that the kids who were in the third grade in the Haitian Bilingual Program—in their third year—had never spent five minutes in a mainstream classroom and had never had a native speaker as a teacher. So here are children that legally have to be exited and they cannot function in an English-speaking classroom because they have never been in such an academic environment. At the same time the bilingual teacher was discovering this, the director of Bilingual Education had this great insight *(laughs)*. "You know," he said, "We really ought to get native English speakers to do ESL in the Haitian Bilingual Program." It's the first time that he has ever said that—he's been doing this job for like fifteen years now and he suddenly realizes this. So now I'm going into grades one through three to help. Well, they have no design to their day. It's not Bilingual Education, it's let's teach the regular curriculum with explanations in Creole. Now, from what I understand, you are supposed to design a Transitional Bilingual Program so that you have, say, forty-five minutes for ESL and forty-five minutes of native language literacy instruction—and then the proportions are to gradually change as the students progress. There's no design to this program. It's just the regular day, you know, reading, spelling, math, and so on. When the teacher needs to, he or she uses Creole. That's not Bilingual Education!

PEPI   Do they theoretically understand what Bilingual Education is?

BETH   I don't think so, I don't think that anyone here does. Most programs don't for that matter. Today I was talking to the Social Studies Department head in another school system. He said to me, "Isn't it true that these Bilingual Programs haven't really been functional?" I responded: "Well, if it is true it's not due to the fact that the idea of Bilingual Education is bad. It's been due to poor execution, and the reality that many people haven't understood that we are trying to develop both content knowledge—through the use of one's native language, and native language literacy, while simultaneously advancing their English." He said, "Oh, thanks for explaining that to me." He's a mainstream teacher, so, under the present circumstances, I wouldn't expect him to know what's up. But, I do expect the director of Bilingual Education, who is getting paid a lot more money than I am, to understand this—but he doesn't have the skills, he doesn't have the knowledge. This is why I want to leave. I cannot work in chaos. I cannot work where there are no policies, where there is no training, where nobody has a clue of what to do. It's certainly not that we can't do what we are supposed to because of logistics. In the mean time, I am doing the best that I can for my kids through all of this.

PEPI   Does it seem like there is a great deal of anti–intellectualism, that people don't want to know, they don't want to read, and they won't attend workshops to expand their understandings of the issues at hand?

BETH   I think that the anti–intellectualism comes mainly from the more mainstream population of teachers and administrators. At least for the Haitian teachers, they seem open and willing to learn. But, if you don't have a boss that is working with you in terms of designing a program, then the results are obvious. In the good Bilingual Programs that I have visited, the director is smart, knowledgeable, and he or she gets involved with what teachers do. They know how the program is organized. Not my director; he doesn't have a clue as to what's going on in any classroom. He says, "Oh, you know what you're doing, do what you want." At first it was nice to have all that autonomy, but after a while, it put us as ESL teachers in a precarious situation. In our building we have 40 students and 3 teachers. In the mainstream, there are 536 students and 26 teachers—so we are a minority. Now if we don't have stuff that's in writing that says what we have to do because this is the job, then we are in a position of having to go negotiate everything with mainstream teachers one-on-one, case-by-case. Well, that takes away a lot of power from us, and I'm sick of it because I don't like negotiating when I'm at a clear disadvantage: when the mainstream teachers are thinking that I don't have a right to be telling them what to do, when they are thinking that I don't really know anything, that I'm not a legitimate teacher. I'm not going to be in that position anymore, it's humiliating. You have to go with your hat in your hand to beg for crumbs.

PEPI   What about any of the other administrators, do they help?

BETH   This year, our principal, who is new, is all into inclusion. The ESL teachers are now going to be part of a close collaboration effort to suddenly include the ESL students in the mainstream courses. Well, she never even told the mainstream teachers who are getting the ESL students that this was going to happen. She just assumed that they would figure it out and that they would be delighted to collaborate. Yeah, right *(laughs sarcastically)*! So she put us in that situation. Here we are in the classroom, in the lion's den with someone who doesn't like us or our kids, doesn't want us in there, and then we are trying to get a little piece of the action. It was horrible. I just finally said, "Look, I'm not doing this, don't put me in this position, I'm not doing it!"

PEPI   Which makes it that much easier to misplace the blame for a lack of integration in the school. Now it can be made to look like you were the unwilling party—never really addressing how you were driven away. Does anyone ever confront the malicious behavior of the mainstream teachers?

BETH   Never, not at all! These things are also happening to the other ESL teachers as well, like the reading teacher. She'll be in this sixth-grade class where she works with including ESL students. She'll be in the middle of a lesson and, I swear to god, the regular teacher will say, "Well, you have to stop now because I have to get back to my math lesson." Can you imagine! I'm telling you that it is too professionally humiliating to be put in that position. I didn't do all that I have done to be put in that situation— I have been certified for seventeen years and I have been in this school system for four. It gets worse every year instead of better. There is this one teacher who is senile. I was going into her class a few days a week to help some Creole-speaking students understand what was going on. The kids could basically cope just fine and didn't need me, but for some reason there was this idea that they did. That's the climate around here, they don't want to deal with these kids if they can avoid it in any way. One day I went in there to get my students to take them out for a lesson, and the teacher said to me, "By the way, could you make me a couple of copies of this paper?" I told her that I didn't have a break until lunch and asked her when her next break was. She responded, still pushing the paper in my direction, "Well, I don't need this until after lunch." This is how she defines inclusion. For god sakes, I'm not a helper!! When things like this happen I just have to go somewhere to vent for like ten minutes.

PEPI   The Multicultural Central Steering Committee, that is in charge of implementing multicultural education systemwide, has been in place for about five years now.

BETH   Has it really?

PEPI   Do you ever see them or the subcommittees that have been established in each school? Do they ever come and talk to people, or hook up with the Bilingual/ESL Programs? Do they have any positive influence that you can see?

BETH   Not that I see. It's clearly an area that needs to be addressed. We have this activity that we have to do each year—the "School Improvement Plan." The entire staff has to work on it, and we have to decide on four areas that we are going to address. The principal of the school has to then report on what we have proposed and accomplished. Every year, since I've been in this building, of the four areas there is always one that deals with diversity. However, there's no more than four people on that committee *(laughs)*—me, the two other ESL teachers, and maybe another person. The other three committees are overflowing.

PEPI   Are there additional forms of professional development around diversity issues?

BETH   All of the people in my building have had this nationally known workshop several times, where you learn not to pat an Asian student on the head *(laughs)*. All of that is really pretty irrelevant if we are talking about racism. To me, racism is just such a hard thing to confront. Even I am not willing to go on record with someone who is not my friend and say this person is behaving in a racist way. Many people don't understand that what they are doing is racist. They are just doing what they've always done. They are using the same old textbook. They are using the same classroom methods that they've always used, and they can't figure out why all of the sudden it is racist to do so. Well, because it excludes some of the kids that you are trying to teach, so you have to change. But these people don't believe that there is any reason why they should change their teaching methods. The attitude is, "You are asking me to change something that I've been doing for twenty-five years, that I am comfortable with, and that has always worked with students." I would venture to say that it has worked with 50 percent of the students. Even twenty-five years ago, there were white, poor, and working-class kids, and they weren't passing the spelling test either. As long as schools always got a certain percentage of "success," and the right ones went on and did well, everything was fine. It's very threatening for these people to be asked to change their attitudes and methods because in a way it's no longer going to guarantee that people like them and their children are going to be successful. It's like saying, "We know what worked for us, let's stick with that, then I know that people that I like are going to get ahead." Now you're asking them to teach something else and they don't know if it works for their choice kids.

PEPI   I call that discrimination, and that's being polite.

BETH   Of course it is, but you cannot explain that to such people; first of all, they wouldn't listen. Unfortunately, teachers, especially those in the mainstream, have been doing what they've been doing for so long that they don't even recognize what their role is in reproducing the current system. They need to be made aware of it if we are going to effectively teach anything, especially a second language.

The Year 2000

The last two years of the millennium would not see much change in Changeton. On December 8, 1998, a teenaged girl was stabbed outside the high school cafeteria. But the response to the violence was not one of public debate. As in the 1960s and 1970s, many people downplayed the problem. As one School Committee member stated, "The schools are safe. . . . There have been some problems in the past, but they are very rare (Boyle, 1998b, p. B12). But according to a state audit that year, Changeton had used "$300,000 in educational reform money for school police" (Hancock, 1998, p. 1). In a response to the three marked cars and eight "male officers with powers of arrest," who during school emergencies wear "bullet-proof vests and carry Glock pistols that shoot hollow bullets," the state's education commissioner told the local papers, "This is totally inappropriate if it is around kids in the school. . . . I support safe schools, but this is not a fort. . . . We do not want a militia" (p. 1).

In March of 1999, a week after the drive-by-shooting of a Changeton High

School student, the new mayor refused to join in with other cities in the lawsuits against gun manufacturers. He argued that Changeton did not need to highlight crime, insisting that if the city joined in the gun suit, the first result would be to put a spotlight on local crime (Hickey, 1999, p. B5). Backing the mayor's decision, an article in the local paper, the *Nosurprise*, stated: "He [the mayor] made a wise decision. The city should be looking ahead to its brightness, not the darkness of the past. It should be highlighting its progress, its growing economy and its safe streets, not its crime rate" (Hickey, 1999, p. B5). Next door to where a seventeen-year-old was found dead in a drive-by shooting (possibly, the police thought, gang related), the neighbor stated, "There's drug deals going down here all the time and a shooting here about every night" (Cornell, Heaney, & Farmer, 1999). Police found bullets embedded in three different houses at the scene of the crime.

On the brighter side, in August of 1998, upon the resignation of the principal who was infamous for his school expulsion rates, Jake (the former member of the CSC) was named the acting head of the Changeton High School, that is, until a replacement could be found. He was "the first African American to become principal—even temporarily—at the high school" (Boyle, 1998b, p. 5). School Committee members applauded the decision.

Nonetheless, public schools in the city continued to be swamped with inhibiting inequities. That same year, the student-to-teacher ratio was 27 to 1, SAT averages remained below the state averages, and only 50 percent of the graduates were going off to four-year colleges (Yahoo! Real Estate, 1998). The average number of classrooms with internet access was 1.7 as compared to the state average of 40.4 (Fanton State Department of Education, 1998). Supported by the teachers union, a charter school (a public institution that is independently managed) was being opened in order to mitigate student dropout rates, although potential enrollees were being referred to by local press in negative ways: "The prospective charter school students are educational misfits in some ways, otherwise they would have succeeded at Changeton High School" (Yarmalovicz, 1998b, p. B8). Throughout the district, Special Education placements increased.

With the horrific outcomes of the FCAS (the Fanton Comprehensive Assessment System's standardized test), which racially subordinated, linguistic-minority, and poor children across the state overwhelmingly flunked, the future of multicultural education in the city is bleak (by the tenth grade, students who do not pass the exam will not be allowed to graduate—they will be awarded a "certificate of attendance"). In 1999, 42 percent of the tenth-grade students in Changeton failed the English Language Arts section, 76 percent failed the Math, and 58 percent failed in Science and Technology.

The two letters in the following chapter, from Changeton teachers who grew up in the community, offer caution, insight, and avenues of agency to local educators on the brink of the twenty-first century.

CHAPTER ELEVEN

Two Letters to Changeton Educators

~

Letter One
November 29, 1999

While in the Changeton Public School System an administrator remarked to me, "You just want to say things to keep people on their toes." The fact of the matter is that I say what I say and write the way I write so as to resist ideologies that attempt to bring me and many students in Changeton to our knees.

Recently, while driving down a local street near the center of the city, I was drawn to a sign posted by the Changeton Education Association which boldly read, "Education Makes America Work – Congratulations Class of 1999." What if we consider the reality that currently 1 percent of the population controls 45 percent of the wealth in the United States, that 1 percent remains primarily male and primarily white, and that: "One out of four children is born into poverty in this, the world's wealthiest nation. That's by the government's own under-counting measure . . . [and that] in lower-income schools [such as Changeton] they are rationing out-of-date textbooks and toilet paper" (Sklar, 1996). The salient question for me is for which part of the United States is education working? Education in Changeton has certainly not worked for most of the friends I grew up with on Nilson and Temple Streets: some have been pushed into the prison industrial complex, most never finished high school, and most remain on the economic cliffs and lifelines of this society.

Education certainly did not work for me growing up in Changeton. Reflecting on my experiences as a Cape Verdean youth, I can recall how most of my time was spent in devising and implementing strategies to resist the indoctrination of a school system and its functionaries that I knew were deeply hurting me. As the struggle to become truly educated was never easy, I often contemplated leaving school so as to evade the omnipresent stigma of negative representations about who I was as a bilingual West African in the world, and suffering downright dehumanization.

By writing this letter, by no means are my intentions to individualize my experiences. A sociohistorical analysis of the (mis)education of African Americans pointedly deconstructs the myth that "Education Makes America Work." James Baldwin (1979) was just one of many black public intellectuals who correctly asserted that "the brutal truth is that the bulk of white people in America never had any interest in educating black people, except as this could serve white purposes" (p. 6). This was true when blacks were relegated to property status during slavery, and it's certainly true today under this current system of economic slavery. The question that we must pose therefore is, for whom is education working? What purposes is education serving?

We exist in a society that invests in the language of freedom, equality, and justice for all, and yet, historically this country has undertaken the most cruel and inhumane treatments of those that it racializes. How can a nation simultaneously subscribe to the ideals of human rights and the ideology of white supremacy? Education, especially the one I came to know intimately in Changeton (yet I have no reason to believe that it is much different across the country), serves primarily to contain subordinated groups and promote the language of exclusion and of white supremacy. As one student recently confided in me, "Changeton High School is not a school, it's a prison!" Although this student was referring mainly to the pervasive structures of punishment constructed mainly to silence students who resist indoctrination, her comment was also indicative of a school system that attempts to restrict the movement of oppositional (or counter-) discourses and social agency. In other words, this is a school system that represses the emergence of voices that could potentially rupture systemic oppression.

In Changeton this policing of discourse is evident in all areas of the public sphere. Recently, Changeton was nominated one of thirty finalists for ten All-America City designations. The All-America City Awards is an event hosted by the National Civic League, which serves the purpose of highlighting progressive practices in cities across the United States. The city of Changeton used the opportunity to window dress progress and use the designation of "An All-America City" to make the city more competitive and marketable with regards to grant procurements. The entire preparation phase for the All-America City Awards was laced with an official suffocation of voices from the margin. In both the preparation phase, as well as the event itself, I cannot count how many times the group was told, "Be positive, smile . . . it sends a positive message, let's hug each other and hold hands." It was clear that the primary objective here was to manufacture consent to lies. In fact, the delegation was told that no one would answer juror questions except "experts." Those experts, of course, were city officials, the superintendent, someone representing the police force, and other "officials" that clearly were invested heavily in the system. The speeches read before the jury did nothing more than blame those who bear the social cost in the city of Changeton for their own predicament.

This type of language fogs reality. What it says is that we should pretend that the mayor of Changeton just one week earlier did not remove thousands of people from the human family by suggesting that immigrants "are Neanderthals. . . . They are not normal people. . . . They are psychos." The mayor's comments were made in light of a shooting where the victim was a Cape Verdean–American youth and the perpetrator was fully American. Clearly, he was not referring to criminal behavior in these statements. The statements were calculated and engineered to assault a specific segment of Changeton's immigrant community, namely the new wave of immigrants such as the Cape Verdean, Haitian, and Latino/a communities. Why were these statements made? The mayor won the support of many bigots in the city who were publicly outraged that Cape Verdeans were part of the delegation to the All-America City Awards. He also eased the fear of a racial transition in Changeton by calling for "deportation sweeps." Lastly, Changeton just won an $18 million grant (the biggest the city has ever received) to be applied to youth work. Why not create a perception of "out of control kids of color" so as to be able to feed all that money to the police force, gang units, the construction of a new courthouse (the most aesthetically pleasing structure in the city), more beds for D.Y.S. (Department of Youth Services) contracted facilities, and governmental "at-risk" troubleshooters. It would not be surprising at all to me, given the city's history of mismanagement, that those funds received are misappropriated.

Nothing calls into question more the pervasive silencing that goes on in Changeton than the school system's handling of a student who courageously spoke out publicly against the mayor's comments. In a graduation ceremony, this student eloquently captured the pulse of the city and demanded that the mayor publicly apologize for comments made against the new immigrant populations of Changeton. The next day, the student returned to Changeton High School, where he is the president of the junior class, and confronts a "gag order issued by the Changeton Public School System." The student was no longer allowed to speak publicly until, as one administrator put it, "he earns our trust back." It seems to me rather ironic that a woman, during the same graduation, would speak of the grandeur of the work of Dr. Martin Luther King, Jr. and the civil rights movement, but when a brilliant young man steps up and engages the spirit of this movement, he is publicly disciplined.

When the Changeton Public School System speaks of diversity, what it in fact wants is a specific type of diversity. It wants someone "of color" who can be easily domesticated into consenting to speak politely and telling nothing but lies. This young man indirectly asked a major question that was not touched on in the graduation ceremonies. While everyone was speaking of "believing in yourself, you can do it if you try" . . . and so on, his questions were, "Where are the structures that will sustain us?" "How can we do it in a city where the highest public figure is attempting to verbally cut us down?" The entire episode pointed to nothing more than a breach of democracy. Democracy is essentially about the opening of public discourse and holding public officials accountable for statements and actions. The silencing of this young man (although the mayor and school officials quickly found that it would be best to remove the "gag order" given the media and community attention this case raised) points to the autocratic nature of our school system and government.

Changeton is part and parcel of the larger social system that distorts histories so as to make it non-threatening to the dominant culture. As far as I'm concerned, the slogan on the billboard mentioned earlier fits neatly into a body of text designed primarily to maintain the dominant groups' doctrinal control.

It's impossible to understand United States history without studying from the many Native-American perspectives, and from other such groups who continue to bear the social cost of this colonial model. Teachers need to understand and engage students on how dominant classes have not only engineered history, but also systematically responded to and subdued counter-memories. Teachers in Changeton (nationwide for that matter) need to understand how even the curricular focus on European glories is flawed because it fails to read into the harsh lived experiences of white peasants and the working classes who also haven't bore [sic] the fruit of "victory." Within this objectifying process, where our very presence is not sociohistorically interrogated, there is this pervasive investment in teaching what Saul Alinsky (1971) called "classic American fairy tales" (p. 89). These depoliticized fairy tales, which fail to speak to the social realities of students in Changeton, present "every problem [as having] already been solved or is about to be solved. Textbooks [and teachers] exclude conflict or real suspense. They leave out anything that might reflect badly upon our national character. . . . Textbooks [and teachers] never use the present to illuminate the past" (Loewen, 1995, p. 28). This is the type of history I was subjected to in Changeton as both a student and a teacher. It's the type of indoctrination still being promoted, with the exception of a handful of critical educators who resist this nonsense.

The role of education in Changeton, both inside and outside of the school walls, represents the ultimate logic of domination in which you have a very pervasive system of segregation. You have a criminal justice system that physically contains groups primarily by maintaining a very visible police force in areas inhabited by Cape Verdeans, Latino/as and African Americans; not to mention "gang" units that harass youth of subordinated backgrounds, and function to restrict physical movement. And, you have an educational system that contains the creative and curious minds of young people. What I'm seeing in this city amounts to nothing less than a carefully thought out form of colonialism.

What's ironic is that multiculturalism has been ingeniously woven into the fabric of this paradigm of colonialism through a liberal language that serves as an anesthetic and functions to control and police marginalized discourses. In short, multiculturalism in this city and country has been co-opted to more adequately fit the doctrinal system. It's not seen or practiced as a vehicle to resist oppression, but rather, one that ultimately sedates and silences the oppressed.

Education in the Changeton Public School System is deadly for the majority of students who traverse its path on a daily basis. It was deadly when I encountered it, and it's more so now than ever. One need only glance at the rate of students pushed out of school today or into suspension closets deliberately built to keep resistant (as if the resistance does not mean something) youths of subordinated groups out of sight and out of mind. One need only take a look at Changeton's tracking system by walking into an advanced and basic classroom at the junior high school in which I studied as a youth, and worked as an adult. The advanced classes are made up by all-white middle- and upper-middle-class faces, and the basic classes are comprised of students from subordinated groups (African Americans, Cape Verdeans, Latino/as, and Haitians), including some impoverished and working-class whites. At this junior high school, there were the advanced classes in the Red Cluster called the "Aces," and the basic classes were officially referred to as the "Deuces." The doctrinal system excitingly parades this type of education around in the name of "excellence" and "fairness." However, unless we are coming from the racist assumption that those of the darker hue, or those who are socioeconomically disenfranchised, are inherently inferior intellectually to whites and the more affluent, this practice is stupendously oppressive and totally unjustified.

At one point in my professional experience in Changeton, I was asked to cover an advanced class and was amazed by the oasis of sameness I confronted. I walked directly into the assistant principal's office to relate my disapproval of this practice, to which he responded, "Well, let's ask the guidance counselor why this is so." Randomly pointing the finger, the guidance counselor—who was more preoccupied with his retirement than education—pointed to the grade schools as the problem and walked away quickly so as to avoid the conversation.

When I reflect on all the institutional obstacles that the youth in Changeton confront, I can't think of a principled reason why they don't drop out. It would seem to me to be an act of resistance rather than failure. In actuality, the conditions are such that students are being forced out. In 1993, the dropout figures among certain groups were visibly astronomical. Today of course, despite the fact that Changeton has a data analyst on staff, all numbers magically disappear. In a telephone conversation with an administrator, I noted a total unwillingness to disclose numbers. When I stated that certainly there were more African Americans, Latino/as and Cape Verdeans dropping out of school than whites, the administrator's response was, "I don't know how you can say that!" His entire position was laced with an "official" obfuscation of reality and outright denial. In his estimation, education works in the city of Changeton. Rather than falling victim to the slogan's dogma, my question remains, *for whom* and *for what* purposes?

If education has worked in the city of Changeton, why is it that we as students, and now as educators, spend so much energy recycling conversations about which teachers to avoid due to their incessant racist and anti-youth attitudes. How was education working when an English teacher pulled me to the side and questioned my competence the first day of his honors English class because of the fact that I am Cape Verdean? How is education working for many other students who have recently come to me stating that this very same English teacher still subjects them to this practice? How was education working when in the majority of social studies classes that I was subjected to, teachers would simply place notes on an overhead projector, have us copy them for about an hour, take a test every week, and call it teaching? How is education working for students of subordinated groups who are force-fed upper-middle-class views of the world through standardized tests, then return to school the next day with their ears ringing from hearing gunshots in the street outside their bedroom window the night before? How is education preparing them to handle their lived experiences? How was education working when a sociology teacher bluntly told me that blacks are inherently less intelligent than whites, and that Asians reigned supreme? At least this particular educator was honest enough to overtly expose feelings that most people have but express in more covert and oppressively creative ways. Such incidents were never isolated. There was always deep-seated and pervasive racism and ethnocentrism that tormented students like me.

Returning in 1997 as an employee, I cannot recall one day that I did not go home physically and mentally drained as a result of at least one racist incident, or as a result of engaging oppressive structures. In fact, I would argue that this investment in oppressive structures is the main reason why the Changeton Public School System does not attract or sustain employees who come from subordinated groups. If the power elite of the city's schools claim that they are looking to diversify the faculty and staff, the fact is it's looking for a specific type of foot soldier "of color" to fill some menial position—someone who is easily domesticated.

Recently an assistant principal asked me, "Do you think these kids misbehave because they feel they are oppressed by whites?" Of course his demeanor, colonial gaze, and former actions placed him in the long line of white supremacists.

Ironically, this particular administrator is Jewish. Nonetheless, he does not see how he benefits from the unearned privilege of white skin, and how he is implicated in reproducing oppressive practices in the Changeton Public School System. Not only did he trivialize oppression, but he proceeded to blame the victim by isolating the way that "they feel as the cause of their problems." A simple analysis of his use of language positions him deeply behind racist walls. The language he should have adopted was, "Are whites oppressing these kids?" Or more concretely, "Am I oppressing these kids?" Of course, he doesn't seem to think so given the fact that he responded to a parent's concern that teachers at the school have no respect for culture, by stating, "Culture has no place here!" After completing his statement he looked to me for affirmation (as whites in power often do in the presence of the "other"). Of course, I proceeded to educate him, but would later find it a useless task, as he looked at me, smiled a colonial smile, and stated, "You showed me that I'm a bigot." Two hours later he would enter the suspension room and look at the brown and black faces before him (two of them he placed in this room for two months) and again state, "It's not about culture. It's not about where you come from. It's about behavior and respect!" This, to me, is clearly an abusive infliction of power. Had he understood, or even cared to understand, the lived realities of students in this society, he would have realized that the very resistance and oppositional strategies of the majority of students against oppression are in fact constitutive of culture. Several weeks later, this same man told me that a full teaching contract would probably not be granted to me given the way I did things; to which I responded, "My work is not a source of money, positions, or contracts. It's a source of dignity."

Very often I wonder whether or not this man (and the white supremacist patriarchal power structure in general) sees itself. I have difficulty believing that such people operate from a position if innocent ignorance. In light of the overwhelming evidence and acts of personal racism and ethnocentrism that I face, and that I see others facing, I believe that Albert Memmi (1963) was correct when he asserted that the oppressor has a "Nero Complex." In other words, he/she consciously oppresses more and more so as to avoid his/her own feelings of evilness. People of this sort not only hide behind power but also abuse it and inflict it in despicable ways that often fall into the realm of sadism. I have a hard time believing that this man simply can't see his complicity in teachers sending a disproportional number of black students to the office for disciplinary action. In a two-month period, he placed about thirty black students, and only two whites, in the in-school suspension room. Most white students, especially those of the middle to upper middle class, are given a little lecture and returned to their rooms, while black students are kept in a closet for weeks for the same behaviors. In a fourteen day period, I sat in five meetings with this man and some white teachers, where the purpose was to convince parents that their children should be placed on Ritalin for hyperactivity (three of these students were Cape Verdean and two were African American). Not only must the system subject those without sustainable power to an education that silences, but it must also recommend the use of sedatives to render students of subordinated backgrounds totally without voice.

With the release of standardized test scores, in which Changeton failed miserably, a new and more morbid culture of silence plagues the city's public school system. New initiatives and programs are constantly introduced to get "those kids" excited about reading. These literacy programs never engage the lived realities of those who bear the social cost of systematic exclusion as an entry point to literacy development. Needless to say, such programs are a mere reproduction of the oppressive practices of the past. They again function to remystify the workings of discrimination, racism, and ethnocentrism (to name only a few social evils) as they are socially sanctioned by perceptions and consequent actions of a "normative" white supremacy (not excluding, of course, male supremacy, heterosexual supremacy, and other forms of perceived "normativeness").

New interpretations of multiculturalism anchored in a liberal mainstream ideology serves most potently to control the discourse on racism, sexism, heterosexism, and classism (to name only a few socially constructed problems). Many liberals hiding behind this "feel-good" brand of pedagogy come from a location where they view the very presence of diverse bodies before them as multiculturalism in practice. In their warped form of thinking, the mere presence of diverse bodies within a physical space will naturally bring people together in ways that they will learn to embrace one another. This position is naïve given the fact that, for example, men and women have shared very intimate spaces for as long as we've known, yet the investment in the ideology of patriarchy is rampant. If these educators weren't suffering from selective amnesia, they would engage history and problematize the fact that often when those in power have come to share spaces with the "other," they have used this space to gain knowledge so as to reinscribe domination. This was certainly the case prior to the enslavement of Africans on the continent. It was the case at the moment they came to know Native Americans. It was the case in Cuba under the Batista regime, where the United States converted the island into a virtual capitalistic entertainment center for affluent white businessmen from the United States. It certainly is the case today with Puerto Rico where the United States is militarily pimping Vieques Island. By no means am I dismissing the fact that some whites have fought racial injustice and collaborated with nationalist struggles to end the hegemony of whites in colonial territories. Nonetheless, we cannot abstract the fact that more evil has been perpetuated than good when whites come to "share" spaces with the "other." Furthermore, if educators problem-posed their very subject position in the classroom, they would understand that their very symbolic presence, if never critically addressed, constitutes a source of tension and threat; especially given the fact that over 90 percent of the teachers in the United States are white.

My point is that the form of multiculturalism into which students in Changeton are pushed is one that damages. It's is a form of multiculturalism that is dehistoricized, one that revictimizes by forcing the release of emotions such as rage and guilt, but never connecting those emotions to positive political projects. It's a form of multiculturalism through which the oppressor dictates a position of comfort. When racism is engaged in Changeton classrooms (which is rare to say the least) it's always isolated to individual storytelling. This storytelling functions to allow the victimizer a space where s/he never has to situate him/herself. The victim proceeds to educate the oppressor through a type of deinstitutionalized and dehistoricized sequence of events and experiences that in the end functions to create what Donaldo Macedo (1994) calls "a form of group therapy that focuses on the psychology of the individual . . . [which] does little beyond making the oppressed feel good about their sense of victimization" (p. 123). We cannot speak of multiculturalism in a meaningful way without analyzing the structures of power in this country. To engage cultural politics without interrogating unequal relations of power is to dishonestly fashion diversity in a manner that renders it nonthreatening to those who reign.

As the demographics of Changeton continue to shift as the so-called minorities are actually becoming the majority, the levers of power continue to rest in the hands of an overwhelmingly affluent white group. The policies and the atmosphere generated continue to point to a fear of racial transition. Local television and radio programming is laced with the theme that Changeton needs to return to its glorious past. In its "glorious" past there were no Cape Verdeans, African Americans, Haitians or Latino/as. At one point I thought that this grand image was being accomplished through the public dissemination of anti–intellectualism. I now know that cannot be correct because a great deal of intellectual energy is spent on denying the existence of a mosaic of cultures that have been living in the city since the plantation's inception, and their lived experience in resisting domination. If there is a cultural celebration promoted by the power structure it's often a distorted picture of culture. This denial severely jeopardizes the city's future because it attempts to counter reality. A great number of cities in this country have traveled that path and I cannot think of one that has won in terms of peace and justice. In this unwillingness to respect groups who are not white, and the diversion of whites who live from paycheck to paycheck away from their connection to other subordinated groups, Changeton will find its own destruction.

Many teachers will criticize my position as Changeton "teacher bashing." Yet those educators and concerned citizens with greater political awareness have applauded my position because I am able to say what they can't because of the repercussions and levels of totalitarianism in the Changeton Public School System.

Clearly, I have met teachers in the system who are exceptionally bright and extremely effective in exposing students to the theoretical languages necessary to navigate and transform the system—creating spaces for students to organize, develop their voice, and work as change agents. However, the number of these teachers is very small. Changeton has already lost many critical educators who have been put in positions where they would have to compromise their values and subject themselves to an unbearable cacophony of cognitive dissonance.

I hope that my small testimony will have an impact on the dehumanizing discourses and oppressive structures currently working through the Changeton Public School System. I hope that in highlighting the truth as I have experienced it, this book will impel action both within and outside the system. I hope that teachers will seriously ask themselves the critical questions: *Who/what* am I teaching, and for *what* purposes? Only when we begin to probe deeply the meaning of these questions, without abstracting them from institutional oppression and the sociohistorical conditions that have brought both students and teachers to this present moment in time, can we arrive and rearrive at a liberatory praxis.

Ricardo Rosa

Letter Two
November 29, 1999

To: Changeton teachers

When I was first asked to share some of my experiences working for the Changeton Public Schools, I was apprehensive. I felt as though I did not have the "right" to critically analyze the institution in a public forum. Fortunately my thinking has evolved to the point where I in fact believe that this is perhaps my sole escape from the psychological dissonance created from a complex love-hate relationship. It is above all, a necessity for alleviating a guilt associated with working for the same system that oppresses which forces me to put things in perspective and on public record. If you're wondering whether this will affect me professionally, you obviously don't know Changeton at all. The mentality here is you are either with us or against us. Of course, for so many working in the system, reality is so obfuscated by those in power that it is difficult to conceive that there may indeed be problems within the institution, hence it is difficult to visualize, let alone materialize, dissent. I feel as though I am running a personal risk that is, strangely enough, immensely purifying spiritually and psychologically comforting.

I suspect that there will be a twofold reaction to the telling of some of my experiences in the Changeton Public Schools. The first will be to chastise me for the sheer arrogance of thinking that I could possibly know about, or have anything to contribute to, the Changeton schools. After all, what gives me the right to even have an opinion about the issues? I should be thankful enough that I was even allowed into the "Club." The other reaction of course will be, "It's a good thing someone is saying something, even though I'm glad I'm not the one doing it." I expect that the latter comment will be confined to those teachers who feel the same oppressive conditions at work, but cannot risk naming the oppressor for fear of professional repercussions. In any case, I truly hope that my experiences as a Cape Verdean, bilingual teacher can contribute to an understanding of the system itself and some of the pressures that the majority of students go through.

Although my professional journey through the Changeton Public Schools [began] at the elementary level, as it does for many other teachers, I now find myself at the high school. It is one of the biggest high schools on the eastern seaboard. With an enrollment of thousands of students, a great percentage is either Cape Verdean, Latino/a, or African American. Within these groups, one can find a multitude of experiences and variations in social and academic backgrounds.

With all the logistical problems faced by teachers and students, perhaps none is as damaging and oppressive as the lack of cultural respect and understanding. The nature of the problem is such that the ones who feel this problem most are those at the bottom of the power pyramid. The best way to illustrate this condition is probably through the recounting of different events that have occurred while I've been associated with the Changeton Public Schools. I'll take just two recent examples out of a long history of oppressive practices that I've witnessed. These two events may in fact give the outsider a glimpse into the ideologies that permeate every level of the institution.

During the 1998 academic year, a Cape Verdean youth named Dino Fernandes was tragically shot and killed in Changeton—another victim of this country's history and culture of cruelty and indifference. Every Cape Verdean at the high school felt the effects of Dino's death. To many of the students it really made no difference that they did not know Dino personally, what mattered was that he was Cape Verdean and that made him part of a "family." Most of the teachers responsible for teaching the Cape Verdean population found themselves assisting students in dealing with the grief and anger of having lost a loved one in such a tragic manner. My understanding is that there was some group counseling available to students in the school's library, but there was little recognition that the event had even happened on a school-wide level. The sense that I felt from many of the staff was that he was only a Cape Verdean youth—just another African, and probably a troublemaker at that. Only one teacher asked me if I knew what had happened and if I knew Dino personally.

At the height of this period of grief, for several days, pleas for assistance for the victims of the tragedy in Kosovo were part of the school morning announcements. The calls for support were emotional, and thankfully and honorably many students responded with financial donations which were then properly distributed to the needy victims. The purpose of bringing this issue forward is not to criticize such noble efforts, but rather to illustrate the double standard that applies to different populations in Changeton.

During this same time period as the crisis in Kosovo, Cape Verdean students requested permission to collect financial donations to assist Dino's family with funeral expenses. The request was flatly refused by the school's administration. Apparently the administration didn't even want to deal with the issue. The order of the day was, "We need to move on." When, at the request of the students, some teachers met with the administration to inquire as to the reasons for the denial, the official response was, "I don't want to set up a precedent. If we do this for the Cape Verdeans then we'll have to do it for every other population." When an attempt was made to correlate the Kosovo issue with the tragedy of the Cape Verdean boy, the administrator stated, "Well that's a whole different ball game." The magnitude of the former warranted the collection of donations, but a Cape Verdean youth in our own city didn't have the same impact in the greater scheme of things.

By the end of the meeting, the administrator "recognized" that the issue was important to the students and advised the teachers to come up with some plan other than collecting donations in the cafeteria and that he would review the plan. What is again ironic is that most clubs in Changeton High School sell flowers or candy in the cafeterias to raise money for one issue or another. The teachers were so discouraged by the stance that the administration was taking that they realized that very little could be done. Nonetheless, the students were encouraged to donate personally to the family. For all those who were able to nobly organize and participate in the efforts to assist the victims in Kosovo, much praise is due; however, it is clear that this group possessed a racial predisposition and the cultural capital to make demands upon the system that Dino's friends and family simply did not.

A few weeks after Dino's death, an article was published in a Changeton newspaper expressing an opinion that Changeton should not seek to prosecute the makers of handguns as many other cities and states across the country were doing because issues of violence were in the "past" and Changeton did not need to bring that type of publicity back into the headlines. Try telling this to Dino's family.

On November 9, 1999, a student of Changeton High School approached me regarding an issue that was, according to him, "morally wrong." As the student was visibly upset, I took every precaution to carefully listen to the problem. Apparently, there was an order by the Yearbook Committee that all captions under the students' photos were to be written "solely in English and in standard English at that." The teacher informed him that there must have been some mistake, as this ruling was in fact illegal according to federal laws governing language discrimination and discrimination based on national origin. The student was reassured that the teacher would follow up and discuss the matter with the Yearbook Committee to assess the "real story" concerning the use of language.

The initial meeting with the chairperson of the Yearbook Committee was one in which the issue of First Amendment rights seemed to be totally irrelevant in the matter, as the maintenance of the yearbook was a privilege and therefore unaffected by such legislation. Apparently what was a bigger factor than the First Amendment was that, "according to some estimates," there are over forty-three languages represented in the school and the printing company could not accommodate all these languages. The meeting ended when the chairperson of the Yearbook Committee resorted to the argument that "What we're trying to do is produce one group capable of using one language."

Several times during the same day, different students approached me, as well as other teachers, complaining of the same situation. In a meeting of a student organization within the high school, I asked the students what they thought of the situation. This diversified group (Latino/as, Cape Verdeans, and a few white and African-American students) immediately expressed their concern over the violation of the rights of different groups to use their native languages. Ideas began to surface as to possible plans of action. By the end of the meeting, a decision had been unanimously taken to resort to writing a petition contesting the language mandate. This would in fact be productive not only as a viable lesson in the development of a civil rights movement, but it would also be a peaceful, going through the channels-type of approach. The petition was in fact written and in the space of two days, 500 signatures were collected. What was impressive was that this was a student initiative both in the conceptual as well as the implementation stage. A veteran staff member delivered the signed petition to the head administrator on Friday, November 10, 1999. This veteran administrator understood the critical nature of the problem and the positive aspect of what the students were trying to accomplish. The students anxiously awaited the decision from above. A meeting with the administrator was scheduled for the following Tuesday.

While preparing for the meeting, the students placed various calls to research the matter so as not to walk into the meeting totally in the dark. At the meeting, the following points were presented as to the reasons for the sudden change in the language statutes concerning the yearbook: "The school represents some forty different languages through the student body and it is virtually impossible for the printing company to accommodate all these languages"; "It is impossible to proofread all the languages to ensure that what goes in the yearbook is appropriate"; "There is no precedent for the use of other languages in the yearbook."

After all the arguments had been made, the teacher representing the students brought up the fact that the printing company had been contacted and that according to them, they could print any language. Further, many conscientious teachers had in fact volunteered to do the proofreading so as to ensure the quality of the yearbook. As a last measure, a past yearbook containing at least three different languages was presented to the administration.

After expressing some surprise that all this research had been done beforehand, the students were assured that after contacting the printing company, and provided that they could in fact accommodate all these languages, the decision would be reversed. What was astonishing was that, evidently the arguments weren't totally investigated by school personnel prior to the meeting. In other words, the arguments had no basis in fact. After a great deal of struggle, and a final realization on the part of the administrator as to the importance of the issue for the language-minority students, the decision was reversed.

I learned several lessons while going through this ordeal. The first and probably the most important was that language is the uniting factor for all the subordinated groups in the school. It represents the most integral part of culture and therefore the self. It is absolutely amazing that an issue of such importance to the different ethnic groups in the city would be taken so lightly by some of the staff. On the other hand, it also demonstrated the ease with which the use of certain languages could be prohibited through simple mandates. I have to say that after meeting with the administrator of the school, I could understand his position in not wanting "codes" in the yearbook; however, native languages should not have been included under this heading and the issue should have been researched in more depth. Having an understanding of the ideology that informs much of the faculty and staff's thinking in the school, I can understand the receptive nature with which the majority of faculty and staff supported the language mandate.

I can't help but ponder the significance of all the world's flags as they hang from the walls of the student cafeterias. If the issue is to represent diversity, I don't believe the objectives are being accomplished. To me they are simple ornaments to decorate and create the illusion that the system accepts difference. What is ironic in all of this is that on November 18, 1999, at the height of this controversy over the simple use of native language as a means of expression, an article appeared in the local Changeton newspaper applauding the multicultural nature of the city and highlighting different upcoming events. How is it possible to speak of multiculturalism while simultaneously discriminating against certain languages? Language, after all, is in fact codified culture.

It has been my experience that Changeton is multicultural to the extent that it has a varied population (sure to be evident in the upcoming 2000 census statistics), and that this variety is fully appreciated insofar as it does not challenge the power structure. For as long as the opinion of some of the staff at Changeton High School is that "What we're trying to do is produce one group capable of using one language," those who are seen as being "deficient" by the proponents of a subtractive form of bilingualism will always be shortchanged. I find some consolation in that there are some staff who can in fact read between the lines and see issues that the majority, by the very nature of their belonging to the power structure or having vested interests in the continued maintenance of unequal power relations, refuse to see and continue to obfuscate by claiming that all is well in the Changeton Public Schools.

It is essential that we critically understand who we are teaching and what their lived experiences may be. Only by listening to our students and opening up spaces for them to organize and dissent if need be, are we engaging multiculturalism. Only by understanding the political nature of education and its relationship to domination can we engage in ongoing multicultural praxis that ruptures systemic oppressions.

Joao Rosa

CHAPTER TWELVE

Challenges for the Future

≈

It is imperative that public educators and concerned citizens, caught in the middle of the culture wars that have been central to the history of the United States, work vigilantly to embrace multicultural education as being fundamental to an informed and critical democratic citizenry. However, as argued and illustrated throughout this book, such materialized theories should not be limited to bits and pieces of the curriculum, or to chic depoliticized and ahistorical methods for teaching students who have been systematically excluded from traditional bodies of knowledge and pedagogical approaches. The conceptual underpinnings of any transformative strategy for public schooling must be systemwide—the philosophy needs to be central to everything that takes place in schools and society. As understood by the Changeton Central Steering Committee, multicultural education should have an impact on employee professional development, curriculum and instruction, and the cultural makeup of the entire faculty and staff. The CSC acknowledged that this type of education is impossible without a creative partnership between the schools and the public. In this sense, the efforts in Changeton were on the right track to realizing more participatory and transformative kinds of learning.

What the committee needs to do from here on out is explore the multiplicity of theoretical and practical insights from across the spectrum of established and emerging camps of multicultural education—conservative, liberal, and critical. These models have an enormous implicit and explicit impact on the national struggles over representation, social relations, pedagogy, and curriculum. However, it is crucial that educators not simply adopt, at face value, such theoretical and practical ideas. Instead, they need to critically appropriate from and reinvent these works in order to adapt them to the historical specificities of their related but unique communities.

Critical multiculturalism is thus by no means a call for educators and an active public to become sponges of existing theory. On the contrary, Critical Multicultural Education is rooted in a democratic project that encourages new theories and languages of critique, resistance, and possibility capable of engaging (critically examining and transforming) the standard academic boundaries and social and educational practices that help to maintain the de facto social code in the United States. These new theories and languages provide the necessary analytic steppingstones for realizing a truly democratic process through which people can better identify the sociopolitical realities that shape their lives, begin to negotiate their differences, and where necessary, transform their practices. But how do we become active theorizers who are capable of making sense of the world for ourselves? While humans are surely biologically predisposed to be creative and curious, we are not endowed with critical thinking, that is, we do not have the proclivity to engage in ideological analysis. Criticicity of this sort comes from rigorous exposure and apprenticing. As such, democratic societies need to provide public spaces and places where these necessary skills can develop. One such site should be teacher education programs. As Ally and Susan [the two bilingual educators interviewed in Chapter Ten] emphasized in their call to democratize public schools, teacher education programs need to be reevaluated and restructured so that they prepare future educators for the complex cultural, economic, and political realities that they will inevitably face. Susan demands, "We really need to start in teacher colleges because educators across the board need to learn how to introduce multiculturalism." Instead of placing the sole accountability on teachers, we need to take a hard look at how they are professionally prepared, and who influences those institutions of higher education.

In my own personal experience, I certainly wasn't prepared to face the cultural politics of everyday life in public schools. When I was a masters and doctoral student at Harvard's Graduate School of Education, it was virtually impossible to explore and discuss how antagonistic sociohistorical and economic conditions are dramatically affecting learning, language acquisition, and literacy. Most professors, and consequently students, made claims to scientific objectivity as a means to discourage substantive debates over such pressing issues as white racism, ideology, class, capitalist social relations, patriarchy, and homophobia (Leistyna, 1999). Such institutions of cultural production—in most cases, cultural reproduction—need to be pushed to democratize the content of their classrooms so that students are exposed to a multiplicity of perspectives. This pedagogy of exposition and not imposition is intended to nurture an informed, flexible, critical and dynamic workforce. This is a far cry from the hegemonic, deskilling, teacher-as-technician paradigm that is currently so deeply entrenched.

Unfortunately, the basic tenets that constitute the core of Critical Multicultural Education have also often been neglected or dismissed within mainstream projects of change. Such efforts are consequently bereft of the dialogue, insights, and contributions that these perspectives offer. Popular endeavors, as embraced in Changeton, can invite surface reforms, but merely recognizing differences, and ignoring, avoiding, or remaining unaware of such related problems as white racism, economic exploitation, patriarchy, heterosexism, ableism, linguiscism, Eurocentrism, and other abuses of power, as a broader set of political and pedagogical concerns, will not lead to a transformation of the exclusionary structural and ideological patterns of this unequal and unjust society. As Peter McLaren (1995) argues, "Multicultural education without a transformative political agenda can just be another form of accommodation to the larger social order" (p. 126).

It is important to note here that Critical Multicultural Education is not simply (as it is often accused of being) some macro, theoretical, abstract undertaking in which realistic applications are beyond reach. On the contrary, as demonstrated in the critiques and suggested extensions of the work in Changeton, there is an inextricable relationship between critical social theory and practice, and most practical applications are not beyond the immediate possibilities of everyday schooling. Critical social theory and cultural studies have direct implications for institutional structures, social relations, methodological considerations, and curricular decisions, all of which should inspire the reconceptualization of different ways of knowing that rupture entrenched epistemologies and social and institutional discriminatory practices. However, in order to effectively put such critical tools to work, the CSC needs to stop ignoring the history of Changeton, its educational institutions, and previous efforts to infuse multicultural education. Unfortunately, the committee did so at its own expense. There were uncanny commonalities between the earlier attempts at the conceptualization and implementation of change tactics and those of 1993, such as:

- Racial balance was a serious motivating force and source of funding.
- There was a central task force/steering committee, as well as working/subcommittees, and school-based committees.
- A mission statement that welcomed diversity was drafted.
- Multicultural education was equated with affirming diversity and working toward integration, rather than with social transformation.
- The general concerns of both movements centered around professional development (which was equated with sensitivity training), curriculum and instruction (in which a cut-and-paste approach to the existing curriculum was attempted through the incorporation of superficial elements of culture), diversifying the faculty (more so for the 1993 efforts), and strategies for soliciting community input and parent involvement.

- There was a concern with assessment of linguistic-minority students (more so for the pre-1993 efforts).
- There were no clear definitions of culture, and instead of engaging a politics of identity and difference, culture was dealt with more as a category for racial and ethnic issues (although both race and ethnicity went undefined).
- There was little, if any, attempt to develop an understanding of the sociopolitical, historical, economic realities that shape educators and students' lives, or the relationship among ideology, power, macro politics, and schooling in everyday life.

As the initial effort to infuse multicultural education in Changeton bore no real fruit, it came as no surprise that little significant change occurred over a six-year period in the second major attempt by the Central Steering Committee. Instead of continuing to echo the shortcomings of earlier endeavors, the CSC needs to begin to reflect on history, realize more progressive ideas and practices that work for social justice, and grasp power so as to be able to implement real change. As Carl argued in Chapter Ten, "Let me say this, they [the CSC] have yet to seize power, they have yet to take power. At this moment they have no power, but there is potential for them to seize and grasp power around the issues that they present."

Hopefully, the CSC will seize the power by hooking up with all those organizations and individuals, especially those in government, who have expressed a deep commitment to change in the streets and the corridors of their city. In fact, this has to become a national trend in public education.

What's key to recognize is that multicultural education does not take place in a vacuum and cannot be understood outside of a recognition and analysis of the larger political landscape and social antagonisms that are reflected in the classrooms and the hallways of schools. If multicultural education doesn't take up the realities of cultural production and the maintenance of symbolic and physical violence in this country, then the opportunities for democratizing change and redistributing economic and political power are beyond realistic reach.

My last trip to Changeton was for jury duty in 2001. We had to make a decision affecting the life of an eighteen-year-old man who, along with a fourteen-year-old, a fifteen-year-old, and two sixteen-year-olds (all Changeton Public School students), was accused of aggravated rape and assault with a deadly weapon during the previous year of two other Changeton High School students. The young woman (seventeen years old) was accosted in a school yard alley, her boyfriend (also seventeen) was beaten and chased away, while she, with a gun to her head and a knife to her breast, was violated from behind. Beyond the immediate, micro-level judicial response, the answer is not to simply provide more police presence in the streets and schools, or to build more prisons (one of the largest growing private industries in the country with over two million people currently incarcerated). On the contrary, when we as a society look to defining and designing multiculturalism, it is imperative that we work counter to the prevailing logic of capital that celebrates greed over human rights. In fact, what is key to our failure as a nation (as evident in Changeton) is how we deal with the majority of students, especially racially subordinated, linguistic-minority, and poor children—how we systematically deny their language, culture, and humanity.

The cultural strife so prevalent in this country will not change on its own. It is with informed struggle and solidarity among significant facets of the public, and with ongoing critical dialogue, that substantive transformation becomes possible, even probable. This is a much more attractive solution than the nihilism and militarism offered up by conservatives, who are working vigilantly toward the kind of social domestication and spectacle in which no one is paying attention to the present social order. It is also a better option than following liberals for that matter, who have been co-opted into hiding behind the very unequal power relations that make a participatory democracy impossible. As Ricardo Rosa argued in his letter to Changeton teachers, "In short, multiculturalism in this city and country has been co-opted to more adequately fit the doctrinal system. It's not seen or practiced as a vehicle to resist oppression, but rather, one that ultimately sedates and silences the oppressed" (p. 270).

The realization and efforts of the Central Steering Committee are evidence of the possibility for the mobilization of agency to effect changes in the world; but the battle is far from over. While grassroots and micro-struggles must persist, it is imperative that they be connected with larger national and global efforts to democratize economic and cultural resources, and once and for all, as the children cry for in the painting on the street wall, "Stop The Violence!"

Appendix

Research Methodology

Theory behind the Research and Analysis

For the primary-analysis stage of the study, which I hoped would result in a description of what the Central Steering Committee had discussed and accomplished, I relied on Barney Glaser and Anselm Strauss's (1967) concept of "grounded theory." As such, the search for underlying patterns in the raw data led to the development of conceptual categories, properties, and tentative hypotheses, which gradually evolved into a core of emerging theory (a simultaneously deductive and inductive process that J. Katz [1983] refers to as "analytic induction").

Collecting the Data

Using qualitative methods of participant observation and document collection, I sat in on and recorded all of the Changeton Multicultural Central Steering Committee meetings (including subcommittee meetings and in-service workshops). The observation notes, which were my central source of data in this study, focused on what was said verbatim at these CSC meetings: ideas presented, issues raised, points of debate, decisions made. I also collected all documents that were shared among the group.

When information discussed during the CSC meetings was not clear, I briefly interviewed the person/s after the meeting. As an observer, I purposefully did not actively participate in any way in the CSC proceedings, other than these clarifying interviews, so that my outside experience would not influence the natural flow of their work.

The Data

CONTEXTUALIZATION DATA. This information provided an historical sketch of the research site. Data was taken from newspapers, town hall records, the local library, the historical society, published books, the school system's accreditation reports, and School Committee meeting minutes. I also conducted an ERIC database search looking for information specific to Changeton. Information about group members was taken from CSC progress reports and introductory documents that were developed by the committee and distributed districtwide to other schools.

PRIMARY SOURCES. The most important data collected for this study consisted of observation notes of all the CSC meetings (round table discussions, about once per month). This data, made up of fifty-four Multicultural Central Steering Committee meetings—including twenty subcommittee meetings and five in-services, was central in describing the developments in the group's work.

SECONDARY SOURCES. This data was collected in order to corroborate my observation notes. It consisted of official CSC minutes taken at each meeting by the committee's chairperson (minutes were also taken at all of the subcommittee meetings), CSC progress reports that were publicly distributed, and clarification interviews.

Data Analysis

CONTEXTUALIZATION DATA. The historical information about the town and the school system was analyzed in order to depict the conditions (such as demographic shifts) within which the impetus was generated for the development of the Changeton Multicultural Central Steering Committee and the system-wide multicultural program.

PRIMARY AND SECONDARY SOURCE DATA (CSC meetings, CSC meeting minutes, CSC official reports). This research was done to answer the question: What are the developments in the work of the Multicultural Central Steering Committee to conceptualize and infuse a system-wide multicultural education program? In order to answer the research question, the data were analyzed on an ongoing basis throughout this study. Analysis of all of the collected data consisted of three steps: coding, data display, and data reduction.

Coding

The Changeton Multicultural Central Steering Committee's areas of focus and inquiry (some of my first research findings) was color-coded in the data: purple marked the development of the committee's formation, basic processes, structures, and functions; red was for any information that spoke of the development of the committee's Mission Statement; yellow pertained to issues of professional development; blue was for any information that pertained to curriculum development; green marked the data that dealt with personnel issues (diversifying the faculty); and orange referred to community outreach efforts.

Such coded information was placed into color-coded folders that represented each of these general categories. The color-coded information in these folders was also accompanied by the actual CSC meeting (subcommittee or in-service) number from which the information came, the page number in my transcribed data, and the sentence number. For example, a piece of information that fell under "community outreach" was marked as o #5, p. 4, 36: this means that it was information about community outreach, taken from the fifth meeting (which is dated in the data), on the fourth page, in the thirty-sixth sentence. The dates/location in the data were important in terms of keeping a chronological record of events. This helped document the developmental changes in the CSC's work, that is, the entire list of information within each folder also showed when an idea originally surfaced, how it developed, when it became a central focus, and how committee attitudes may have shifted over time.

Subcategories were generated out of the more general categories and helped with more specific analyses. For example, under the purple code for the committee's basic processes, structures, and functions, more specific emerging concerns such as membership and funding were individually coded with a number and the first letter of the color that they fell under. As such, an example of a comment about funding would be coded as Fp #25, p. 7, 35: the number "F" is the subcategory, which in this case signifies funding; the letter "p" stands for the purple category of processes, structures, and functions; "#25" marks the Multicultural Central Steering Committee meeting number; "p. 7" indicates the page on which the information can be found in the transcribed observation notes; and "35" stands for the numbered sentence and where it can be located on the page. Again, the dates/location in the data were important in terms of keeping a chronological record of events.

Data Display

After cutting and pasting all the data into appropriate folders, the contents of each folder was displayed in a matrix chart. These charts placed the primary and secondary data sources side by side. For example, as purple marked the development of the committee's formation, basic functions and structures, I juxtaposed the following data: my purple coded observation notes from the CSC meetings (which included aftermath clarification interviews), the chairperson's minutes of the CSC meetings, and the CSC's progress reports. Each of these categories was individually portrayed in an effort to depict the developments therein.

Data Reduction

I worked primarily from the six matrix charts: purple (CSC's formation and basic processes, functions, and structures), red (CSC mission statement), yellow (professional development), blue (curriculum development), green (personnel issues), orange (community outreach). Within each of these coded areas of inquiry, I looked for general patterns of development.

After those major categories had evolved, and I was able to piece together the three-year study, I put together a literature review on the plethora of approaches to multicultural education. In this way, I would be able to do a secondary analysis through which I could situate and critique the efforts of the Changeton Multicultural Central Steering Committee. As discussed in Chapter One, the basic theoretical tenets of Critical Multicultural Education provided a lens through which to interpret my findings.

Reliability/Dependability

As a qualitative researcher, one should never hide behind the positivist notion that makes claims to a researcher's objectivity in defense of a scientific basis for the study of culture (Giroux, 1981; Hall, Held, Hubert, & Thompson, 1996; Rosaldo, 1993; Wright Mills, 1959). As explorers of the world around us, we are compelled to develop a sociohistorical lens that works from the assumption that human beings are never independent of the social and historical forces that surround us—we all inherit ideologies (that is, values and beliefs) that inform our desires, interests, perceptions, and actions. In that any examination of social reality is inherently subjective, this sociohistorical lens is crucial to understanding how our subject position informs our observations and interpretations. While we can't be objective, the question is can our work be reliable?

In the traditional sense of the word, "reliability" refers to the extent to which one's findings can be replicated. Because qualitative research is highly contextual, in flux, and influenced by the collector and interpreter, achieving reliability in the traditional sense is impossible (Merriam, 1991). For the sake of semantics, I prefer Y. S. Lincoln and E. G. Guba's (1985) choice of the term "dependability."

Regardless of the type of research, reliability/dependability can be approached through careful attention to the study's conceptualization and the way in which the data are collected, analyzed, and interpreted. I used three of the basic strategies, readily found in the literature, with which a researcher can ensure validity/dependability: triangulation, member checks, and peer examination.

My main source of data came from CSC meeting notes (which included sub-committee meetings and in-service workshops). The triangulation of data in this research project was conducted by comparing my transcribed observation notes of the Changeton Multicultural Central Steering Committee meetings with the official minutes taken at every meeting by the CSC chair and with the CSC official progress reports. These official minutes and CSC reports provided the only information available to corroborate my observation notes.

By virtue of the CSC's working format, in which each individual had to present his or her point of view to the group of seventeen-plus people on the committee, ambiguities (in terms of a person's voiced position on an issue) were generally cleared up by questions from colleagues. In the case of a lack of clarity during committee discussions, I conducted after-meeting clarification interviews.

I recognized that my own subjectivities would inevitably come into play in the collection process, analysis, and interpretation of the data. In an attempt to achieve a coherent depiction of the Changeton Multicultural Central Steering Committee's endeavors, during the descriptive stage of this research (capturing what the group discussed and accomplished), I had the CSC's approval to select members to read over my written descriptions of the committee's efforts to make sure that they were, in some respect, on target. In other words, on a regular basis, I took my descriptive data back to the source and asked the people about the results. This technique allowed the solicitation of alternative perspectives on what transpired.

During member checks, in order not to influence the reader's participation with the CSC, I did not reveal my critical interpretations of the data. My interpretation and discussion notes were protected in the research proposal clause that stated that I could maintain a private journal. The reason for this journal was not simply secrecy (as if I were hiding something), but rather, it was to ensure that my comments and insights would not have an influence on the CSC's natural flow of work.

A colleague had been trained in my coding scheme. As such, she was able to double-check and comment on the accuracy and consistency of my categorical assumptions as they emerged.

Confidentiality

As agreed upon in the site negotiation proposal, the school system, the city, and all of the participants involved in this study will remain anonymous. Pseudonyms have been created in order to protect all identities.

Notes

⌒

Introduction

1. Some of this research at the time this project in Changeton began include a Columbus, Ohio, district's system-wide program to develop curricula (Miranda, 1992); Cambridge, Massachusetts, Public School's K-12 efforts at staff sensitivity training and diversifying subject matter (Brown, 1992; Downey & Stern, 1989); New York State's implementation of its Curriculum of Inclusion (New York State Special Task Force on Equity and Excellence in Education, 1989; Singer, 1992; Wiles, 1992), and California's K-12 history/social science curriculum, of which Diane Ravitch was principal writer.

2. While every educational context is different and thus requires individualized approaches to such an infusion (as opposed to monolithic recipes), nonetheless, models are helpful in providing insight, generating ideas, and inspiring hope.

3. Virtually all references to the state, county, city, former names of the town, schools, research and published books about the area, newspaper names, school personnel, members of the committee, roads, area cities and towns, colleges, in-service organizations and facilitators, community organizations, companies, and so forth, have been given pseudonyms throughout this book, including the references. Thus Changeton, Nobel, and Fanton are not real names.

Chapter One

1. It is important to note that only four of Sleeter and Grant's (1988) models are being used. The fifth approach, Education that is Multicultural and Social Reconstructionist, has been incorporated and expanded in the pending discussion of critical pedagogy/multiculturalism.

2. In fact, assimilation is not the real long-term goal of reactionary models of education. Assimilation is merely used as a mechanism to get people to lose the only tools of resistance to domination that they possess—culture and language. Groups that are marked by race, class, gender, and so forth, are meant to be segregated and exploited.

3. Whereas many of the early theories of cultural reproduction were based solely on social class analysis, the idea of "hidden curriculum" here is also meant to include the specific

social practices, discourse styles, and representations that maintain discrimination along the lines of race, sexual orientation, gender, health, and so forth. Social class does cut across these other categories—categories that are multiple and interconnecting.

4. The use of "ideological construction" is not meant to dismiss the biological aspects of these categories, especially sexual orientation. The point is that dominant perceptions of these social markers (as opposed to genetic makeup) lead to oppressive practices. It is also important to point out that the words "gender" and "sexual orientation" are problematic. "Gender" only implies biology and is often used in reference to women, as if men are not gendered. The preference for "gendered" is because it assumes an agent, that is, someone is ascribing the characteristics onto others. "Sexual orientation," on the other hand, gives the immediate impression that the complex cultural identities of gay, lesbian, bisexual, and transgendered people can be reduced to acts of sex. There are similar issues with the connotations in the descriptor "disabled." It falls within a deficit model that should not be supported.

5. It is interesting to note that the word "ignorance" contains the word "ignore." Only people in positions of privilege have the possibility of turning their backs on oppression.

6. People of any background can speak in solidarity with others, and to or about issues, but they should never speak for people whose experiences are not their own. The reader also shouldn't assume that the medical metaphor implies that nature is at play here and that the oppressed are sick and in need of healing. In fact, they have been victimized.

7. With a long history of global colonization and continued imperialism, the relational aspects of cultural development are also important to recognize. Culture must also be examined as being contingent. That is, cultures emerge out of particular contexts, for example, the culture of the bus, the classroom, the school, the corporation, the nation, and so on. Often, power relations shift in these contexts and resituate social identities and positions of subordination and dominance. From this perspective, power can be understood as much more multifaceted than simply a monolithic binarism of the haves and the have nots. In some contexts certain people are the oppressors and in others they oppress (Freire, 1970).

8. In writing this chapter, I am deeply indebted to Christine Sleeter and Carl Grant for their painstaking research and insight. As all interpretations of their models are mine, I hold myself accountable for any potential variation that may occur in the initial descriptions. This is not an attempt to take credit for their work—it is simply to hold myself responsible for any interpretations that they may not have intended.

Chapter Two

1. Splack is a pseudonym.

2. For an in-depth look at this process, see Noel Ignatiev's (1995) *How the Irish Became White*. New York: Routledge.

3. One of the only bright spots during that period of time was that a Changeton man developed a successful sewage disposal plan for inland cities—the first in the country. As Kane (1982) writes, "The system of intermittent downward filtration became interna-

tionally famous and engineers and other visitors (including the King of Siam) came from everywhere to marvel at the works" (p. 9). In 1896, is was also the first city to abolish train grade crossings; forcing the rich railroads to pick up the overwhelming majority of the bill for finding alternative routes.

4. Contrary to the dreary economic news, Kane (1982) notes that by the turn of the century, Changeton was the world leader in the production of splack. "There were 48 splack firms and the value of the product in 1900, according to the U.S. Census, was $19,844,397" (p. 11). This statistic foreshadows the kind of market logic and class warfare that General Motors in Flint, Michigan, used in the 1980s: the corporation was making profits in the billions and was still laying off workers by the thousands. Both of these cities put virtually all of their eggs in one industrial basket. Given that corporations are only accountable to the profits of stockholders, and not to the well-being of the community and the very citizens that helped the industry grow, their futures were inevitably bleak.

5. In the autumn of 1938, to honor the Irish, French, Lithuanian, and Italian people of Changeton, four homes were erected at the Changeton Fair. This is rather ironic given that in 1923, the poor Irish (and later Italian) neighborhood/community, which had developed over a period of fifty years in the heart of the city, was destroyed so that a new road system could come through.

6. In 1952, he would return to Changeton in order to support Adlai Stevenson, Democratic candidate for president. As Stevenson had already campaigned in Changeton, the Republicans felt compelled to send Richard Nixon in order to support Dwight Eisenhower, the Republican candidate.

7. Sennett (1982) has the total population in 1970 at 83,499. Statistics should always be observed with great caution. As research is inherently subjective, how one counts, or who one counts, has political implications.

8. The end of the 1950s would also see the beginning of the death of the Eastern Fanton Street Railway. On November 17, 1958, the bus drivers went on strike, hoping to gain a 25-cents raise per hour. After 199 days out, the strikers "accepted a 33-month contract calling for a 10 cent an hour raise" (Kane, 1982, p. 28). While Kane seems to hold the strikers responsible, it is more reasonable to assume that the new road ways, the introduction of the automobile, the power of General Motors, Firestone Tires, and the big fuel companies to dismantle public transportation in the name of increased profits, are the culprits.

9. By 1994, the per capita public library materials budget was sixty-one cents.

10. According to one of the school's history teachers, the project was highly successful. He explained that they used a United Press International teletype machine through which "each student feels personally involved in today's world happenings."

11. Notice the gendered language in these comments.

12. This is the same superintendent as when this three-year study began. There would be total of two during the study.

13. In early February of 1994, there were three fires set inside Changeton High School. On that very day, a special needs student was removed from school after a fire was set in a wastebasket in a third floor corridor (Blotcher Guerrero, 1994, p. 1).

14. The school system has no METCO Program.

15. In 1982, the city museum put on an exhibition called "Black Changetonians." This exhibit depicted the lives of black Changetonians from 1881 to 1923, and emphasized the important roles that blacks have played in the city over the years. Along these same lines, in 1987 "a 250-year-old sycamore, which was once used as a signpost of freedom along the Underground Railroad for slaves escaping from the South, received nationwide recognition as a 'Landmark of Democracy'" (Carroll, 1989, p. 32).

16. To give an idea of the numbers, the Appleton School increased its racially subordinated student enrollment from 199 to 320.

17. The Gopmore School, though excluded from the state statistics, had 33 percent racially subordinated students in 1984.

18. Unlike research conducted with the Multicultural Central Steering Committee, information and interpretations of pre-1993 efforts are based solely on the literature available on the subject.

19. While the literature chooses to use the term "minority," it is not an accurate descriptor. As Lilia Bartolomé (1994) asserts, "This is not entirely accurate to describe these students as 'minority' students, since the term connotes numerical minority rather than the general low status (economic, political, and social) these groups have held and that I think is important to recognize when discussing their historical academic underachievement" (p. 174). In making a general reference to these groups, the preferential use of racially subordinated or oppressed will be used. The dominant group in U.S. society is in fact a minority. As B. A. Sizemore (1979) points out, "In a nation of minorities, the preferred minority is still the affluent white Anglo-Saxon Protestant male . . . the sorting mechanisms continue to work in his favor" (p. 354). Nonetheless, the term has been used only to refer to racially subordinated groups.

20. Proposition Two-and-a-Half was an attempt to level the property tax structure statewide so that schools would not be victimized by their community's tax base. However, in an attempt to save the middle class from bearing the brunt of local expenses, this proposition failed to demand more contributions from the corporate sector and, in doing so, depleted local educational budgets. This in turn resulted in many cuts in public/educational services. In one budget year, Changeton lost 120 teachers.

21. As community involvement was diminishing, the task force began a serious advertising campaign, in multiple languages, to regain interest and wider participation in their efforts.

22. In a different attempt to deal with the demographic shifts of their ever changing community, and to meet the requirements of state and federal law, Changeton school officials proposed in the mid-1980s to develop magnet schools. Chapter 636 funds were used unsuccessfully to help attract white students to the schools largely populated by racially subordinated students. They also attempted to increase the enrollment of such students in the academically talented program (Fanton State Department of Education, Bureau of Equal Educational Opportunities, 1984a, p. 3). However, this plan had been passed over "in favor of an approach based upon moderate redistricting" (Glenn, 1987, p. 48). Changeton was looking at the possibilities of a controlled choice plan and received $248,337 in state funds to implement such ideas.

23. Information Publications (1993) has the per pupil expenditure in 1989 as $3,512; 1990 as 3,566; 1992 as $3,201; and 1993 as $3,462. These numbers are significantly lower than the others presented.
24. On August 10, 1998, this principal resigned.

Chapter Three

1. It is important to note here that the category "youth" is not a monolithic entity. In fact, it is a complex analytic distinction that is cut across by a politics of identity and difference.
2. In the last two years (1999–2000), this landscape has changed as a massive muti-block court house has been constructed.
3. The national organization's campaign of painting buildings and picking up trash was problematic. The young people present, who were paid very little for their services, were being exploited. It wasn't as if the participants in the program were encouraged by the administrators or core leaders, except for Liz, to sit down and critically discuss their worldview, needs, interests, and concerns. Even though words like "bitch" and "fag" flew around like mosquitoes in the warm spring air, the teams were never encouraged to engage in a discussion of sexism and homophobia. The program seemed to be solely about discipline and job responsibility.
4. The local paper reported that the nineteen-year-old, who was a recording artist for East/West Records America—with whom he had signed a $500,000 recording deal, was shot to death at 2:20 A.M. on a Sunday. The police reported that at least eighteen shots were fired into the car. There were no drugs or weapons found inside the car. Three hooded men were seen fleeing from the crime scene.

Chapter Four

1. The difference between Cape Verdean-American and Cape Verdean is that Carl and Raul were born in the United States and Juan was born in Cape Verde. These were self-described categories.
2. Although the two superintendents during the three-year period supported the efforts of the CSC, neither of them played an active role in the committee's work, beyond positive formal public statements and motivational letters to individual school principals.
3. The descriptor "people of color" is used here because the CSC referred to racially subordinated people as such. "Racially subordinated" is preferred in that "people of color" assumes that white is not a color, rendering whiteness invisible and beyond question. A lack of analysis of the dominant referent that situates difference in society is debilitating.
4. The committee used the term "minority" interchangeably with "people of color" throughout the three years of research. Luis wrote a letter to the CSC contesting the use of this word, finding it "degrading." Nonetheless, the CSC continued using it.

Chapter Five

1. In terms of the general seating arrangement: the majority of individuals sat in different places each session. The two black men (one African American and the other Cape Verdean-American—the only dark-skinned members of the group) had a tendency to sit side by side. Eva, the chair of the committee, always sat at the end of the table.

2. The article that was photocopied and passed around was "An Analysis of Multicultural Education in the United States" by Christine Sleeter and Carl Grant, from the *Harvard Educational Review* (November 1987). Jackie cited the most critical of the models—Education that is Multicultural and Social Reconstructionist.

3. Jake was a high school housemaster. The CSC should have analyzed and transformed the black educator's title of "housemaster," which is an ideologically loaded term given the history of slavery.

4. It is interesting to note that these three committee members, the only ones to mention such issues, all eventually left the CSC.

5. Up through the January of 1993 meeting, only one of the male committee members specifically mentioned the inclusion of women. On the contrary, all but one of the women talked of including gender. Most of these women also specifically listed other groups in their discussions and written draft of goals and philosophies.

6. Fortunately, issues of gender did appear in the lists of multicultural activities in some Changeton schools, for example, guest speakers on the contributions of black women writers, "Up from Slavery with Black Women" was presented, one school celebrated "Women's Month," another examined women in history through reports.

7. As previously discussed in the deconstruction of disabilities, there is also the dichotomy in, "Those others, gays for example." The "us" and "them" surfaces again, which serves the purpose of shaping otherness.

Chapter Six

1. While the majority of the articles distributed during the three-year period would fall into mainstream models of multicultural education, there were some elements of Critical Multiculturalism that surfaced—discussions of dominant power relations, the social construction of whiteness, ideology, liberatory pedagogy, education for social reconstruction, and so on. The Sleeter and Grant article that was handed out earlier to the CSC should have provided, for the most part, a research lens for the CSC in its overall understanding and approach.

2. Globe of Human Differences does classroom, community, and workplace workshops on issues of diversity.

3. It is important to note that GHD conducted and complied the evaluations. As such, the inclusiveness of the report is not certain. It's disconcerting that there was not a single negative comment from any participant in the distributed version of the evaluations.

4. Often, multicultural professional development efforts only include teachers and administrators, at the exclusion of the rest of the school community. Ostensibly, the CSC didn't want to make this same mistake. Unfortunately, by the end of the third

year of the study, the committee had yet to develop and push for the implementation of workshops for the school cafeteria and office workers, custodians, and so on.

5. This woman's comment points to the importance of teachers being sensitive. When she states that she "can't know everything about religions and cultures," she is absolutely right. However, she can be sensitive to the fact that those differences exist among her students and that if she uses the people directly in front of her as part of the educational process, then she is embodying a facet of Critical Multicultural Education.

6. Globe of Human Differences, even though it is a non-profit organization, relies on having a good reputation in order to continue its work. One is thus compelled to question whether or not, as a business, the facilitators were concerned about acceptance, even at the expense of a real exchange of ideologies—which would require serious confrontation.

7. The concept of white supremacy came up rarely in the CSC's discussions. The most pertinent example was the news story that a white supremacist group had stolen the football dummies so that they could practice violent acts. But in this way, white supremacy was seen as something that only extremists participated in, rather than the society as a whole.

8. There is also the risk of collapsing into a deficit-model orientation when the cultural capital of students is interpreted as "baggage."

9. The original theoretical model wasn't presented as a means to blame the victim, but rather, it was used to make the case that blacks have strong redeeming qualities that whites don't themselves possess.

Chapter Seven

1. This was the first substantial reference to pre-CSC efforts to infuse multicultural education.

2. They should also consider current fashion (like baggy pants and their connection to prison life), tattoos, body piercing, and hair styles that speak to the struggles of particular political movements such as punks, Rastafarians, hip hop, and so forth. They also need to examine the ways in which such movements are co-opted and cleansed of any political insight (Gelder & Thornton, 1997; Mercer, 1994). Discussions should also take up marketing to youths and how so many young people become walking advertisements, freely celebrating the names of companies on their clothing. Supporting engagement with popular culture, Giselle thought that graffiti should be recognized as "a mosaic of multicultural achievement." Graffiti artists, as they spray-paint murals and their names (or "tags"), are taking a creative political stance by "inscribing their otherwise contained identities on public property" (Rose, 1994, p. 22).

3. By no means does this imply that deviant behavior is non-existent. Nor is this discussion intended to simply romanticize resistance, which when disarticulated from a positive political project can be self-destructive.

4. This points to the positive impact that media can have if properly used.

Chapter Eight

1. The deep concerns over cuts in the budget and the workforce were grounded in the layoff of 200 teachers across the city in the early 1990s (Blotcher Guerrero, 1991; Hoey, 1991c). A clear example of losing quality workers was the release of Jackie Robinson, who was the department head of Chapter 636 and the sanctioned multicultural specialist for the Changeton Schools in the mid-1980s—a position created during the resurgence of the Racial Imbalance Plan.
2. According to Eva, 25 percent was the school system's de facto minority quota goal.
3. As argued in Chapter Five, the CSC should also avoid a color-coordination approach to diversification. The idea is to also have ideological diversity. The most illustrative example of the CSC's propensity to essentialize identities can be found in their efforts to diversify the multicultural committee itself. By December of 1993, members of the committee were showing some discomfort with the organization's makeup. Struggling with membership, a typical CSC discussion sounded like this: "What about the Asian populations?" "There's Crester." "Is her personal life associated with that culture?" The CSC should avoid categorizing a multiplicity of groups within one homogenous term. "Crester" becomes the potential voice for something that she does not fully represent; that is, how does a Chinese person speak to the realities, needs, and concerns of a Korean student? Or, as Carl revealed and contested earlier, what can a Thai translator in the guidance office be expected to do for a Vietnamese student in need—let alone necessarily help communicate across issues of class, gender, sexuality, health, etc.
4. It is important to note that the CSC and the Professional Development Committee discussed developing an evaluation/questionnaire for gaining students' perspectives. However, this instrument was never created.
5. The Heath School in Brookline, Massachusetts, includes youths in community meetings that have "evolved into a community-building entity as well as a forum in which participatory problem-solving occurs" (Mosher, Kenny Jr., & Garrod, 1994, p. 160).

Chapter Nine

1. The CSC should have encouraged other schools to emulate the Appleton School's grade three "integration of bilingual and mainstream education to study Puerto Rican geography, history, art, music, customs, food, and literature."
2. These services were generally unpaid labor. This infuriated many multilingual people who were more than willing to provide their services to help children and their families, but who felt used by the school system (an example of this is in Chapter Ten).

Chapter Ten

1. In a racist and discriminatory society, the use of "management of diversity," while perhaps well-intentioned, invokes a strange image of containment and control. It also

illustrates how the ideology behind privatized corporate language has made its way into the discourse around public education.

2. As mentioned in Chapter Two, the report was commissioned by the school system because of the notification from the State Department of Education "that a number of Changeton elementary schools are racially imbalanced" (p. 2). NEDAC was looking to balance the racial/ethnic, linguistic, and socioeconomic composition of the district's total school population within individual school zones and buildings. According to the report (1995), there was fear that failure to develop a desegregation plan "could result in a state-imposed or court-ordered mandatory reassignment plan to achieve racial balance" (p. 3). The consultants from NEDAC assisted school personnel in the process of developing a new student assignment plan by conducting observations, and meeting with citizens of the community: School Committee members, parents, principals, business, religious, and political leaders, racial and ethnic minority groups, labor representatives, and others. School Department staff also visited nearby urban school systems that had successfully implemented new state sanctioned, controlled choice, student assignment plans.

3. Given that the most downtroddened schools house the bilingual children, an interesting study would have been to see how the race to desegregate schools worked to dismantle the progress of Bilingual Education by attempting to "mainstream" linguistic-minority students as fast as possible so as to be able to send them to other less integrated buildings around the city. One of NEDAC's (1995) goals, "when feasible," was to give Bilingual Education students a choice of schools that provide "Transitional Bilingual Education classes or Two-way Bilingual Education Programs for their primary language group" (pp. 28–29).

4. By 1998, the white population would decrease in total size to 47.5 percent. The African-American population would rise to 36.3 percent. However, as will be noted in the following dialogue with teachers, it is not clear where the ever-growing population of Cape Verdean students was being placed in the racialized categories.

5. By this time, 7.55 percent of the city's students were attending private schools (Fanton Department of Education, 1997b). Intradistrict choice and the opportunity to participate in a magnet school were now being offered.

6. The preliminary report was released to the mayor, the school committee, and the superintendent in 1996. The official report was released in 1997. It is unknown whether or not the report was ever intended to be made public; regardless, it was somehow released to the local press.

7. This perhaps confirms Carl and Jake's skepticism of the superintendent's support of the CSC's efforts, regardless of his powerful speeches against discrimination. With so much power, he should have been able to ensure more action—unless he felt that the work of the CSC was coming to fruition. . . . The African-American interim superintendent who followed, who, according to many teachers, was supportive of real substantive change, was run out of town after an extensive scrutiny of his past. Unwilling to be subjected to further unwarranted indignities, he stepped down.

8. The names of these three teachers have been changed in order to protect their identities. Those involved were afraid that there would be some serious reprisals if they

publicly spoke the truth about what they had been experiencing. In the year of the interview, the ESL instructor would leave the school system.

9. "Low-incidence" refers to those linguistic groups who are below the necessary population size that would render them eligible for mandated bilingual services. They are consequently taught in an all-ESL environment.

References

Abelov, H., Barale, M. A., & Halperin, D. (Eds.) (1993). *The Lesbian and Gay Studies Reader* New York: Routledge.

Alberts, G. (1994). "On Connecting Socialism and Mathematics: Dirk Struik, Jan Burgers, and Jan Tibergen." In: *Historia Mathematica*. Vol. 21, pp. 280–305.

Allen, T. (1994). *The Invention of the White Race*. London: Verso.

Amin, S. (1998). *Spectres of Capitalism: A Critique of Current Intellectual Fashions*. New York: Monthly Review Press.

Anyon, J. (1980). "Social Class and the Hidden Curriculum of Work." In: *Journal of Education*. Vol. 162 (winter), pp. 38–51.

Anzaldua, G. (1990a). "How to Tame a Wild Tongue." In: *Out There: Marginalization and Contemporary Cultures*. (Eds.) Ferguson, R., Gever, M., Minh-ha, T. T., & West, C. Cambridge, MA: M.I.T. Press.

———. (1990b). *Making Face, Making Soul/Haciendo Caras: Creative and Critical Perspectives by Feminists of Color*. San Farancisco: Aunt Lute Books.

Apple, M. (1990). *Ideology and Curriculum*. New York: Routledge.

Apple, M. (1996). *Cultural Politics and Education*. New York: Teachers College Press.

Aronowitz, S. (2000). *The Knowledge Factory: Dismantling the Corporate University and Creating True Higher Learning*. Boston: Beacon Press.

Austin, J., & Willard, N. (Eds.) (1998). *Generations of Youth: Youth Cultures and History in Twentieth-Century America*. New York: New York University Press.

Bacon, D. (2000). "Unions Take on Immigration-Related Firings." In: *Z Magazine*. (July/August), pp. 25–28.

Bakhtin, M. M. (1981). *The Dialogic Imagination*. Austin: University of Texas Press.

Baldwin, J. (1985). *The Price of the Ticket*. New York: St. Martin's Press.

Banks, J. (2000). *Cultural Diversity and Education: Foundations, Curriculum, and Teaching*. Boston: Allyn & Bacon.

Barthes, R. (1972). *Mythologies*. London: Cape.

Bartolomé, L. (1994). "Beyond the Methods Fetish: Toward a Humanizing Pedagogy." In: *Harvard Educational Review*. Vol. 64, No. 2 (summer), pp. 173–194.

Bascia, N. (1994). *Unions in Teachers' Professional Lives: Social, Intellectual, and Practical Concerns*. New York: Teachers College Press.

304 | *References*

Bauman, Z. (1998). *Globalization: The Human Consequences.* New York: Columbia University Press.

Bell, D., & Kennedy, B. (2000). *The Cybercultures Reader.* New York: Routledge.

Bender, G., & Druckrey, T. (Eds.) (1994). *Culture on the Brink: Ideologies of Technology.* Seattle: Bay Press.

Bennett, C. (1998). *Comprehensive Multicultural Education: Theory and Practice.* Boston: Allyn & Bacon.

Bennett, W. (1992). *The De-Valuing of America.* New York: Summit.

Bhabha, H. (1994). *The Location of Culture.* New York: Routledge.

Biagioli, M. (1999). *The Science Studies Reader.* New York: Routledge.

Bloch, M., & Tabachnick, B. (1994). "Improving Parent Involvement as School Reform: Rhetoric or Reality." In: *Changing American Education: Recapturing the Past or Inventing the Future.* (Eds.) Borman, K., & Greenman, N. New York: SUNY Press.

Blotcher Guerrero, A. (1990). "Parents Differ in Perception of High School Violence." In: *Nosurprise,* April 10, pp. 1, 5.

———. (1991). "Incumbents in Election Expected to Do Well Despite Fiscal Troubles." In: *Nosurprise,* November 3, p. 4.

———. (1994). "Fire Destroys Two CHS Classrooms: Three Blazes Called Suspicious" In: *Nosurprise,* February 5, p. 1.

———. (1996a). "Report: School Officials 'Out of Touch': Disturbing Practices by Changeton Teachers Also Cited." In: *Nosurprise,* April 25, p. 8.

———. (1996b). "Reaction to Report Muted." In: *Nosurprise,* May 3, p.2.

———. (1996c). "Changeton School Plan OK'd." In: *Nosurprise,* July 14, p.1.

Boone, S., McGrath, D., & Dupuy, A. (1996). "CHS Students Bring Home Gold from Regional History Contest". In: CHS Notebook, *Nosurprise,* February 16, p. 7.

Bourdieu, P. (1996). On Television. New York: The New Press.

Bourdieu, P., & Passeron, J. (1977). *Reproduction in Education, Society, and Culture.* London: Sage.

Bowles, S., & Gintis, H. (1976). *Schooling in Capitalist America: Educational Reform and the Contradictions of Economic Life.* New York: Basic Books.

Boyd-Barrett, O., & Newbold, C. (Eds.) (1995). *Approaches to Media: A Reader.* London: Arnold.

Boyle, M. (1998a). "Jake Named Acting Head of CHS." In: *Nosurprise,* August 12, pp. A1, A6.

———. (1998b). "Despite Spotlight, School Violence Rare." In: *Nosurprise,* December 9, p. B12.

Brandt, R. (1989). "On Parents and Schools: A Conversation with Joyce Epstein." In: *Educational Leadership.* Vol. 47, No. 2, pp. 24–27.

Brown, B. (1992). "Designing Staff/Curriculum Development Content for Cultural Diversity: The Staff Developer's Role." In: *Journal of Staff Development.* Vol. 13, No. 4 (spring), pp. 3–7.

Bullard, P. (1973). *Noble Herald,* October 28, p. 10.

Carey, A. (1995). Taking the Risk out of Democracy: Corporate Propaganda Versus Freedom and Liberty. Chicago: University of Illinois Press.

Carlson, D. (1992). *Teachers in Crisis: Urban School Reform and Teachers' Work Culture.* New York: Routledge.

———. (1997). *Making Progress: Education and Culture in New Times.* New York: Teachers College Press.

Carroll, W. (1989). *Changeton: From Rural Parish to Urban Center: An Illustrated History.* Northridge, CA: Windsor Publications.

Castells, M. (1996). *The Rise of the Network Society.* Oxford: Blackwell.

Castenell, L., & Pinar, W. (1993). *Understanding Curriculum as Racial Text: Representations of Identity and Difference in Education.* New York: SUNY Press.

Changeton Desegregation Planning Team (1995). "A Long-Range Voluntary Desegregation and Educational Equity Plan for the Changeton Public Schools. (Draft 2/7/95).

Changeton Safe Neighborhood Initiative (1995). Committee sponsored by District Attorney Michael J. Sullivan, Attorney General Scott Harshbarger, et al. Photocopied Report.

Cheney, L. (1988). *Humanities in America: A Report to the President, the Congress, and the American People.* Washington, DC: National Endowment for the Humanities.

Chernoff, J. M. (1979). *African Rhythm and African Sensibility: Aesthetics and Social Action in African Musical Idioms.* Chicago: University of Chicago Press.

Cherryholmes, C. (1988). *Power and Criticism: Poststructural Investigations in Education.* New York: Teachers College Press.

Childs, J. B. (1996). "Street Wars and the New Youth Peace Movement." In: *Z Magazine.* (November), pp. 9–12.

Chomsky, N. (1993). *Year 501: The Conquest Continues.* Boston: South End Press.

———. (2001). *9–11.* New York: Seven Stories Press.

Chomsky, N., Leistyna, P., & Sherblom, S. (1995). "A Dialogue with Noam Chomsky." In: *Harvard Educational Review.* Vol. 65, No. 2 (Summer), pp. 127–144.

———. (1999). "Demystifying Democracy: A Dialogue with Noam Chomsky." In: *Presence of Mind: Education and the Politics of Deception.* Boulder, CO: Westview.

Clark, R. (1994). "The Development of Schools that Practice Reflection." In: *Chartering Urban School Reform: Reflections on Public High Schools in the Midst of Change.* (Ed.) Fine, M. New York: Teachers College Press.

Cole, W. (1968). *Changeton: A History of the Decline of a Splack, Manufacturing City, 1900–1933.* Ph.D. dissertation, Nobel University.

Collins, C., Hartman, C., & Sklar, H. (1999). "Divided Decade: Economic Disparity at the Century's Turn." In: *United for a Fair Economy.* Internet website: www.stf.org.

Collins, S. (1996). *Let Them Eat Ketchup! The Politics of Poverty and Inequality.* New York: Monthly Review Press.

Conley, V. A. (1993). *Rethinking Technologies.* Minneapolis: University of Minnesota Press.

Cooper, L. (2000). "Youth Activists Fight Prop 21." In: *Against the Current.* Vol. 15, No. 2 (May/June), pp. 12–13.

Cornell, J., Heaney, J., & Farmer, T. (1999). "Changeton Shooting Leaves Teen Dead." In: *Nosurprise,* March 18, p. 5.

Current, R., Williams, T., Freidel, F., & Brinkley, A. (1983). *American History: A Survey.* New York: Knopf.

D'Ambrosio, U. (1990). "Ethnomathematics and Its Place in the History and Pedagogy of Mathematics." In: *For the Learning of Mathematics.* Vol. 5, No. 1, pp. 41–48.

Darder, A. (1991). *Culture and Power in the Classroom: A Critical Foundation for Bicultural Education.* New York: Bergin & Garvey.

de Certeau, M. (1984). *The Practice of Everyday Life.* Berkeley: University of California Press.

Debord, G. (1988). *Comments on the Society of the Spectacle.* London: Verso.

Dines, G., & Humez, J. (1995). *Gender, Race, and Class in Media: A Text-Reader.* London: Sage.

Downey, J., & Stern, A. S. (1989). "Staff Development: An Approach to Curriculum Reform in Cambridge, Massachusetts." In: *Equity and Choice.* Vol. 5, No. 3 (May), pp. 4–8.

D'Souza, D. (1995). *The End of Racism.* New York: Free Press.

DuBois, W. E. B. (1935). *Black Reconstruction in America, 1860–1880.* New York: Atheneum.

Durham, M. G., & Kellner, D. (Eds.) (2001). *Media and Cultural Studies: Keyworks.* Oxford: Blackwell.

Dyer, R. (1988). "White." In: *Screen.* Vol. 29, No. 4, pp. 44–64.

———. (1993). *The Matter of Images: Essays on Representations.* New York: Routledge.

Dyson, M. E. (1993). *Reflecting Black: African-American Cultural Criticism.* Minneapolis: University of Minnesota Press.

———. (1996). *Between God and Gansta Rap.* New York: Oxford University Press.

Faltis, C. (1995). "Building Bridges Between Parents and the School." In: *Policy and Practice in Bilingual Education: Extending the Foundations.* (Eds.) Garcia, O., & Baker, C. Philadelphia: Multilingual Matters Ltd.

Fanon, F. (1952). *Black Skin, White Masks.* London: Pluto.

———. (1961). *The Wretched of the Earth.* London: Penguin.

Fanton State Department of Education, Bureau of Equal Educational Opportunities (1984a). *Desegregation in Fanton, 1983 Annual Report.* Nobel: Fanton State Department of Education.

———. (1984b). *Equity and Choice Conference Report—The Pursuit of Excellence: Improving the Quality of Our Urban Schools through Desegregation, Equity, and Choice.* Fanton: Fanton State Department of Education.

Fanton State Department of Education. A letter to the School Committee from Maureen M. Wark, Civil Rights Specialist; January 25, 1995.

———. (1997a). *English Language Arts Curriculum Framework.* Nobel: Fanton State Department of Education.

———. (1997b). *School District Profile.* Nobel: Fanton State Department of Education.

———. (1998). *Changeton Public Schools, School District Profile, 1997–1998.* Nobel: Fanton State Department of Education.

Feagin, J., & Vera, H. (1995). *White Racism.* New York: Routledge.

Featherstone, L. (1999). "Hotwiring High Schools: Student Activists across the Country Experiment with Organizing by Internet." In: *Nation.* Vol. 268, No. 23 (June 21), pp. 15–20.

Ferrell, J., & Sanders, C. (1995). *Cultural Criminology.* Boston: Northeastern University Press.

FitzGerald, F. (1986). *Cities on a Hill: A Journey through Contemporary American Cultures.* New York: Simon & Schuster.

Foster, M. (1993). "Resisting Racism: Personal Testimonies of African-American Teachers."

In: *Beyond Silenced Voices: Class, Race, and Gender in United States Schools.* (Eds.) Weis, L., & Fine, M. New York: SUNY Press.

——. (1994). "Effective Black Teachers: A Literature Review." In: *Teaching Diverse Populations: Formulating a Knowledge Base.* (Eds.) Hollins, E., King, J. E., & Hayman, W. New York: SUNY Press.

Foucault, M. (1972). *Power/Knowledge.* Brighton, England: Harvester.

Frankenburg, R. (1993). *The Social Construction of Whiteness: White Women, Race Matters.* Minneapolis: University of Minnesota Press.

——. (1997). *Displacing Whiteness: Essays in Social and Cultural Criticism.* Durham, NC: Duke University Press.

Fraser, N. (1989). *Unruly Practices: Power, Discourse, and Gender in Contemporary Social Theory.* Minneapolis: University of Minnesota Press.

——. (1994). "Rethinking the Public Sphere: A Contribution to the Critique of Actually Existing Democracy." In: *Between Borders: Pedagogy and the Politics of Cultural Studies.* (Eds.) Giroux, H., & McLaren, P. New York: Routledge.

——. (2000). "Rethinking Recognition." In: *New Left Review.* No. 3 (May), pp. 107–120.

Freire, P. (1970). *Pedagogy of the Oppressed.* New York: Seabury Press.

——. (1985). *The Politics of Education: Culture, Power, and Liberation.* New York: Bergin & Garvey.

Freire, P., & Leistyna, P. (1999). "Presence of Mind in the Process of Learning and Knowing." In: *Presence of Mind: Education and the Politics of Deception.* Leistyna, P. Boulder, CO: Westview Press.

Freire, P., & Macedo, D. (1987). *Literacy: Reading the Word and the World.* Westport, CT: Bergin & Garvey.

——. (1996). "A Dialogue: Culture, Language, and Race." In: *Breaking Free: The Transformative Power of Critical Pedagogy.* (Eds.) Leistyna, P., Woodrum, A., & Sherblom, S. Cambridge, MA: Harvard Educational Review Press.

Fusco, C. (1988). "Fantasies of Oppositionality." In: *Afterimage Magazine.* (December), pp. 3–6.

Garofalo, R. (1992). (Ed.) Rockin' the Boat: Mass Music & Mass Movements. Boston: South End Press.

Gay, G. (2000). *Culturally Responsive Teaching: Theory, Research, and Practice.* New York: Teachers College Press.

Gee, J. P. (1996). *Social Linguistics and Literacies: Ideology in Discourses.* London: Taylor & Francis.

Gelder, K., & Thornton, S. (Eds.) (1997). *The Subcultures Reader.* New York: Routledge.

Gerdes, P. (1999). *Geometry from Africa: Mathematical and Educational Explorations.* Washington, DC: Mathematical Association of America.

Gibson, M. A. (1976). "Approaches to Multicultural Education in the United States: Some Concepts and Assumptions." In: *Anthropology and Education Quarterly.* Vol. 7, pp. 7–18.

Gilroy, P. (1987). *The Ain't No Black in the Union Jack: The Cultural Politics of Race and Nation.* Chicago: University of Chicago Press.

——. (1993). *The Black Atlantic: Modernity and Double Consciousness.* Cambridge, MA: Harvard University Press.

308 | *References*

Giroux, H. (1981). *Ideology, Culture, and the Process of Schooling.* Philadelphia: Temple University Press.

———. (1983). *Theory and Resistance in Education: A Pedagogy for the Opposition.* South Hadley, MA: Bergin & Garvey.

———. (1992). *Border Crossings: Cultural Workers and the Politics of Education.* New York: Routledge.

———. (1994). "Insurgent Multiculturalism and the Promise of Pedagogy." In: *Multiculturalism: A Critical Reader.* (Ed.) Goldberg, D. Cambridge, MA: Blackwell.

———. (1996). "Doing Cultural Studies: Youth and the Challenge of Pedagogy." In: *Breaking Free: The Transformative Power of Critical Pedagogy.* (Eds.) Leistyna, P., Woodrum, A., & Sherblom, S. Cambridge, MA: Harvard Educational Review Press.

———. (1999a). "Multiculturalism: Substituting Prisons for Schools." In: *Z Magazine.* Vol. 12, No. 4, pp. 46–49.

———. (1999b). *The Mouse that Roared: Disney and the End of Innocence.* Boulder, CO: Rowman & Littlefield.

Giroux, H., & Penna, A. (1979). "Social Education in the Classroom: The Dynamics of the Hidden Curriculum." In: *Theory and Research in Social Education.* Vol. 7, No. 1 (spring), pp. 18–27.

Glaser, B. G., & Strauss, A. L. (1967). *The Discovery of Grounded Theory.* Chicago: Aldine.

Glenn, C. (1987). "The Evolution of School Desegregation in Fanton." In: *Equity and Choice.* (fall), pp. 46–52.

Goldfield, M. (1992). "The Color of Politics in the United States: White Supremacy as the Main Explanation for the Peculiarities of American Politics from Colonial Times to the Present." In: *The Bounds of Race.* (Ed.) LaCapra, D. Ithaca, NY: Cornell University Press.

Goodlad, J. (1994). *Educational Renewal: Better Teachers, Better Schools.* San Francisco: Jossey-Bass.

Gordon, J. (2000). "Immigrants Fight the Power: Workers Centers Are One Path to Labor Organizing and Political Participation." In: *Nation.* (January 3), Vol. 270, No. 1, pp. 16–20.

Gould, S. (1981). *The Mismeasure of Man.* New York: W. W. Norton & Company.

Greene, M. (1996). "Plurality, Diversity, and the Public Space." In: *Can Democracy Be Taught?: Perspectives on Education for Democracy in the United States, Central and Eastern Europe, Russia, South Africa, and Japan.* (Ed.) Oldenquist, A. Bloomington, IN: Phi Delta Kappa Educational Foundation.

Grimes, P., & Register, C. (1991). "Teacher Unions and Black Students' Scores on College Entrance Exams." In: *Industrial Relations.* Vol. 30, p. 3.

Grossberg, L. (1996). "History, Politics and Postmodernism." In: *Stuart Hall: Critical Dialogues in Cultural Studies.* (Eds.) Morley, D., & Chen, K. New York: Routledge.

Haar, C. (1998). "The Teacher Unions: Enemies of Reform." In: *Crisis in Education.* (winter/ spring), pp. 30–40.

Habermas, J. (1962). *The Structural Transformation of the Public Sphere: An Inquiry into a Category of Bourgeois Society.* Cambridge, MA: M.I.T. Press.

Hall, S. (Ed.) (1997). *Representation: Cultural Representations and Signifying Practices.* London: Sage.

Hall, S., Held, D., Hubert, D., & Thompson, K. (1996). *Modernity: An Introduction to Modern Societies.* Cambridge, MA: Blackwell.

Hall, S., & Jefferson, T. (Eds.) (1975). *Resistance Through Rituals: Youth Subcultures in Post-War Britain.* New York: Routledge.

Halliday, M. A. K. (1976). *Language as a Social Semiotic.* London: Edward Arnold.

Hancock, M. (1993a). "Principal Finds Much to Praise in Changeton." In: *Nosurprise*, June 12, pp. 1, 5.

———. (1993b). "Changeton Students Learn about Hunger." In: *Nosurprise*, October 15, p. 13.

———. (1993c). "School to Investigate Reports of Marijuana Use." In: *Nosurprise*, October 24, p. 17.

———. (1994). "Preventing Dropouts at CHS: School Lost a Tenth of Its Population Last Year." In: *Nosurprise*, October 10, pp. 1, 4.

———. (1998). "Changeton School Police Defended." In: *Nosurprise*, January 16, pp. 1, 6.

Harding, S. (1994). "Is Science Multicultural? Challenges, Resources, Opportunities, Uncertainties." In: *Multiculturalism: A Critical Reader.* (Ed.) Goldberg, D. T. Cambridge, MA: Blackwell.

Hassan K. (2000). "The Future of the Left." In: *Monthly Review.* Vol. 52, No. 3 (July/August), pp. 60–82.

Heath, S. B. (1983). *Ways with Words: Language, Life, and Work in Communities and Classrooms.* Cambridge: Cambridge University Press.

Hebdige, D. (1987). *Cut 'n Mix: Culture, Identity and Caribbean Music.* London: Methuen.

Herman, E., & Chomsky, N. (1988). *Manufacturing Consent: The Political Economy of the Mass Media.* New York: Pantheon Books.

Herrnstein, R., & Murray, C. (1994). *The Bell Curve: Intelligence and Class Structure in American Life.* New York: Free Press.

Hickey, C. (1999). "Changeton Does Not Need to Highlight Crime." In: *Nosurprise*, March 22, p. B5.

Hill, M. (1997). *Whiteness: A Critical Reader.* New York: New York University Press.

Hirsch, E. D. (1996). *The Schools We Need, Why We Don't Have Them.* New York: Doubleday.

Hoey, J. (1990a). "Under the Influence: Things Are Better . . . . Things Are Awful." In: *Changeton Magazine*, January 28, pp. 1, 14.

———. (1990b). "Students at Alternative School Resent Use of Metal Detector." In: *Nosurprise*, April 6, pp. 1, 6.

———. (1991a). "Changeton Minorities Organize for Election." In: *Nosurprise*, June 22, pp. 1, 5.

———. (1991b). "Open Crime Records to Landlords." In: *Nosurprise*, August 1, p. 13.

———. (1991c). "Campaigns Over, the Work Begins." In: *Nosurprise*, November 7, p.1.

hooks, b. (1981). *Ain't I a Women: Black Women and Feminism.* Boston: South End Press.

———. (1990). *Yearning: Race, Gender, and Cultural Politics.* Boston: South End Press. See especially, Chapt. 15: "Choosing the Margin as a Space for Radical Openness."

———. (1992). *Black Looks: Race and Representation.* Boston: South End Press.

———. (1994). *Teaching to Transgress: Education as the Practice of Freedom.* New York: Routledge.

Information Publications (1986–94). *Fanton Municipal Profiles.* Wellesley Hills, Fanton: Information Publications.

Institute for Wisconsin's Future (1996). *Are Teacher Unions Hurting American Education: A State-by-State Analysis of the Impact of Collective Bargaining among Teachers on Student Performance.* Milwaukee, WI: Institute For Wisconsin's Future.

James, D. (1995). *That's Blaxploitation: Roots of the Baadasssss 'Tude.* New York: St. Martin's Press.

Jameson, F., & Miyoshi, M. (Eds.) (1999). *The Cultures of Globalization.* Durham: Duke University Press.

Jenkins, H. (1998). "Childhood Innocence and Other Modern Myths." In: *The Children's Culture Reader.* New York: New York University Press.

Jhally, S. (1991). *The Codes of Advertising: Fetishism and the Political Economy of Meaning in the Consumer Society.* New York: Routledge.

Johnson, S. M. (1984). *Teacher Unions in Schools.* Philadelphia: Temple University Press.

———. (1990). "The Primacy and Potential of High School Departments." In: *The Context of Teaching in Secondary Schools: Teachers' Realities.* (Eds.) McLaughlin, J. W., Talbert, J. E., & Bascia, N. New York: Teachers College Press.

Jones, L. (1963). *Blues People: The Negro Experience in White America and the Music that Developed from It.* New York: Morrow Quill.

Kane, R. (1982). *Changeton 1881–1981: A Pictorial History.* Changeton, Fanton: Changeton 100.

Karp, S. (2000). "Rethinking Teacher Unionism." In: *Z Magazine.* October 14, pp. 1–3.

Katz, J. (1983). "A Theory of Qualitative Methodology: The Social Science System of Analytic Fieldwork." In: *Contemporary Field Research.* (Ed.) Emerson, R. M. Boston: Little Brown.

Kelly, E. (1995). *Education, Democracy, and Public Knowledge.* Boulder: Westview Press.

Kerchner, C. T., & Mitchell, D. E. (1986). "Teaching Reform and Union Reform." In: *Elementary School Journal.* Vol. 86, No. 4, pp. 449–70.

Keysar, A. (1986). *Out of Work: The First Century of Unemployment in Fanton.* New York: Cambridge University Press.

Kimbal, R. (1990). *Tenured Radicals: How Politics Has Corrupted Our Higher Education.* New York: Harper Perennial.

King, J. E. (1994). "The Purpose of Schooling for African-American Children: Including Cultural Knowledge." In: *Teaching Diverse Populations: Formulating a Knowledge Base.* (Eds.) Hollins, E., King, J. E., & Hayman, W. New York: SUNY Press.

Kingman, B. (1895). *History of Changeton, Devend County, Fanton, 1656–1894.* New York: D. Mason & Company.

Kleiner, M., & Petree, D. (1988). "Unionism and Licensing of Public School Teachers: Impact on Wages and Educational Output." In: *When Public Sector Workers Unionize.* (Eds.) Freeman, R., and Ichniowski, C. Chicago: University of Chicago Press.

Knijnik, G. (1992). "An Ethnomathematical Approach in Mathematical Education: A Matter of Political Power." In: *For the Learning of Mathematics.* Vol. 13, No. 3, pp. 23–26.

Koch, K. (1994). "Latino Students Form New Club at Changeton High School." *Nosurprise,* November 23, p. 17.

Kuhn R. (1998). "Rural Reaction and War on the Waterfront in Australia." In: *Monthly Review.* Vol. 50, No. 6 (November), pp. 30–44.

Laclau, E., & Mouffe, C. (1985). *Hegemony and Socialist Strategy: Towards a Radical Democratic Politics*. London: Verso.

Lakes, R. (1996). "Youth Leadership." In: *Youth Development and Critical Education: The Promise of Democratic Action*. New York: SUNY Press.

Lankshear, C., & McLaren, P. (1993). *Critical Literacy: Politics, Praxis, and the Postmodern*. New York: SUNY.

Lash, S., & Urry, J. (1987). *The End of Organized Capitalism*. Madison, WI: University of Wisconsin Press.

Leistyna, P. (1999). *Presence of Mind: Education and the Politics of Deception*. Boulder, CO: Westview Press.

Leistyna, P., & Woodrum, A. (1996). "Context and Culture: What Is Critical Pedagogy." In: *Breaking Free: The Transformative Power of Critical Pedagogy*. (Eds.) Leistyna, P., Woodrum, A., & Sherblom, S. Cambridge, MA: Harvard Educational Review Press.

Leistyna, P, Woodrum, A., & Sherblom, S. (1996). *Breaking Free: The Transformative* Power of Critical Pedagogy. Cambridge, MA: Harvard Educational Review Press.

Levin, D. (1996). "Immigrant Worker Organizing in New York's Underground Economy: Latino Workers Center Experience." In: *Against the Current*. Vol. 11, No. 4 (Sept.), pp. 13–17.

Levin, M. A. (1987). "Parent-Teacher Collaboration." In: *Critical Pedagogy and Cultural Power*. (Ed.) Livingston, D. New York: Bergin & Garvey.

Lieberman, H. (1997). *The Teachers' Unions: How the NEA and AFT Sabotage Reform and Hold Students, Parents, Teachers, and Taxpayers Hostage to Bureaucracy.* New York: Free Press.

Lincoln, Y. S., & Guba, E. G. (1985). *Naturalistic Inquiry*. Newbury Park, CA: Sage.

Lipsitz, G. (1994). "We Know What Time It Is: Race, Class and Youth Culture in the Nineties." In: *Microphone Fiends: Youth Music, Youth Culture*. (Eds.) Ross, A., & Rose, T. New York: Routledge.

Loewen, J. (1995). *Lies My Teacher Told Me: Everything Your American History Textbook Got Wrong*. New York: New Press.

Lott, T. (1994). "Black Vernacular Representation and Cultural Malpractice." In: *Multiculturalism: A Critical Reader*. (Ed.) Goldberg, D. Cambridge, MA: Blackwell.

Louis, K. S. (1990). "Social and Community Values and the Quality of Teacher Work Life." In: *The Context of Teaching in Secondary Schools: Teachers' Realities*. (Eds.) McLaughlin, J. W., Talbert, J. E., & Bascia, N. New York: Teachers College Press.

Ludwig, M. (1997). "The Cultural Politics of Prevention: Reading Anti-Drug Public Service Announcements." In: *Understanding the Ad: Reading Culture in Advertising*. (Ed.) Frith, K. T. New York: Peter Lang.

Lyotard, J. (1979). *The Postmodern Condition: A Report on Knowledge*. Minneapolis: University of Minnesota Press.

MacCannell, D. (1992). *Empty Meeting Grounds: The Tourist Papers*. London: Routledge.

Macedo, D. (1994). *Literacies of Power: What Americans Are Not Allowed to Know*. Boulder, CO: Westview Press.

MacLeod, J. (1991). "Bridging School and Street." In: *Journal of Negro Education*. Vol. 60, pp. 41–56.

Martinez, E. (2000). "The New Youth Movement in California." In: *Z Magazine*. (May), pp. 1–14.

Marx, K. (1859). *Grundrisse: Foundations of the Critique of Political Economy.* New York: Penguin.

Mascaro, M. E. (1990). "The *Goodfield* School Initiative: About the Program." In: *W.I.S.E.: Winners in Sharing Education.* (Eds.) Mitchell, E. G., & DePlacido, A. Conference booklet presented at WISE at the University of Fanton.

May, S. (1994) (Ed.) *Critical Multiculturalism: Rethinking Multicultural and Antiracist Education.* Philadelphia: Falmer Press.

McBrien, J. L., & Brandt, R. (1997). *The Language of Learning: A Guide to Education Terms.* Alexandria, VA: Association for Supervision and Curriculum Development.

McCaleb, S. P. (1994). *Building Communities of Learners: A Collaboration among Teachers, Students, Families, and Community.* New York: St. Martin's Press.

McCarthy, C. (1993). "After the Canon: Knowledge and Ideological Representation in the Multicultural Discourse on Curriculum Reform." In: *Race, Identity, and Representation in Education.* (Eds.) McCarthy, C., & Crinchlow, W. New York: Routledge.

McChesney, R. (1997). *Corporate Media and the Threat to Democracy.* New York: Seven Stories Press.

McClintock, A., Mufti, A., & Shohat, E. (Eds.) (1997). *Dangerous Liaisons: Gender, Nation, and Postcolonial Perspectives.* Minneapolis: University of Minnesota Press.

McDonnell, L. M., & Pascal, A. H. (1988). *Teacher Unions and Educational Reform.* Washington, DC: RAND Corporation.

McIntosh, P. (1990). "White Privilege: Unpacking the Invisible Knapsack." In: *Independent School.* (winter), pp. 31–36.

McIntyre, A. (1997). *Making Meaning of Whiteness: Exploring Racial Identity with White Teachers.* New York: SUNY Press.

McLaren, P. (1994). "White Terror and Oppositional Agency: Towards a Critical Multiculturalism." In: *Multiculturalism: A Critical Reader.* (Ed.) Goldberg, D. Cambridge, MA: Blackwell.

———. (1995). *Critical Pedagogy and Predatory Culture: Oppositional Politics in a Postmodern Era.* New York: Routledge.

———. (2000). *Che Guevara, Paulo Freire, and the Pedagogy of Revolution.* Boulder, CO: Roman & Littlefield.

Mercer, K. (1994). *Welcome to the Jungle: New Positions in Black Cultural Studies.* New York: Routledge.

Merriam, S.(1991). *Case Study Research in Education: A Qualitative Approach.* San Francisco: Jossey-Bass.

Metz, M. H. (1990). "How Social Class Differences Shape the Context of Teachers' Work." In: *The Context of Teaching in Secondary Schools: Teachers' Realities.* (Eds.) McLaughlin, J. W., Talbert, J. E., & Bascia, N. New York: Teachers College Press.

Minh-ha, T. T. (1989). *Woman, Native, Other.* Bloomington, IN: University of Indiana Press.

Miramontes, O., Nadeau, A., & Commins, N. (1997). *Restructuring Schools for Linguistic*

Diversity: Linking Decision Making to Effective Programs. New York: Teachers College Press.

Miranda, A. H. (1992). "The Implementation of a Comprehensive Multicultural Program." In: *Journal of Staff Development.* Vol. 13, No. 2 (spring), pp. 18–25.

Mohanty, C. T., Russo, A., & Torres, L. (1991). *Third World Women and the Politics of Feminism.* Indianapolis: University of Indiana Press.

Morisson, T. (1992). *Playing in the Dark: Whiteness and Literary Imagination.* New York: Vintage.

Morley, D. (1992). *Television Audiences and Cultural Studies.* New York: Routledge.

Mosher, R., Kenny, R. A., Jr., & Garrod, A. (1994). *Preparing for Citizenship: Teaching Youth to Live Democratically.* Westport, CT: Praeger.

Munōz, J. E. (1999). *Disidentifications: Queers of Color and the Performance of Politics.* Minneapolis: University of Minnesota Press.

New England School Development Council. (1997). *Changeton Public Schools Administrative Reorganization of the Central Office, August 1997.* Marlborough, MA.

New England Desegregation Assistance Center. (1995). *A Long-Range Voluntary Desegregation and Educational Equity Plan for the Changeton Public Schools.* Providence: Brown University.

New York State Special Task Force on Equity and Excellence in Education. (1989). "A Curriculum of Inclusion: Report of the Commissioner's Task Force on Minorities—Equity and Excellence." New York: New York State Special Task Force on Equality.

Nieto, S. (1992/2000). *Affirming Diversity: The Sociopolitical Context of Multicultural Education.* New York: Longman.

Norton-Pierce, B. (1993). "Social Identity, Investment, and Language Learning." In: *TESOL Quarterly.* Vol. 29, No. 1 (spring), pp. 13–25.

Nosurprise. (1906). February 15, pp. 1, 2, 5.

Ogbu, J. (1987). "Variability in Minority Responses to Schooling: Nonimmigrants vs. Immigrants." In: *Interpretive Ethnography of Education.* (Eds.) Spindler, G., & Spindler, L. Hillsdale, NJ: Lawrence Erlbaum Associates.

Ogren, K. (1989). *The Jazz Revolution: Twenties America and the Meaning of Jazz.* New York: Oxford University Press.

Osayande, E. (1996). *Gangsta Rap Is Dead: Ciphers, Poems, and Prophecies on the War for Black Youth and Hip Hop.* Philadelphia: Talking Drum Communications.

Pang, V. (2000). *Multicultural Education: A Caring-Centered Reflective Approach.* New York: McGraw Hill.

Parekh, B. (2000). *Rethinking Multiculturalism: Cultural Diversity and Political Theory.* Cambridge, MA: Harvard University Press.

Parent Access Information Center, Executive Office of Education. (1990–95). *School District Profile: Changeton.*

Peterson, B., & Carney, M. (1999). *Transforming Teacher Unions: Fighting for Better Schools and Social Justice.* New York: Rethinking Schools.

Phillips, P. (2001). *Censored 2001.* New York: Seven Stories Press.

Pongonis, J., & Malonson, J. (1983). "The Changeton Battery: A Special Needs Assessment for Bilingual Students." *Minority Parents and Special Education: Advocacy, Placement, Programs* (Report on Over/Under Representation Project).

Ponvert, P. (1998). "Putting the Power of Video in the Right Hands: The Chiapas Youth Media Project." In: *Against the Current.* Vol. 13, No. 2 (May/June), pp. 22–23.

Powel, A. B., & Frankenstein, M. (Eds.) (1997). *Ethnomathematics: Challenging Eurocentrism in Mathematics Education.* New York: SUNY Press.

Pratte, R. (1983). "Multicultural Education: Four Normative Arguments." In: *Educational Theory.* Vol. 33, pp. 21–32.

Prazniak, R., & Dirlik, A. (2001). (Eds.) *Places and Politics in an Age of Globalizations.* Boulder, CO: Rowman & Littlefield.

Ravitch, D. (1995). *Debating the Future of American Education: Do We Need National Standards and Assessments?* Washington, DC: Brookings Institute.

Reardon, M. (1995). "Putting All the Pieces Together: Principal's Take on Changes in Education." In: *Nosurprise,* September 17, pp. 17, 24.

Reddy, N. (2000). "The Right to Organize: The Working Children's Movement in India." In: *Cultural Survival Quarterly.* (summer), pp. 52–55.

Ro, R. (1996). *Gangsta: Merchandizing the Rhymes of Violence.* New York: St. Martin's Press.

Roberts, G. (1999). *The American Cities and Technology Reader: Wilderness to Wired City.* New York: Routledge.

Robinson, C. (1994). "Ota Benga's Flight through Geronimo's Eyes: Tales of Science and Multiculturalism." In: *Multiculturalism: A Critical Reader.* (Ed.) Goldberg, D. T. Cambridge, MA: Blackwell.

Roediger, D. (1991). *The Wages of Whiteness: Race and the Making of the American Working Class.* London: Verso.

——. (1994). *Towards the Abolition of Whiteness.* New York: Verso.

Rosaldo, R. (1993). *Culture and Truth: The Remaking of Social Analysis.* Boston: Beacon Press.

Rose, F. (2000). "Prospects for a Working- and Middle-Class Alliance." In *Coalitions across the Class Divide: Lessons from the Labor, Peace, and Environmental Movements.* Ithaca, NY: Cornell University Press.

Rose, T. (1994). *Black Noise: Rap Music and Black Culture in Contemporary America.* London: Wesleyan University Press.

Ross, A. (Ed.) (1996). *Science Wars.* Durham: Duke University Press.

Ross, A., & Rose, T. (1994). *Microphone Fiends: Youth Music, Youth Culture.* New York: Routledge.

Said, E. (1981). *Covering Islam: How the Media Experts Determine How We See the Rest of the World.* New York: Vintage Books.

——. (1993). *Culture and Imperialism.* New York: Knopf.

Saltman, K. (2000). *Collateral Damage: Corporatizing Public Schools—A Threat to Democracy.* Boulder, CO: Roman & Littlefield.

Scaglione, D. (1990). "More Drug Use in Growth Areas." In: *Changeton Magazine,* January 28, pp.1, 14.

Schlesinger, A., Jr. (1991). "The Disuniting of America: What We All Stand to Lose if Multicultural Education Takes the Wrong Approach." In: *American Educator.* (winter), pp. 14–33.

Schlosser, E. (2001). *Fast Food Nation: The Dark Side of the All-American Meal.* Boston: Houghton Mifflin Company.

Scott, J. (1990). *Domination and the Arts of Resistance: Hidden Transcripts.* New Haven, CT: Yale University Press.

Sedgwick, E. K. (1990). *Epistemology of the Closet.* Berkeley: University of California Press.

Sennett, K. (1982). "Second Year Validation Studies of the Changeton Battery: A Special Needs Assessment for Linguistic-Minority Students." Paper presented at the CEC: National Topical Conference on Bilingual Special Education, Phoenix, AZ (November 2).

Shaheen, J. (1997). Arab and Muslim Stereotyping in American Popular Culture. Washington, DC: Center for Muslim-Christian Understanding.

Sholle, D., & Denski, S. (1994). *Media Education and the (Re)Production of Culture.* Westport, CT: Bergin & Garvey.

Singer, A. (1992). "Multiculturalism and Democracy: The Promise of Multicultural Education." In: *Social Education.* Vol. 56, No. 2 (February), pp. 38–49.

Siskin, L. S. (1994). *Realms of Knowledge: Academic Departments in Secondary Schools.* London: Falmer Press.

Sizemore, B. A. (1979). "The Four M Curriculum: A Way to Shape the Future." In: *Journal of Negro Education.* Vol. 47. pp. 51–63.

Sleeter, C. (1993). "How White Teachers Contruct Race." In: *Race, Identity, and Representation in Education.* (Eds.) McCarthy, C., & Crinchlow, W. New York: Routledge.

Sleeter, C., & Grant, C. (1988). *Making Choices for Multicultural Education: Five Approaches to Race, Class, and Gender.* New York: Merrill.

Sloan, L. (1986). "Video Commentary." In: *Ethnic Notions.* Riggs, M. San Francisco: California Newsreel.

Snauwaert, D. (1993). *Democracy, Education, and Governance: A Developmental Conception.* New York: SUNY Press.

Spivak, G. C. (1987). *In Other Worlds: Essays in Cultural Politics.* New York: Routledge.

Steinway, S. (1992). *The Nobel-Area School Report Card.* March.

———. (1994). "Report Card: How Does Your High School Stack Up?" In: *School.* (October), p. 3.

Strinati, D. (1995). *An Introduction to Theories of Popular Culture.* New York: Routledge.

Sullivan, E. (1990). *Critical Psychology and Pedagogy: Interpretation of the Personal World.* New York: Bergin & Garvey.

Suina, J. (1988). "Epilogue: And Then I Went to School." In: *Linguistic and Cultural Influences on Learning Mathematics.* (Eds.) Cocking, R., & Mestre, J. Hillsdale, NJ: Lawrence Erlbaum Associates.

Szkudlarek, T. (1993). *The Problem of Freedom in Postmodern Education.* London: Bergin & Garvey.

Temple, J. (1999). "Noise from Underground: Punk Rock's Anarchic Rhythms Spur a New Generation to Political Activism." In: *Nation.* Vol. 269, No. 12 (October 18), pp. 17–20.

The Group of Green Economists. (1992). *Ecological Economics: A Practical Program for Global Reform.* London: Zed Books.

Torres-Guzman, M. E. (1995). "Recasting Frames: Latino Parent Involvement." In: *Policy* and *Practice in Bilingual Education: Extending the Foundations.* (Eds.) Garcia, O., & Baker, C. Philadelphia: Multilingual Matters, Ltd.

Torres-Guzman, M. E., Mercado, C. I., Quintero, A., & Rivera Viera, D. (1994). "Teaching and Learning in Puerto Rican/Latino Collaboratives: Implications for Teacher Education." In: *Teaching Diverse Populations: Formulating a Knowledge Base.* (Eds.) Hollins, E., King, J. E., & Hayman, W. New York: SUNY Press.

Vallance, E. (1973). "Hiding the Hidden Curriculum." In: *Curriculum Theory Network.* Vol. 4, No. 1, pp. 68–77.

Villegas, A. M. (1988). "School Failure and Cultural Mismatch: Another View." In: *Urban Review.* Vol. 20, No. 4, pp. 23–34.

Voloshinov, V. N. ([1929] 1986). *Marxism and the Philosophy of Language.* Reprinted, Cambridge, MA: Harvard University Press.

Vygotsky, L. S. (1978). *Mind in Society: The Development of Higher Psychological Processes.* Cambridge, MA: Harvard University Press.

Walker-Moffat, W. (1995). *The Other Side of the Asian American Success Story.* San Francisco: Jossey-Bass.

Wallace, M. (1990). *Invisibility Blues: From Pop to Theory.* New York: Verso.

West, C. (1993). "The New Cultural Politics of Difference." In: *Beyond a Dream Deferred: Multicultural Education and the Politics of Excellence.* (Eds.) Thompson, B., & Tyagi, S. Minneapolis: University of Minnesota Press.

Wiles, D. (1992). "Diversity Curriculum in Public Schools without Minority Pupils." New York: New York Board of Regents.

Willams, Janice A., Associates (1996). *Central Office Assessment, Reorganization Option and Recommendations.* Hopkington, MA.

Williams, R. (1958). *Culture and Society.* New York: Columbia University Press.

Willis, P. (1977). *Learning to Labor: How Working Class Kids Get Working Class Jobs."* New York: Columbia University Press.

Wilson, W. (1985). "Chapter 636 and the Changeton Public Schools." In: *Equity and Choice.* Vol. 2, No. 1 (fall), pp. 75–80.

Winant, H. (1995). "Dictatorship, Democracy, and Difference: The Historical Construction of Racial Identity." In: *The Bubbling Cauldron: Race, Ethnicity, and the Urban Crisis.* (Eds.) Smith, M. P., & Feagin, J. R. Minneapolis: University of Minnesota Press.

Wright Mill, C. (1959). *The Sociological Imagination.* London: Oxford University Press.

Yahoo! Real Estate (1998). "The School Report." Internet website: theschoolreport.com.

Yarmalovicz, S. (1998a). "Another Chance for Troubled Students." In: *Nosurprise,* April 17, p. 1.

———. (1998b). "Consultant: It's No Reform School". In: *Nosurprise,* November 19, p. B8.

Zinn, H. (1980). *A People's History of the United States.* New York: Harper & Row.

———. (1990). *Declarations of Independence: Cross-Examining American Ideology.* New York: Harper Perennial.

———. (1999). "An Interview with Howard Zinn." In: *Transforming Teacher Unions: Fighting for Better Schools and Social Justice.* New York: Rethinking Schools.

Zwerling, H., & Thomason, T. (1994). "The Effects of Teacher Unions on the Probability of Dropping Out of High School." In: *Journal of Collective Negotiations in the Public Sector.* Vol. 23, No. 3, pp. 239–250.

Index

Abelove, H., 120
Accreditation Report, 113, 117
Achieving Community Involvement in Organizing (ACTION), 217
Administration, 65
"Administrative Reorganization of the Central Office," 247
Affirmative Action Plan, 113, 117
African-Americans: cultural deprivation interpretation, 165; in early Changeton, 36, 37, 40–41; essentializing, 164; popular representations of, 181; school control over, 164; school enrollment, 58, 58*tab;* unemployment and, 69
Afrocentrism, 164
AIDS, 186
Alberts, G., 181
Allen, T., 24, 150, 161
Amin, S., 187
Anti-Semitism, 43
Anyon, J., 15, 16, 161
Anzaldua, G., 118, 234
Apple, M., 13, 15, 16, 161
Aronowitz, S., 188
Ashport, L., 40

Asians: school enrollment, 58, 58*tab*
Assimilation, 15, 293*n2*
Atus, J., 40
Austin, J., 162
Awakened Awareness and Development of Self, 50
Awareness: raising, 124–125

Bacon, D., 215
Bakhtin, M., 235
Baldwin, J., 24
Banks, J., 128, 142
Barthes, R., 182
Bartolomé, L., 21, 296*n19*
Bascia, N., 211
Bauman, Z., 187
Behavior: deviant, 299*n3;* discriminatory, 144; individual, 143; links to oppressive social practice, 163; oppositional, 155; oppressive, 147; pathologizing, 143; racial stereotypes and, 141; resistant, 165; shaping, 165; social construction of, 30; standards of, 193; theorizing about, 147; unacceptable, 193
Behavior Adjustment Program, 141, 164

Williams, R., 28
Willis, P., 162
Wilson, W., 57, 61–62
Winant, H., 150, 213
"Working and Living in Culturally Diverse
    Environments" (conference), 140

World Food DayAwareness Project, 187

Yarmalovicz, S., 241, 265

Zinn, H., 34, 183, 216
Zwerling, H., 209